This map is repeated in back of book

THIS work examines and affirms the claim that the Catholic founders and settlers of Maryland established in this country both religious and civil liberty, those principles so inseparably a part of American tradition. In tracing this heritage from its roots in the Magna Charta through the policies of the first Lord Baltimore and his colonial charters, to the Catholic colony of Maryland and eventually to the Constitution, Mr. Ives who is a non-Catholic and a lawyer, adds an important chapter to American history.

The Maryland charter recognized the right of self-government, and provided the foundation for a representative democracy which is now so firmly embedded in the political ideals of our country. The author points out that the care exercised by Lord Baltimore in drafting this document was due to the perilous situation of Catholics in England, and a desire to provide a haven not only for them but for the persecuted of all other creeds and sects.

The part played by the first Lord Baltimore in the court of James I, and the far-reaching influence of George Calvert's policies are amply covered. The author also traces the influence of the English foreign policy of that time as embodied in the proposed Spanish marriage and the final alliance between Charles I and Henrietta Maria on the treatment accorded Catholics.

To the Carroll family the author devotes a large portion of his book. Coming to America after the overthrow of the Baltimore government by the Protestant revolution of 1688, the Carrolls became the real successors of the Catholic Calverts and, until the dawn of the New Republic, preserved the fundamental principles and ideals of the first Lord Baltimore. In these ideals and principles, Mr. Ives sees the social and political philosophy of Saint Thomas Aquinas, as reinterpreted by Suarez and Bellarmine.

A book to be recommended to all students of American history because of its real interest, its sincerity, and its painstaking scholarship.

To

M. G. I.

George Calvert, The First Lord Baltimore

THE *ARK* AND THE *DOVE*

The Beginning of Civil and Religious Liberties in America

BY

J. MOSS IVES, LL.D.

LONGMANS, GREEN AND CO.
LONDON · NEW YORK · TORONTO
1936

LONGMANS, GREEN AND CO.
114 FIFTH AVENUE, NEW YORK
221 EAST 20TH STREET, CHICAGO
88 TREMONT STREET, BOSTON

LONGMANS, GREEN AND CO. LTD.
39 PATERNOSTER ROW, LONDON, E C 4
6 OLD COURT HOUSE STREET, CALCUTTA
53 NICOL ROAD, BOMBAY
36A MOUNT ROAD, MADRAS

LONGMANS, GREEN AND CO.
215 VICTORIA STREET, TORONTO

IVES
THE ARK AND THE DOVE

First Edition January 1936
Reprinted February 1936
April 1936

PRINTED IN THE UNITED STATES OF AMERICA

FOREWORD

A LITTLE more than three centuries ago, in the late autumn of the year 1633, two ships set sail from the Isle of Wight and, with a favoring wind, headed for the open sea. As it was too late in the season to venture in a direct course to the Chesapeake Bay Country whither they were bound, these ships chose a southwesterly course to avoid the storms that were sure to come on the North Atlantic before a crossing could be made. The larger of the two ships was the *Ark* of three hundred tons burden. The other was the *Dove,* a little ship of only fifty tons and of the type of the old English pinnace. Her ability to cross the sea was measured by the sturdiness of her crew.

It so happened that the names of these two ships were strikingly significant of the motive that prompted the voyage. The sailing of the *Ark* and the *Dove* took place at a time when there had long been a misalliance of religion and politics. Sir Philip Sidney during the Elizabethan reign had said that the highest political wisdom was to be found in the dictum that religion and politics must never be separated. This was the view of his day and it cast its shadow well along into the seventeenth century.

There was much religious persecution that had its source in politics. Of real religion there was little. In the words of Dean Swift, most men had just enough to make them hate one another and not enough to make them love one another. Bigotry was enthroned, and its rule suffered no dissent and granted no freedom.

Toleration was little understood. Lord Stanhope in the debate on the repeal of the Test and Corporation Act in 1827 made the comment that the "time was when toleration was craved by dissenters as a boon, it is now demanded as a right, but the time will come when it will be spurned as an insult." In the days before the sailing of the *Ark* and the *Dove* mere toleration would have been a welcome blessing to those who could not conform to a faith that was not theirs but which the government insisted should be imposed upon them.

There were few men in England at the time who had any sympathy for toleration, much less any conception of the idea of freedom of conscience. But because of these few the voyage of the *Ark* and the *Dove* was made possible. It was the ideal of religious freedom transmitted from father to sons and put into actual practise when the voyage was ended that bore rich fruit on Maryland soil.

It may be easy to attribute other motives for this venture, but to the father who conceived it and to the sons who led it the need of a greater freedom was very real. It was the realization of this need and the desire for the attainment of this ideal that accomplished the end they sought.

There could have been no religious freedom where those who having gained it for themselves, denied it to others. God-fearing men and women, sturdy and courageous, had crossed the sea in ships in order that they might worship God after their own fashion, but the truth as they saw it forbade them to grant to others the same privilege they sought for themselves. In such a gain of freedom there was little of value for posterity.

Those who set sail from the Isle of Wight in the late autumn of 1633 sailed under orders that proclaimed religious freedom for all who might seek sanctuary at the journey's end. On these two ships were men of different faiths and creeds and these faiths and creeds were to be equally respected before the law. Herein the voyage of the *Ark* and the *Dove* was quite without a precedent in the history of the Christian era.

History has quite generally ignored the *Ark* and the *Dove*.

Their names are not familiar and there is scant mention of them by most historians. History as it has been written has been more than kind to the *Mayflower,* which thirteen years before the departure of the *Ark* and the *Dove* sailed from old England to new England. In fact it may be said that the name "Mayflower" is a household word in America and has been widely used and recognized in many ways. Yet after all is said and done, the *Mayflower* really brought little to America, for it was overladen with the spirit of the Old Dispensation with a goodly mixture of rigid Calvinistic theology. Fortunately, the Maryland *Ark* of the old covenant was leavened with the mildness and charity of the *Dove,* the spirit of the New Dispensation.

On the voyage of the *Ark* and the *Dove* were three missionaries of the Society of Jesus, two priests and a lay brother. They did not take passage until the day of final departure. Jesuits in the England of those days had to be wary of their comings and goings and it would not have been prudent to have had their departure heralded so that everyone might know of it. The influence of the English Jesuit mission on the foundation of this most interesting of the thirteen colonies needs to be told. Out of the English mission came the first American Jesuit mission which constitutes the Maryland-New York Province of this great religious order.

American historians, notably Bancroft and Parkman, have not failed to pay tribute to the heroic missionaries who came to New France to suffer privation and unspeakable cruelties in order that they might carry the Message of the Cross to the natives of the North American wilderness, and they have painted a soul-stirring picture for their readers to behold and admire, yet there has hardly been mention made of the holy influence of the little band of Jesuit missionaries sent out on the voyage of the first colonists of Maryland and those who followed them, to bring to America not bigotry and intolerance, but the message of peace and good will.

The seeds of both religious and civil liberty were planted

on the banks of the St. Mary's after the landing of the *Ark* and the *Dove*. There was not only freedom of religious worship in early Maryland. There was equality before the law and a representative democracy wherein the people became the real source of power. The electoral franchise was freely given and was dependent neither upon church membership nor ownership of property. In later years there was much to retard the growth from that early planting, but the harvest time came finally with the American Constitution and the first amendments thereto. It was a long time from seed-time to harvest—a little over a century and a half. It is some of the events of this period and the great silent forces that gave rise to these events that the following pages attempt to portray.

* * *

For the use of the map of St. Mary's City and Bay and for the drawings of the *Ark* and the *Dove* I am indebted to Mr. Swepson Earle of Baltimore, author of *The Chesapeak Bay Country*.

J. Moss Ives

September 8, 1935

CONTENTS

BOOK ONE: ANTECEDENTS AND PREPARATIONS

BOOK TWO: THE PLANTING

BOOK THREE: THE HARVEST

LIST OF ILLUSTRATIONS

THE *ARK* AND THE *DOVE*

BOOK I
ANTECEDENTS AND PREPARATIONS

CHAPTER I

THE ENGLISH MISSION FIELD

FORTY years after Ignatius Loyola founded the order which became known as the Society of Jesus, and as many years after Henry VIII, for the love of Anne Boleyn, broke from the See of Rome to become the head of his own ecclesiastical establishment, two English-born Jesuit priests returned to their country to attempt to restore it to the old faith. It was likewise forty years since Edmund Campion first saw the light of day in London. Now in the year 1580, with his companion, Robert Persons, he was returning to his native land, to minister to the faithful and within a year to suffer a martyr's death on the gallows of Tyburn. Graduate of Oxford, former Anglican, brilliant in intellect, eloquent of speech and of attractive personality, Campion had abandoned the path of opportunism and preferment to take the vows of poverty, chastity and obedience. Persons, also an Oxford man, had been fellow and tutor at Balliol and had attained eminence in scholarship.

It was a dangerous time for these priests to come back to their native country, for England had placed their church under the ban of persecution and had outlawed all Catholic priests. Three years before, Cuthbert Mayne, a Cornwall priest, was found guilty of denying the spiritual supremacy of the Queen and saying Mass. He became the first member of the Catholic clergy to suffer capital punishment in England.

The exercise of his priestly functions was construed as an act of treason. With Father Mayne, there had been convicted as aiders and abettors of his treason, sixteen of his parishioners, including the owner of the house where Mass was said, for which heinous crime he languished in prison for twenty-eight years and his estate was seized by the crown.

The majority of the English people were Catholic by tradition and by choice, and had desired no change in the established religion of the realm. Elizabeth, who had been half inclined to be a Catholic herself, would not have persecuted her Catholic subjects of her own will, but behind the throne was her wily minister, William Cecil. It was the hand and mind of this able politician that ruled the land. It was he who decided there should be no return to the ancient faith. With the aid of a powerful minority that, like its leader, had become immensely wealthy from the loot of the churches and the confiscation of monastery and friars' lands, he had his way and England became and remained Protestant. This came about not because of any hatred of the Catholic religion, but because Cecil and his followers were determined to protect their fortunes—they were fearful lest the plunder they had amassed would be lost to them if the old religion was restored.[1]

Pope Pius V had played into the hands of these men when he issued his bull of excommunication against the English Queen. Elizabeth had feared it, but when it came it only angered her and made it all the easier for Cecil to bend her to his will. It served the cause of the English Catholics poorly and made their lot the harder. Anti-Catholic legislation of the most drastic nature was enacted. Conformity to the national church was made the dividing line between patriotism and treason and the oath of supremacy was the means whereby conformity was enforced.

There were more Catholics in England all through the reign of Elizabeth than most historians have ever been willing

[1] Belloc, *Charles the First,* 43.

to admit. These two Jesuit missionaries had come to satisfy what they had reason to believe were the longings and desires of the larger part of their fellow countrymen. They knew that their task would be a difficult one and fraught with danger. Prior to their coming every jail in England numbered among its inmates Catholics who were imprisoned solely for their religion. Many of these had died while they were incarcerated, so foul were the conditions that were allowed to exist in all the jails. Death had annually thinned the ranks of the secular clergy who had remained in the face of persecution and who were endeavoring as best they could to minister to those who like themselves had kept true to the faith. Following the fate of Father Mayne, priests were tortured and put to death. There was a call for help to save the faith. These Jesuit missionaries like him who crossed from Troas to Philippi and heard the cry to "come over into Macedonia and help us" obeyed the summons and had no fear of persecution or death.

At the Jesuit residence at St. Omer's where the missionaries stayed on the eve of their departure, the fathers tried to dissuade them from attempting to enter England. Their coming had been known for some time. News had been received that full particulars of both Campion and Persons had been furnished to the Queen's council and that portraits of the expected Jesuits had been sent to all the government searchers at the ports. Persons insisted that if their entrance was dangerous now it would only be more so later on. They had made deliberate choice and no fear of danger or peril to themselves could now deter them.

It was decided that Persons should first make the attempt and if he succeeded he would send for Campion. By adopting clever disguises they were able to elude the cordon of spies and watchers that had been thrown out to prevent their landing. Persons was disguised as a soldier and obtained consent for his friend to follow him. Campion came over a few days later disguised as a merchant. When it became known that the Jesuits were actually in England and had outwitted the police, there was consternation in the Privy Council. Cecil had both respect and fear for "the light cavalry of the Pope" and had made up his mind that there would be no work of the counter-reformation in England to thwart his ends. He knew Campion. He had been captivated by the eloquence of the young priest as had Elizabeth herself, when Campion was a student at Oxford and he had called him "one of the diamonds" of England. He now had reason to fear his power and influence. A royal proclamation was issued which warned all persons who knew or heard of any Jesuit in the kingdom and did not reveal where he was concealed, that they should be prosecuted and punished as abettors of treason.

Within a few days after the landing of Persons and Campion, had come the close of the session of Parliament in the twenty-third year of the reign of Elizabeth. With its closing was passed the usual act of grace and pardon covering every crime from murder to petty larceny, but there was one exception. The new crime of non-conformity was not to be condoned, nor the offender pardoned. To this land of persecution overshadowed and overlorded by the greatest archplotter in English history came these Jesuit missionaries with the fond purpose at heart to restore their native land to the orthodox faith.

As Jesuits had been accused of complicity in every plot against established rule in Protestant countries, it is not surprising that in the reign of Elizabeth they should be accused of plotting to overthrow the English government. Secrecy and the use of disguise necessarily surrounded the labors of the mission priests, but these had nothing to do with political intrigues and plots of assassination. There was no trace of secular intrigue in the reports of the early missionaries sent to Rome. "About parliament," writes one of them to his superior, "I say nothing as I desire my letter like my soul to have nothing to do with matters of state."

Had not the mission kept clear of politics in the way it did, Professor Meyer says, "it could not have achieved its great religious success." [2]

There may have been at times exceptions to this rule. Even Catholic writers have claimed that Persons was guilty of political intrigue, but if he was they admit "he threw obedience to the winds." [3] The general of the order had given the English missionaries specific instructions not to interfere with matters of government and directly forbade them to discuss political questions. When he arrived in London, Persons assured the secular clergy that he had come only to treat of religion "in truth and simplicity, and to attend to the gaining of souls without any pretense or knowledge of matters of state." [4] If Persons did stoop to intrigue it was in disobedience to orders. Exceptional cases always attract the attention of historians because they *are* exceptions, but are seldom noted as such.[5]

As the persecution became more severe more priests came to England to brave death in the perilous mission field. In their panic the Protestants magnified the little group of missionaries into a host of disguised Jesuits. The invasion of this imaginary host was met by the seizure of as many priests as the government could lay hands on and the imprisonment of hundreds of lay Catholics throughout the country.[6] This was followed by the calling of an assembly of parliament early in 1581. The parliament solemnly enacted that:

> All persons pretending to any power of absolving subjects from their allegiance or practising to withdraw them to the Romish religion with all persons after the present session willingly so absolved or reconciled to the See of Rome, shall be guilty of High Treason.

Hiding by day and going forth only by night and under disguise, seldom spending more than one night under the

[2] Meyer, *England and the Catholic Church under Queen Elizabeth,* 204.
[3] Taunton, *English Black Monks of St. Benedict* I, 240.
[4] Simpson, *Edmund Campion,* 183.
[5] LaFarge, *Jesuits in Modern Times,* 141.
[6] Green, *History of the English People,* II, 396.

same roof, the mission priests were tracked and hounded by the agents and spies of Cecil. "We shall not long be able to escape the hands of the heretics," wrote Campion from one of his hiding places, "so many eyes are centered on us, so many enemies beset us. I am constantly disguised, and am constantly changing both my dress and my name." So hot was the pursuit that Persons was forced to flee to the continent while Campion was apprehended within a year from the time he crossed the Dover channel. Persons never returned to England or he would probably have suffered the same fate as Campion.

Father Campion suffered a cruel martyrdom. England had borrowed her methods of torture from the Spanish Inquisition after these had long been abandoned, and put them into service in the torture of Catholic priests. After his arrest Campion was racked and tortured with the utmost barbarity. Brought before the Queen to speak in his own defense it was seen that when he was making a gesture in his speech all the finger nails had been torn by force from the flesh. A vain attempt was made to have him implicate others in a plot concocted in the fertile imagination of Cecil. He was finally brought to trial with no less than twelve secular priests and one layman. To their astonishment they were indicted for a conspiracy to murder the Queen and overthrow the government. There was no evidence to support such a charge. The trial was a travesty. Hallam acknowledged that "it was as unfairly conducted and supported by as slender evidence as can be found in our books." [7]

One was remanded, the others, including Campion, were found guilty and condemned to suffer the death of traitors. This was the sentence pronounced:

> You must go to the place from whence you came, there to remain until ye shall be drawn through the open city of London upon hurdles to the place of execution and there to be hanged and let down alive, and your privy parts cut off and your entrails

[7] *Constitutional History of England,* (5th Edition, N. Y., 1870), 92.

taken out and burnt in your sight; then your hands to be cut off and your bodies to be divided into four parts to be disposed of at Her Majesty's pleasure. And God have mercy upon your souls.

Upon hearing the sentence Campion burst out into the triumphant hymn, *"Te Deum laudamus. Te Dominum confitemur,"* in which the others joined. He was carried back to the tower and put in irons. His keeper said he had a saint to guard. Friday, December 1st, was fixed for the execution. The day was dismal and raining. Campion and two secular priests, Sherwin and Briant, were led out and tied to the hurdles. Through the mud and slush they were dragged with a rabble of ministers and fanatics beside them. The three priests, with faces lit with the internal joy that filled their hearts, actually laughed as they neared Tyburn, and many of the onlookers wondered how this could be. It is said that several converts to the Catholic faith were made that day.

The executions were unnecessarily cruel. Before his death Campion forgave his persecutors and prayed for the Queen whom he acknowledged to be his sovereign. "We are come here to die, but we are not traitors," he said upon the scaffold. "I am a Catholic man and a priest. In that faith I have lived and mean to die. If you consider my religion treason, then I am guilty. Other treason I never committed as God is my judge."

The heroism of the martyred priests won the respect of many Protestants, and when they saw one of the hated Jesuits go to his death with a prayer for the excommunicated Queen on his lips, they questioned whether a system that could send to death such a man as this could prevail. Some there were who gave warning that too many martyrs were being made for the Church of Rome. Henry Walpole came as a Protestant to witness the death of Campion. He went away inwardly convinced of the truth of the martyr's faith. He afterwards became a Catholic and a Jesuit and suffered a similar fate to Campion. Cecil afterwards issued two pamphlets to explain and justify the severities and tortures that were used in the cases of Campion and the other priests who suffered with him, but his excuses were so weak that Hallam says they only served to "mingle contempt with detestation."

The protests that came as the result of these executions did not stay the hand of Cecil. The persecution went on and "the rack seldom stood idle in the Tower for all the latter part of Elizabeth's reign." No Catholic could longer enjoy liberty of worship. There was risk of torture and death for the priest and imprisonment and confiscation of property for the layman. Pursuivants and recusants now became familiar terms in English history. To the pursuivants, officers of the humblest rank in the college of heraldry, but with powers and emoluments by no means humble, was given the privilege of tracking down the Catholic non-conformists and for reward they received one-third part of the property confiscated. In this way there was raised a zealous army of heresy hunters and to each was given "a sense of importance in being an assistant district attorney of God, to prepare indictments for the last judgment, together with the excitement of playing the amateur detective in uncovering mysterious evil doers." [8]

Spying came to be considered an honorable means of livelihood, and the sport of tale-bearing became more popular than ever, now that it was placed on a paying basis. The Catholic victims of these heresy hunters became known as recusants, and their refusal to conform to the national religion made a rich living for the army of pursuivants. Their homes were subject to search and their property to seizure at any hour of day or night. Names of recusants in each parish, amounting to about fifty thousand, had been returned to the Privy Council, and the jails were filled with persons suspected of being priests or harborers of priests.

Next to enter upon the scene of the Elizabethan drama was the "provocateur," a sinister creation of Walsingham,

[8] Van Dyke, *Ignatius Loyola,* 109.

Cecil's chief ally and organizer of the spy system. There had to be Catholic plots with which to frighten the Queen and win her over to the Cecilian policy. As there were no real plots, some had to be manufactured. The provocateurs were fewer in number than the pursuivants, but their rewards were greater as the result of their work was more momentous. There were more of these creatures than has been revealed, for they moved stealthily behind the scenes of history, and the names of only a few ever came to light. When a plot was needed, a provocateur was ready at hand to instigate one, and once instigated, it was carefully nurtured until the time came for the great exposé.

When Campion came to England on his perilous mission the luckless Mary, Queen of Scots, was held a prisoner in the land where she had sought a refuge. She threw herself on the mercy of Elizabeth, only to become a victim of the wiles of Cecil. Elizabeth's promised help for the exiled Scottish Queen was not forthcoming. Cecil stood in the way. It did not fit in with his policy to permit a possible Catholic successor to the English throne to be at large. Mary had become the rallying point for the hopes and ambitions of the English Catholics who had good reason, if they saw fit, to attempt her liberation, for there was nothing to justify her imprisonment. There had been a Catholic uprising in the north country which was poorly organized and quickly and ruthlessly put down. In order to convince Elizabeth that her life was in danger as long as the Scottish Queen was living, there was a plot needed which should have for its double purpose the liberation of Mary and the assassination of Elizabeth. No such plot as this had been forthcoming, but Walsingham, the fabricator of plots, was equal to the occasion. The necessary provocateur was found in the person of one Gilbert Gifford, whose perfidy, aided by the cunning of Walsingham and directed by the finesse of Cecil, was soon to bring the Scottish Queen to the block and rid England of a Catholic heir-apparent to the throne of the Tudors.

There was a strong spiritual bond between the missionaries and the lay-Catholics which had been riveted by their common dangers and perils. It is safe to say that it was the work of the missionary priests that saved the Catholic faith from being utterly exterminated in England. Their most difficult task was to strengthen the faith of those who were easily frightened into conformity to the new religion. The attacks upon the Catholic Church and its priests were making headway with the weaker members of the flock. It was a case of the survival of the most devout. Those who did survive were those whose faith was real, and whose spiritual lives had only been deepened by the experiences and sufferings they had undergone. These numbered many of the best families of the nobility and for them to remain true to their faith meant far more than to others who had less to lose.

The loyalty of the English Catholics met a severe test when Philip of Spain sent his Armada to drive Elizabeth from the throne. The militant faction of the Catholics was mostly on the continent, receiving many recruits from the ranks of the English refugees, and there can be no doubt but that this faction planned and hoped for a Catholic uprising in England to aid the Spanish forces in placing a Catholic on the English throne. Cardinal Allen was leader of this faction, and attempted to enlist support for the Spanish invasion of his native country. Persons' forced exile on the continent and the Spanish influence to which he was subjected unfortunately led him to take the side of Allen. He was betrayed by the hope of regaining England through the intervention of Spain, rather than through the toil and sacrifice of the missionaries. Not all the exiles, however, favored the armed intervention of Spain. Many of these viewed with disapproval "the sight of ministers of a kingdom not of this world dabbling in politics to the certain disgrace of their cause." [9] Flanders was the great place of refuge of the English exiles

[9] Taunton, *History of the Jesuits in England,* 104.

who "were not by any means all favorable to the Spanish policy of aggrandisement under the plea of religion." [10]

Only a few, if any, of the Catholics in England, gave encouragement to the invaders. There was a Catholic uprising when the Armada neared the English coast, but it was an uprising in support of the Protestant Queen.

All religious differences were forgotten and all Englishmen, Protestant and Catholic alike, rallied to the standard of their Queen. The persecuted, and even the imprisoned Catholics, laid aside all resentment for their past treatment and offered their services to the government, but it was the Queen and not her ministers, to whom they pledged their support. The Catholic prisoners in Ely signed a declaration of their readiness to fight in defense of their sovereign against "all her enemies, were they kings or priests or pope or any other potentate whatsoever." The ministers themselves in a report published later stated that "no difference could be found on this occasion between the Protestants and Catholics," and mentions the Catholic Viscount Montague, who, with his son and grandson, presented himself before the Queen "at the head of two hundred horse that he had raised for the defense of her person." [11]

"The Catholic gentry who had been painted as longing for the coming of the stranger," says Green, "led their tenantry to the muster at Tillbury. The loyalty of the Catholics decided the fate of Philip's scheme." [12] The Catholic lords on Allen's list of those from whom help for the invading forces might be expected, Cumberland, Oxford and Northumberland, brought their vessels alongside the English naval fleet as soon as the Armada appeared in the channel.

After the defeat of the Armada the Catholics received no reward for their loyalty through any cessation of the persecution. There was no recognition in any way of the part

[10] Ibid, 108.
[11] Lingard, *History of England.* 4th Edition. VIII, 277, note.
[12] *History of the English People,* II, 422.

they had taken in the defense of their queen and country, and no gratitude shown. The persecution was continued with renewed severity, and from the defeat of the Armada to the death of Elizabeth, fourteen years later, no less than sixty-one priests, forty-seven laymen and two women suffered capital punishment for their religion. On one fateful day in August 1588 no less than thirteen men—six priests and seven laymen—suffered death on the scaffold.

The persecution spared neither age nor sex. "Religious fanaticism was at its height," writes Professor Meyer, and it "developed traits hitherto foreign to the character of the English people. In the ferocity with which they treated women and children Englishmen acted contrary to their true character, even more than by resorting to unscrupulous espionage." [13] It was not uncommon for women and children to be arrested while hearing mass and cast into prison.[14] A Catholic boy was racked and tortured to make him betray his friends and died a traitor's death. According to Willis-Bund, *State Trials,* he was only thirteen years of age. The executions continued to be featured with unspeakable cruelty. In addition to this, the penalties of recusancy, heavy fines, frequent search and seizure and imprisonment visited nearly all who remained true to their faith. There was more need than ever of the ministrations and sacrifices of the mission priests.

There were always recruits ready to fill vacancies in the ranks caused by the deaths of the martyrs. These came from the young men who had left their homes in England to receive their training and education in the colleges in France and Belgium, and then to return to brave the perils of the mission field. The dawn of the new century found the missionaries gaining in numbers and influence, and all this was to be needed, for the end of the Tudor dynasty was not to mark the end of the persecution.

[13] Op. cit., 176.
[14] Strype, *Annals,* II (1824), 11, 660, 662.

CHAPTER II

BETWEEN TWO FIRES

JAMES VI, King of Scotland, only off-spring of the unfortunate marriage of Mary, Queen of Scots, and Lord Darnley, paid a price for the English throne and so became James I of England. The price paid was his tacit consent to his mother's execution.[1] In addition to receiving the promise of his succession to Elizabeth, he received, to boot, a liberal pension and six pairs of bloodhounds. When his mother's life was in peril and she needed the support of her son, he abandoned her to her fate. Soon after her sentence he sent envoys, one of whom was a pensioner of the English court, to request that proceedings against his mother be stayed until he could be made acquainted with her offense. It was suggested that Mary's life be spared on condition that she resign her rights to her son. This would secure Elizabeth from the fear of a competitor and the established church from the danger of a Catholic successor. When it was replied that Mary had no rights to resign, the envoys represented that their master would be compelled in honor to avenge his mother's death. One of the envoys assured Elizabeth, however, that James had sent them merely to save appearances and that whatever he might pretend, he would be easily pacified with a "present of dogs and deer." [2] On the receipt of the news of his mother's execution, he wept and talked of vengeance, but when members of the Scottish parliament on their bended knees implored him to avenge his mother's death, he put them off by saying he must consult his allies. His resentment, such as it

1 Belloc says: "Young King James of Scotland who was, by that time, in Cecil's pay, consented to his mother's removal by the axe." *A History of England,* IV, 378.

2 Egerton, *Life of Lord Egerton,* (1802) 116.

was, soon evaporated. It was believed at the time that he looked upon the death of his mother as a personal benefit for it relieved him from his fear of a rival for the Scottish throne.[3]

In justice to Mary Stuart it can be said that her son inherited more from his father than from his mother. He inherited nearly all of Darnley's weak traits, including a trait of cowardice. He had read and studied much but had learned little. Of what little learning he had, he made a great show. He claimed, with some excuse, to be a great theologian but religion to him, as to most of those who were to help him rule his new kingdom, was a matter of politics.

When he came to England, James had three choices of outward religious faith, Anglican, Catholic and Puritan. Presbyterianism offered him no choice. He knew that if he espoused the cause of the state church he would be its head. This appealed to his pride and vanity, and of these traits there was far more in his character than any real religion. There were reasons why he should be inclined toward a policy of toleration. It was for his interest to effect a compromise among the opposing factions. He had shown favor to Catholics and had promised to relieve the severity of their fines. The Pope looked favorably upon him and ordered the missionary priests to countenance no action against him.[4] There were two factors, however, that militated against a change of religious policy and shattered the early hopes of the Catholics for a lessening of the persecution.

While there had been a change of dynasties in the English monarchy, from the House of Tudor to the House of Stuart, there was no change in the power behind the throne. When Walsingham died in 1590, the first Cecil, Lord Burghley, had his son, Robert, become his assistant. Upon the death of the father, the younger Cecil took control of the invisible government, and true to his father's policy, he saw to it that

[3] Lingard, op. cit., VIII, 255.
[4] Belloc, op. cit., IV, 439.

England remained anti-Catholic. It was Robert Cecil who placed James on the throne, as his father before him had given the throne to Elizabeth. Without the new king being quite aware of what it was all about, his prime minister became master of the government, and the first Stuart king yielded unconsciously to the dictatorship of the House of Cecil, as had the last of the Tudor monarchs.

Robert Cecil was aware of the danger to his power and fortune that would come if James were allowed to grant toleration to the Catholics. Then there was the slowly rising tide of Puritanism which was as inimical to Catholicism as was the government under the sway of Cecil. The Catholics soon found themselves between two fires, the stern repressive policy of the government, prompted by political and mercenary motives, and the enmity of the Puritan party motivated by religious bigotry and prejudice. It is difficult now to see which was the worse for them.

Although James was at first inclined to be tolerant toward his Catholic subjects, it was not long before he was accused of being at heart a "Papist," and this was a little more than he could stand. In order to remove the impression that he had any leaning toward the Catholic faith, he issued in the second year of his reign a proclamation enjoining the banishment of all Catholic missionaries and the magistrates were ordered to put the penal laws of the Elizabethan reign into effect. As a result, between five and six thousand Catholics had to surrender two-thirds of their estates and incur enormous fines. Many forfeited their entire personal property.[5]

In the star chamber James avowed his detestation of the Church of Rome and declared he wanted no child of his to succeed him on the throne if that child should become a Catholic. He did not put to death as many Catholics as did his predecessor, but he made the lot of the living so miserable that they might just as well have suffered martyrdom by death. Then in 1605 came the gun-powder plot, and this did

[5] Gardiner, *History of England,* I, 224-9.

not help matters any. For the incredible folly of a few hot-headed fanatics, the great body of loyal Catholic subjects, who had never countenanced resort to force and violence, had to suffer. The plot was so clumsily executed that it was soon discovered. Then there followed what might have been expected. Cecil's power became supreme, England as a nation became definitely Protestant, and Catholics were placed under a ban of suspicion which lasted for over a century.[6]

In 1606 new and more severe penal laws were enacted. Under the provisions of an "Act for the Better Repressing of Popish Recusants" [7] a fine of twenty pounds each month was imposed on all over the age of sixteen who refused to attend the services of the Church of England, or in lieu of a fine, to suffer forfeiture of two-thirds of their lands. Power was given to the king to refuse the fine and seize the lands at will. The fine of twenty pounds a month was exacted only of those who were possessed of large estates. At the accession of James there were not more than sixteen Catholics whose landed estates were large enough to allow them to escape forfeiture of their lands by paying fines. Upon the less wealthy fell the hardest exaction of all: the forfeiture of two-thirds of their lands. Those without landed estates were mulcted of their personal property. When the fine of twenty pounds a month was exacted for non-conformity, it was made to cover a period of a year, a demand which reduced many families to absolute beggary.[8]

The pursuivants were not forgotten. A supplementary bill was passed providing that anyone discovering Mass being said or relief being given to a Jesuit missionary priest, should receive a reward of one-third of any fine imposed or one-third of the property forfeited. Again the heresy hunter stalked

[6] Belloc says: "From that date, May 9th., 1606, begins a new chapter in the story of English religion. For it was the gun-powder plot which turned the tide, left great masses of the Catholic body doubtful of their own position, and made them all criminals in the eyes of those hitherto indifferent." Op. cit., IV, 448.

[7] 2 and 4 Jac. I, caput 4.

[8] Lingard, op. cit., IX, 31.

through the land. Catholic subjects were at the mercy of these paid spies. They knew not whom to trust among their friends and neighbors, for friendship was often used as a cloak to hide the work of the informer seeking his reward.

Added to the army of pursuivants were the King's indigent favorites. It was a chance for them to obtain money and property which they very much needed. Catholics were "farmed out" to these needy courtiers who were allowed to make such terms with the recusants as they might please.

Many of these courtiers so favored were men who had come with the king from Scotland. There had been intense jealousy between the two kingdoms, and these Scotch favorites were looked upon as foreigners. For the king to place English subjects at the mercy of these Scottish minions was only to add insult to injury. King James did not hesitate to enrich his own purse at the expense of his Catholic subjects and before he allowed his favorites to receive plunder, he saw to it that he had some for himself. By his own account, he received a net income of thirty-six thousand pounds per annum from fines and forfeitures imposed on Catholics.

It was not in money and property alone that the English Catholics suffered in the reign of James. They were deprived of most of the rights and liberties which were dear to them as English freemen. No Catholic who refused to conform could seek redress in a court of law or equity. He could not hold public office nor be an officer in the army, nor could he practise law or medicine. Any Catholic married except in the Church of England was disabled to have any estate of freehold in the lands of his or her wife or husband. He could not educate his own children. Catholic children sent to foreign Catholic schools or colleges forfeited their inheritance to their Protestant next of kin. Furthermore, when parents tried to send their children to seminaries on the continent, the English schools and colleges being barred to Catholics, the state interfered, took the children from their parents and had them educated in the homes of Protestant clergymen, at their parents' expense. The right to search homes was greatly abused. Armed with warrants anyone could visit a Catholic home under the pretext of enforcing the law and then exact bribes. From the poor, the pursuivants usually seized furniture and cattle. The old common law maxim that "a man's house is his castle" gave no protection to a non-conforming Catholic. Even after death, his troubled soul was not suffered to rest in peace. His body could not be buried in consecrated ground, but in the burial ground of the established church. The right of holy sepulchre was denied him. In death as in life, he was pursued by the grim specter of conformity.

After the exposure of the gun-powder plot, Robert Cecil was at the zenith of his power, but his reign was only to last six years longer. In 1616 came his death, but with it did not come the end of the Catholic persecution. The Cecilian policy, selfish and mercenary, had sapped the economic strength of the monarchy and, contemporaneous with it, had come the gradual ascendancy of the Puritan party. James, after the death of his minister, found himself greatly handicapped by what the House of Cecil had taken from him. The monarchy, weakened not only in power and influence, had lost heavily in worldly estate. As the church lands had been confiscated and sold by the elder Cecil, the royal lands had been sold by the younger Cecil on a ruinous scale.[9]

James was now forced to compromise with the Puritan taxpayers and to meet the pressing needs of royal rule, he must now yield to the policies of the new parliamentary party. Little pressure was brought to bear on the throne by the English churchmen who were not particularly hostile to the old church. The Catholic persecution under the Cecils was ostensibly to protect the established church, but it was based more on political and economic grounds than on religious. The Church of England had tried to take a middle ground between Rome and Geneva, but leaned more toward Rome. But there was no middle ground for the Puritans.

[9] Belloc, op. cit., IV, 449.

It was an uncompromising, relentless persecution so far as they were concerned, and James did not dare to show any favor to his Catholic subjects, although there were times after the death of Cecil when he seemed disposed toward a mild toleration. Although never enforced with uniform rigidity, the penal laws were always on the statute books as ready weapons that could be used at any time.

Persecution was relaxed when the crown prince Charles was suitor for the hand of the Catholic Infanta Maria of Spain. As an indication of how the prisons were crowded with Catholics "so that there was little room for thieves," no less than four thousand prisoners obtained their discharge when the King in 1616 preparatory to the Spanish match, granted liberty to Catholics under the penal laws.[10] As soon as the Spanish match was broken off, the persecution which had temporarily abated, began again with renewed vigor.

Even during periods when enforcement of the penal laws was relaxed, a Catholic was never better off than a paroled prisoner. He was always circumscribed in the exercise of his religion. He had no church to attend and could only worship in secret. So all through the reign of James the tide of persecution ebbed and flowed, sometimes abating, at other times setting in with increased severity, but never ceasing. Through all these years the missionary priests remained at their posts to be shepherds of the little flock of the faithful.

In the face of tremendous odds the mission had a phenomenal growth. In 1610, thirty years after two solitary priests came to England to establish the mission, the membership was so large that there were fifty-three in England, all being priests except one lay brother who was in prison. The roll of death showed the martyrdom of sixteen members at Tyburn, St. Paul's church-yard, or on the rack. In 1623 the mission was enlarged into a province and ten years later was to send its first missionaries to America. At this latter time no less than three hundred and thirty-eight members referred

[10] Lingard, op. cit., IX, 157.

to the province as their own, although they were not all in England.[11] Many of the priests had been banished and some of these returned at the risk of being executed in accordance with the statute prohibiting the return of priests from exile. According to Bishop Challoner, forty-seven mission priests were sent into perpetual banishment at various times.[12] It was long before the sending of the first missionaries from the English province to America that groups of English Catholics made attempts to migrate across the sea to escape the double fire of persecution.

11 Hughes, *History of the Society of Jesus in North America,* I, 162.
12 *Memoirs of Missionary Priests,* (revised edition, 1924) 282.

CHAPTER III

EARLY ATTEMPTS AT CATHOLIC MIGRATION

IT WAS not long after the first Jesuit missionaries came to England that the colonization of the North Atlantic seaboard began. With the closing years of the Tudor dynasty a new era was to bring to an end the days of discovery and adventure. Men were no longer to seek an easy passage to the sea of India, and fabulous tales of gold and treasure were no longer to lure them to America. With the Turks blocking the overland route to India, English adventurers had ever been on the lookout for a western passage to the Orient and, in search of this, they heard stories of hidden riches. The discovery of a vast new continent had aroused the spirit of adventure and tainted it with a good bit of greed. Ralph Lane, governor of Raleigh's first colony on the coast of what is now North Carolina, believed that the Roanoke River was the gateway to the South Seas. Both he and his colonists at the same time gave credence to the wild tales brought to them by Indian interpreters, of great treasure and of a town the walls of which were made of pearls, near the headwaters of the river. Raleigh did turn his mind to the settlement of an agricultural colony, but his followers were soon distracted by stories of mysterious rivers and hidden gold. Colonization could not be permanent, nor could foundations of a stable government be laid when men were victims of phantasies and delusions.

With the turn of the century there came the end to the days of adventure and discovery. The time for permanent colonization had come. It was to be no longer love of adventure, nor the seeking of gold, nor a search for a new route to the Orient, that was to send ships from England across the sea. There was to come a change in the impelling force of the English exodus. Permanent settlement was to be largely motivated by the desire to escape conditions that made life at home intolerable. Discriminatory laws and persecution were to turn the eyes of many to a possible refuge beyond the sea. With the exception of the early settlements of Virginia, religion had much to do with the settlement of the American colonies.[1]

The last quarter of the sixteenth century witnessed the beginning of a Catholic exile movement to America. As early as 1574 Sir Humphrey Gilbert, half-brother of Sir Walter Raleigh, conceived a plan of colonization which was to have the support of two Catholic gentlemen, Sir George Peckham and Sir Thomas Gerard. A state paper hinted that he was hand in glove with "the Papists" in looking for relief to a new world. Sir Humphrey was not a Catholic but he was glad of support from this quarter. It was not until four years later that he was able to obtain a grant to discover and colonize any land in North America then unsettled.

At the time of this venture there was in force a statute with the true Cecilian flavor, called "An Act against Fugitives over the Sea" which was designed to prevent the migration of Catholic recusants. Any Catholic successful in escaping persecution by flight was told to return at once to the privileges and blessings of his native land, repent and conform to the state religion, and for failure so to do, would suffer disfranchisement and the confiscation of all property. Cecil did not intend to let the Catholic recusants slip from his grasp. He and his favorites had looted the Catholic churches and enriched themselves by confiscating monasteries and abbeys, lands and buildings. When there was no more church property to loot and appropriate, they pounced upon the Catholic laity and had their share of fines and forfeited estates.

1 Woodrow Wilson, *History of the United States,* I, 126; Eggleston *Beginners of the Nation,* 220; Charles McLean Andrews, *The Colonial Period of American History,* I, 66.

Sir Humphrey evidently had his eye on the fugitive statute, since he succeeded by some process of political legerdemain in having a saving clause inserted in his charter exempting all members of the expedition from the provisions of this law. He, with Gerard and Peckham, presented a petition to Walsingham, the secretary of state, to be allowed to take "recusants of ability" whose finances would enable them to discharge the "penalties due to her Majesty," and such others who were not able to pay the fines and penalties of their religion but might be able to pay them later. Walsingham seeing no diminution in the revenue from wealthy Catholics and anticipating further revenue from the new colony, favored the plan and prevailed upon the Queen to sign Gilbert's patent.[2]

In November 1578, Gilbert, with Raleigh in command of the *Falcon,* sailed with seven ships and 350 men for America. Encounters with the Spaniards and storms forced them to return three months later without having attained their objective. It is safe to infer that the majority of the voyagers were Catholics and that the purpose of the expedition was to found a Catholic colony in America. Another attempt at a similar voyage was made early in the following year, but owing to the fact that Raleigh had had a dangerous sea fight with the Spaniards, the Council forbade Gilbert to sail.[3]

Six years had been allotted to Gilbert within which to launch his colony. The failure of his first expedition caused him financial embarrassment, and then there came opposition from an unexpected source. Many of the English Catholics did not agree with their brethren on the continent including many of the refugees from England, in the method of combating the persecution. They thought they saw a way of giving political allegiance to the crown without violating the tenets of their faith. The so-called Spanish party, which had

2 William J. P. Powers, "The Beginnings of English Catholic Emigration to the New World," *Records of the American Catholic Historical Society of Philadelphia,* XI (March, 1929), 15.

3 Ibid, 16.

only a few adherents in England, favored constant opposition to the Protestant English government and a resort to force if need be to bring about the restoration of the Catholic faith. The Spanish government at that time did not look with favor upon Catholics founding an English colony in America. Mendoza, the Spanish ambassador to England, as head of the Catholic Spanish party, did all in his power to dissuade Catholics from supporting Gilbert's expedition, not for want of sympathy with the persecuted Catholics, but rather because he foresaw a menace to Spanish supremacy in the New World.[4]

Notwithstanding this opposition the English Catholics, led by Peckham and Gerard, continued their efforts to plant a Catholic colony under the Gilbert grant. In 1582 they renewed their contract with Sir Humphrey and made plans for another expedition. At this time a zealous informer with hope of reward submitted to Walsingham secured information to this effect:

> There is a muttering among the Papists that Sir Humphrey Gilbert goeth to seek a new found land; Sir George Peckham and Sir Thomas Gerard goeth with him. I have heard it said among the Papists that they hope it will prove the best journey for England that was made these forty years.[5]

Walsingham still adhered to his policy to allow Catholic recusants to accompany the expedition provided they made provision for the payment of their fines. On June 11, 1583, Sir Humphrey's fleet of five ships and some two hundred men, with Catholic recusants on board, sailed from Plymouth to America. Four of the five ships arrived at St. John's, Newfoundland, after a voyage of two months. Finding the climate unsuitable for colonization, Gilbert sailed for the coast of Maine, August 20, 1583. Off Cape Race he lost all his supplies in his best ship. He then set sail for home. At midnight September 9, during a heavy storm, the ship on which he

[4] Ibid, 19.
[5] Hughes, op. cit., I, 147.

was sailing went down with all on board. The *Golden Hind,* under command of Captain Edward Hayes, finally reached Falmouth with the first tidings of the disaster. This ended the second attempt of the English Catholics to find a refuge in America from persecution. Father Powers says that from the Catholic viewpoint:

> The importance of these voyages lies in the fact that by them was abrogated the law of 1571, by which Catholics were forbidden to leave the realm, thereby setting a norm for all future exile movements. The words of the letters patent were to the effect that in Sir Humphrey was vested the authority to make all laws, political and religious, for his colony, provided, of course they were not against the true Christian faith, i.e., the Church of England. The phrase "the true Christian Faith" was a stock phrase taken from Magna Charta of 1215 and it was capable of being interpreted, as it was by Calvert in 1634, to mean the Catholic faith.[6]

For twenty years no more was heard of a Catholic migration. When it became known that King James I was not to grant toleration to the English Catholics, plans were again made for the planting of a colony on the Maine coast. Based largely on the report of James Rosier who had accompanied Bartholomew Gosnold on a voyage to New England in 1602, a Catholic gentleman by the name of Winslade interested Lord Thomas Arundel, Baron of Wardour, a wealthy Catholic nobleman in a colonization venture.[7] Winslade consulted Father Persons who did not give his approval. Such a project, he said, would cause prejudice to be done to the cause of Catholicity by exasperating the public authorities who would proceed to tighten the restraints upon priests and interfere more effectually with students passing over to the seminaries on the continent.

Despite Persons' objections the plans went forward, and on Easter Sunday 1605, the good ship *Archangel* under the com-

[6] Op. cit., p. 17.

[7] Lord Arundel afterwards became the father-in-law of the second Lord Baltimore.

mand of Captain George Weymouth set sail from the Downs headed for the Maine coast. Rosier accompanied this expedition and wrote an interesting "relation" of the voyage as he did of the Gosnold expedition.[8] There is reason to believe he was a Catholic priest and probably a Jesuit. The religious tone of his letters indicates this and there is no doubt but that he was sent on both expeditions by Lord Arundel.

The *Archangel* made its first landing on the beautiful island of Monhegan ten miles off the Maine coast and here a cross was planted which remained for several years being found by a subsequent expedition.[9] The landing was made on Saturday, May 18 ("Whitsun eve") and Rosier says the island was "the most fortunate we ever discovered." The next day the *Archangel* sailed into what is now Boothbay Harbor. This was named Pentecost Harbor, the landing being made on Pentecost Day. After exploring one of the large rivers, probably the Penobscot, and planting another cross on an island at its mouth, which was named *Insula Sanctae Crucis,* the expedition returned to Monhegan. For some unknown reason, no permanent settlement was made and the *Archangel* sailed back to England. Knowledge of this expedition is very meager and all the information is that given in Rosier's Relation. It is certain, however, that it represented another effort on the part of English Catholics to find a refuge from persecution.[10]

For a period of eighty years after Sir Humphrey Gilbert's first venture, no less than fifty-nine colonial charters were granted by the British crown. The settlements so authorized ranged in territory from the Gulf of St. Lawrence to the mouth of the Amazon. Nearly all of the early charters were avowed to be granted for the purpose of propagating the Christian religion among people as yet living in darkness. The light of the gospel which was to come to those in dark-

[8] Rosier's Relation of the Weymouth voyage is found in *Purchas His Pilgrimes,* (Glasgow, 1906) XVIII, 335 et seq.

[9] Proper, *Monhegan the Cradle of New England,* Portland, 1930, 78.

[10] Powers, op. cit., 30; J. T., Adams *Founding of New England,* 38.

ness, however, was to be filtered through the windows of the established church. These charters were strongly inoculated with the anti-Popery virus. As a specimen, an enlargement of the Virginia charter in 1609 declared:

> Because the principal effect which we can desire or expect of this action, is the conversion and reduction of the people in those parts unto the true worship of God and Christian religion, in which respect we would be loathe that any person should be permitted to pass that we suspected to affect the superstitions of the Church of Rome, we do hereby declare that it is our will and pleasure that none be permitted to pass in any voyage from time to time into the said country but such as first shall have taken the oath of supremacy.[11]

In the closing days of the reign of James I, it remained for a Catholic convert who had received preferment from Robert Cecil and advancement from the king, who had been a member of the Privy Council and a Secretary of State, to obtain a liberal charter permitting a Catholic migration to America. This charter was to be a variant from previous charters in that there were to be no disabling clauses barring Catholics and no restrictions preventing those "living in darkness" from hearing the gospel as it was preached by St. Augustine to the Britons. Furthermore there was to be religious liberty accorded to all Christian sects and creeds.

11 Hughes, op. cit., I, 151.

CHAPTER IV

GEORGE CALVERT—THE FIRST LORD BALTIMORE

In the same year that saw the coming of the first Jesuit missionaries to England, a son was born to Leonard and Alicia Calvert, farmer folk living in the little Yorkshire village of Kiplin in the valley of the Swale. Events of later years will show this to have been an interesting coincidence.

Little is known of the boyhood of George Calvert. It is maintained by some authorities that he was a Catholic from his early youth, by others that he was born in that communion. But as the first record we have of him is his matriculation as a commoner at Trinity College, Oxford, he must at that time have been a conformist to the Church of England, for at Oxford since 1581, subscription to the thirty-nine articles of religion had been required for matriculation.

The north of England was the stronghold of the Catholics during the reign of Elizabeth, and the county of York was the scene of the revolts of 1569, when the Catholic forces gathered for the attempted liberation of the Queen of Scotland. According to Sussex, Elizabeth's general in the north, "there were not ten gentlemen in Yorkshire that did approve of her procedure in the cause of religion." It was said that the valley of the Swale was filled with devoted followers of Mary the Queen and Mary the Virgin. The influence of the environment of his youth may have had an effect on young Calvert's life which counter-influences, great though they were, did not eventually overcome.

The North Riding of Yorkshire contained much pasture-land and Leonard Calvert was a cattle farmer, so later those who envied his son's rise to power had opportunity to sneer at him as "the son of a grazier." But this humble grazier was prosperous enough to give his son the advantage of a good education. His preliminary education may have been at the grammar school at Ripon founded by Queen Mary. At the early age of thirteen he entered Oxford, and received his bachelor's degree in 1597. At college it is said that he excelled in the languages, Greek and Latin, French, Spanish and Italian. He completed his education, as was the custom, by travel on the continent. It was during this time that he was afforded the opportunity of a public career, for by a strange irony of fate, he came into the favor of Robert Cecil, who was on an embassy from Queen Elizabeth at the court of Henry of Navarre.

Cecil saw in this young Oxford graduate not only promise of ability, but traits of character that were unusual in young men of his day, and determined to make use of him in the affairs of state. This adroit politician had an ingratiating way with him which would readily influence a young man of talent and ambition. This influence started a cross-current in the life of Calvert, which was not to spend its force until some years later, when he openly confessed his allegiance to the church which his patron had persecuted.

When he returned to England Calvert became secretary to Cecil "being esteemed a forward and knowing person in matters relating to state." After the death of Elizabeth he had a seat in parliament as a member from Bossnay, a small fishing village on the Cornish coast. He was employed by Cecil at this time in the management and settlement of certain estates included in the jointure of Queen Anne of Denmark, the consort of James. In 1605 he received his master's degree at Oxford on the occasion of the first visit of the new king to this ancient seat of learning. The master's degree was conferred upon forty-three candidates, including many members of the nobility, upon lay and ecclesiastical lords, and on Cecil himself who had already received a master's degree at Cambridge.

In 1606, Calvert was appointed Clerk of the Crown and of assize and peace in County Clare, Ireland. This was an office of importance resembling that of attorney-general, and it was Calvert's first relationship with the affairs of this oppressed country. He was afterwards to hold considerable estates in Ireland and to occupy a place on the roll of its nobility. In 1610, the year of the accession of Louis XIII to the throne of France, after the assassination of Henry IV, he was sent on a mission to the French court to bring about friendly relations with the new king. The mission was apparently successful. He returned the next year and declared that it was with difficulty he was able to withdraw his mind from the pleasant memories of the Faubourg St. Germain.

After the death of Cecil, Calvert still had the favor of the King, and his advancement in the affairs of government continued. In 1613 he was appointed clerk of the Privy Council and was entrusted with all the official Spanish and Italian correspondence. The next year it was reported that he would be sent as Ambassador to Venice, but a contemporary wrote that he "was not likely to effect such a journey, being reasonably well settled at home and having a wife and many children, it would be no easy carriage for him." Calvert had married Anne, daughter of George Mynne, Esq., of Hertfordshire. She bore him eleven children. He was devoted to his wife and children, and his family life was singularly happy.

In 1617, George Calvert was knighted in recognition of his public services and two years later he was elevated to the office of Secretary of State and became a member of the King's Privy Council. There were two incumbents of this office at the time of Calvert's appointment and he succeeded Sir Thomas Lake. It was deemed necessary to remove Sir Thomas on account of the indiscretion of his wife, who had talked too much, and who, with her daughter, had become involved in a court scandal. A contemporary writer, referring to the dismissal of Lake, says that "the Papists were much dejected at his fall, . . . for the Secretary had given much satisfaction to the Catholic element," and his own private chaplain was a suspected priest. This was not the real reason for his removal however. Lady Lake had talked her husband out of his office. In a speech in the star chamber a day or two after Lake's dismissal, James discoursed on the danger of secretaries entrusting their wives with secrets of state, and referred to Lady Lake as Eve, and to her daughter as the serpent in the Garden of Eden.

James, who was now solicitous about the wives of his secretaries, asked Calvert questions as to Lady Calvert. One of the answers to these questions shows that like her husband, the wife of the new secretary had virtues quite rare in the royal suite. "She is a good woman," he said to the King, "and has brought me ten children; and I can assure Your Majesty that she is not a wife with a witness."

There is justification for the belief that one of the chief reasons that prompted James to select Calvert for Secretary of State had to do with the negotiations for the proposed marriage of the Crown Prince Charles with the Spanish Infanta, Donna Maria. Not long after his appointment, Calvert was given the delicate and difficult task of continuing the negotiations already begun. He was well qualified for this undertaking, and thoroughly in sympathy with the plan. It would not have done to have trusted the negotiations to anyone with strong anti-Catholic views. Gardiner states that Calvert's opinions fitted him to be "the channel of communications which could not be safely entrusted to one who looked with extreme favor upon the Continental Protestants," and that while Calvert "was anything but a thorough-going partisan of the Spanish monarchy, yet he had no sympathy whatever with those who thought a war with Spain was to be desired for its own sake." [1]

The King knew that Calvert had tolerant views on the subject of religion and this was all the more reason for his

[1] *Prince Charles and the Spanish Marriage*, 1617–1623, I, 164.

selection. An old authority, the *Biographica Britannica* says that:

> Calvert was the only statesman who being engaged to a decried party, managed his business with that great respect for all sides that all men who knew him applauded him and none that he had anything to do with complained of him. He was a man of great sense, but not obstinate in his sentiments, taking as great pleasure in hearing others' opinions as in delivering his own.

The negotiations for the Spanish marriage treaty began as early as 1614, when after the dissolution of Parliament, James addressed a proposal of marriage to the Spanish court. Spain, playing a waiting game, slowly fed the hopes of the English monarch. Both the Crown Prince and the Infanta were young, and the marriage would have to wait for some years. In the meantime, while negotiations were pending, there would be hope of relief for the oppressed Catholics who were suffering from the persecution following the exposure of the gun-powder plot. Moreover James would be kept from giving aid to the German Protestants. The real significance of the negotiations and the part taken therein by Calvert cannot be fully appreciated without taking into consideration the religious situation in Germany and the smoldering fire that was soon to break out into the Thirty Years War.

Just before he died, Robert Cecil planned the marriage of James' daughter Elizabeth to Frederick, the successor-apparent to the Palatine-Electorate and one of the leaders of the German Protestant Princes. Cecil intended to give the support of the English government to the Protestant cause in Germany and the proposed alliance with Catholic Spain would not have been in keeping with his policy.

But now that Cecil was dead, James proposed to act as his own minister. Spain's star of empire was gradually declining. Since the defeat of the Armada, she was no longer powerful on the sea, but she was still the strongest power in Europe, believed to be by far the richest, still in the lead in the settlement and colonization of the Americas, and still regarded as a strong ally in peace and a dreaded opponent in war. An alliance with Spain appealed to James' sense of pride. Then there was the bride's dowry which was to be considered, as the royal treasury was low. James must be given credit at least for his reluctance to be drawn into the threatening religious war in Germany. There was a strong war party arising in England, and it was an anti-Catholic party determined to give aid to the German Protestant cause.

The Protestant war party besought James to come to the support of his son-in-law when the nobles of Bohemia, invoking the penalty of fenestration, threw the Catholic Ferdinand's deputies from the windows of the palace at Prague and called the country to arms. Bohemia had been Protestant since the days of John Huss. In 1619, when Calvert was appointed Secretary of State, Ferdinand became emperor. The nobles of Bohemia declared the realm vacant and chose Frederick as their king. This was at variance with James' pet idea of the divine right of kings. He regarded Frederick as an usurper and advised him to renounce his kingship and return to the Palatinate. Frederick disregarded this advice, but he was only "king for a winter." The next summer he was defeated by the army of the League before the walls of Prague and driven a fugitive to north Germany. The following year saw the Spanish battalions marching up the valley of the Rhine, for Spain, now powerless on the seas, must have a highway to the Netherlands in order to hold what was left to her in the low countries. Fierce passions were aroused and the Thirty Years War that was to desolate Central Europe had begun.

Calvert now became an open and zealous advocate of the alliance with Spain, and he encouraged the King to adhere to his policy of peaceful intervention through a Spanish alliance, rather than to become involved in the European war. Calvert was by nature a man of peace and opposed to war, but this fact alone cannot account for his reversal of the traditional policy of his old patron, Cecil. The only reasonable explanation for his course was his natural inclination toward the old religion. His predisposition drew him toward the Catholic side.

In England during the negotiations with Spain the line between Catholics and anti-Catholics was sharply drawn. The war party had its adherents, not alone in the Paliament, but also among the King's ministers and councillors. Calvert was the leader of the Spanish cause in the Council.

At a meeting of the Privy Council held in the year 1619, the Bohemian representatives, in urging the claims of the Palatine, told how they had inflicted the penalty of fenestration upon their enemies. One of the councillors whispered to another that it would give him pleasure to see some of the Hispaniolized members present treated to the same reward. Streeter, Maryland historian, says that "had the penalty been carried out in English Council, as intimated, several among the members would have found it necessary to make their exit by another way than the door, and among them, Sir George Calvert." [2]

When Parliament reassembled in 1621, after its seven years' recess, the storm of opposition against the Spanish match broke loose. There was a demand for the repudiation of the proposed alliance, coupled with a demand for a Protestant marriage, as the parliamentary party would brook no plan that would place a Catholic queen on the throne of England. The war party was active for a declaration of war against Spain and an alliance with the German Protestants. There was also a demand "for the better execution of the laws against Jesuits, seminary priests and Popish recusants." The King refused these demands and declared he would govern according to the common weal, and not according to the common will.

Calvert had a seat in this parliament, having been elected to represent his old home county of Yorkshire. As Secretary

[2] *The First Lord Baltimore,* mss.

of State he was given the unpopular rôle of spokesman for the King. It was a trying experience, but his "unruffled and conciliatory demeanor and his fairness in debate" frequently disarmed his opponents. He was accused of undue favoritism toward Count Gondomar, the Spanish ambassador, with whom he was brought in close relationship during the negotiations for the Spanish marriage. Although he realized he was not on the popular side of the controversy, he did not waver in his course. "He did not follow the king blindly," says Wilhelm, "nor from sordid motives. He recognized and accepted the issue." [3]

In 1622 there were negotiations with Rome. A dispensation for the marriage had been solicited from the Pope by the Spanish king, through the agency of his ambassador and of the Padre Maestro, one of the Catholic clergy attached to the Spanish legation in London. Calvert had charge of all the correspondence relating to the English part of the negotiations. He sent George Gage, an English Catholic, to Rome with letters for the Pope. Father Bennett, an English Catholic priest, was later sent for the same purpose. He went as a representative of the secular clergy. To the requests of these envoys, the Pontiff replied that he could not dispense with the canons unless it were for the benefit of the Church, that James had promised much, but had done nothing, so let him first relieve the Catholics from the pressure of the penal laws, then there would be sufficient ground for the dispensation.

James lost no time in acting on the suggestion. He ordered the lord keeper to issue under the great seal pardons for recusancy to all Catholics who should apply for them in the course of five years, and instructed the judges to discharge from prison, during their circuits, every recusant able and willing to give security for his subsequent appearance. This indulgence awakened the fears of the zealots. To silence their complaints Williams, a member of the council, ex-

[3] *Sir George Calvert, Baron of Baltimore;* Fund Publication No. 20, Maryland Historical Society (1884), 71.

plained that some modification of these severities had become necessary to satisfy the Catholic princes who threatened to enact against the Protestants in their dominions, laws similar to those against Catholics in England.

While these explanations appeased the Protestants, they alarmed the Catholics and there was a suspicion that James had acted with duplicity. If Gondomar boasted in Spain that four thousand Catholics had been released from confinement it was replied that "they still had the shackles about their heels" and would enjoy their liberty no longer than might suit the royal convenience.[4]

It was during the time that Calvert was carrying on negotiations with the Papal court that he had the misfortune to lose his wife by death. Lady Calvert died August 8, 1622, after giving birth to a son, the eleventh child of this happy pair. Her husband had a tablet placed in the Hertingford Church as a memorial of her virtues. There is every reason to believe that Calvert's decision to enter the Catholic Church was made not long after the death of his wife. Just what direct effect his wife's death had upon his decision may be conjectural, but there are unmistakable evidences that within a year thereafter he showed a strong leaning toward the Catholic faith, and that it was during this period he definitely made up his mind to take the step which he later publicly announced when resigning office.

The negotiations for the Spanish marriage reached their climax when the Crown Prince and Buckingham went on their secret mission to the Spanish court, where Charles appeared in person as the suitor for the hand of the Infanta. Calvert was one of the few who knew of this hurried trip, but it is not known whether he approved of it. The plan is said to have originated with Gondomar. It is certain that it did not meet with the approval of Bristol, the English ambassador at Madrid, with whom Calvert was corresponding.

While Charles was urging his suit in Spain a "solemn and

[4] Lingard, op. cit., IX, 200.

royal entertainment" was given to the Spanish representative at Whitehall. The proposed marriage treaty had been prepared in Latin by Calvert and was read to the assembly in the royal chapel. He had been careful to include a clause granting full religious liberty to the Catholics of England and freedom from further persecution. This clause provided that "no particular law against Roman Catholics or general laws under which all are equally included, if they are of the kind that are repugnant to the Roman Catholic religion should be executed as regards the said Roman Catholics, at any time, in any way on any occasion, directly or indirectly." [5]

A Catholic education for the children of the marriage, a Catholic household for the Infanta, and a Catholic chapel at the English court, were all guaranteed. "We are building a chapel to the devil," said the King, but he signed the treaty with due solemnity. A secret treaty granting further concessions was signed later at the home of the Spanish ambassador and when the oath was taken by James, he exclaimed: "Now all the devils in hell cannot hinder it." But he reckoned without Buckingham and the Crown Prince. Whatever hope he had for a happy consummation of the marriage treaty was dashed by the excursion to Spain. Buckingham and Charles made a mess of the negotiations which had been handled so skillfully by Calvert and which would probably have reached a successful conclusion had it not been for their conduct at the Spanish court.

Buckingham was indiscreet and offensively arrogant. Charles was too glib with his promises. There was offense given and taken by both sides, and the final result was failure, the prince and his envoy returning without the bride.

On their journey to Spain, Charles and Buckingham had stopped off at Paris where the prince had seen Princess Henrietta Maria, who afterwards became his bride, dancing gracefully at a court ball. She may have had more attraction

[5] For the Latin text of this clause in the treaty, see Lingard, op. cit., IX, 216-217, note, citing Prynne, 44; Hardwick papers, I, 428, 430.

for him than the young Spanish Infanta, and this may account for the reason that his heart did not seem to be in his wooing at Madrid. Their return to England was made the occasion of great rejoicing by all who were opposed to the Spanish marriage and the streets of London were lighted with bon-fires as the pair made their way to the palace. But there was no joy for George Calvert. He knew that his cause was lost and that his days of influence and usefulness to his king and country were over.

Buckingham, quick to sense the popular feeling, abandoned the Spanish party. The King also soon forgot his enthusiasm for the Spanish match and turned his mind toward an alliance with France. Charles no doubt had told him of the pretty French princess he met on his journey to Spain. A contemporary wrote that the King was "almost as much in love with France as with Spain and is merry and jocund." Several of the advocates of the Spanish cause had gone over to the other side and more were wavering, ready to desert their party when opportunity arose. Calvert, now practically alone, still remained loyal to the cause he favored.

The anti-Catholic party had its opportunity when James called a session of parliament at the suggestion of Buckingham. Calvert had opposed such action, fearing it would mean a declaration of war with Spain. His whole effort had been to keep his country out of war. Buckingham and the prince supported a demand for the repudiation of the treaty with Spain and a declaration of war. It was as if the King had abdicated and turned over the government to his son and favorite.

Calvert had a seat at this session, representing the University of Oxford. He was astounded to hear the King in his speech from the throne repudiate his oath and declare that he never in any treaty public or private promised to dispense with the execution of the penal laws against Catholics. Calvert thereafter took little interest or part in the proceedings of parliament. It is recorded that he quite frequently absented himself on the plea of illness. It is not difficult to diagnose the nature of the ailment.

At a general conference held between the two houses, Buckingham delivered a long and misleading address narrating the negotiations at Madrid. The only man who could have exposed the falsity of his statements was the Earl of Bristol, English ambassador to Spain and a Catholic. Bristol had incurred the enmity of Buckingham and was ordered to return home after the failure of the negotiations, to repair to his house in the country and consider himself a prisoner. All his entreaties were fruitless. The disgraced minister was not suffered to visit the court or take his seat in parliament during the remainder of the reign of James.[6]

The Spanish ambassadors protested against the speech of the Duke, but in vain. The two houses defended the conduct of Buckingham, and in an address to the throne, pronounced their opinion that neither the treaty for the Spanish marriage nor that for the restoration of the Palatinate, could be continued with honor or safety.

James, now drifting helplessly with the tide, in answer to the address, said that his debts were enormous and his exchequer was empty, but that if a vote of a grant of money were passed, he would carry on a war with Spain which would not end until he was advised by Parliament. The King asked for seven hundred thousand pounds to begin the war, and an annual supply of one hundred and fifty thousand pounds toward the liquidation of his debts. This demand made the parliamentary leaders gasp, but the Prince and the Duke assured them that a smaller sum would be acceptable, and three hundred thousand pounds were finally voted, coupled with an address vindicating Buckingham and followed by a royal proclamation announcing that both the treaties with Spain were at an end. Parliamentary orators told of the "alarming growth of popery in the land," and declared that "connivance of the evil would beget tolerance."

[6] Lingard, op. cit., IX, 217.

In the eyes of these men tolerance was, of all things, to be abhorred.

After the Easter recess a joint petition was presented to the King, praying him to enforce the penal statutes against Catholic recusants. James once more called God to witness that he never intended to dispense with those laws, and promised that he would never permit in any treaty the inclusion of a clause granting indulgence to Catholics.

A proclamation was issued commanding all missionaries to leave the kingdom under penalty of death. The judges and magistrates were ordered to put into execution the laws as in former times. The lord mayor was directed to arrest all persons coming from Mass in the houses of foreign ambassadors. All Catholic children were to be taken from their parents and brought up as Protestants. The tide of persecution which had abated during the years of the Spanish negotiations was setting in once more.

After Buckingham had secured the vote of confidence of Parliament he set about to crush the leaders of the Spanish party. A former associate of Calvert in the treasury commission, Cranfield, Earl of Middlesex, received the brunt of Buckingham's first attack. He had done all in his power to prevent a rupture with Spain and continued to urge a peaceful policy. This was enough for Buckingham. Cranfield was impeached, heavily fined and removed from office. Gardiner says that as Lord Treasurer, Cranfield had "done more than any other man to rescue the finances from disorder." James did not favor his impeachment, but lacked the courage to intervene. He told the Duke he was a fool for "making a rod for his own breech" and warned his son that he would live to have his "belly full of impeachments." Little did he realize the ominous portent of his warning, for Charles unconsciously had aided Buckingham in giving to Parliament the weapon that was finally to be used to end his own fateful career and bring his head to the block.

Calvert was saved from attack only because it was known

that he had the favor of the King in greater degree than any others of the council. The Duke could not resist the opportunity however to obtain from Calvert by a false promise, a paper he wanted for his own use. The secretary had in his possession a copy of a letter sent to the Pope to secure approbation of the Spanish marriage. Buckingham wanted this to use as a model for another letter to the Pope in reference to the French marraige, and he obtained the copy by assuring Calvert that he would be asked to serve the King in the French treaty negotiations. "If this be a lie," wrote Buckingham to the King, "as I am sure it is, then you may begin to think with a little more study I may cry quittance." [7]

A list of the names of Catholic lords and knights employed in the governmental service had been presented by the Commons to the King with the strong intimation that their removal would be exceedingly gratifying to the people. Calvert's name was not on the list, but there was no disguising the fact that the parliamentary leaders were trying to force his hand as it was generally known at this time that he was favorably inclined toward the Church of Rome. In his capacity as secretary Calvert was named on a commission to try recusants and with other members of the commission was instructed to "examine parties charged with errors in matters of faith, tending to schism against the established church, who refused to have their children baptized or allowed that ceremony to be performed by a Jesuit or popish priest or were guilty of any offense against the established church." These instructions were aimed not only at Catholics, but at Puritans and Baptists as well.

Calvert now bowed to the inevitable. He refused to serve on the commission and publicly announced his allegiance to the Catholic Church. He had no difficulty in convincing the King, now on the verge of death, that the duties of his office were no longer compatible with his religious belief. The King respected his wishes and suffered him to resign from

[7] Wilhelm, op. cit., 103.

office and retire to private life. He held large estates under royal grant, and anticipating that he would not be allowed to longer hold these lands without taking the oath of supremacy, he surrendered them. He was willing to pay a heavy penalty for his change of faith. The King in gracious recognition of the loyalty and worth of Calvert, restored his estates with the religious clause omitted and asked him to remain as a member of the Privy Council. Although Calvert knew that the King was favorably disposed toward him, he also recognized the growing power of the Protestant party and realized that he could no longer hold public office.

In one particular at least James rose superior to his predecessor on the throne. Elizabeth, when she turned on the English Catholics who had come to her support when the Armada threatened the kingdom, showed that she was unworthy of the full measure of loyalty which her Catholic subjects had given her. James may have been a coward, but he was no ingrate. He did not forget the loyalty and devotion of George Calvert. One of the last acts of his reign was to elevate his faithful minister to the Irish peerage as Lord Baltimore, in recognition of his "singular gifts of mind, candor, integrity and prudence as well as benignity and urbanity toward all men."

When George Calvert made public confession of his faith it was a step that could only have been taken by a man of rare courage. It meant for him the surrender of high office with all the privileges, emoluments and influence that went with it. It meant liability of incurring the penalties and disabilities of the penal laws now to be enforced with greater rigor. He saw in the rising tide of anti-Catholicism in parliament, the prospect that the ancient faith would soon be driven from the realm of England. To this faith, notwithstanding, he gave his support and allegiance.

No historian has ever been heard to say that Calvert's open profession of faith was not sincere and not the result of inward conviction. Bancroft says:

In an age when religious controversy still continued to be active and when increasing divisions among Protestants were spreading a general alarm, his mind sought relief from controversy in the bosom of the Roman Catholic church and preferring the avowal of his opinions to the emoluments of office, he resigned his place and openly professed his conversion.[8]

According to Wilhelm:

Calvert's conversion to the Catholic religion was thorough and honest though the change of belief had been gradual. At a crisis in his career he made an open profession of his adherence to the papacy and accepted the consequences... The Church of Rome offered him, in his distress of mind, a surer peace than the deeply stirred Church of England or the aggressive fold of the Puritans.[9]

There is the testimony of some of Calvert's contemporaries and those not of his faith that he had been a Catholic at heart for some time prior to his resignation from office. Archbishop Abbott of Canterbury, who was secretly opposed to the Spanish marriage, yet willing to put his signature to the treaty, wrote that "Secretary Calvert hath never looked merrily since the Prince's coming out of Spain," and that he had "apparently turned Papist which he now professeth, this being the third time he hath been to blame that way." [10] The Anglican Bishop Goodman wrote:

He was thought to gain by the Spanish match and did what good offices he could therein for religion's sake, being infinitely addicted to the Roman Catholic faith, having been converted thereto by Count Gondamar and Lord Arundel, whose daughter, Secretary Calvert's son had married. And it was said the Secretary did usually catechize his own children, so to ground them in his own religion and in his best room having an altar set up with chalice, candlesticks and all other ornaments, he brought all strangers thither, never concealing anything as if his whole joy and comfort had been to make open profession of his religion.[11]

There is no reason to believe that Count Gondomar had any influence upon Calvert so far as his change of faith is

[8] *History of the United States,* 18th edition, I, 239.
[9] *Sir George Calvert, Baron of Baltimore,* 158, 168.
[10] *Negotiations of Sir Thomas Roe in his Embassy to the Ottoman Porte,* (1621–28) 372.
[11] *The Court of King James,* I, 376.

concerned. His attitude on the question of the Spanish treaty was largely the result of his own convictions, and he had evidently decided to make open profession of his real faith regardless of the result of the negotiations. It is far more likely that he was influenced by Lord Arundel as there was the closest relationship between the two families. According to the Aspinwall Papers, he began to turn towards the Catholic faith in 1620 but nothing was revealed of his state of mind until February 1625, when "he made known his change of faith to the King and then went to the north of England with Sir Tobias Matthews to be received into the church." [12] Matthews was an old schoolmate of Calvert. He was the son of the Anglican Bishop of Durham but had himself become reconciled to the Catholic religion much to the disgust of his father. The same authority states that Matthews was a Jesuit, but his name does not appear in the lists in the Jesuit archives. He had been knighted by King James for his services in connection with the Spanish treaty negotiations, and was one of the witnesses of George Calvert's last will.

On his retirement from public life we find the figure of George Calvert, the first Lord Baltimore, standing out in bold relief against a dark and sinister background of political intrigue and religious animosities. That he remained aloof from the partisan influences that surrounded him is revealed by his life and character. He was tolerant in a day of intolerance, open-minded during a reign of bigotry, kind and considerate of others when cruelty was easily excused and quickly condoned, charitable in his opinions of his fellowmen when harsh judgment was the order of the day, and above reproach in his family and private life when a refined immorality spread its thin veneer over the lives of men and women. He became easily reconciled to withdraw from public life and to seek a refuge from political strife and religious controversy beyond the seas.

[12] *Massachusetts Historical Collections,* 98-99.

CHAPTER V

WESTWARD HO FOR AVALON

IN THE year 1620 when the Pilgrims of the *Mayflower* landed on New England's stern and rock-bound coast, George Calvert purchased from a former classmate at Oxford, Sir William Vaughn, a plantation on the stony coast of Newfoundland. It would seem as if the voyage of the *Mayflower,* which came within his official purview as Secretary of State, had turned his attention to the need of a colonial refuge for the religiously oppressed. Sir Edwin Sandys had already sent his invitation to the Pilgrim exiles in Holland to repatriate themselves to America, but there was no progress made with the plan until after Calvert became secretary of state. Matthew Page Andrews in his *History of Maryland,* has brought out that there is a logical inference at least "in the light of other events that as secretary of state, Calvert must have aided the Separatists directly or indirectly in obtaining their patent, which unfortunately is among the missing documents of history." [1]

It would not have been possible for any such migration as that of the Pilgrims of the *Mayflower* to have been arranged without the knowledge and consent of the Privy Council, and much would have depended, so far as any favorable action was concerned, on the recommendation of one of the secretaries of state. Calvert's colleague in the secretaryship, Robert Naunton, who was subsequently disgraced and deprived of office, was given mostly routine matters to attend to, while the more important matters having to do with foreign and colonial affairs were entrusted by the King to his new secretary. It was no easy matter for any large

[1] Loc. cit., 7. See also *The Founding of Maryland,* by the same author, 22.

group to secure permission to settle in the American colonies.

A band of Huguenots, who had fled to the Netherlands to escape persecution in France, tried to obtain permission from the English government to settle in America, and being unsuccessful in this, came over under Dutch auspices to settle New Amsterdam. It was not a foregone conclusion by any means that the English separatists who had gone to Holland to escape conformity in England would be permitted to make an English settlement in America. From all that is known of Calvert and his tolerant views, it is more than probable that he was largely responsible for granting permission to the *Mayflower* pilgrims to settle in New England.

Calvert received a grant of the entire island of Newfoundland in 1622. The entry in the state paper simply reads: "grant to Sir George Calvert and his heirs of the whole country of Newfoundland." This was held by him only a few months. He applied for and received in April 1623, the charter of Avalon, the name he gave to his new colony. This was one of the earliest instruments for the organization of English colonists on the North American coast. The document was prepared by Calvert himself and later was made by him the model for his charter of Maryland. It introduced for the first time in English colonial history a palatine form of government. This system of government for minor principalities came into use in England during the thirteenth century, the counts or earls palatine ruling over entire counties as independent princes, swearing homage and fealty to the King. At the time of the granting of the charter, the bishopric of Durham was the only instance of a complete county palatine in England. The same rights were given to Calvert and his heirs "as any bishop within the Bishopric or County Palatine of Durham in our Kingdom of England ever hath." The ancient bishopric of Durham, with its majestic Norman cathedral mirrored in the clear waters of the Wear, had long been a semi-independent government.[2] The American colonists, however, were given under the Avalon charter more liberty in self-government than was enjoyed by the freemen in the Durham bishopric, since an elective assembly curbed the sovereignty of the proprietary.[3]

Oldmixon, an early English authority on colonial history, throws interesting light on the Newfoundland grant to Calvert:

> This gentleman being of the Romish religion was uneasy at home and had the same reason to leave the kingdom as those gentlemen had who went to New England, to enjoy liberty of conscience. He therefore resolved to retire to America and finding that the Newfoundland company made no use of their grant, he thought of this place for his retreat; to which end he procured a patent for that part of the land that lies between the Bay of Bulls in the east and Cape Mary's on the south.[4]

According to this same authority Calvert was a Catholic when he procured the grant, and he gives this as the reason why the colony was called by him *Avalon,* out of veneration to the memory of Joseph of Arimathea who is fabled "by the Papists to have landed in Britain and to have built a chapel for the Britons at Glastonbury, Somersetshire, then called Avalon."

An old legend gives a little different version for the name, for it says that *Avalon* was named in honor of Avalonius, a monk who was supposed to have converted the British King Lucius and his court to Christianity. In memory of this event the Abbey of Glastonbury was said to have been founded.

There is a strong presumption that the name of Avalon was suggested to Calvert by a member of the Catholic clergy, as it was hoped that the gospel according to the ancient faith would be practiced and preached for the first time in the

[2] Fiske, *Virginia and Her Neighbors,* I, 259.
[3] Adams, *March of Democracy,* 34.
[4] *British Empire in America* (London, 1708), I, 8.

English colonies in America at Avalon. Dr. John G. Morris, Lutheran clergyman and historian, says:

> As one of the oldest historians of Newfoundland attributes Sir George Calvert's design in planting his colony at Avalon to the desire of making a place of retreat for English Catholics, in which he is followed by other subsequent historians, such motive being founded on strong probability, may be safely admitted.[5]

Calvert was preparing his Avalon charter during the fall and winter of 1622, after the death of his wife and while he was engaged in the negotiation for the Spanish marriage treaty. He was in sympathy with the plans for the relief of the English Catholics from persecution and discriminatory laws, but he knew that if the negotiations were not successful, and there was no certainty that they would be, there would be little hope for the Catholics obtaining the relief they sought, and in that event, the colony of Avalon would be a place of refuge for them. At the very time he was drafting the clause in the treaty for the equal administration of the laws on religion and exemption from persecution, he was at work on the charter of Avalon with its broad provisions in the matter of religion. These facts show that the trend of his mind at this time was in the direction of a greater toleration, and that his chief purpose of securing the Newfoundland charter was to provide an American sanctuary for the English Catholics who were as much in need of it as the Puritans who then were migrating to New England.

In the early colonial charters, Catholics were barred by provisions which carried the disabilities of the Elizabethan laws to the colonies. The Virginia charter of 1609 required the oath of supremacy to be taken by all settlers. In the confirmation of the charter in 1612 instead of the oath of supremacy, King James' oath of allegiance could be taken, the colonial officials having the power to administer either or both, and so were enabled, if they chose, to debar Catholics.

[5] *The Lords Baltimore,* Fund Publication No. 8, Md. Hist. Soc., 19.

This power was invoked in 1629 to keep Lord Baltimore out of the colony when he came there from Newfoundland.

All anti-Catholic restrictions and disabilities were kept out of the charter of Avalon because the draftsman intended to omit them so that he might open the door of his colony to Catholic settlers. Calvert was familiar with the provisions of the Virginia charters. He had been a member of the second Virginia company in 1609, and he was also one of the provisional council for the management of the colony after the revocation of its charter. He had had experience in charters and charter drafting and he knew what he was doing.

Father Hughes has given an interesting commentary on the religious feature of the Avalon charter:

> The intolerance which had introduced test oaths into civil existence and which was fostering the growth at that moment on the soil of the new world, was not to be found in Calvert's earlier charter for Avalon. Nor had any mention been made there of the Anglo-American formulas about the superstition of the Church of Rome. Calvert had merely spoken of "God's Holy and True Religion" which like allegiance to civil authority, was to suffer no prejudice or diminution. All other artificial elements or odious incidents of an ancient people that had known strife and sorrow, like the laws of police and revenue, such as are enforced by penalties, the mode of maintenance for the established clergy, the jurisdiction of spiritual courts and a multitude of other provisions, were neither necessary nor convenient for them, and therefore were not in force. And so with respect to the whole network of penal laws, the Catholic proprietary left in their native habitat those sanguinary and predatory intrigues which still found England a happy hunting ground and were to keep Ireland a rich preserve for two centuries to come. And keeping a free hand for equipping conscience and religion with their rights, he assured civil freedom of a respectable and genial home.[6]

Under section IV of the Avalon charter, Calvert had a provision inserted which gave him the "patronage and advowsons of all churches which as the Christian religion

[6] Op. cit. I, 243. Eggleston says that the charter of Avalon naturally left open a door for the toleration of the faith to which he was already attached. *Beginners of the Nation,* 226.

shall increase within the said region isles and limits, shall happen thereafter to be erected." Here was privilege only, which he could exercise or not as he saw fit. It did not prevent the erection of any Christian church, Catholic or Protestant. The provisions relating to churches and religion in both the Avalon and Maryland charters are somewhat vague and indefinite and this fact has led some non-Catholic historians to charge Calvert with having a secret understanding with the King with whom he connived for the purpose of "blinding the public mind." [7] He may have been disingenuous. Possibly there was a secret understanding between him and the King. But if so, it was all quite proper and justified. It was well that the real meaning of the charter was hidden, else the enemies of tolerance would have thwarted an accomplishment that was commendable and ideal. The non-Catholic historian Cobb has said if circumstances ever "justified a deceptive turn of words, they certainly justified this 'blinding purpose' of Baltimore." [8]

Calvert made no definite plans to visit Avalon until he retired to Ireland after his resignation and became Lord Baltimore. At that time, according to Archbishop Abbott, he bought a ship of four hundred tons. This was undoubtedly the *Ark,* which afterwards made two trips to Avalon, and then sailed with the *Dove* to Maryland. His visit was postponed for two years, for some unknown reason, and, in the meantime, affairs in England had assumed a more threatening aspect. James had died soon after elevating Calvert to the peerage and his ill-fated son had come to the throne as Charles I.

Before the marriage of Charles to Henrietta Maria, Cardinal Richelieu had insisted that the same concessions should be made for the English Catholics as were promised in the case of the proposed Spanish marriage. This demand coming so soon after the orders of King James to the judges and

[7] Anderson, *History of the Church of England in the Colonies,* 113.
[8] *Rise of Religious Liberty in America,* 365.

magistrates, and his promises to parliament, created a difficulty which was finally compromised by a secret treaty granting to Catholics as great a freedom of religion as they would have had if the Spanish marriage had been consummated. Both James and Charles signed this and ratified it with their oaths. Faced by a hostile parliament soon after his coronation Charles determined to violate the treaty. Every provision was violated, even those relating to the Queen's household. The penal laws were put into execution and again Catholic recusants were fined and imprisoned. The King of France remonstrated, but Charles dared not face his opponents in parliament and as an excuse to Louis, he said he had never considered the stipulations in favor of Catholics as anything more than an artifice to obtain the papal dispensation for the marriage. Lord Baltimore then heeded the call of "Westward Ho for Avalon."

In a letter to his friend Wentworth, dated May 21, 1627, Baltimore wrote that he had finally received the royal consent to cross the ocean and that he would soon have the pleasure of carrying out his long deferred desire of visiting Newfoundland. He promised to remain but a few months and to return not later than Michaelmas. He took with him on this first trip two Catholic priests of the secular clergy, Fathers Rivers and Longavilla. Father Rivers was a former Jesuit. Later Jesuit missionaries were sent. As soon as he announced his change of faith, Baltimore had applied for missionaries to be sent to Avalon and had partly arranged for sending members of the Order of Discalced or Barefooted Carmelites, but this arrangement was never carried out as the two priests of this order who were to have gone were then in prison, there having been a sudden flare of persecution in England against the Catholic clergy.

It must be clear that Baltimore's reasons for now going to Avalon were mainly religious. Although he may have hoped that the colony would prosper and that the fishing industry would be profitable, there is nothing to indicate that it was purely a money-making venture with him. The establishment of a colony as far north as Newfoundland could have offered little hope or inducement in a financial way. In fact, the colony caused its founder to suffer a loss of over twenty thousand pounds sterling. The *Biographia Britannica* said of him that he differed with others who were planning American settlements at the time in that he was for converting the Indians instead of exploiting them, that he was for taking "the soberest people to these places while others were for taking the lewdest," and while others were for making present profit, he was satisfied with a reasonable expectation.

Both Protestant and Catholic clergy accompanied the colonists to Avalon and were granted the fullest freedom in the matter of religious worship. The first Protestant incumbent was the Reverend Richard James, a clergyman of the established church who was sent over in 1622 with the first party of settlers. Having tried it with "its eight or nine months of winter," he abandoned it for the more congenial post of librarian to Sir Robert Colton in England. In a document of Jesuit missionary relations released by the Nuncio at Brussels in 1630 is found this report of the settlement at Avalon: "As to the practice of religion that was carried on under Calvert's roof, in one part Mass was said according to the Catholic rite, in another the heretics performed their functions." Here, indeed, was an unheard of measure of religious liberty, with Catholics and Protestants worshipping under the same roof.

Lord Baltimore was greatly misled in respect to the natural advantages of Newfoundland. No high pressure land salesman of this day could have painted in more glowing colors the attractions of a prospective realty development than Captain Richard Whitbourne described the imagined beauties of Newfoundland in his *Westward Ho for Avalon,* which was published in 1622. Whitbourne describes the island as a veritable earthly paradise where raspberries, strawberries, pears and cherries grow in abundance and flowers of every kind, including red and damask roses, make meadow-lands beauteous to behold. The woods are vocal with songbirds that rival the nightingale, the wild beasts are "gentle and humane," the harbors eminently good and in St. John's harbor had been seen a mermaid. Baltimore may have been impressed with this glowing description, but he was soon to be sadly disillusioned for he found that "it was not always June in Avalon." The bleak coast had been made to blossom with names of beauty. There was the "Bay of Plesaunce," the "Bay of Flowers" and the "Harbor of Heartsease." As Eggleston says, when winter time came "the icy Bay of Plesaunce and the bleak Bay of Flowers mocked him with their names of delight."

Although on his first trip, Baltimore came at the most favorable season of the year and his stay was short, he failed to find the Garden of Eden described by Captain Whitbourne. He found only a small strip of land fitted for cultivation and "all behind the little plantation lay this region of wild savagery of bleak and hopeless desolation and in front was the wild, stormy and inhospitable sea." And he had yet to see the northern winter.

In the summer of 1628 the ships of Lord Baltimore again crossed the sea to Avalon. This time he brought Lady Baltimore, his second wife, and several members of his family. With him also came forty colonists, including three Jesuit missionaries. Trouble soon came. First a French fleet came to attack the colony, England being at war with France. Baltimore was not a fighting man, but fight now he must. There was no other recourse. He fitted his ships, one of them the *Ark,* as men-of-war, and they were so well handled by the English seamen that with the help of the *Unicorn,* an English man-of-war, the attacking French fleet soon had the worst of it. How distasteful all this was to him is shown in a letter written at the time to Buckingham, in which he said: "I came to build and set and sow, but am fain to fighting with Frenchmen who have disquieted me."

The war with France was of Buckingham's making, and after the smoke of battle cleared, Baltimore wrote to the favorite saying, "whether the French gentleman may return again when the ships are gone, I know not, but if he do we shall defend this place as well as we are able," and asked that two men-of-war be allowed to remain all the year. Before the letter reached its destination Buckingham had been assassinated. The *St. Cloud,* one of the captured ships, was loaned to Baltimore, "in consideration of his good services," and was brought out to him by his son Leonard, afterwards Governor of Maryland.

Then bigotry raised its head in the person of a Puritan minister, the Reverend Erasmus Stourton. Whether this clergyman came by invitation or as an unbidden guest, is not disclosed, but come he did and found hospitality and sanctuary. This did not deter him, however, from stirring up trouble for his host. He was horrified because Jesuit priests said Mass every Sunday and used "all other ceremonies of the Church of Rome in as ample manner as is used in Spain," and he had seen with his own eyes a Presbyterian child actually baptised by a "Romish priest." This was enough to send him back to England on trouble bent. As soon as he landed he went straight to the mayor of Plymouth with his tale of "Popish doings." The magistrates of Plymouth were greatly shocked and sent the informer to the Privy Council. Fortunately Baltimore had friends in the Privy Council to whom differences in matters of religion meant little. Nothing more was heard of the complaint.

Bigotry had failed in its purpose and the tale-bearer had spent his shaft, but the worst enemy of all was soon to come, and this was the northern winter. Baltimore in his own words tells of the sufferings of his colony in the long cold winter of 1628-9. In a letter to his King written in the following summer he says:

I have met with difficulties and incumbrances here which in this place are no longer to be resisted, but enforced me presently to quit my residence and to shift to some other warmer climate of the new world where the winters will be shorter and less rigorous.

From the middle of October to the middle of May he writes:

There is a sad fare of winter upon all this land, both sea and land so frozen for the greater part of the time as they are not penetrable, no plant or vegetable thing appearing out of the earth until about the beginning of May, nor fish in the sea, besides the air so intolerable cold as it is hardly to be endured.

His house had been a hospital all through the long winter, a hundred persons sick at a time, and because of his own illness he was not able to minister to the wants of others. Ten had died during the winter. Broken in health, and with a considerable loss of fortune, he was almost on the point of giving up further plans of colonization. That there was some deep underlying motive, other than the expectation of profit that led him to make another attempt, is indicated in the following, which appears in his letter to the King:

Hereupon I have had a strong temptation to leave all proceedings in plantations and being much decayed in my strength, to retire myself to my former quiet; but my inclinations carrying me naturally to these kind of works and not knowing how better to employ the poor remainder of my days than with other good subjects, to further the best I may, the enlarging your Majesty's empire in this part of the world, I am determined to commit this place to fishermen that are able to encounter the storms and hard weather and to remove myself with some forty persons to your Majesty's dominion Virginia; where if your Majesty will please to grant me a precinct of land with such privileges as the king, your father, my gracious master, was pleased to grant me here, I shall endeavor to the utmost of my power to deserve it.[9]

It is to be noted that Baltimore was careful to include in his request for a new grant the same privileges which King James had granted to him in the Avalon Charter. Without these his main purpose in affording an asylum for the religiously oppressed would have been defeated.

9 Browne, *Calverts,* 24, 25.

Charles wrote in reply, reminding Baltimore that men of his condition and breeding were fitter for other employment "than the framing of new plantations which commonly have rugged and laborious beginnings and require much greater means in managing them than usually the power of one private subject can reach unto." The King advised him to give up the further prosecution of his plans and return to England "where he would enjoy both the liberty of a subject and such respect from us as your former services and late endeavors do so justly deserve." There was a gracious side to the character of Charles revealed in this kindly letter to a loyal subject of another faith, but in those days it would have taken more than the favor and respect of a king to insure to a Catholic "the liberty of a subject." Charles' advice was not heeded, for before the letter was written Lord Baltimore had set sail from Avalon for a sunnier clime.

CHAPTER VI

THE PROMISED LAND

Lord Baltimore and his little band of colonists sailed from the bleak hills of Newfoundland and came to the coast of Virginia in the summer of 1629. It is believed that two Catholic priests accompanied the party, but whether these were secular priests or Jesuits is not certain.

He found the southern climate much warmer than his welcome at Jamestown. Virginia was at this time under royal grant, the charter of the Virginia Company having been revoked. When Baltimore arrived the assembly was in session. He was not long in finding out that he had come into a stronghold of conformity where no Catholics were wanted.

The Virginians hated Papists more than they did the Puritans. Here was a "Popish recusant" in their midst and a nobleman of rank and prestige who was known to be in the favor of the King. When they saw that he seemed "well affected" toward their part of the country and had plans for a colony where Papists would be granted a refuge from the restraints of the recusancy laws in England, great was their dismay, but they were sorely perplexed to know just what to do. To have a Roman Catholic set up a colony in their midst or even on their borders was to them unthinkable. Theirs was a colony from which Catholics had been carefully excluded and where the provisions of their laws aimed at strict religious uniformity.

They soon made it apparent that they did not wish to have Lord Baltimore for a neighbor, and a way was discovered to get rid of him which they believed would be legally justifiable. The oath of supremacy was the modus operandi. This oath went further than the oath of allegiance, which Catholic subjects were willing to take. The oath of supremacy was specially designed to make Catholics refuse to recognize the spiritual supremacy of the Pope and to recognize the King of England as the head of the church. It was the chief weapon of enforced conformity. Baltimore offered to take a modified form of oath which would have recognized the supremacy of the King in all temporal matters, but this he was not allowed to do. Mere allegiance to the King in matters temporal was not enough; he must swear subservience to the King in matters spiritual as well, and acknowledge him as the titular head of the church. They knew that he would not take this form of oath. As a matter of fact they exceeded their legal powers in trying to compel a visiting nobleman to subscribe to the oath of supremacy, and it is doubtful if the assembly had any power to compel the oath, as this power was in the charter of Virginia which had been annulled.

The acting governor of Virginia at this time was Dr. James Potts. Sir George Sandys had written a letter to a friend in London that the doctor "kept company too much with his inferiors who hung upon him while his good liquor lasted." He was afterwards charged with abusing his powers by pardoning a culprit who had been convicted of wilful murder. In addition to this he was convicted of stealing some of his neighbors' cattle and sentenced to jail. He was later released on a pardon because he was the best physician in the colony and "skilled in epidemicals." [1] Although he loved his neighbors' cattle he had little love for his neighbors. He was extremely bitter against Catholics and determined that none of that faith should abide in Virginia. He was the first signer of a letter to the Privy Council setting forth the reasons why Lord Baltimore was not allowed to take the oath of allegiance in lieu of the oath of supremacy, so anxious was he to demonstrate to the authorities at home that he was a loyal churchman. "We could not imagine," the letter states, "that so

[1] Fiske, op. cit., I, 253.

much latitude was left us to decline from the prescribed form so strictly exacted." The letter then goes on to expatiate on the Virginia idea of religious freedom:

> Among the many blessings and favors for which we are bound to bless God and which this colony has received from his most Gracious Majesty, there is none whereby it hath been made more happy than in the freedom of our religion, which we have enjoyed and that no papists have been supposed to settle their abode amongst us, the continuance whereof we most humbly implore from His Most Sacred Majestie.[2]

Baltimore, fully realizing that Virginia was no place for him or his colonists, made plans for returning to England, but before his departure he had to suffer a personal indignity. It is a matter of record that one Thomas Tindell was pilloried "for giving my Lord Baltimore the lie and threatening to knock him down." This punishment however was not meted out until Baltimore's departure and after Governor Harvey had arrived in Virginia. Governor Harvey was a friend of Baltimore. Anticipating Harvey's early return to the colony, Baltimore left his wife and children at Jamestown, knowing that the governor would not suffer them to be treated unkindly. He expected to return to America and join his family in a new colony which he hoped to be able to establish near Virginia, but finding that there were to be hindrances and delays before he could obtain a new charter, he sent for them to return to England.

The ship on which his wife and children sailed was lost in a storm at sea. Nearly all historians state that the lives of the passengers were saved. The better evidence however is that they were lost with the ship. His son Cecil, the second Lord Baltimore, in a letter written several years later, stated that his father, finding that the cold of the winters in Avalon disagreed with his constitution, went from there to Virginia in the year 1629, where he found a much better climate and:

> leaving his lady (his then second wife) and some of his children by her, there, comes himself to England to procure a patent of

[2] *Archives of Maryland,* III, 17.

some part of that continent; and some while after sends for his lady, who together with her children who were left with her, were unfortunately cast away in their return.

After his return to England, Lord Baltimore took up his residence at Lincoln's Inn Fields. He kept this same residence until he died and he would not have kept these lodgings had his wife and children returned in safety. Furthermore, there is no record of the death or burial of his second wife and the children by her. This can only be accounted for by the fact that she was lost at sea on her return from Virginia. In a letter of condolence to Wentworth (the Earl of Stafford), expressing sympathy for his friend's loss of his wife, he refers to his own personal affliction and to the loss of his wife and children. He wrote:

There are few perhaps can judge of it better than I, who have been a long time myself a man of sorrows. But all things, my lord, in this world pass away; statum est; wife, children, honor, wealth, friends and what else is dear to flesh and blood. They are but lent us till God please to call for them back again, that we may not esteem anything our own, or set our hearts upon anything but Him alone, who only remains forever. I beseech His almighty goodness to grant that your lordship may for His sake, bear this great cross with meekness and patience, whose only son, our dear Lord and Savior bore a greater for you; and to consider that these humiliations, though they be very bitter, yet are they Sovereign medicines ministered unto you by our heavenly physician, to cure the sicknesses of our souls.

In the same year (1630), Baltimore wrote another letter to Wentworth which reveals his spirit of tolerance. Writing on the occasion of the birth of a son to King Charles, he tells how the Spanish court, which had no reason whatever to rejoice over affairs concerning the English court and the Anglo-French Queen Henrietta Maria, did nevertheless rejoice exceedingly and "solemn Masses and prayer" were said for his (the young prince's) health and prosperity everywhere. "Thus," he adds, "your Lordship sees that we Papists want not charity towards you Protestants whatsoever the less understanding part of the world think of us." [4] This letter was written at a time of discouragement, after the failure of the colony of Avalon, after his rude reception in Virginia, and when the persecution of the Catholics was most bitter. Charity towards those of another religious faith was a rare thing in the England of his day.

There is no record of Lord Baltimore's second marriage nor of the birth of his children by his second wife. This is not at all surprising, but it has afforded the opportunity welcomed by a few historians to intimate that Baltimore was never married a second time, that the woman referred to as Lady Baltimore was his mistress and that his children by her were illegitimate. If these same historians had cared anything for fairness or truth, by glancing at contemporary English history they would have found no difficulty in explaining why so little is known of his second marriage and the birth of his children by his second wife. When he remarried he was undoubtedly married in the Catholic faith, and probably the ceremony was performed by one of the Jesuit missionary priests. In England at this time Catholic marriages had to be performed in secret, in order to avoid the Protestant marriage service which was made compulsory and "women about to become mothers hid themselves in places where no one could take their child away from them to receive the dreaded baptism of heretics." [5]

His second marriage took place probably some five or six years after the death of his first wife, and after he had made known his change of faith. The first record we have of his second wife is when he took her on his voyage to Newfoundland in 1628. In his letters he refers frequently to his wife and in a deed of trust to his son Cecil, under date of March 20, 1628, it is declared that "for this purpose Sir George Calvert and his wife Joan will levy a fine at Westminster on all the said lands." [6]

[4] Hughes, op. cit. I, 207.
[5] Meyer, op. cit., 170.
[6] Russell, *Land of Sanctuary*, 517.

With his Catholic friend, Lord Arundel, Baltimore applied to the Attorney General in February, 1630, for a grant of land south of the James River, within the boundaries of the province of Carolina "to be peopled and planted by them with the permission to erect courts." Lord Arundel died in November of 1630, and the benefit of his coöperation was lost. After the death of Arundel, a patent of territory extending southward from the James River as far as the Roanoke and reaching from the Atlantic westward to the mountains, was granted to Lord Baltimore. But in the meantime the Virginia colonists had sent commissioners to England to keep watch on Baltimore and see that he did not trespass on their preserves. So vigorous was the opposition of these commissioners, as well as that of several of the most influential members of the dissolved Virginia company, that he decided to return the grant; otherwise he would have been the founder of the Carolinas.

At the time he was meeting with the opposition of the Virginia commissioners, Baltimore found time to reenter the domain of state-craft, but only to dissuade the King from taking up arms in the cause of his sister's husband, the discrowned king of Bohemia, and thus becoming involved in the Thirty Years' War. Gustavus Adolphus had begun the invasion of Germany and there was danger of England being drawn into the war. It was just prior to the era of the newspaper. Public opinion was expressed in tracts and pamphlets printed and circulated by their sponsors. Several vigorous pamphlets had appeared attacking the foreign policies of the King for not taking the part of the German Protestants. These were: "Tom Tell-Troth or a Free Discourse touching the Manners of the Times," "Lamentations of the Kirke," and the "Practise of Princes."

The first appeared when Calvert was secretary of state. He conceived it to be his duty to answer these attacks and uphold the policy of non-intervention. His tract which was entitled "The Answer to Tom Tell-Troth, the Practise of

Princes and the Lamentations of the Kirke," was intended only for private circulation and primarily for the guidance of Charles to whom he felt a duty to explain his views. It was not published until after Baltimore's death, and is interesting as revealing his views on the religious and political questions of the day. A manuscript copy is in the records of the Maryland Historical Society.

This is one of the few printed records of the writings of Lord Baltimore and reveals him as a man of peace urging the King to avoid a policy that would bring upon his people the miseries of the Thirty Years' War. Charles took Baltimore's advice and followed his father's policy. Although he raised six thousand men for Gustavus Adolphus, this was done in the name of the Marquis of Hamilton and the neutrality of England was preserved.

After Baltimore had refused to take the oath of supremacy at Jamestown, he went on a voyage up the Chesapeake in quest of unoccupied territory and beheld for the first and only time the meadowlands and hills of the future colony of Maryland. He had pleasant memories of this cruise and believed the land he saw "was fit to be the home of a happy people." After deciding to surrender the Carolina grant, he asked for a grant north of the unsettled portion of Virginia to include the lands he had seen on his cruise up the Chesapeake. The original grant included more than what is now the State of Maryland. The northern boundary was the fortieth parallel of latitude. On the west the boundary was the meridian line from this parallel to the most distant fountain of the Potomac, thence southeast by the right bank of the Potomac to the Chesapeake Bay, and thence northwardly by the Delaware Bay and river to the fortieth parallel. It included all of the present state of Delaware, a large tract now forming part of Pennsylvania, and a smaller tract now a part of West Virginia.

The country beyond the Potomac was then untenanted except by scattered Indian tribes. The Dutch were preparing to occupy this country so the grant to Baltimore was one way of securing this territory for an English settlement. Now that the Virginia patents had been canceled, the King had ample power to sever a province from the colony of Virginia to which he at first assigned so vast a territory and it "was not difficult," says Bancroft, for Baltimore "a man of such moderation that all parties were taken with him, sincere in his character, disengaged from all interests and a favorite with the royal family, to obtain a charter for domains in that happy clime."

The first Lord Baltimore was destined to suffer the fate of Moses, for although he had beheld the promised land, he was never "to set his foot thereon."

CHAPTER VII

THE FIRST LORD BALTIMORE AND THE JESUITS

A GREAT change had come over the religious situation in Europe since Fathers Campion and Persons first entered the English mission field. The Protestants had weakened their cause by useless controversy and senseless persecution. They had lost the effect of the death of their martyrs by making martyrs for the Church of Rome. They had attacked the union of state and church but had neglected no opportunity to make political alliances and establish state churches wherever and whenever they could. The very abuses they decried they adopted. They finally awakened from their dream of a Protestant Church Universal to find a Protestant Church divided against itself.[1] Calvinists quarrelled with Lutherans, and both persecuted divers new sects with divers new creeds and consequently added to their growth and number. In England the Puritans had broken from the established church but in their intolerance found common ground with the more intolerant of the Anglicans in persecuting the Catholics who with them had refused to conform to the state religion.

In the meantime the Catholic Church had rallied the faithful behind the Council of Trent. The great work of the Counter-Reformation had begun. The vanguard of this movement was the Society of Jesus, organized by its founder for the very purpose of combating the new schism and winning back adherents to the ancient faith.[2] It was sending its

[1] Lecky in his *Rationalism in Europe,* II, 58, makes a strong indictment against the Protestant Church in its early days.

[2] Dr. Guilday says: "The Counter-Reformation becomes a living reality when the history of the Jesuits is known. The one spells the other." *The English Catholic Refugees on the Continent* (1914), 121.

missionaries far and wide and there was no peril too great to hold them back from their endeavors and sacrifices. The deaths of their martyrs were, in the words of the poet Southwell, "the spring showers that watered the field of the church." As the Catholic cause was gaining strength on the continent, strength in turn was given to the little Jesuit mission in England, and as the years went by, recruits were being constantly added to the ranks of the mission priests.

The order of Loyola was making a strong appeal to the youth of England. Many were found to be ready and eager to risk the dire penalties imposed by the laws of their native land by going to the novitiates in France and Belgium to be educated for membership in the order. During the reign of Elizabeth, all manner of laws were passed to prevent English students from attending Catholic colleges on the continent. At one time an act was passed whereby all students in the colleges and seminaries abroad were ordered to return within six months or else be regarded as traitors.[3] The story of these young men, who entered the order during the period of the Cecilian persecutions and went through years of arduous training to prepare themselves for probable martyrdom and certain hardship, persecution and peril, all for the cause of religion, is one of the brightest chapters in the history of the society.[4]

The learning and scholarship of the Jesuits soon came to the front in the Counter-Reformation. They expounded the teachings of the schoolmen and applied them to existing conditions, thereby giving an impulse to liberal principles of government. Lecky says that the Jesuits "saw what no others in the Catholic Church seem to have perceived, that a great future was in store for the people and they labored, with a zeal that will secure for them everlasting honor, to hasten and direct the emancipation." [5]

The Jesuit philosopher, Suarez, contended that the inter-

[3] 27 Eliz., c.i. and ii.
[4] Guilday, op. cit., 139.
[5] Lecky, op. cit., II, 147.

ests of the sovereign should at all times be subordinated to the interests of the people and that civil sovereignty was through the natural law directly received from God by the people.[6] The Jesuit cardinal, Bellarmine, in his famous *De Controversis* held to a principle of government which will sound strangely familiar to American ears: "It depends on the consent of the people to decide whether kings or consuls of other magistrates are to be established in authority over them." [7]

It was at the time when young George Calvert had a seat in the first parliament of James, that Bellarmine challenged the doctrine invoked by the English King, of the divine right of kings and insisted that "the people never so transfer their power to the king as not to retain habitual power in their own hands." James, making a great show of what he was pleased to call his learning, attempted to answer Bellarmine but his wits were no match for the brilliant intellect of the Jesuit scholar, and his writings were the laughing stock of Europe.

Whether this controversy had any influence upon the future founder of Maryland can only be a matter of inference, but the significant fact remains that in the charter of his colony, Baltimore wrote in a clause that the law making powers of the proprietary should be "of and with the advice, consent and approbation of the freemen." There was to be no government in the colony of Maryland without the consent of the governed.

Father Henry More was one of the first fathers of the English mission and had a long period of activity in the mission field. He attempted to write a history of the mission, during the last years of his life spent in the Low Countries. He confined himself to the records, and this was unfortunate as he was an eye-witness of many important events and happenings. He found many of the records, especially the

[6] Ryan and Millar, *The State and the Church*, 79.
[7] *De Laicis or the Treatise of Civil Government*, Fordham Press, 1928, 27.

annual letters, missing, and he wrote little of the Maryland project although he had an active part in it.

There is a dearth of Jesuit records from 1625 to 1633. These were important years in the formative period of the colony and included the years Lord Baltimore was preparing his charters and completing his colonization plans, but the curtain is drawn on much that would have been of great historic interest. Some of the missing records may be accounted for by the violence of the persecution at various times. A Jesuit chronicler, soon after the Titus Oates Plot, writes:

> Much more could be said about our English mission but the violence of the last persecution did away with almost all our documents; while whole libraries of ours were pillaged; all our desks with their papers and notes were robbed; so that it is not strange if much is wanting here which we hope is written in the Book of Life.[8]

The opposition of the Parliamentary party and the Virginians made it necessary that most of the planning be carried on without publicity. There is little written evidence of all that was done, particularly relating to the part taken by the Jesuits. It is known that Father Henry More was one of the chief advisers of Lord Baltimore, as he was in later years of his son. More was a great-grandson of the martyred Chancellor, Sir Thomas More, author of the *Utopia,* and there are several historians who agree that it would be strange indeed if the story of Utopus and his ideal state in which peace and concord reigned supreme, did not have some bearing and influence in the formation of the plans for the new colony and the carrying out of those plans.[9]

This much is certain, the law of Utopia, that "every man might be of what religion he pleased and might endeavor to draw others to it by the force of argument and by amicable

[8] Hughes, op. cit., I, 66.

[9] Russell, op. cit., 24, 26. Johnson, op. cit., 12. Andrews, *History of Maryland,* 13.

and modest ways but without bitterness against those of other opinions,"[10] did become the unwritten law of early Maryland and guided the founders of the colony and their successors until the Revolution of 1688. There was a period in the first years of Maryland when there was a nearer approach to a Utopia than there ever has been since in American history.[11]

The outstanding figure of the English Jesuits during the time plans were being laid for the Maryland colony was Father Richard Blount. When the English mission was made a vice-province in 1619, he became the vice-provincial or superior. He was vice-provincial from 1619 to 1632, having charge of all Jesuits' affairs in England, subject only to the general of the society. This covered the period when Lord Baltimore first became active in American colonization and prepared the Avalon and Maryland charters. When a province was created in 1632, he was made provincial. This office he retained until 1635 when he was succeeded by Father Henry More. It was to him the first Lord Baltimore applied for missionaries to be sent to America, and to him the second Lord Baltimore went for advice and assistance after the death of his father.

Father Blount was a member of one of the ancient families of England and of the nobility. He had close, if not blood relationship, with Lord Baltimore's co-laborer, Lord Arundel of Wardour. In his veins ran the blood of the houses of Norfolk, Howard and Warwick.[12]

Father Blount was a graduate of Oxford and a classmate of Laud, Archbishop of Canterbury. Upon his graduation from Oxford he entered the English College at Rome. After finishing his courses in philosophy and theology he was or-

10 Morley, *More's Utopia*, 151.

11 Fülop-Miller in his *Power and Secret of the Jesuits*, 298-302, tells of a "Forest Utopia" established by Jesuit missionaries in Paraguay in the eighteenth century and says that "if we compare the Jesuit Republic with the Island of Utopia which was invented by the English Lord Chancellor, More, we find remarkable coincidences."

12 Johnson, op. cit., 12.

dained to the priesthood. In 1591 he was sent back to his own country, but because of the severe persecution of Catholic priests he was obliged to enter under the disguise of a sailor. He found a refuge in Scotney Castle in County Sussex, the home of Sir Thomas Darrell, a Catholic nobleman. Here he remained in hiding for several years, living in a secret chamber, keeping himself out of the sight of servants who could not be trusted because of the bribes offered to informers, and always leaving and returning under cover of night. He made it a rule to leave the castle only when he had an errand of duty saying that "if I am taken, I should like to be taken as a priest and not as an idler." While living at Scotney Castle he had several narrow escapes from capture and death. When Father Robert Southwell was apprehended in 1599, Father Blount was on his way to meet him at Harrow, and it so happened that he was disappointed in a horse which was to have been provided for him and thus spent a night longer on the road than he anticipated. The delay saved his life. Father Southwell was later condemned to death and suffered a barbarous execution.

Five years elapsed between the time of Father Blount's return to England after his ordination and his entrance into the Society of Jesus. He spent his entire novitiate in the English mission at its most perilous time. Like Father Campion, he had an attractive personality that won the hearts of many outside of his own faith. Father Morris says that he combined in a remarkable degree "the most perfect gentleness of manner and sweetness of disposition with an inflexible firmness and persevering courage." He converted Thomas Sackville, Earl of Dorset and Lord High Treasurer under Elizabeth. Later he received into the church Anne, Queen Consort of James I. Anne was a native of Denmark and was brought up in the Lutheran Church. In Scotland she was required to forsake the Lutheran Church for the Calvinist faith, and on coming to England was asked to change once more and conform to the established church. It is no wonder that in religion she was said to be doubtful. Just before the birth of one of her children she asked Father Blount to give her the sacraments of the Catholic Church, which he did, much to the dismay of the King.

Father More records in his history that in 1624, when Father Blount was appointed provincial "two thousand six hundred and thirty persons were numbered who had been brought over from heresy to the Catholic faith since the persecution had moderated somewhat in view of the Spanish match." [13] He was held in such high esteem by some of the English clergy who had known him at Oxford that one of them, Archbishop Abbott of Canterbury, interceded for him when his arrest was threatened.

Not long after Lord Baltimore announced his allegiance to the Catholic Church, Father Blount was confronted with a most trying situation that involved the whole future of the Jesuit mission. This was due to the pretensions of Dr. Richard Smith, who had been appointed Bishop of Chalcedon and Vicar Apostolic of England. Baltimore came to the aid of Father Blount in the controversy that arose, and took the side of the Jesuit missionaries.

The new bishop exercised the powers of his office in such a way as to greatly disturb the English Catholics, especially so by creating a tribunal before which he required wills and testaments to be produced with judicial supervision over pious legacies, marriages and baptisms, together with the power of visiting the private houses of Catholics. The jealousy of many within the Catholic Church toward the Society of Jesus came to the surface in the policy and regulations of the new bishop. He quite ignored in his appointments the Jesuit mssionaries who had been performing their hazardous duties and keeping alive the spark of the old faith in the face of the persecution. In 1628, so great an opposition had arisen to the action of the bishop that a number of the Catholic lords and gentry signed a letter of remonstrance.

[13] Hughes, op. cit., I, 61.

Among the signatures to the remonstrance are the names of earls, viscounts and barons, the last being that of Lord Baltimore. The letter was prepared by Baltimore before leaving for Newfoundland. In it strong and vigorous exception is taken to the establishment of a tribunal as proposed by the Bishop, stating that it would be perilous for the Catholic laity to submit to such a power. There was a flood of pamphlets and papers on each side of the controversy and those who wrote for the bishop were "reinforced by all the anti-Jesuitism of the Gallicians and Jansenists of France, including the whole body of the Sorbonne." [14]

Then came the edict of silence, and the Jesuit forces were recalled from the field of controversy by their general. This was in keeping with the instruction of the founder of the order "to preach positive doctrine and avoid controversy." The Jesuits, as was often the case, were not allowed to say anything in their own defense against unjust attacks and wilful misrepresentation, but they found an able and fearless advocate in Lord Baltimore. He, with others of the Catholic nobility, sent a brief to Rome, setting forth that the interests of the Catholic laity would be imperilled, and praying that the Jesuits be exempted from the pretended authority of the Bishop since they are "bound to the Holy See canonically and especially by vows and privileges in a way beyond the duty of the faithful and they have no fortunes at stake since they possess nothing." The Bishop had gone so far as to recommend the expulsion of the Jesuits and since they had monasteries outside of England they "should betake themselves thither." When he heard that Lord Baltimore and his associates had sent in a brief remonstrance to Rome he resigned his dignity with the hope that it would not be accepted. It was quickly accepted, however, and for the next half century the Bishopric of England was vacant. The Jesuits were allowed to remain at their posts on the mission field

[14] Hughes, op. cit., I, 207.

and this was largely through the influence of Lord Baltimore.[15]

In the last years of Lord Baltimore one of the Jesuit mission priests came into close association with him in his plans for the Maryland colony. This was Father Andrew White, afterwards to become the saintly "Apostle of Maryland," and whose name is justly entitled to preeminence among the pioneer missionaries of the American colonies. He was born in London in 1579. At the age of sixteen he entered St. Alban's College at Valladolid, one of the seminaries founded by Father Persons to supply priests for England. Later he attended the college at Seville. In the year 1605, when he was twenty-six years of age, he was engaged in the ministry in the English mission field, and after the discovery of the gunpowder plot, was caught in the storm that followed and with forty-five other priests was sent into "perpetual banishment." [16] While in exile in France he applied for admission into the Society of Jesus.

Father White, on being accepted to membership, entered the novitiate of St. John at Louvain. This novitiate was the first to be established for English Jesuits and was opened the year of Father White's admission. He was the second novice entered, the first being Father Thomas Garnett, who a few years later was to suffer martyrdom at Tyburn. Father Henry More entered later in the same year. It was a noble company of English youth that made up this first novitiate, most of them coming from the best families of England and educated in English schools and universities.

For these novices it was necessary to not only serve the two years' apprenticeship followed by eight years of practice in the ministries of the society, but in addition thereto they were required to pursue courses in the higher studies of

[15] There are records which show that shortly before the close of this controversy Lord Baltimore incurred the risk of heavy penalties by sending two of his sons to the Jesuit college of St. Omers. Hughes, op. cit., I, 206.

[16] Challoner, *Memoirs of Missionary Priests,* 282.

philosophy and theology, making a total of seventeen years of training, ministry and study, before the final profession could be granted. Father White, having pursued his higher studies before entering the priesthood, was not required to follow the entire seventeen years of preparation as in the case of those entering the novitiate without previous theological education. It was twelve years, however, before he took the final vows of profession.

On completion of his course at Louvain in 1609, Father White took his first vows of religion and was then sent back to the labors and dangers of the English mission field. It was not altogether an auspicious time for a Catholic priest to reenter England. Only the year previous three priests were executed for their refusal to take the oath of supremacy. Little is known of his activities, as they were necessarily shrouded in secrecy. His name does not appear in the list of the fathers then laboring in England, yet two years later he was in London. At about this time he was sent to Lisbon to the seminary founded by Father Persons. The remainder of his time was largely spent in the duties of a professor, teaching Sacred Scripture, Theology, Greek and Hebrew, and he was in charge of the higher courses as Prefect of Studies at Louvain and Liège. At intervals he was engaged on the English mission in Suffolk, Middlesex, Devonshire and Hampshire. It was at the residence of St. Thomas in the district of Hants that he was stationed when deputed for the American mission.

Although Father White attained eminence as a scholar and theologian, the strongest appeal of the order to him was the opportunity for work in the mission field. The spirit of Xavier was always beckoning to those members of the order who were more disposed to active service than to studies and carrying them to fields of hardship and sacrifice.

It was while Father White was in the English mission that he met Lord Baltimore and became acquainted with the plans for the American colony. During the winter of 1629-30, while Baltimore was in Newfoundland, he wrote to Father White that he was willing to share with him "every and the last bit." It was soon after receiving this letter that Father White applied for the Maryland mission.

Prior to this in 1629, when Lord Baltimore made his last visit to Avalon, he took with him two Jesuit priests, so it is probable that there had already been negotiations regarding a Jesuit mission in America. It is not known who these missionary priests were. They may have been Fathers Alexander Baker and Lawrence Rigby, but this is not certain.[17]

After Lord Baltimore's return from Virginia in 1630, there is evidence to show that from that time on until his death, Father White was in close touch with him and had an active part in the plans for the new colony. It is now a well established fact that Father White wrote the famous *Declaratio Coloniae,* outlining the purposes of the colony and the terms and conditions offered to settlers. This was published in the early part of the year 1633, after the death of the first Lord Baltimore, but was prepared sometime before his death and contains all the plans outlined by him. Copies of this were printed in Latin and English. The Latin version was intended for Father White's superiors in the Society of Jesus; the English copies were used for circulation in England to attract colonists.

A fac-simile of the tract printed in English from the only copy now in existence was published by the Baltimore Press in 1929, and contains an interesting foreword by Lawrence C. Wroth. The tract was clearly of Jesuit authorship, and now it is admitted beyond question that it was written by Father White. Tracts of this nature commonly appeared in the early stages of a colonization project, and as Mr. Wroth states, "in the case of Maryland, with religious complications hindering the enterprise, there was need for a clear statement of the purpose of the proprietary of the proposed colony." Mr. Wroth refers to the "known close relationship of Father

[17] Hughes, op. cit., I, 199.

White to Lord Baltimore" in the formation years of the project, and his intense interest in the proposed colony and "its potentialities for the faith," and he adds that it is a tribute to the integrity behind the project that "the document employed to gain the cooperation of the General of the Society of Jesus should have been printed and distributed practically without restriction to attract adventurers and settlers from among the English people." Father White, the General of the Society of Jesus, and the English Provincial, Father Blount, all must have known that Protestants, as well as Catholics, were invited to the new colony. Father Hughes has pointed to the Spiritual Exercises of St. Ignatius as the source of the spirit and of the phraseology employed in the tract, even in the part which sets forth the practical terms and conditions offered to prospective settlers by the "zealous and unworldly Father White."

The tract is entitled *A Declaration of the Lord Baltimore's Plantation in Maryland nigh upon Virginia, manifesting the nature, quality, condition and rich vitalities it containeth.* Father White states the primary and secondary objects in view as:

> First and chiefly, to convey into the said land and neighboring parts, the light of the Gospel and of the truth, where it is certain no knowledge of the true God has ever shed its beams; secondly, for this purpose too that all who take part in the voyage and the labors may have their share in the profit and honors and that the sovereignty of the King may be more widely extended.

This statement reveals not only that religion was the primary objective, but also that this Jesuit priest who had been exiled from his native land still regarded himself as a loyal subject to his King. Father White then goes on to develop the first point, the spiritual object in view, as follows:

> The first and chief purpose of the Right Honorable Baron is that which should be first also in the minds of others who shall be in the same ship with him; and it is that in so fruitful a land, the seeds be sown not so much of fruits and trees as of religion

and piety. Such a purpose is in truth worthy of Christians, worthy of angels, worthy of Englishmen; and never has England though ennobled by so many triumphs of old, taken up a project more noble or more glorious than this. See, the country lies white for the harvest; it is ready to receive the seed of the Gospel in its fruitful bosom! Since all men have not such enthusiastic souls and noble minds as to think of nothing but divine things and to consider nothing but heavenly things, because most men are more drawn secretly or openly by pleasures, honors and riches, it was ordained by the wonderful wisdom of God, that this one enterprise should offer to men every kind of inducement and reward.

The *Declaratio Coloniae* is Father White's dedication of the new colony and well has he been called "The Apostle of Maryland." [18]

[18] There is a marked similarity between the writings of Father White, especially those relating to the religious purpose of the expedition, and the narratives of James Rosier in the earlier Catholic expedition to Maine. This has been pointed out by several historians. Charles McLean Andrews, op. cit., I, 80; Baxter, *Sir Ferdinando Gorges and His Province of Maine,* I, 65.

CHAPTER VIII

THE ROYAL CHARTER AND ITS ANTECEDENTS

THE Maryland charter has never received the attention that its importance and significance in relation to both English and American constitutional history have justified. It was the outgrowth of the development of democratic institutions in England and transplanted on American soil all of the great principles of Magna Charta and of the many confirmations of and additions to the charter which had been making English constitutional history for the previous four centuries. It secured all of the rights and liberties that had been wrested by English freemen from unwilling kings. It guaranteed to the freemen of the colony the franchises of free-born Englishmen, including the right to participate in person and as individuals in their own form of government. An assembly of freemen was established and the laws passed by this assembly did not need the approval of king or parliament. It recognized as no other colonial charter did the principle of no taxation without representation. It went a step further than the constitution and laws of England and opened wide the door for the establishment of real religious liberty.

It is a document that should have a preeminent place in American colonial history, but its true historical significance cannot be fully appreciated without a study of its antecedents considered in the light afforded by the panorama of English history. It might be inferred from a hasty reading of the charter that it was concerned chiefly with the giving of broad rights to the proprietary, but a closer examination will disclose among the provisions dealing with the domain of Lord Baltimore, clauses recognizing for the first time in a colonial grant, certain fundamental and natural rights of the colonists which are briefly but clearly defined. In the tenth section is to be found full acknowledgment of the ancient rights and privileges of freeborn Englishmen which had come down from Magna Charta and its various confirmations. These rights were to be held and enjoyed without "impediment, molestation, vexation, impeachment or grievance" of the king or his successors on the English throne, "any statute, act or ordinance or provision to the contrary thereof notwithstanding."

No doubt in the preparation of both the Avalon and Maryland charters Lord Baltimore had assistance and advice. This aid came largely from Lord Arundel, who had been interested in the Weymouth expedition and who but for his death would have shared in the Maryland venture, and from members of the English Jesuit mission with whom Lord Baltimore had the closest relations. It is not to be wondered at that English Catholics should have sought to perpetuate the rights and liberties of the Great Charter. With their liberties restricted by the recusant statutes passed in the reign of Elizabeth and re-enacted in the reign of James, they naturally looked upon Magna Charta in the light of a sacred heritage which had been obtained for them as well as for all Englishmen by a great primate of their church.

It is to Stephen Langton, Archbishop of Canterbury, more than to any other one man, that England owes her Magna Charta. From the moment he assumed his duties as Primate of England, he became the mighty champion of the rights of the English people. He used all the power and influence of his position in the church to uphold the ancient customs of the realm against the personal despotism of the King. "As Anselm had withstood William the Red, as Theobald had withstood Stephen, so Langton prepared to withstand and rescue his country from the tyranny of John." [1] It was Langton who compelled the King to deal with the barons not by the force of arms, but by process of law and it was he who made pos-

[1] Green, op. cit., I, 226.

sible the meeting of the King and barons on the field of Runnymede.

"It is to Langton," says Maurice, "to whom the most trustworthy authorities point as the procurer of peace and the mediator between king and barons at this famous meeting. Here was the result of Langton's influence, that the formal assertion of the separation of church and state had become the strongest bond between them and the liberties of the church had become united with and almost absorbed with the liberties of the nation." [2]

England needed a man of God to deal with the most despotic of all her kings. Langton knew King John better than did the Pope, who had had some previous dealings with him and had brought him to terms. Innocent III listened to the claim of the King that the barons had extorted concessions from him by the use of illegal force and he ordered the excommunication of the barons if they did not relinquish the charter and resort to peaceful measures to gain their ends. The archbishop refused to publish the bull of excommunication. For this he was suspended from the primacy and made his way to Rome. Langton, who was a native born Englishman, was just stubborn enough not to yield an inch from the position he had taken, even though he knew that by so doing he would continue to incur the disfavor of the Pope. On the death of Innocent, Langton gained the favor of Honorius III, and was permitted to return to England, but not before he had obtained the promise that so long as he lived no other papal legate should be sent to the English church.

As soon as Langton returned to power in the reign of Henry III he lost no time in demanding a fresh confirmation of the charter. When one of the King's councillors protested that it had been extorted by force and was of no validity, Langton warned him not to "throw a stumbling block in

[2] Maurice, *Stephen Langton,* 194.

the way of the peace of the realm." [3] The wrathful insistence of the archbishop was sufficient to make the King and his councillors promise and grant confirmation and obedience.

Although Magna Charta was considered fundamental law, it became always expedient and sometimes necessary to secure confirmation in succeeding reigns. Sir Edward Coke reckons thirty-two instances where the charter was solemnly ratified. After the death of Langton, it was due to the zeal of the Catholic clergy, sometimes in the face of Papal protection granted to the kings that the many confirmations of the Great Charter were obtained.[4]

Additional religious character and solemnity were given to the charter by the frequent pronouncement of excommunication upon all who violated its provisions. During the reign of Edward I, the pronouncement became a regular ceremony at each session of parliament and was so worded that the penalty would fall not only on those who invaded the rights of the church under the charter, but likewise on those who violated any rights of the people.[5] This religious background of Magna Charta and the support given to it by the church offered provocation during the Protectorate when there was intense prejudice against anything that had to do with the Church of Rome, for a writer to disparage the importance of the charter by referring to it as "this Magna Charta intended for the advancement of the powers of Anti-Christ." [6]

It was Stephen Langton who made Magna Charta more than a mere redress of the grievances of the barons. He gave it the heart and soul that made it a living entity fostering the growth of constitutional law in England. He had the vision to foresee that a formal recognition of natural rights was needed for the administration of justice and for the protection not only of the barons, but of all the freemen of the

[3] Green, op. cit., I, 240.
[4] Hallam, *Middle Ages* (1904), II, 554.
[5] Mott, *Due Process of Law*, 38.
[6] Ibid, 53, note 31.

realm. He refused to separate the freedom of the church from the freedom of the laity, and he extended the liberties of the church to the common people, for he considered "the cause of the whole people was worthy to be considered the cause of God and Holy Church." [7]

During the lifetime of Archbishop Langton there was fast growing up a school of philosophy which was showing the true relation of man to the will of God and bringing divine law to bear upon the affairs of men so as to afford protection to person and property. This philosophy has come to be generally known as the teaching of the schoolmen of the middle ages. It was a teaching designed to force upon kingship a sense of responsibility towards its subject, to instill in subjects an appreciation of their dignity and worth and to resurrect in a lethargic church a realization of its divine mission in order that the principles of natural justice might prevail.

This philosophy which affords the real background of Magna Charta has been too often clouded in the study of the growth and development of democratic institutions of government. It is here that the real genesis of the great principles of self-government that guided the framers of the American constitution is to be found.

Not only Langton who was schooled in this philosophy, but many of the clergy who followed him, including the great religious orders, endeavored to apply these teachings to the affairs of government, and so gradually freed the English people from the thraldom of despotic kings. It was just after the death of Langton that the friars of St. Dominic and St. Francis came to England to spread the teachings of the schoolmen in the towns and centers of learning. Green has pointed out the influence and value of this when he says:

> Politically indeed the teaching of the schoolmen was of immense value, for it set on a religious basis and gave an intellectual form to the constitutional theory of the relations between

[7] Maurice, op. cit., 272.

the King and People, which was slowly emerging from the struggle with the crown. In assuming the responsibility of a Christian king to God for the good government of his realm, in surrounding the pledges whether of ruler or ruled with religious sanctions, the mediaeval church entered its protest against any personal despotism. The schoolmen pushed further still to the doctrine of a contract between king and people; and their trenchant logic made short work of the royal claims to irresponsible power and unquestioning obedience.[8]

Some three centuries after Magna Charta and nearing the time when Lord Baltimore and his advisers were framing the charters of Avalon and Maryland, the followers of St. Ignatius were found interpreting this same philosophy. Green, in a later chapter of his history, says in reference to the new influences following the Elizabethan Renaissance:

> Writers and statesmen were alike discussing the claims of government and the wisest and most lasting forms of rule, travelers turned aside from the frescoes of Giorgione to study the aristocratic policy of Venice *and Jesuits borrowed from the schoolmen of the middle ages a doctrine of popular rights which still forms the theory of modern democracy* (Italics ours).[9]

The Jesuit influences behind Lord Baltimore's project of American colonization are not to be overlooked. Their full extent will probably never be known, for it is always difficult to accurately appraise the value of silent forces that affect the deeper currents of thought and action.

The Maryland charter recognized the right of self-government and provided the foundation for a representative democracy. It gave to Lord Baltimore and his heirs "for the good and happy government" of the province, free, full and absolute power to make, ordain and enact laws, but "with the advice, assent and approbation of the freemen of the same province or of the greater part of them or of their delegates or deputies whom we will, shall be called together for the framing of laws when and as often as need require."

[8] Green, op. cit., I, 251.
[9] Op. cit., III, 9.

In tracing the antecedents of representative government we again go back to the middle ages and find its origin in the church. The germ of this form of government was the rule established in the Cistercian order, where each monastery had to send a representative to attend the annual chapter. There was a further and greater development of the idea in the Dominican order founded early in the thirteenth century. From their original base at Oxford the Dominicans spread all over England with houses at all the important centers of population. To the provincial chapter, the national parliament of the order, each house sent representatives. These representatives consisted of the prior of each house and one additional representative chosen by the members of the community. Professor Henry J. Ford, of Princeton, in his *Representative Government* says:

> The Dominican representative system supplied a model that was imitated extensively by other orders and deeply affected the constitution of diocesan synods which also assumed a distinctly representative character during the thirteenth century. It is certainly a reasonable inference that the analogous change which took place in the constitution of parliament in the same period was similarly inspired. All civic organization was then pervaded by clerical influence. When the burgesses were summoned to send their representatives they could know what to do for the clergy were there to tell them.[10]

Professor Ford further points out that when Simon de Montfort led the barons in their revolt against the exactions of Henry III, he participated in the arrangements made by the barons for governing the country through committees chosen by them, which broke with all constitutional traditions. De Montfort, who had Dominican advisers, consented to these arrangements and when he obtained individual control of the situation, there is found new parliamentary arrangements which reflect Dominican practise. "The Church originated representative institutions, the state adopted them."

[10] Loc. cit., 108, 111.

There was no provision in the Maryland charter that the laws adopted by the assembly of freemen should have the approval of either king or parliament. For the administration of law, power was given to establish courts of justice, including courts of final appeal and last resort. Soon after the colony was formed the assembly of freemen demanded and the lord proprietor yielded the right to initiate all legislation.

In the first code of laws passed by the assembly of Maryland is found this provision, which is quite explicit: "The inhabitants of this province shall have all the rights and liberties according to the Great Charter of England." [11] These rights were already recognized and protected under the Maryland Charter although no specific reference was made to Magna Charta. The freemen of Maryland under Section X were granted the same privileges, franchises and liberties as were enjoyed by the freemen of England.

For more than four centuries Magna Charta had exerted a powerful influence upon the constitutional history of England and now this same influence was being transferred to the jurisprudence of the American colonies. All the colonies claimed the rights and liberties under the Great Charter, if not by express grant, at least by implication. Through colonial laws, and later through state and federal constitutions, the classic wording of the pledge of King John in the thirty-ninth article of Magna Charta that "no free man shall be taken and imprisoned, or disseized or exiled or in any way destroyed, nor will we go upon him or send upon him except by the judgment of his peers or by the law of the land" finally took form in the great concept of "due process of law" which is the very foundation of the American government.[12]

There is one feature that is not only peculiar to the Maryland charter, but is of the greatest interest to the student of constitutional history and that is the provision exempting the colony from taxation by the English government. This is

[11] *Archives of Maryland,* I, 82.
[12] Mott, op. cit., 136.

found in the twentieth section. The King bound himself, his heirs and successors that:

> At no time hereafter will we set or make or cause to be made, any importation, custom or other taxation, rate or contribution, whatsoever, in or upon the dwellers and inhabitants of the aforesaid province or upon their lands, tenements, goods or chattels within the said province, or upon the goods or merchandise within the said province to be laden within any ports or harbors of the said province.

There was to be no taxation without representation in Maryland. The power of assessing taxes no longer rested with the King or parliament, but was placed directly in the hands of the colonists themselves. There was also a provision in the charter that the grant itself should be received as a "sufficient and lawful discharge, payment and acquittance," if any attempt were ever made at any future time to levy a tax upon the free colony of Maryland.

To appreciate the full significance of the incorporation of this principle in the Maryland charter it is necessary to consider the antecedents of the principle itself. This was no original idea of Lord Baltimore nor of his advisers. It was but the reaffirmation of a right demanded and obtained by another Catholic Primate from another unwilling English king. In the reign of King Edward I, with "the clergy outlawed, the baronage in arms and the merchants beggared," by reason of the King's heavy impositions to meet the multitude of his necessities, there came a train of events that led to armed resistance. It was largely due to the action of Archbishop Winchelsey, then Primate of England, that there was obtained from the King the "Confirmatio Chartarum," next to Magna Charta the most important document in English constitutional history.

This charter was used as a model for all subsequent confirmations of the Great Charter. It was a reaffirmation of Magna Charta and the Charter of the Forests, and, in addition, contained a set of laws which deprived the crown of its assumed right of arbitrary taxation. By the provision of one of these laws, the King granted "to arch-bishops, bishops and other folk of Holy Church, as also to earls, barons and to all the commonalty of the land, that for no business from henceforth will we take such manner of aids, tasks, nor prises but by the common consent of the realm and for the common profit thereof, saving the ancient aids and prises due and accustomed." [13]

Although King John at Runnymede had been called upon to relinquish the claim to levy taxes without the consent of the nation, yet the concession was not lived up to and had become a dead letter. The concession was thought to bear so heavily upon the crown that in the first confirmation of the charter early in the reign of Henry III, it had been reserved for future consideration.[14] Green attributes the omission of the article restricting the royal power of arbitrary taxation to the temporary absence of Archbishop Langton.[15] Langton's suspension had proved a severe blow to the barons, leaving them without a leader when the success of their efforts were dividing them. The law that no taxes should be levied by the king "without the consent of the realm" first became effective nearly eighty years after the victory of "The Army of God and Holy Church" at Runnymede.

Here was the real birth of the principle of no taxation without representation. It was mainly due to the "combined courage and prudence" of the English barons, "and to the patriotic exertions of Archbishop Winchelsey," says Taswell-Langmead, "that we owe the addition of 'another pillar to our constitution not less important than the Great Charter itself.' " [16]

Lingard points out:

If we are indebted to the patriotism of Cardinal Langton and the barons of Runnymede, the framers of the great charter, we

[13] Palgrave, *Parliamentary Writs,* I, 63.
[14] Lingard, op. cit., III, 264.
[15] Op. cit., I, 240.
[16] *Constitutional History of England,* 2nd Edition, 252.

ought to equally revere the memory of Archbishop Winchelsey and the earls of Hereford and Norfolk. The former erected barriers against the abuse of the sovereign authority; the latter fixed the liberties of the subject on a sure and permanent foundation.[17]

As Archbishop Langton had extended the rights and liberties of the church and barons under Magna Charta to the freemen of the realm, so his successor, Archbishop Winchelsey, was careful to extend the grant of freedom from arbitrary taxation to "all the commonalty of the land."

Thus did these two great Primates of the Church show their holy zeal for the rights of the common people. Unless we bear this in mind we lose the real significance of a Catholic lord acting largely on the advice of Catholic clergy obtaining this same important concession for all the freemen of his American colony. The principle of no taxation without representation is the very foundation of political freedom. "Only when this principle of justice was first practically recognized," wrote John Fiske, "did government begin to divorce itself from the primitive bestial, barbaric system of tyranny and plunder and ally itself with the forces that in the fullness of time are to bring peace on earth and good will to men." [18]

When the right of the English government to tax the American colonies was challenged by the leaders of the colonists, they at first turned to Magna Charta for the justification of their stand. As the Revolutionary movement gained momentum, they appealed more to the spirit than to the letter of the charter, and finally they had recourse to the doctrine of natural rights as expounded by the schoolmen and by Bellarmine and Suarez. "Side by side with the idea of the common laws as an element in the English constitution had arisen the conception of natural law and natural right. The doctrine of natural law was elaborated by such thinkers as Suarez and Grotius." [19] The English had appro-

17 Op. cit., III, 269.
18 Fiske, *Beginnings of New England,* 31.
19 Mott, op. cit., 47.

priated this doctrine and endeavored to weave it into the warp of common law.[20] This same trend is found in the American revolutionary period. Evidence of this is in the declaration of Hamilton that "the sacred rights of mankind are not to be rummaged for, among old parchments or musty records. They are written as with a sun-beam in the whole volume of human nature by the Hand of Divinity itself and can never be erased or obscured by mortal power." [21]

Maryland was the only colony that could claim the stamp act was in direct violation of the terms of its charter. One of the courts of Maryland held that the act was unconstitutional, being in contravention to the royal charter. The first successful resistance to the enforcement of the stamp act was in Maryland.[22] Franklin at one time claimed that the Pennsylvania charter prohibited parliament from taxing the colony, but when asked to point out the specific provision to support this claim he was unable to do so, and fell back on the assertion that the act violated the rights of Englishmen as declared by Magna Charta and the Petition of Right. While similar exemptions were granted to other colonies, these were for short periods, but under the Maryland charter the period was perpetual.

Chalmers, English lawyer and Royalist, who spent several years in the colonies in the pre-Revolutionary period, wrote several interesting treatises on colonial affairs. He says that the exemption in the Maryland charter gave "peculiar strength to the Maryland claim," but contended that the exemption was not intended to operate against the powers of Parliament, being nothing more than the reassertion of the principle maintained by the House of Commons against the royal Prerogative in the Petition of Right of 1628, which ante-dated the Maryland charter. He overlooked the fact

20 *Ibid.*

21 Alexander Hamilton, *The Farmer Refuted,* Works of Hamilton by Lodge, I, 113.

22 Riley's *History of the General Assembly of Maryland,* 277; Andrews, *History of Maryland,* 279.

that the same exemption was in the Avalon charter which in turn ante-dated the Petition of Right by four years. As a matter of fact the exemption from taxation in the Maryland charter was clearly intended to operate to the entire exclusion of all taxation by the English government.[23]

Under the royal charter Maryland, like Avalon, became a colony palatine. Under this form of government the lord proprietary stepped into the place of the King, but an elective assembly being provided for the sovereignty of the proprietary was limited and safeguarded. The colonists retained all the rights and privileges of English subjects with the right to hold, inherit and acquire lands, and they were free to trade with England or with any friendly foreign power. The colony of Maryland was not only a miniature England, as one historian has described it, but it was practically an independent government and under the rule of a wise and beneficent lord proprietary, the charter provided the best form of government possessed by any of the colonies.

On the question of religion the charter was more remarkable in what it omitted than in what it contained. There was no provision making it mandatory to establish a state church, nor was there anything to prevent separation of church and state. Mere "license and faculty" were given to found churches and when and if founded, they were to be constituted and dedicated according to the laws of England. The Church of England was not mentioned and other churches than the established church could be erected and maintained.

In the early days of the colony chapels were erected for both Catholic and Protestant worship and this was clearly permissible. The grant was given as in the Avalon charter, to receive "the patronages and advowsons of all the churches," but this too, was optional and not mandatory. The grant was never exercised while the House of Baltimore remained in the Catholic faith. There was no necessity for an established church, or of a state religion in Maryland, and no church was

[23] McMahon, *Historical View of the Government of Maryland,* 163.

established until after the overthrow of the proprietary government. Under the broad terms of the charter the Lords Baltimore established for the first time in America a free religion in a free state.[24]

[24] This chapter previously appeared under the title of "Catholic Antecedents of Maryland Liberties" in an article by the author in *Thought* (September 1932).

CHAPTER IX

FROM FATHER TO SON

BEFORE the Charter of Maryland passed the great seal, Lord Baltimore, whose health had been weakened by the rigors of the winter at Avalon, died at the age of fifty-two years. His death occurred at his lodgings in London, April 15, 1632. His remains were interred in the chancel of the Church of Dunstan, Fleet Street, an Anglican church. Under a law in force at that time, a "popish recusant" could only be buried in a church or churchyard of the established church.[1] This church has since been destroyed by fire and there is no adequate memorial either in England or in this country of the life and services of this great and good man.

Of all the tributes paid to the first Lord Baltimore the greatest was made by the New England historian, Bancroft, who said that he deserved to be ranked among the most wise and benevolent lawgivers of all ages, for

> he was the first in the history of the Christian world to seek for religious security and peace by the practise of justice and not by the exercise of power; to plan the establishment of popular institutions with the enjoyment of liberty of conscience; to advance the career of civilization by recognizing the rightful equality of all Christian sects. The asylum of Papists was the spot where in a remote corner of the world, on the banks of rivers which as yet had hardly been explored, the mild forbearance of a proprietary, adopted religious freedom as the basis of the state.[2]

Upon the young shoulders of Cecil Calvert, twenty-six years of age when his father died, suddenly fell the full responsibility for carrying on the plans for the new colony.

[1] *Great Britain, Statutes at Large,* Remington Edition, III, 48.

[2] *History of the United States,* 18th edition, I, 244. This passage is found in no less than twenty-four editions of Bancroft, the first appearing in 1834. It is not to be found in the abridged edition of 1883.

CECIL CALVERT, THE SECOND LORD BALTIMORE
Reproduced by permission of the Maryland Historical Society

The charter already engrossed was made to read in the name of Cecil, who on the death of his father became the second Lord Baltimore. The charter now made him Lord Proprietary of the Colony of Maryland. How the young Lord Baltimore in the face of great odds and bitter opposition, carried out the plans of his father and established for the first time a government where the principle of religious liberty had full recognition and practical application, makes one of the most interesting but at the same time one of the most neglected chapters of early American history.

Little is known of the early life of Cecil Calvert. Like his father, he became a student at Trinity College, Oxford. There is a record of his matriculation in 1621, when he was fifteen years of age. There is no record of his graduation but this is not surprising. His father announced his conversion to the Roman Catholic faith just before the son would have been graduated. It is not certain when Cecil became a Catholic, but it was probably before his father announced his conversion. An explanation why he did not receive his degree may be found in the fact that "at Oxford, subscription to the thirty-nine articles had been required of students since 1581; and dissenting students had been thus excluded from the university. It was a university set apart for the English church." [2]

In 1628 he married Lady Anne Arundel, daughter of Thomas, Lord Arundel of Wardour, the Catholic nobleman who was a close friend of his father and sent out the expedition to Maine under Captain Weymouth in 1605. His married life was most happy. His wife was a woman of great beauty, as shown by her portrait by Van Dyck, which is carefully preserved at Wardour Castle.

For the accomplishment of so great a task as was his, the second Lord Baltimore was well endowed. He inherited not only his father's estate, but his purposes and ideals as well The same spirit of charity and forbearance which charac

[2] May, *Constitutional History of England,* III, 195.

terized the father was found in the son. He knew of his father's plans and his determination to open the door of Maryland to all who might seek sanctuary there, was prompted by his father's intention already revealed to him.

Johnson states that soon after the granting of the charter the second Lord Baltimore had, "in some proclamation or public declaration" inviting colonists to settle in Maryland, promised among other things, that they "would be secure in the enjoyment of their religion." [3] There is apparently no record of any printed proclamation containing any such specific promise. Andrews says that Baltimore was determined to make religious toleration the "unique distinction of his new plantation; but this alone, for reasons of public import, he could not advertise." He could only include it in his instructions to those who were actually to take up their abode in the province and this he did.[4]

To Father Richard Blount, Provincial of the English Jesuit Province, the second Lord Baltimore went for counsel and advice, knowing that his father had previously applied to the Provincial for missionaries to be sent to Maryland. The sending of Jesuit missionaries was a most important part of the original plans, but this made the whole project extremely hazardous. Naturally there is little record to show Father Blount's connection with the undertaking, but there is one record which is enough to establish the fact that as provincial he gave his full support and that of the English province to all the plans that had been formulated.

The Lords Baltimore had no idea of establishing a colony for Roman Catholics alone, as the Puritans had created in New England an exclusive refuge for themselves. The liberal provisions of the charter and those exempting the colony from the operation of the statute laws and from parliamentary legislation, were specially designed for opening the door of religious liberty to all sects. But even under these conditions

[3] Op. cit., 36.
[4] *Founding of Maryland,* 53.

there was opposition to Catholics being allowed to enjoy toleration and freedom from persecution. The enemies of the Maryland project were continually referring to it as a "popish colony" dangerous to the cause of English Protestantism. Then there were some narrow-minded Catholics who seriously questioned whether one of their faith should openly tolerate the exercise of the Protestant religion and grant religious liberty to all sects and denominations.

To be able to answer these critics, Baltimore submitted to Father Blount, certain propositions covering the various objections raised. The answers to these objections were prepared either by Father Blount or by one of the mission priests under his direction. Johnson says the answers were prepared by Father Blount but Foley in his *Records of the English Province, S.J.*, says that they were probably written by Father Andrew White and sent through the provincial with his approval.[4a] It really matters little who actually prepared the answers. They bore the stamp of approval of the English Province and of Father Blount. The objections and answers are reproduced in full by Johnson in his *Foundation of Maryland* who states that:

> This paper proves that the charter of Maryland was then considered and treated as securing liberty of conscience to Roman Catholics. It proves further that the Society of Jesus undertook to further and extend the planting of the colony, with full knowledge that the principle of religious toleration was to be adopted as one of the fundamental institutions of the Province and toleration for Roman Catholics carried with it of necessity, toleration for all Christians. The Provincial of the Jesuits therefore agreed to assist in adopting and applying this principle in Maryland.[5]

In answer to the first objection that a license for Catholics "to depart this kingdom and to go into Maryland, or any country where they may have free liberty of their religion, would take away all hope of their conformity to the Church

[4a] Vol. III, 362.
[5] Page 30.

of England," which was the purpose of the laws then in force against Catholics, is found this answer:

> Conversion in matters of religion, if it be forced should give little satisfaction to a wise state, for those who for worldly respects break their faith with God will do it on a fit occasion much sooner with men.

Here is evidence that the English Jesuits were among the first to recognize the utter futility of conversion by force. They had seen how the cause of the Catholic Church in England had not been served by the persecution of Protestants under Queen Mary. They had not failed to catch the message of the Spanish friar (the confessor to Philip, Mary's consort), Father de Castro, who had raised his voice as one crying in the wilderness in opposition to the sanguinary measures that were being taken to stamp out heresy in the realm. To the amazement of the court, the friar pronounced persecution to be contrary not only to the spirit but to the text of the Christian gospel, and declared that it was not by severity but by kindness that men were to be brought into the fold of the church. This appeal did not fall altogether on deaf ears. For a period, at least, the execution of prisoners was suspended and it was some time before the advocates of severity could obtain permission to rekindle the fires of Smithfield.[6]

It has been the occasion of surprise and wonder to some that any policy of toleration or religious liberty should be favored by Roman Catholics, but as a matter of fact there was just as much reason to expect at this time a movement in the direction of religious liberty to come from Catholics as from Protestants. The early Protestant church was a persecuting church and it did not hesitate to mete out the traditional punishment for heretics. Religious liberty was not born of the Protestant Reformation.[7]

[6] Lingard, op. cit., VII, 193.

[7] Charles C. Marshall in his *Roman Catholic Church in the Modern State,* says: "Of course no claim is made here that the extirpation of

Lecky, who says that there were more instances of toleration being advocated by Catholics than by orthodox Protestants, calls attention to the fact that:

> L'Hôpital and Lord Baltimore, the Catholic founder of Maryland were the two first legislators who uniformly upheld religious liberty when in power; and Maryland continued the solitary refuge for the oppressed of every Christian sect till the Protestant party, who were in the ascendant in its legislature basely enacted the whole penal code against the co-religionists of the founder of the colony. But among Protestants it may, I believe, be safely affirmed, that there was no example of the consistent advocacy or practise of toleration in the sixteenth century, that was not virulently and generally denounced by all sections of the clergy and scarcely any till the middle of the seventeenth century.[8]

L'Hôpital, referred to by Lecky, was the Catholic chancellor of France in the latter part of the sixteenth century. He stood far in advance of his day in his advocacy of religious liberty. He maintained that to "bring back heretics to the fold, charity, patience and prayer are the only arms which the Divine Founder of our religion used to draw nations to him." He prevented the introduction of the Inquisition in France and issued the Edict of Romorantin in 1562 which authorized the free exercise of Protestant worship.

Lord Montague, one of the leaders of the English Catholics during the reign of Elizabeth, made a speech in the House of Lords in opposition to the statute, providing that a Catholic who for a second time should refuse to subscribe to the oath of supremacy, should incur the pains and penalty of high treason. Hallam says that this speech "breathed such abhorrence of persecution as some erroneously imagine to have been unknown to that age." Montague declared:

> This law is not necessary, forasmuch as the Catholics of this realm disturb not, nor hinder the public affairs of the realm,

heretics or religious persecution of any kind was limited to the Latin church. In certain aspects, Protestantism was a greater offender, at least in theory." 191, note 22.

[8] Op. cit., II, 58.

neither spiritual nor temporal. They dispute not, they preach not, they disobey not the Queen, they cause no trouble or tumult among the people; so that no man can say that thereby the realm doth receive any hurt or damage by them. They have brought into the realm no novelties of doctrine or religion. This being true and evident, as it is indeed, there is no necessity why any new law should be made against them. And where there is no sore nor grief, medicines are superfluous and also hurtful and dangerous. I do entreat you whether it be just to make this penal statute to force the subjects of this realm to receive and believe the religion of the Protestants on pain of death. This I say to be a thing most unjust, for it is repugnant to the natural liberty of men's understanding; for understanding may be persuaded but not forced.[9]

The Society of Jesus did not lend itself to the persecution of those outside the faith. The teaching of the founder did not countenance conversion by force. It was not long after the foundation of the order that the Papacy abandoned the mediæval weapons of religious warfare. Ignatius Loyola, during his last days, prayed for Henry VIII and Martin Luther and ordered Masses to be said and prayers offered for England and Germany. The Jesuits, writes Dr. Paul Van Dyke "were peace-makers; one of their most common and fruitful efforts was to inculcate in preaching and also by private conversations, the fundamental precept of Christ: 'If ye forgive not men their trespasses, neither will your Heavenly Father forgive your trespasses.' "[10] Francis Xavier wrote to Ignatius:

The Company of Jesus, it seems to me, is nothing but a company of love. Harshness on one side, fear on the other, ought to be far from us. No one ought to be retained by any constraint. On the contrary, those lacking the necessary virtues ought to be rejected even though they wish to stay; and those who have these virtues— it is love alone which should bind them together.[11]

It made no difference with many of the opponents of the charter that Lord Baltimore had promised religious freedom and offered to take Protestants as well as Catholics to Maryland and protect them in the exercise of their religion. Re-

[9] Hallam, *Constitutional History of England*, 5th edition, 75.
[10] *Ignatius Loyola*, 185.
[11] Ibid, 260.

ligious freedom of this kind was so inconceivable to them that Baltimore was not taken at his word, and his offer of security for Protestants was looked upon as only a guise to lure them into a Roman Catholic stronghold.

At this time prospects for both civil and religious liberty in England were at their darkest. Absolutism reigned supreme in state and church. In 1629 when Charles dissolved parliament, Catholic recusants were persecuted and fined and this continued until the sailing of the *Ark* and the *Dove*. It is false interpretation of English history to claim, as some have, that, during the period preceding the first voyage to Maryland, there was little inducement for Catholics to leave the realm of England. Charles may have been averse to an active persecution but to placate the parliamentary party, which was strongly determined to destroy Catholicism in England, he supported the anti-Catholic policy and broke the treaty with France in more ways than in the treatment of the Queen's household.[12]

The influence of Henrietta Maria on account of her religion has been exaggerated. It is a mistake to make the Queen's influence responsible for whatever leniency Charles may have desired to show to his Catholic subjects.[13] The Queen had little political influence, and even the King himself gave little consideration to her when it came to the matter of religion. He "hated the Queen's religion heartily, it was a sentiment in which he never wavered and in foreign policy she did not perceptibly interfere." [14] After sending back to France most of her household, he carefully excluded all English Catholics from her chapel at Somerset House. His dislike of the Catholic religion and his steadfast loyalty to the established church, however, did not lead him really to desire to persecute his Catholic subjects. It was a matter of necessity, at least he so regarded it.

12 Belloc, *Charles the First,* 116.

13 Meyer, "Charles I and Rome," *American Historical Review,* XIX (October, 1913), 13.

14 Belloc, op. cit., 172.

Charles was always in need of funds, and had it not been for his lack of money he would willingly have discharged Catholics from the obligation of their fines under the recusancy laws, as well as from their danger to life and liberty, but he could not afford to do this.[15] The law left it optional with him to exact a fine of twenty pounds a month or to take two thirds of the estates of lay recusants, but in lieu of these penalties he allowed them to compound for a fixed sum to be paid annually. The amount of the composition was determined at the pleasure of the commissioners.

The Catholic by the sacrifice sometimes of one-tenth, sometimes of one third of his yearly income, purchased, not the liberty of serving God according to his conscience (that was still forbidden under severe penalties), but the permission to absent himself from a form of worship which he disapproved. The exaction of such a sacrifice was irreconcilable with any principle of justice, but inasmuch as it was a mitigation of the severities inflicted by the law, the recusants looked upon it as a benefit, the zealots stigmatized it as a crime in a Protestant sovereign.[16]

The King repeatedly ordered the magistrates and judges to enforce the penal laws against priests and Jesuits. Many were apprehended and some were convicted. Although the King was reluctant to shed their blood on account of their religion, one priest suffered the penalty of treason and others perished in prison or were sent into banishment.[17]

Charles did show favor to Lord Baltimore in the granting of the charter with its broad powers and in his consent to a Catholic migration to America. Here may have been one possible instance of the influence of the Queen, for he expressed the desire to have the colony named in honor of his Catholic consort, *Terra Maria* (Mary Land). This favor he at all times continued to show. But notwithstanding this there was every reason for the desire of this group of English Catholics to leave the mother country and find refuge not

[15] Meyer, op. cit., 20.
[16] Lingard, op. cit., IX, 308.
[17] Ibid, 307.

only from the policy of the King but from the ominous portent of more severe treatment at the hands of the parliamentary party striving for power.[18]

The colony of Virginia again entered the list of opponents and made strong objections to the Maryland charter which they claimed invaded its territory and infringed upon its rights. In one breath these opponents claimed that the palatinate powers granted to the proprietary were too extensive and were dangerous to the liberties of the people, and in the next breath said that the privileges and franchises granted were so great that they would attract settlers from other colonies and so depopulate them.

The privy council sustained the Maryland grant, and Virginia colonists were advised to live in peace with their neighbors, advice which they had no mind to heed. The hostility of the Virginians remained bitter and persistent, and they continued for years to attack Lord Baltimore and to misrepresent his motives. They never relaxed their opposition, and Browne says "dyng bequeathed their vindictiveness to their successors and their calumnies to posterity, and the hereditary animosity was kept up for a century and a half, if indeed it is yet entirely extinguished."

It was no easy task that confronted the young Lord Baltimore when the death of his father found the preparations for the first voyage to Maryland hardly started. There were financial as well as political difficulties to be overcome. The ill-fated Newfoundland colony had made serious inroads on the Baltimore fortune. Although Cecil Calvert inherited a large landed estate from his father, he was in fact "land poor," for the personal estate that came to him was appraised at only nine thousand, seven hundred pounds.[19] The new

[18] In the pamphlet which was written by the first Lord Baltimore in answer to "Tom Tell Troth" he thus described the condition of the English Catholics at the time (1631): "The poor afflicted Catholics of England have their grievances daily multiplied, their estates spoiled, their persons disgraced." This was only two years before the sailing of The *Ark* and the *Dove*, see *supra* 62, 63.

[19] Browne, *George and Cecilius Calvert*, 31.

plan of colonization needed the financial help of others to make it possible, since it was not an investment that promised great or quick returns. Baltimore required the help of those who were influenced by the same motives that had prompted his father to make the undertaking and this help was given.[20] He later testified before the House of Lords, when he was called upon to answer his enemies and defend his charter, and he "engaged the greatest part of his fortune in Maryland." [21] Chalmers says that "the transportation, necessary stores and provisions, during the first two years cost the nobleman upwards of forty thousand pounds, which if estimated according to the value of money and the price of all things, must be allowed to have been a considerable sum." [22]

When it came time to make the final plans for the voyage of the *Ark* and the *Dove,* Father White discovered that Lord Baltimore would not be able to make any adequate provision for the missionaries and that the new mission would have to be practically self-sustaining. This did not deter him, however, from going ahead with his plans, nor did it serve to dampen his ardor. Father Knott, who succeeded Father More as the English provincial, in a letter written to the Belgian Nuncio, some years later, throws light on the hard conditions Father White at the last moment was obliged to assent to. The most difficult problem for solution was the providing of means of subsistence for the missionaries as there was no hope of their living on alms in the new country. It was decided that the fathers should accept the same terms as the other colonists. Father Knott reported:

> This seemed a hard condition to the fathers and not in conformity with their institute, involving a number of difficulties for which they could not discern any easy remedy in the future. Still such as it was, it seemed a necessary condition to accept for fear they should look like deserting the cause of God and souls.[23]

20 Andrews, *The Founding of Maryland,* 54.
21 *Archives of Maryland,* III, 180.
22 *Annals,* I, 208.
23 Hughes, op. cit., I, 255.

In view of the above, Father Hughes comments:

And so on the first occasion within a hundred years when priests were to be sent out of reach of persecution and yet to be on the soil belonging to England—when Catholics would be able to deal fairly and a Catholic government treat openly with them—the priests so honored were among the first instances of Christendom, whether Catholic or Protestant, if not the very first, who were left to shift for themselves by the government that asked for them and who were put on the footing of mere lay citizens in a community of farmers and traders.[24]

It is hardly to be expected that Lord Baltimore would offer favorable terms to the Jesuit missionaries, and the wonder is that he was able to offer any terms at all as Jesuit priests were under the ban of the penal laws. According to Professor Meyer, King Charles hated both Jesuits and Puritans. The Jesuits he termed "the Puritans of Rome." [25] It is very doubtful if he consented to or even knew of the Jesuit missionaries accompanying the voyagers, and this partly accounts for the secrecy surrounding their departure. Father Hughes does not seem to be fairly justified in his comment that Lord Baltimore may "have taken the measure of the Jesuits quite exactly; not only for the influence which they might exercise and for the possible amount of the contribution which they might throw into the settlement."

If Lord Baltimore had provided funds or means directly or indirectly for outlawed Jesuit priests, he would have incurred the penalties of the English statutes in force at the time and would have wrecked his whole colonial enterprise at the very outset. As it was, he was taking no little risk in allowing the Jesuits to accompany the voyage, for if this had become known to some of the zealots, the claim would no doubt have been made that he was harboring Jesuit priests within the meaning of the penal statute. Lord Baltimore was walking on thin ice and he had to be wary. It is to be borne in mind that after all, it was a Protestant kingdom

24 Ibid, 257.
25 Meyer, op. cit., 24.

that was sponsoring this colony and a kingdom where all Catholics and more especially Jesuit priests were being persecuted. It adds to the glory and honor of the new American mission that it accepted these hard conditions without question or complaint and in a spirit of willing self-sacrifice.

No sooner were the preparations for the voyage completed than the busybodies and trouble makers made one final attempt to head it off. The *Ark* had already left Gravesend when one particularly industrious zealot rushed to the Star Chamber and informed that body that the crew had not taken the oath of allegiance, and reported all the rumors that had been started by evil tongues to encompass the failure of the expedition. It was assumed that all Catholics were in league with Spain, and one of the rumors had it that the ships were not to sail for America until they had visited Spain where a conspiracy to take possession of the English colonies was to be hatched. It was also reported that soldiers and Catholic nuns were hidden on the ship for passage to Spain.

All this created a great fuss, and Secretary Coke became very much excited and sent an order to Admiral Pennington, commanding the Channel fleet, to stop the ships at Dover. This dispatch was forwarded by a relay of couriers and the original dispatch had the endorsement "haste" ten times repeated with the addition of "post haste" and "all speed." The various endorsements record the time the dispatch was received by each courier, indicating that all speed records were broken. The last courier arrived in time. The *Ark* and the *Dove* were found lying off Tilbury. Watkins the London "searcher" reported that he had boarded the ship and administered the oaths to 128 emigrants. He found no soldiers nor nuns. The final attempt to prevent the sailing of the *Ark* and the *Dove* had failed.

The young Lord Baltimore, exasperated by all this commotion, showing as it did, the persistency and determination of his enemies, wrote, after the ships had sailed, to his friend, the Earl of Strafford:

My ships are gone, after having been many ways troubled by my adversaries, after they had endeavored to overthrow my business at the council board, after they had informed some of the Lords of the Council that I had intended to carry over nuns into Spain and soldiers to serve the King (which I believe your Lordship will laugh at as I did) and after they have gotten Mr. Attorney-General to make an information in the Star Chamber that my ships were departed from Gravesend without any cockets from the custom house, in contempt of all authority, my people abusing the King's officers and refusing to take the oath of allegiance. As soon as I had notice of it I made it appear unto their Lordships that Mr. Attorney was abused and misinformed and that there was not any just cause of the complaint in any of the accusations and that every one of them was most notoriously and maliciously false; whereupon they were pleased to restore my ships to their former liberty.

The foregoing bears evidence of the manner in which English Catholics were annoyed and harassed even when engaged in a legitimate enterprise under royal authority. The letter then goes on with a recital of further last minute opposition and discloses that Lord Baltimore had the aid of others in his undertaking:

After they had likewise corrupted and seduced my mariners and defamed the business all they could by their scandalous reports to discourage men from it, and used all the means they could both publicly and privately, to overthrow it, I have as I said, at last by the help of some of your Lordship's good friends and mine, overcome these difficulties and sent a hopeful colony into Maryland with a fair and probable expectation of good success, however without danger of any great prejudice unto myself, in respect that others are joined with me in the adventure. There are two of my brothers gone, with very near twenty other gentlemen of very good fashion, and three hundred laboring men well provided in all things.[26]

The activity of his enemies caused Lord Baltimore to change his plans at the eleventh hour and decide not to go

26 Browne, op. cit., 41.

with the expedition as he had intended, but to remain at home where he could better guide the destinies of the colony and protect his charter rights. It was a wise decision. It is doubtful if the project would have been at all successful had Baltimore not remained at home where he could exercise the vigilance which was to be the price of safety. So, following the fate of his father, he was destined never to set foot upon the promised land. Command of the voyage and of the colony was given to Leonard Calvert, his younger brother, another worthy son of the father.

After deciding not to accompany the expedition, Lord Baltimore carefully prepared a letter of instructions to the colonies which was given to Leonard Calvert to take with him on the voyage. The original manuscript is now in the possession of the Maryland Historical Society, being among a large collection of Calvert papers obtained by the society in 1888 from a descendant of the last Lord Baltimore. This is a paper of great historic interest for it was the first declaration of religious liberty to come to America.

The first instruction is very simple and couched in plain language but it is weighted with wisdom and justice. It reads as follows:

> His Lord required his said governor and commissioners that in their voyage to Maryland that they be very careful to preserve unity and peace amongst all the passengers on shipboard and that they suffer no scandal nor any offense to be given to any of the Protestants whereby any just complaint may hereafter be made by them in Virginia or in England and that for that end they cause all acts of the Roman Catholic religion to be done privately as may be and they instruct all the Roman Catholiques to be silent upon all occasions of discourse concerning matters of religion and that the said Governor and Commissioners treat the Protestants with as much mildness and favor as justice will permit. And this to be observed at land as well as sea.[27]

After all this was only a bit of sensible advice, and the following of sensible advice is all that is needed to establish peace among Christian sects. In plain language it meant that

[27] Hall, *Narratives of Early Maryland,* 16.

each man when it came to the matter of religion was to "mind his own business." Here was religious liberty of a very practical sort.

In later years statutes and laws were passed recognizing in one way or another the spirit of tolerance and well sounding provisions forbidding discrimination by reason of religion, but none were so effective and none so wise and salutary as these simple instructions given to a band of voyagers who caught the spirit of their leader and had the understanding to know that his advice was good to follow.

CHAPTER X

THE VOYAGE

Sails were spread on the *Ark* and the *Dove* in the early morning of November 22, 1633, and with a favoring wind the ships put out to sea. The departure was from Cowes on the Isle of Wight. The number of voyagers and the proportion of Catholics and Protestants have been questioned. In his letter to Strafford, Lord Baltimore gives the number as approximately three hundred and twenty—including his two brothers—"near twenty other gentlemen," and three hundred laboring men. This letter is dated January 10, 1634. He should have known how many accompanied the voyage and he would have no reason to overstate the number. At Cowes according to Browne [1] they took on board the Jesuit mission priests and "a number of other emigrants raising the total to about 320 souls."

The London "searcher" administered the oath to 128 persons, all he found. This was while the ships were at Gravesend. If the oath given included the form of the oath of supremacy it was not taken by the Catholic emigrants so it is a fair assumption that none were on board at that time. Evidently the authorities did not know that the ships were to make another stop at the Isle of Wight. In view of the efforts made to prevent the voyage, secrecy had to surround the taking of Jesuits and Catholic recusants. There is every reason to believe, therefore, that in order to avoid taking the oath of supremacy the Catholic emigrants did not embark until after the ships had dropped down to Cowes. This being so the Catholics constituted a majority of the voyagers, although this has been seriously disputed.

[1] Op. cit., 45.

Leonard Calvert was in command of the voyage. Another brother, George Calvert, was a member of the expedition. Thomas Cornwaleys and Jerome Hawley, both Catholics, were commissioned as counsellors. Cornwaleys belonged to an old London family from which descended Earl Cornwallis who surrendered to Washington at Yorktown.

No Protestant ministers went over on the first voyage and some historians have not failed to comment on this fact. There was some reason for the omission. The first Lord Baltimore had had trouble with Protestant clergymen in Newfoundland. In view of this his son might well have thought twice before inviting a Protestant minister on the voyage to play the role of an informer. Then, too, it would have been a difficult matter to have found any Protestant clergyman at that time who was a believer in religious toleration and not addicted to controversy. "Controversial discourse concerning matters of religion," was the one thing to be avoided according to the letter of instructions.

Lord Baltimore may have heard or read of the experience of Champlain when on his expedition to New France earlier in the century. The explorer had taken both a Catholic priest and a Huguenot minister along in order to promote peace between Catholics and Protestants with the result that "the clergymen disputed heartily on the way." Champlain wrote that he had seen "our curé and the minister fall to with their fists on questions of faith." For the sake of unity and peace among his colonists, it was quite the sensible and politic thing for Lord Baltimore not to have included clergy of both faiths on the *Ark* and the *Dove*. The Protestants did not suffer any neglect in the exercise of their religion, for according to their own doctrine and practise, they could worship without the aid of clergy. They had lay readers, were provided with a chapel after a settlement was made, and Protestant clergy were provided later.

In *Savin's Reprints* (No. II), in the Peabody Library at Baltimore, seventeen names are given "of the gentlemen adventurers that are gone in person to this plantation." They are:

Leonard Calvert, Governor, and George Calvert, his Lordship's brothers; Jerome Hawley, Esquire; Thomas Cornwaleys, Esquire; Commissioners; Richard Gerard, son to Sir Thomas Gerard, Knight and Baronet; Edward Wintour and Frederick Wintour, sons of Lady Anne Wintour; Henry Wiseman, son to Sir Thomas Wiseman, Knight; John Saunders, Edward Cranfield, Henry Greene, Nicholas Fairfax, John Baxter, Thomas Dorrell, Captain John Hill, John Medcalf, and William Saire.[2]

Brother Thomas Gervase, a Jesuit lay brother, accompanied Fathers Andrew White and John Altham and these three comprised the original Maryland Jesuit mission.

The two ships were owned by the first Lord Baltimore and had been in his service for several years. They had each made at least one trip to Newfoundland. Most writers describe the *Ark* as of three hundred ton burden, but Father White described her "as strong as could be made of oak and iron, four hundred ton burden, King built, making fair weather in great storm." Apparently the *Dove* had been rechristened the *"Dove of Maryland"* before the voyage, for in a deed from Cecil Calvert bearing his seal, under date of October 15, 1633, conveying a one-eighth part of the ship to his brother Leonard Calvert, it is described as "the vessel called the Dove of Maryland of forty tunne or thereabouts, now in the River Thames, London."

The Reverend William McSherry, S.J., discovered in the archives of the Society of Jesus in Rome, in 1832, the original manuscripts of the *Declaratio Coloniae* and also the *Relatio Itineris in Marylandiam,* the latter being the narrative of the voyage of the *Ark* and the *Dove,* written by Father Andrew White. Father McSherry carefully copied both manuscripts and these copies are now in the library of Loyola College in Baltimore. A copy of the manuscript of the narrative of the voyage in Latin, together with an English trans-

[2] Sarah Redwood Lee, "The Maryland Influence in American Catholicism," *Records, American Catholic Historical Society of Philadelphia* (Dec. 1930), 6.

lation, was published by the Maryland Historical Society in 1874 as *Fund Publication,* Number 7.

Another version of the report or "relation" of the voyage to Maryland is found in an original manuscript now in the possession of the Maryland Historical Society, acquired in 1894 and published in 1899 as *Fund Publication,* Number 33. This manuscript was sent by Leonard Calvert to one of his partners in London. It was enclosed in a letter sent from Point Comfort, May 30, 1634, a little more than two months after the landing of the colonists at St. Mary's. It was sent on the first return voyage of the *Ark* to England. Governor Calvert describes the English manuscript as having been written by a "most honest and discreet gentleman" and it is safe to attribute its authorship to Father White.[3]

Father White kept a journal of the voyage from which he afterwards prepared his relation in Latin to send to his superiors for recording in the archives of the society at Rome. At the same time he prepared the English manuscript for use by Governor Calvert. The following excerpts from the narrative of the voyage are taken from the translation of the original Latin manuscript found by Father McSherry. As John Fiske says, it is written in "quaint and very charming Latin." [4] The piety of the narrator and his devout faith in Divine favor and protection are manifest all through the story. He sees the hand of God in every escape from pirates, shipwreck and the perils of the sea, which were met with in the voyage of four months. As the winter was coming on, the trip was not made directly across the Atlantic and a southwesterly course was taken by way of the Barbados.

Thus begins the narrative:

On the twenty-second of the month of November in the year 1633, being St. Cecilia's day, we set sail from Cowes in the Isle of Wight, with a gentle east wind blowing. And after committing the principal parts of the ship to the protection of God espe-

[3] Hall, *Narratives of Early Maryland,* 28.
[4] *Virginia and Her Neighbors,* I, 260.

cially, and of his most Holy Mother and St. Ignatius, and all the guardian angels of Maryland, we sailed on a little way between the two shores and the wind failing us, we stopped opposite Yarmouth Castle, which is near the southern end of the same island (Isle of Wight). Here we were received with a cheerful salute of artillery.

There was evidently still danger that the ships would not be allowed to get away safely even after they had set sail. The enemies of the voyage to Maryland were resourceful and persistent. This is disclosed as the narrative continues:

Yet we were not without apprehension, for the sailors were murmuring among themselves saying that they were expecting a messenger with letters from London and from this it seemed as if they were conniving to delay us. But God brought their plans to confusion, for that very night a favorable wind arose and a French cutter which had put into the same harbor with us, being forced to set sail, came near running into our pinnace. The latter, therefore, to avoid being run down, having cut away and lost an anchor, set sail without delay; and since it was dangerous to drift about in that place, made haste to get further out to sea. And so that we might not lose sight of our pinnace, we determined to follow. Thus the designs of the sailors, who were plotting against us, were frustrated. This happened on the 23rd of November, St. Clement's day who, because he had been tied to an anchor and thrown into the sea, obtained the crown of martyrdom. "And showed the inhabitants of the earth, how to declare the wonderful things of God."

That some of the sailors were "conniving" to delay the voyage indicates that Lord Baltimore had not been thorough in eliminating from the crew all who had been "corrupted and seduced" by his enemies before the voyage started. After passing the western cape of England the little *Dove* soon dropped behind, for with her small body of sail she could not keep up with the *Ark*. So the *Ark* shortened her sail in order to keep her little consort in sight, fearing that if "we left the pinnace too far behind us, it would become the prey of the Turks and pirates who generally infest the sea." One of the thrills of the old sailing days was given to the voyagers on the third day out when the *Dragon,* a merchant ship of six hundred tons sailing from London, overtook the *Ark* and the two ships had a lively race "with a great noise of trumpets" to see which ship with fair weather and a favorable wind could outstrip the other. "Our ship would have beaten the other," boasts Father White, "though we did not use our topsail," but the *Ark* was obliged to wait for the little *Dove* which was slower, and "so we yielded the palm to the merchant ship and she sailed by us before evening and passed out of sight."

On the first Sunday of the voyage there was fair sailing until evening when the wind suddenly changed to the north. The storm that followed was so severe that the merchant ship *Dragon* was soon driven back on her course and returned toward England, but the *Ark* and the *Dove* held to their courses. Those on the *Dove,* losing confidence in her strength, sent out a warning that if they apprehended shipwreck they would hang out lights from the masthead.

> We meanwhile sailed on in our strong ship of four hundred tons, a better could not be built of wood and iron. We had a skillful captain and so he was given his choice whether he would return to England or keep on struggling with the winds; if he yielded to these, the Irish shore close by awaited us, which is noted for its hidden rocks and frequent shipwrecks. Nevertheless, his bold spirit and his desire to test the strength of the new ship which he had then managed for the first time, prevailed with the captain. He resolved to try the sea, although he confessed that it was the more dangerous on account of being so narrow.

As the winds increased and the sea became angrier, the voyagers on the *Ark* suddenly saw in the distance the fateful signals—two lights on the mast of the *Dove*. "Then indeed," writes Father White, "we thought it was all over with her and that she had been swallowed up in the deep whirlpools, for in a moment she had passed out of sight." The sea was so heavy that the *Ark* could not go to the rescue of her little sister-ship, which was given up as lost with all on board. Then the narrator hastens to inform his readers in order not to keep them in suspense, that:

God had better things in store for us, for the fact was that finding herself no match for the violence of the waves, she had avoided the Virginian ocean with which we were already contending by returning to England, to the Scilly islands. And making a fresh start from thence in company with the *Dragon,* she overtook us, as we shall relate, at a large harbor in the Antilles. And thus God who oversees the smallest things, guided, protected and took care of the little vessel.

It was to be six weeks before the voyagers on the *Ark* saw the *Dove* again and "being ignorant of the event, were distressed with grief and anxiety which the gloomy night filled with manifold terrors." The storm abated somewhat the next morning, but for three days the winds were so strong and variable that the ship made little progress. Then the next day, "which was the feast of Andrew the Apostle," the weather took a turn for the worse. The following is Father White's graphic description of the recurrence of the storm which nearly shipwrecked the *Ark:*

The clouds accumulating in a frightful manner, were fearful to behold before they separated, and excited the belief that all the malicious spirits of the storm and all the evil genii of Maryland had come forth to battle against us. Towards evening, the captain saw a sun-fish swimming with great effort against the course of the sun, which is a very sure sign of a terrible storm; nor did the omen prove a false one. For about ten oclock at night a dark cloud poured forth a violent shower. And such a furious hurricane followed close upon it, that it was necessary to run with all speed to take in sail; and this could not be done quickly enough to prevent the mainsail, the only one we were carrying, from being torn in the middle from top to bottom. A part of it was blown over into the sea and was recovered with great difficulty.

At this juncture the minds of the bravest were struck with terror. The sailors acknowledged that they had seen other ships wrecked in a less severe storm. The hurricane "called forth the prayers and vows of the Catholics in honor of the Blessed Virgin Mary and Her Immaculate Conception, of St. Ignatius, the Patron Saint of Maryland, Saint Michael and all the guardian angels of the same country." And each one hastened to "purge his soul by the sacrament of penance." All control of the rudder was lost, and the ship drifted about like a dish in the water, at the mercy of winds and waves. Then "God showed a way of safety." The narrative continues:

At first, I confess, I had been engrossed with the apprehension of the ship's being lost, and of losing my own life; but after I had spent some time in praying more fervently than was my usual custom, and had set forth to Christ the Lord, to the Blessed Virgin, St. Ignatius, and the angels of Maryland, that the purpose of this journey was to glorify the Blood of Our Redeemer in the salvation of barbarians, and also to raise up a kingdom for the Saviour (if he would condescend to prosper our poor efforts) to consecrate another gift to the Immaculate Virgin, His Mother, and many things to the same effect; great comfort shone in upon my soul, and at the same time a conviction that we should be delivered, not only from this storm but from every other during that voyage, that with me there could be no room left for doubt. I had betaken myself to prayer, when the sea was raging its worst and (may this be to the glory of God) I had scarcely finished, when they observed that the storm was abating. That indeed brought me to a new frame of mind and filled me at the same time with great joy and admiration, since I understood much more clearly the greatness of God's love towards the people of Maryland, to whom your Reverence has sent us. Eternal praises to the most sweet graciousness of the Redeemer!

Father White had reason to believe in the efficacy of fervent prayer for not only did the storm abate but from this time to the journey's end, three months in all, there was not one hour of bad weather, so "that the captain and his men declared they had never seen it calmer or pleasanter."

The first stop was made at the Fortunate (now the Canary) islands. Then after sailing two hundred miles on a southerly course the *Ark* changed her course to the westward and sailed across the Atlantic headed for the West Indies. Barbados was reached January 3, 1634, and here the *Ark* was joined by her consort, the *Dove*. "We came again to enjoy our pinnace," writes Father White, "for before we saw her in the harbor we gave her up for lost in that hideous storm. Herein God's mercy showed toward us."

After stopping at several islands including Montserrat where was found a large group of Irish Catholic refugees, the vessels turned their courses northward toward their final destination. The three months' journey came to an end on February 24, 1634, when the *Ark* and the *Dove* dropped anchor at Point Comfort, Virginia.

BOOK II
THE PLANTING

CHAPTER I

THE LANDING OF THE PILGRIMS

THE same rumor of a Spanish plot which had delayed the departure of the *Ark* and the *Dove* from England greeted them on their arrival in America. It had made quicker passage than the ships. After the attack of the Armada, it was always easy to start a rumor of a Spanish plot in connection with any activity where Catholics played a part, and it was remarkable how fast such a rumor could travel. This rumor had it that six ships were coming and "everything was to be reduced under the power of Spain." It was given little credence by the English, although it started from among their number, but care was taken to spread it among the native Indian tribes through interpreters. As a result the Indians were all in arms when the ships arrived. In this way it was hoped by those who started the rumor to frustrate the plans of Lord Baltimore and lead him to abandon the idea of founding a colony near Virginia. The rumor soon spent its force. The Jesuit missionaries were able to convey a message of peace and good-will to the natives, and to win their confidence and friendship.

Father White records that the voyagers when they first landed at Virginia were "full of apprehension lest the English inhabitants who were much displeased at our settling, should be plotting against us." Their fears of a hostile reception were somewhat allayed for they were kindly received by the colonial authorities, and were able to obtain many things which were necessary in establishing their first settlement. Father White discovered that this unexpected cordiality was due largely to the fact that the governor of Virginia hoped he "would easily recover from the royal treasury a large sum which was due him."

In making a landing at Point Comfort, the voyagers for some unexplained reason, disregarded the warning of Lord Baltimore that they should not be persuaded under any circumstances to go to Jamestown or to come within the command of the fort at Point Comfort, unless "they should be forced unto it by some extremity (which God forbid) for the preservation of their lives and goods and that they find it altogether impossible otherwise to preserve themselves." He had instructed them to send a messenger who was conformable to the Church of England to Governor Harvey and after reminding him of the long acquaintance and friendship the governor had with the first Lord Baltimore and of the friendly letters he had written to the second Lord Baltimore, since he had learned of the latter's intention to be his neighbor, to present him with a "butt of sack" [1] from His Lordship.

After several days spent at Point Comfort, the *Ark* and the *Dove* entered the Chesapeake and then turned toward the north to reach the Potomac. Of the Potomac Father White writes that he had never beheld "a larger or more beautiful river—the Thames seems a mere rivulet in comparison with it." It was not disfigured with swamps, but had firm land on each side and "fine groves of trees appear, not choked with briers and bushes and undergrowth but growing at intervals as if planted by the hand of man, so that you can drive a four horse carriage wherever you choose through the midst of the trees."

The natives were observed to be in arms, and at night fires blazed through the whole country. Reports that a canoe "like an island" had come with as many men as there were trees in the woods, spread wild alarm. The Indians however never made any armed resistance, for it was not long before the peace-

[1] Choice white wine.

ful intentions of the settlers were made known to them.

On St. Clement's Island the Maryland colonists made their first landing on the territory included in the Baltimore grant and here on March 25, 1634, occurred a solemn and memorable event. It is best told in the words of Father White:

> On the day of the Annunciation of the Most Holy Virgin in the year 1634, we celebrated the mass for the first time, on this island. This had never been done before in this part of the world. After we had completed the sacrifice, we took upon our shoulders a great cross, which we had hewn out of a tree, and advancing in order to the appointed place, with the assistance of the Governor and his associates and other Catholics, we erected a trophy to Christ the Saviour, humbly reciting, on our bended knees, the Litanies of the Sacred Cross with great emotion.[2]

Exception has been taken by some historians to what they term an over-emphasis upon this particular ceremonial. They have been apprehensive lest this religious ceremony be taken as an official act and be construed as a church establishment which was far from the purpose and intention of Lord Baltimore. Nothing could have been more natural and fitting than an act of religious worship upon the first landing of these colonists coming at the invitation of a Lord Proprietor who had announced as his chief purpose the planting of seeds of piety and religion. It was to have been expected that the ceremony would partake of the Catholic form of worship, for this was the faith of the founders of the colony and of a majority of the settlers. It was no more an act of church establishment than a Protesant ceremony would have been. It is difficult therefore to see why there should be any misapprehension as to its true meaning. The fact that the ceremony was a Roman Catholic mass which was prohibited in

2 There is a painting by Emanuel Leutze, the same artist who painted the famous "Washington Crossing the Delaware," which hangs in the state house at Annapolis of "The Landing of the Pilgrims" on St. Clement's Island, showing the large wooden cross in the background and standing in front of it, the black-robed figure of Father White, with outstretched arms bestowing blessing and benediction upon the group of colonists and Indians gathered about the scene. This painting is not as familiar as the allegorical paintings of the landing of the Pilgrims of the *Mayflower* and has found its way into few histories, even histories of Maryland.

the Mother Country in itself indicated that here in Maryland there was to be full liberty of religious worship.

So far as violating the letter of instructions is concerned, there could have been no offense taken by the Protestants, nor does it appear that any such offense was taken. There certainly can be no harm in properly emphasizing this ceremony which was as natural as it was devout and in giving to it, its true significance, not as an official act of church or religious establishment, but as the expression of the faith of an early band of American settlers whose faith had made them free.

There was an official ceremony later at the place of final settlement, attended by military pomp and the salute of guns, but this humble and devout homage to the Prince of Peace came first as well it should have done.

On March 25, 1934, three hundred years after the celebration of the first mass on Maryland soil, a great cross, forty feet high was dedicated with appropriate ceremony on St. Clement's Island, so no longer will the scene of this historic event be neglected. The bronze panel on the base of the cross bears this inscription:

> St. Clement's Island. To this Island in March 1634, Governor Leonard Calvert and the first Maryland colonists came in the *Ark* and the *Dove*. Here they landed. Here they took possession of the Province of Maryland, a cross of Maryland wood was erected and the Holy Sacrifice was celebrated. Here they first brought to the New World those principles of religious liberty which have been the chief glory of this State.

Governor Calvert had been advised not to make a permanent settlement until he had explained the purpose of his coming to the Chieftain of the Indian tribes and had gained his good-will. With this intention he sailed on the *Dove* further up the river, leaving the *Ark* at the island of St. Clement. He landed on the southern side of the river and when he learned that the Indians had fled inland he went to a village which took its name from the river, Potomac. Father White had been left with the larger part of the voyagers on St.

Clement's Island and Father John Altham accompanied the governor. At the village the party met the young chieftain's uncle who was his guardian and took his place at the head of the tribes. He is described by Father White as a "sober and discreet man." Father Altham through an interpreter explained that the white people had come "not to make war, but out of good-will toward them," to impart civilized instruction and to show them the way to heaven. The guardian gave them to understand that they were welcome and if they returned as he wished them to, "we will eat at the same table, my followers too shall hunt for you and we will have all things in common."

Going from this place further up the river to Piscataway several hundred natives equipped with bows and arrows were found awaiting the approach of the *Dove*. After signals of peace the chief of the tribe came on board of the pinnace and when he heard of "our friendly disposition towards those nations, he gave us permission to dwell wherever we pleased in his dominions." In the meantime the natives on St. Clement's Island grew more friendly, and mingled freely with the group which remained there. Father White writes that "it was pleasant to hear them admiring everything, especially wondering where in the world a tree had grown large enough to be carved into a ship of such huge size" as the *Ark*.

The governor had taken with him as a guide and interpreter one Henry Fleet, "a captain from the Virginia colony, a man especially acceptable to the savages, well versed in their language and acquainted with the country." This man was first described as being very friendly, but afterwards according to Father White he was misled by "evil counsels," became hostile and tried to excite the natives to "anger against us by all the means in his power." While he was on friendly terms he pointed out to Governor Calvert "a spot so charming in its situation that Europe itself can scarcely show one to surpass it."

After the *Dove* rejoined the *Ark,* the voyagers, guided by Fleet, came to the St. Mary's river which Father White described as a harbor and this he consecrated "to the Blessed Virgin Mary." On a high bluff on the easterly shore of this river the first permanent settlement was made. Here the plan of a village was laid out, it being named by Father White, St. Mary's.

There was an Indian village on the site but there was no taking of land by force. Payment was made neither in firearms nor fire-water, which too often had been the medium of exchange between white settlers and Indians, but in implements of husbandry. These the Indians "accepted kindly and freely gave consent." This was half a century before William Penn used the same method of negotiations in purchasing the soil of his first Quaker settlement in Pennsylvania.

Father White told in his narrative how the names of Catholic saints were used to christen all the places of interest, but much of the christening was in vain, for few of the names survived the Protestant revolution of later years. Even the name of St. Mary's had a narrow escape. In the year 1644 the Puritan government, then in temporary power, voted to change the name of St. Mary's County to Potomac "upon the theory that too much honor should not be given to the Blessed Virgin." [3] When the colony was restored to Lord Baltimore the name was changed back again to St. Mary's.

American history has bestowed the title of "Pilgrims" upon the little band of English separatists who landed unexpectedly on the coast of New England on a bleak November day in 1620. It has therefore been difficult to give this name to any other group of colonists. Both the first settlers of Massachusetts and Maryland had come to America seeking religious liberty and freedom from persecution. The English Catholics, however, had suffered more from persecution than had the Puritans and this may have been one of the reasons why those who came on the *Ark* and the *Dove* had a broader conception

[3] Swepson Earle, *The Chesapeake Bay Country,* (2nd Ed.) 106.

of the ideal of religious liberty than those who came on the *Mayflower*.

As a matter of fact, neither the voyagers on the *Mayflower* nor those on the *Ark* and the *Dove* came within the strict dictionary definition of the word "pilgrim," but in a broader sense both groups were pilgrims, for religious motives were dominant in both voyages. Some recent writers vigorously contend that the coming to America of the *Mayflower* Pilgrims was purely a commercial enterprise, that these English separatists had found in Holland the freedom from persecution and the religious sanctuary they sought, but as their lot had become a hard one, bowed down as they were by poverty, it was solely to better their material condition that they decided to migrate to America. While this is true to an extent yet it is not all. They were under a foreign rule, strangers in a strange land. Their children were being led away from the faith of their parents, intermarrying with their Holland neighbors and they saw the danger, if they stayed in Holland, of finally losing their nationality, their language and their faith.[4] So it was they sought an asylum in America where they would be free to worship God in their own fashion, remain English subjects and preserve their nationality and their language.

With the strong religious background of the voyage of the *Ark* and the *Dove,* the effect of the first Lord Baltimore's conversion to the Catholic faith on his plans of colonization and the solemn dedication of the project by Father White in his *Declaratio Coloniae* to the cause of the Christian religion, it seems idle to contend that the religious motive was not the dominant factor in the first migration to Maryland. Those who came on the *Ark* and the *Dove* came on a pilgrimage to a land of sanctuary, where the hand of persecution was stayed. They chose to call themselves "The Pilgrims of St. Mary's," and by this name they are entitled to be known.

[4] Howe, *The Puritan Republic,* 4.

CHAPTER II

OLD ST. MARY'S

IT WAS a pretty bit of country that the Pilgrims of St. Mary's had chosen for their home in America, and no one ever described it so well as Father White. To him it was indeed the land of promise, a land flowing with milk and honey. He sang the praises of Maryland with a heart full of joy and gladness. Not only did he see the fields as white for the harvest of the gospel but he had an added interest which came from his knowledge and love of natural history. He described the equable climate, the mildness of the winter, the glory of the springtime, the luxuriance of the summer, the beauty of the autumn, and the long Indian summer that lingered between autumn and winter. He told of fallow fields and gentle sloping hills, of broad streams and rich meadow lands, of safe harbors, of inlets and estuaries that afforded means of transportation and plenteous yield of fish, of strange and beautiful trees in the woods and forests, of medicinal herbs and of the crops of Indian maize. He told also of birds of brilliant plumage such as the settlers had never seen before, the scarlet tanager and the American oriole dressed in rich gold and black, the colors of the House of Baltimore, and "henceforth to be dear to Maryland eyes."

There was little that escaped his observation. In his *Relation of Maryland,* written in English when the voyage was ended, he concluded:

I will therefore end with the soyle, which is excellent so that we cannot sett downe a foot but tread on strawberries, raspires, fallen mulberrie vines, acchorns, walnutts, saxafras, etc. and those in the wildest woods. The ground is of a readish colour. All is high woods except where the Indians have cleared for corne. It abounds with delicate springs which are our best drinke. Birds diversely feathered there are infinite, as eagles, swans, hernes, geese, bitters duckes, partridge, read, blew, partie coloured and the like, by which will appear, the place abounds not alone with profit, but also with pleasure. *Laus Deo.*

As soon as the Pilgrims had established their settlement at St. Mary's, it was time for the early spring planting. The seed corn, which they had brought from Barbados, was placed in the soil where before the Indians had harvested their crops. The squaws showed their white sisters how to make bread from the Indian maize. The braves instructed the white men how to hunt the game that was abundant in the forests and accompanied them in the chase. Gardens were planted with seeds brought from England and before the summer was over, the wooded bluff of St. Mary's was transformed from an Indian village to a thriving English settlement. In six months Maryland had advanced more than Virginia had done in as many years.[1]

As St. Mary's was the capital of the colony, it was afterwards incorporated as a city and is generally referred to as St. Mary's City, yet it never lost its character as a little English village. The houses at no time exceeded sixty and were located at some distance from each other in the manner of English town houses.

James Walter Thomas of the Maryland Historical Society devoted much patient research to the early settlement days, and in his *Chronicles of Colonial Maryland* he gives a pleasant picture of the little capital. "A gentle slope from the eastern hills, then a spacious plateau of singular beauty, elevated about forty feet above the water and terminating in a bold bluff between two broad expanses of the river," formed the site of St. Mary's City.

A river possessing more enchanting scenery than the Saint Mary's may not easily be found, and at no place along its banks is this displayed to greater advantage, than at the site of old Saint

1 Bancroft, op. cit., I, 247.

Mary's. Looking from thence, either towards the north where its clear and glittering waters are first seen winding down the blue vista of the distant hills, with its sloping banks and intercepted by its long narrow capes and jutting cliffs; or towards the south where its waters, growing bolder and deeper with its high grassy banks, upland slopes, abrupt declivities, white winding beach, pebbly shore, and as seen from the direction of its mouth, its interlocking promontories, giving it the appearance of a series of lakes, rather than a stream of regular width, it presents a picture of rare and exquisite beauty.[2]

At first the Pilgrims found shelter in the homes of the Indians, but it was not long before houses were built. The first houses were log cabins with hand-hewn frames and clapboards siding thatched with crude green shingles.[3] These cabins had brick chimneys and later houses of brick were built. Although some brick was imported from England, most of what was used came from the clay soil of the surrounding country, which was found to be excellent material for the purpose.

Under Lord Baltimore's instructions, the colonists were directed after having selected a suitable place for their permanent settlement "to seate a towne," in which they were to cause streets to be marked out and to require the buildings to be erected in line with such streets and "neare adjoining one to another," all the houses to be constructed in "as decent and uniform a manner" as circumstances permitted, the land in the rear of the houses to be used for gardens. The first choice of lots was to be "a fit place and a competent quantity of ground for a fort," and near to this was to be a house with a church and a chapel adjacent "for the seate of his Lordship or his Governor."

A survey and plot of the town was to be made and sent to Lord Baltimore. Thomas states that it is to be regretted that "no chart of the city of the Calverts was made before it had disappeared, except in name and memory, from the banks of St. Mary's." From original surveys and grants, ancient trans-

[2] Page 20.
[3] Wilstach, *Tidewater Maryland,* 62.

fers and re-surveys, together with many natural boundaries and landmarks still visible, a map was platted which was printed in the appendix of the *Chronicles of Maryland.* By this data, obtained after exhaustive research, the outlines of the city and the location of its public as well as its more prominent private buildings have been preserved.

The first permanent building of any size to be erected was St. Mary's Fort. This was built in 1634 on a small bluff at the mouth of Key's Creek, between the governor's lot and the chapel land. According to Thomas, at the time the fort was built the settlers were in the midst of building their houses but becoming alarmed by the war-like attitude of the Indians, they ceased building and at once set to work to erect a fort for their better security. This they completed in about six weeks. Governor Calvert described it as a "pallaizado of one hundred and twentie yards square with fower flanks." Thanks to the labors of the Jesuit missionaries there were no Indian attacks. The fort, being the only building of considerable size, was used for more peaceful purposes than intended. For several years it was used as a state house and for the transaction of public business. The first three colonial assemblies were held there.[4]

Adjoining the Fort on the south and east was "Saint Mary's Chapel Yard," while on the north and west was the land of Governor Leonard Calvert known as "Governor's Field." On this land the Governor's residence was built, but of its architecture little is known. In the inventory of his estate it is described as "a large frame building." Subsequently the lower or northern portion of this land came into possession of Hugh Lee, one of the early colonists who built a brick house upon it, which in 1662 was purchased by the Province for a "government house" and was used as such until the State House was erected in 1876. This was the first real estate ever owned by the Colony of Maryland, and that part of the lot known as St. Mary's bluff became the site of

[4] Op. cit., 25.

the public buildings, and later the State House. Here was erected a house later described as the "Old Court House," which contained the Secretary's office, Council Chamber and "St. Mary's Room."

On St. Mary's bluff stood the historic mulberry tree. Under its spreading branches the Pilgrims of St. Mary's first assembled in accordance with the instructions of Lord Baltimore to "assemble all the people together in a fit and decent manner," to hear the royal charter read and to listen to a declaration of "his Lordship's intentions which he means to pursue in this his plantations," the first of which was for "the honor of God, by endeavoring the conversion of the savages to Christianity."

According to traditionary history it was under the shade of this tree that the Catholic Pilgrims assembled for their first Mass at St. Mary's, and it was here that a treaty was made between Governor Calvert and the Yaocomico Indians. The tree was used for many years as the official sign-post, for on it were nailed the proclamations of the governor and other public notices. Thomas, writing in 1913, said that "within comparatively recent years even, curious relic hunters were able to pick from its decaying trunk, the rude nails which there held the forgotten state papers of two centuries and more ago." He further said:

> This aged tree had watched over the city in its infancy; in its developement and prosperity and in its pride and glory as the metropolis of Maryland, it had seen it stripped of its prestige and honors and lose its importance and its rank; it had witnessed its battle with adversity and its downfall and decline and it has mourned the departure of nearly every symbol of its existence and memorial of its glory, which under the winning game of time, had one by one faded and passed away.[5]

In the *Relatio Itineris,* Father White after describing the wigwams of the Indians which were used as temporary abodes by the white settlers until dwellings could be erected, told

[5] Op. cit., 32.

how one of the "cabins" of the chieftains had "fallen to me and my associates in which we are accommodated well enough for the time until larger dwellings are provided. You would call this the first chapel of Maryland, *primum Marylandiae sacellum,* though it is fitted up more decently than when the Indians lived in it." To this wigwam of an Indian chieftain in the primitive village of St. Mary's in 1634, the Roman Catholic Church in the United States can trace its juridical beginning.

It is not known just when the first chapel was built but it was probably during the first two or three years of settlement. Lord Baltimore indicated, in his instructions, that a house and a church and a chapel for "the seate of his Lordship or his Governor" should be built. It is to be assumed that such a church or chapel would be a place of worship for those of the Catholic faith. There was nothing in the royal charter to prohibit the erection of Catholic chapels or churches, and King Charles, whose wife was allowed to have a Catholic chapel on the royal premises, was no doubt fully aware as were the members of the Privy Council that Lord Baltimore would expect to erect a Catholic place of worship for all those of his faith who were to make their homes in Maryland.

A description of the location and general character of the chapel is thus described by Thomas:

> On the south and east side of the Fort was the "Chapel Land." It extended from Key's Creek across the plateau to the fresh waters of Saint John's (above tide-water, called Mill) Creek. The Chapel itself, stood near the intersection of Middle and Mattapaney streets,[6] fronting northeast and on the former street. It was a brick building and judging from its foundation lines (visible until a recent period) it was about eighteen by thirty feet. Over the altar, was a carved representation of clouds and of the flames of Pentecost. The exact date of its erection has not been ascertained, but it was prior to 1638 and it was undoubtedly (barring the little wigwam fitted up by Father White

6 Middle and Mattapaney streets were the names of the two main thoroughfares laid out in St. Mary's City.

and called by him the "first chapel in Maryland") the first church built by the Maryland colonists.[7]

A few years ago, Father John LaFarge, S.J., who spent several years in educational work in the mission parishes of Southern Maryland, including St. Mary's, and Professor Daniels, principal of the Cardinal Gibbons Institute at Ridge, were able to definitely locate the foundations of the first chapel at St. Mary's and found it to be at the location given by Thomas. They discovered one of the corners of the foundation, and by means of soundings were able to trace all the foundation walls. The exact dimensions of the chapel building were found to be 32½ x 28½ feet, somewhat larger than the dimensions given by Thomas.

It has been suggested that in proof of the harmony and concord existing between the Catholics and Protestants in early Maryland, this chapel was built by their joint contributions and was used in common between them as a union chapel. No proof of this kind is needed, however, to show that there was religious concord in the early days of the colony. There is reason to believe that from the beginning this chapel was used exclusively as a Roman Catholic place of worship. The Protestants who came over on the *Ark* and the *Dove* were for the most part Anglicans and called themselves English Catholics. They were no doubt admitted to and did worship in the Catholic chapel, but there is no proof that Protestant services were held there or that it was in that sense a union chapel.

The chapel lot was first surveyed by Father John Brooke who became superior of the American Jesuit mission. The deed to the land was taken in the name of Thomas Copley, a Jesuit mission priest, who was known officially as Father Philip Fisher. It contained twenty-five acres and was bounded "on the east by Saint Peter's; south by Giles Brent's land; west by Key's Branch and north by a line drawn from Key's

[7] Op. cit., 37-8.

Branch at the 'Vayle' to the brook where Saint Peter's ends, being about forty-five perches above the mill." [8]

The fact that this was a Roman Catholic chapel and under the charge of the Jesuit missionaries, is indicated by two letters written by Father Copley (Fisher). In 1638, he asked Lord Baltimore "that the church and our houses may be sanctuarie." [9] In 1643, he wrote to his superior inquiring whether "our public chapels not consecrated as yet but only dedicated, have the privileges of those indulgences granted to other churches of the Society." The answer to this query was in the affirmative, that the ceremony of consecration was not necessary for the purpose of giving to a church or chapel the character and privileges of a Jesuit church. Neither the request for sanctuary nor the question about consecration would have been relevant if the building had been a union chapel or general meeting house.[10]

There are a few relics of old St. Mary's and the first Catholic chapel in the museum at Georgetown University. These include, among others, an old pewter chalice and paten which were used by Father White in the Mass on St. Clement's Island and later in the chapel, a cross made of the wood of the old mulberry tree, the bell which is said to have been used in the chapel and a picture of Ignatius Loyola which was brought over by Father White in the *Ark*. When, under order of the Governor's council in 1704, the Catholic Chapel was closed to public worship, the bricks and furniture were taken to Saint Inigoes' mission and afterwards the manor house there was built of the bricks.

The first Protestant church or chapel was erected in 1642. It was probably built of wood and of its architecture it is only known that it had an arched ceiling after the design of which the State House ceiling was subsequently modeled.[11]

With the exception of the monument erected to com-

[8] Op. cit., 38, note 7.
[9] *Calvert Papers,* I, 166.
[10] Hughes, op. cit., I, 540.
[11] Thomas, op. cit., 36.

memorate the life and services of Governor Leonard Calvert and a small memorial tablet on the bluff, for three hundred years there was little to mark the site of the first settlement. The tercentennial year brought among other memorials the reproduction of the first State House which accords with the specifications laid down by the General Assembly of 1674.

Just two hundred years after the landing of the Pilgrims, Bancroft wrote that "religious liberty obtained a home, its only home in the wide world, at the humble village which bore the name of St. Mary's." The site of the old City of St. Mary's should long ago have been made one of the shrines of American history, for here surely is hallowed ground.

CHAPTER III

CHRISTIAN AND HEATHEN NEIGHBORS

THE Pilgrims of St. Mary's were a kindly and friendly folk who desired to be on good terms with their neighbors. It so turned out, through no fault of theirs, that the only neighbors whose friendship they could cultivate were the Indians. Their Christian neighbors did not care to have cordial relations with them. Even in their new home the Catholic colonists found themselves again between two fires, with the Puritans on the north with their hatred both of prelacy and papacy, and Cavaliers on the south with their antagonism both toward dissenters and papists.

In the summer following the settlement of St. Mary's, Governor Leonard Calvert tried to open friendly trade relations with the Puritan colony of Massachusetts. Late in August of 1634, the little *Dove* was sent to Boston with a cargo of corn which it was expected would be exchanged for a cargo of fish. Massachusetts was already famous for its cod. The *Dove* carried a friendly letter from Governor Calvert and also one from Governor Harvey of Virginia. The Virginia colonists had already opened trade relations with Massachusetts, and the Maryland colonists had no reason to anticipate any difficulty in establishing similar relations which would be mutually profitable, so when the *Dove* set sail for Boston with her cargo of corn and her friendly letters, there was no expectation of the rude reception she would receive.

As soon as it became known after the arrival of the *Dove* at Boston harbor that the crew was mostly Catholic, some of them deigning to call the Puritans their "holy brethren" and that in the Maryland colony from whence the *Dove* sailed they "did set up Mass openly," there was at once evident a feeling of unfriendliness and suspicion, which soon took shape in open hostility, Hildreth says:

> Just as the ship was about to sail the super-cargo happening on shore was arrested in order to compel the master to give up the "culprits." The proof failed and the vessel was suffered to depart, but not without a special charge to the master to "bring no more such disordered persons." [1]

The corn sent to Massachusetts was from the first planting of the old Indian fields, the Indians having helped both in the planting and harvest. The Puritans were quite willing to trade with the heathen, but refused to exchange fish for corn with their Christian neighbors who did not happen to be of their own denomination.

Undeterred by this incident, we find Governor Calvert several years later (1643), sending a commission to Captain Gibbons of Massachusetts offering "free liberty of religion" to such of the people of New England as were willing to remove to Maryland. The invitation was not accepted. "There were those in New England at that time," says Eggleston, "who longed for a more genial climate but to settle under the authority of a Papist was to them like pitching a tent on the confines of perdition."

Reverend Francis Hawks, D.D., formerly rector of St. Thomas' Church in New York, in his *Rise and Progress of the Episcopal Church in Maryland,* makes caustic comment on the Puritan rejection of Governor Calvert's invitation:

> This letter to Gibbons reached Boston about the time of a transaction which it were to be wished, could not be written upon the records of New England's history. The inhabitants of Massachusetts had but just been thrown into pious consternation by the stupid and unintelligent ravings of Gorton and his followers, which merited nothing but contempt and were now settling down to repose produced by a sentence upon the poor sufferers which purposed to cure heresy with fetters. At such a

[1] *History of the United States,* I, 209.

time to offer liberty of religion to men who were congratulating themselves upon the successful application of their iron preservative of orthodoxy, doubtless provoked a sneer at the stupidity which could present toleration merely as a temptation to removal. Human ingenuity could not have devised a better timed or keener rebuke than is contained in this offer of religious freedom from the persecuted Papist to his Protestant fellow sufferer and human wit could not have made the memory of that rebuke more lasting than it is made by the scornful rejection of the offer.[2]

While Catholic Maryland was opening the door to Puritans as well as to all other Christian sects, Puritan Massachusetts closed her doors to all who were not of her own particular faith. If a Catholic priest came into the colony, he was to be banished. If he returned, he was to be hanged.

Of all those who made trouble for Lord Baltimore and the early colonists of Maryland, Captain William Claiborne of the colony of Virginia showed the greatest amount of pertinacity and kept up his opposition longer than any one else. Like many another long continued controversy started and kept up by a single individual, it all had to do with the question of the ownership of land.

Claiborne was not particularly interested in religion, but he made capital of religious prejudices and fanned the flames of bigotry in order to serve his own purpose. At different times he espoused the cause of Cavalier, Roundhead, Anglican and Puritan; it mattered little to him who his allies were or what cause he served. One writer of the day said it was not religion "he stood upon, it was that sweet, that rich, that large country," he coveted.[3]

On the east shore of the Chesapeake was a large island known as Kent Island. Claiborne claimed to own it. He arrived in Virgina in 1621, and immediately applied for and received the office of surveyor of the colony. He was industrious and acquired a considerable estate. He engaged in a prosperous trade with the Indians and established his trad-

[2] Pp. 27-30.

[3] Hammond, "Leah and Rachel," *Narratives of Maryland*, 304.

ing headquarters on Kent Island. He never had a grant of land, all he had was the right of a squatter. He claimed that the island was not included in the Maryland patent and as some of the leading colonists of Virginia had opposed the Maryland grant, he was able to enlist their sympathy in his attempt to oust Lord Baltimore from possession. He became a member of the Virginia council and later was appointed Secretary of State for Virginia, so he was able to command considerable influence.

Kent Island was clearly within the Maryland grant, and Claiborne was never able to prove his title, but for twenty years he became the proverbial thorn in the flesh of the Calverts and he showed all the persistence of the confirmed litigant. He was the most active enemy of the Maryland colony and twice nearly brought it to destruction.

Governor Calvert made every effort to have friendly relations with Claiborne, offered to give him such trading rights as he might desire and grant him possession of as much land as might be reasonably necessary for him, but all to no avail. Claiborne wanted absolute ownership or nothing. Lord Baltimore had learned of Claiborne's claim to Kent Island before the sailing of the *Ark* and the *Dove,* and instructed his commissioners to treat him courteously and to invite him to a friendly conference. Claiborne spurned all offers of an amicable settlement. He seemed to prefer hostility.

Governor Calvert attempted to bring about trade relations with Virginia and although he had the cooperation of Governor Harvey his efforts were thwarted. Governor Harvey had been instructed to assist the Maryland colonists in every way possible. In the fall of 1634 he wrote to the Privy Council that he counted it as part of his happy days any service that he did to Lord Baltimore, but he found that he had almost all against him when he proposed to do anything for Maryland. Notwithstanding "the obligations of Christianity and His Majesty's commands" to assist the new colonists, "many are so averse" that they declared "that they would rather knock their cattle on the head than sell them to Maryland." [4]

Governor Harvey finally sent cattle of his own to Maryland and said that he would do his best to procure anything else they might stand in need of. As Harvey made it manifest that he was friendly to Lord Baltimore and anxious to serve his colony, Claiborne made plans to weaken the governor's power, claiming he was a "friend to papists." This was enough to stir up all the smouldering fires of bigotry in the colony, and Harvey soon found that his power and influence were gone. He was sent back to England to answer charges Claiborne had made against him. Even before his departure a new governor was chosen in his place.

Captain Thomas Young, in command of a trading vessel, wrote to a friend in England that in Virginia "it was counted as a crime almost as heinous as treason, to favor, nay almost to speak well" of Maryland, and he observed a "palpable kind of strangeness and distance between those of the best sort in the country who have formerly been very familiar and loving one to another, only because the one hath been suspected, but to have been a well wisher to the Plantation in Maryland." [5]

It is related that one Samuel Matthews, on reading a letter from England, advising friendly relations with the colonists of Maryland, threw his hat on the ground and shouted, "A pox upon Maryland!" [6]

In the spring of 1634, Claiborne sent an armed sloop very appropriately named the *Cockatrice* to St. Mary's with orders to capture any Maryland vessels that might be found. Hearing of this, Governor Calvert fitted out two pinnaces, under the command of Captain Thomas Cornwaleys, to repel the invaders. Claiborne's men first opened fire, killing one man and wounding several. Captain Cornwaleys returned the fire

[4] Letter of Gov. Harvey to Privy Council, Sept. 18, 1634. *American Catholic Historical Researches,* XIX, 28.
[5] Hall, op. cit., 58.
[6] Archives of Maryland, III, 30.

with such effect that Captain Warren who was in command, and two others, were killed and the *Cockatrice* surrendered. Thus ended what was said to be the first naval engagement to be fought in American waters. There was another engagement the following month in the harbor of Great Wighoocomoco in which Claiborne's men evidently had the best of it, for he gained temporary possession of the island. In neither of these engagements was Claiborne present. In fact whenever there was any fighting to be done he was always conveniently absent.

Claiborne never made good his title to Kent Island. In 1637 the dispute was submitted to the Commissioners of Plantations. At the head of the body was the Archbishop of Canterbury, who could not be accused of partiality to the Catholic Proprietary. In the minutes of this commission it is found after a full hearing that the Isle of Kent was within the bounds of Lord Baltimore's patent, and that Claiborne's commission was only a license to trade with the Indians in such places where the trade had not been formally granted to another, which commission did not extend nor give any warrant to Claiborne to trade within the precincts of Lord Baltimore's patent, nor did he have any right or title to the Isle of Kent.[7]

After all, Claiborne would not have been able to have gone as far as he did in his opposition to Lord Baltimore and the Maryland colonists had it not been for the slumbering prejudice against Catholicism which he succeeded in awakening in order to serve his own ends. A Virginia historian in referring to the antipathy of the English settlers toward Catholics says "this narrow and impolitic spirit qualified in the mother country by a thousand circumstances which softened its rigor and severity, had the fullest scope in the colonies for displaying its malignity." [8] Chancellor Kent points to the "astonishingly fierce and unrelenting"

[7] Ibid, III, 72.
[8] Burk, *Virginia,* II, 24.

public prejudice against the Catholic Church, as "a psychological phenomenon in colonial history." [9] Father Hughes says:

> The American colonies took after the mother country. Just as in England from Land's End to Berwick-on-the-Tweed, so in America from Cape Cod to the Ashly River, the dulness of life was varied and enlivened with the resonance of "Popish plots." These came echoing from England and re-echoing from Barbados and Jamaica and most of all from the "back" of the plantations where the Indians and the French were supposed to be. And thence dim and far came whispering Popish plots and Jesuit intrigues from every cliff and scar of the Alleghanies.[10]

When we turn to consider the relations of the Maryland colonists with their heathen neighbors we find a far different and happier picture.

At the very time the *Ark* and the *Dove* were bringing the little band composing the first Maryland mission to fields white for the harvest, the Society of Jesus was beginning to send mission priests into the forests of Canada and northern New York, to fields that were also white for the harvest but soon to become red with the blood of the martyrs. The story of those great heroes of the faith as first told in the Jesuit Relations, and retold by historians both Catholic and non-Catholic, seems quite incredible in an age of materialism. Not since the days of the early Christian martyrs had there been such fortitude under protracted suffering, such a willingness to undergo unspeakable cruelties and such a spirit of self-abnegation. Their own church now after nearly three centuries has given them just but tardy recognition by placing the names of their martyrs among the names of the saints.

It did not matter whether these missionaries were French or English, their mission was the same, their objective identical. Allegiances to different earthly kings and kingdoms did not set them apart. The Count de Frontenac, Governor of Canada, cautioned the missionaries to make the Indians,

[9] *Commentaries,* 73.
[10] Op. cit., I, 101.

subjects of the French king and not merely "subjects of Jesus Christ." The caution itself is the best proof of the fact that the Jesuits recognized no boundaries of earthly kingdoms. Their field of labor was the Kingdom of God.

The secret of the Jesuits' knowledge and understanding of the American Indian lay in the fact that they recognized the red men as members of the human family, and treated them not as outcasts and barbarians but as friends and brothers. Thus they learned of their ways, mastered their language, and joined with them in their life of the forests. By patient labor they came to have an understanding of Indian character without which their sacrifices would have been in vain. Their work and influences were the envy of the clergy and missionaries of the English settlements who could not quite understand just how it was done.

Father Hughes tells of the "tenacious memory" of the Indians years after the Jesuits had departed, which did justice to the traits of what they had witnessed in the missionaries of the past. A report to the Propaganda from America says of the tribes evangelized in former times:

> They have great veneration for the Black Robes (so do they call the Jesuits). They tell how the Black Robes slept on the ground, exposed themselves to every privation and did not ask for money. When a Protestant comes to convert them the savages have not a little to say, concluding: "go ye and learn; do as the Black Robes did, then we shall believe what you say." [11]

Happily for the lot of the Maryland missionaries, the Indians with whom they came into contact cared more to fish and hunt than to follow the war-path, although there was always a threat from the neighboring Susquehannocks, a powerful tribe of Iroquois stock, but not on friendly terms with the five nations. This tribe was a foreign intrusion into the Algonquin region, and having possessed itself of the lake region near Ontario, it reached down to the Chesapeake through the natural line of travel of the Susquehanna

[11] Op. cit., II, 262.

River.[12] The Susquehannocks made several raids, slaying some of the friendly Piscataways and making an attack on one of the mission stations. At the time of these raids the missionaries were ordered to remain near the settlement, but these orders were irksome to the Jesuits who knew no danger and, disregarding orders, they made excursions to the Indian settlement in boats. When they were allowed to dwell among the Indians, Father White chose the most distant and perilous post.

The reports of the missionaries show the use of the same methods of preparation for their work of evangelization and the same intelligent effort to familiarize themselves with the habits and customs of the Indians so to gain their confidence and friendship, as were employed by the mission priests of New France. The result was the same. The Indians became the friends of the "Black Robes," and knew that they would not betray their confidence.

Father White, by patient study, mastered the language of the tribes among which he worked and prepared for them a catechism, grammar and vocabulary in their own language. The missionaries made many conversions among the Indians. On one occasion the chief of the tribe and his squaw were baptised in a little chapel of birch bark made for that purpose. This ceremony was attended by the governor, his council and many of the colonists. In the afternoon the couple were "united in matrimony in the Christian manner," and then a great cross was erected, "in carrying which to its destined place," the governor and other officials "lent their shoulders and hands, two of us in the meantime chanting before them the litany in honor of the Blessed Virgin."

When famine prevailed among the Indians on account of a great drought, the missionaries gave freely of their allotment of food, "although corn was scarce and selling at a great price." Due to the privations which he suffered during this famine, Father White contracted a severe fever and

[12] Op. cit., II, 128.

Father Gravener became ill and died, being the first priest to give his life on the American mission field.

Such were the relations between the Indians and the Maryland colonists, largely the result of the labors of the missionaries, that on one occasion, when the Governor and Council had been having a parley with one of the native tribes, it is said that the chief when he took his leave made this statement to the governor:

> I love the English so well that if they should go about to kill me, if I did so much breathe as to speak, I would command my people not to revenge my death, for I know that they would not do such a thing except it were my own fault.[13]

There was never any exploiting of the natives in early Maryland. They were protected in their dealings with white men by laws which strictly forbade any advantage being taken of them, and it was made a serious offense to sell either liquor or firearms to an Indian. These friendly relations were never broken. Treaties were made and renewed and when treaties of peace were made with some of the northern tribes, the "Friend Indians" as the neighboring tribes were called, were always included in the stipulations.

When in later years the natives who lived near St. Mary's became reduced in number and wasted by sickness and reported that they were unable to bring their annual gifts, the governor replied that he only desired to continue in peace and amity with them, and would not cast them off because of their poverty.

Scharf says that while the New England colonist "ploughed his fields with his musket on his back" always in fear of Indian raids, the settlers of St. Mary's accompanied the red-men to the chase and learned his art of woodcraft and the Indians coming to the settlement with wild turkey or venison, "found a friendly reception and an honest market." [14]

[13] Hawkes, *Relation of Maryland,* 11, 12.
[14] Op. cit., I, 97.

The labors of the Jesuit mission priests among the Indians bore fruit a hundredfold, for in no other colony not even in Pennsylvania where in later years William Penn dealt with the Indians in the same Christian manner, were the relations between the two races so friendly and mutually helpful.

CHAPTER IV

REAL RELIGIOUS LIBERTY

UNDER the broad terms of the royal charter, Lord Baltimore had freedom of choice between a real religious liberty and a policy which would have restricted the right of worship to those of his own faith. Although Section IV of the charter empowered the proprietary to erect and found churches and to cause them to be dedicated and consecrated according to the ecclesiastical laws of England, it did not compel him to do so, and did not prevent him from building or permitting to be built and maintained churches of other faiths. The proviso of section XXII that no interpretation of the charter should be made whereby "God's holy and true Christian religion" may suffer prejudice, was purposely vague and cannot be held to either establish the Church of England or to prohibit the exercise of any other worship. It was not so construed by the crown, by the proprietary or by the people. Baltimore would never have accepted a charter making mandatory the establishment of the Church of England nor a charter which prohibited Catholic worship.[1]

Contention has often been made that Lord Baltimore's policy was prompted solely by self-interest, and that it would have been impossible for him to have done otherwise than to have granted religious freedom to non-Catholics. On the other hand there is justification for the belief that if Maryland in its early days had been kept as a sanctuary for Catholics alone there would have been little interference from the mother country. The Puritans who were feared more by king and court than were the Catholics, had no difficulty in

[1] Brantley, "The English in Maryland," in Winsor's *Narrative and Critical History of America,* III, 523.

making the church of the Puritans the established church of Massachusetts and in denying the right of suffrage to all who were not members of that church. The Church of England was outlawed by the Puritan oligarchy. The King and his party were too busy with troubles at home to bother with questions of church and state in the colonies and the Puritans were allowed to do as they pleased in the matter of religion.

There is at least room for inference that what the Puritans were doing in Massachusetts the Catholics could have done in Maryland. Even Cromwell did not interfere with the religious affairs of Maryland during the Commonwealth. There would always have been the opposition of the Puritans but that was bound to be in any event. This is the view of two Maryland historians, one Protestant, the other Catholic.

In his *History* of Maryland, Bozman says:

> The English government through all its vicissitudes as well as those of the New England colonies, from their first planting to their Declaration of Independence, tolerated the Congregational or Independent sect as the established religion of New England and by connivance permitted them to persecute and exclude from their civil government as well as hierarchy every presumptuous intruding heretic. It is probable that the English government would have acted in the same manner by the Roman Catholics of Maryland.

Scharf agrees with Bozman when he says:

> Indeed but little did King or Parliament heed the state of the colonies, not rich enough to plunder and not strong enough to fear. Men's minds in England were then too much occupied with the upheaving of the popular ocean whose rising surges were already menacing the church and the throne, to care much what was going on in the forest settlement across the Atlantic. Had it been the will of the early settlers of Maryland they could have done with equal facility, impunity and completeness what was done in the northern colonies. When Parliament triumphed it brought them all together under the same yoke but when the royal authority was restored, the Marylander was again tolerant,

the Virginian again exclusive and the Puritan again a persecutor.[2]

A more recent Maryland historian (Brantley), holds to the view that:

> Apart from the supposed agreement between Baltimore and the king, the persecution of Conformists in the Province would have been extremely impolitic; it would have resulted in the speedy loss of the patent, but Baltimore could without danger have prohibited the immigration of Puritans and could have discouraged in many ways the settlement even of Conformists. Not only did he not do any of these things but he invited Christians of every name to settle in Maryland. It is the glory of Baltimore and of the Province that from the first, perfect freedom of Christian worship was guaranteed to all comers.[3]

The fact remains that both Lord Baltimore and his brother Governor Calvert went far beyond what was expected or required of them in affording sanctuary to all the religiously oppressed. This they did not have to do in order to save their charter or preserve their rights. There have always been writers to question the sincerity of Lord Baltimore and belittle his motives. A man's motives are best determined by what he accomplishes.

The first official act recognizing and establishing religious liberty in the Maryland colony after the arrival of the *Ark* and the *Dove* was the form of oath which Lord Baltimore required of his governor. This oath was first administered in 1636 and reads as follows:

> I will not by myself or any other, directly or indirectly trouble, molest or discountenance any person professing to believe in Jesus Christ for or in respect to religion. I will make no difference of persons in conferring offices, favors or rewards for or in respect of religion, but merely as they shall be found faithful and well deserving and endued with moral virtues and abilities; my aim shall be public unity and if any person or officer shall molest any person professing to believe in Jesus Christ, on account of his religion, I will protect the person and punish the offender.[4]

[2] *History of Maryland,* I, 162.

[3] In Winsor's history, op. cit., 524.

[4] Chalmers, *Political Annals of the United Colonies,* (1780) 235; McMahon, *Historical View of Maryland,* 226. For a similar form of oath required in 1648, see Archives, III, 210.

This oath gave legal force and effect to the announced policy of Lord Baltimore and to his letter of instructions. It was intended to be lived up to and it was. The claim that it was a mere idle gesture and resulted only in a bare tolerance being granted to the non-Catholic emigrants who had little or no religion and who had no real desire to be protected in their right to worship, is not substantiated by the records in the archives. These records disclose that there was a considerable group of Protestants who were religiously minded, to whom religion meant something and who were quick to assert their rights when the exercise of their religion was interfered with.

On a hot summer's day in the year 1638, four years after the first settlement, two indentured servants at St. Inigoes manor were engaged in reading aloud from a book of Protestant sermons. These men were Francis Gray and Robert Sedgrave. At that time there was no Protestant clergy in the colony and the Protestants who were mostly Anglicans relied on the use of the English prayer book and books of sermons for their worship. The particular sermon which was being read was a sermon which had been preached in England by the Reverend Mr. Smith and like most Protestant sermons of the day it had something to say of the Pope and the Jesuits which was not complimentary. Whether by accident or design, the reader raised his voice sufficiently loud so that some words of the sermon caught the ears of one William Lewis the overseer of the manor, a Catholic. Unfortunately the words that caught the hearing of Lewis expressed the sentiment that the Pope was Anti-Christ and that all Jesuit priests were anti-Christian. Lewis, being a good Catholic, took exception to these sentiments and injected himself into the proceedings. Just what Lewis said on this occasion became afterwards a moot question but whatever he did say was said forcibly and accompanied with gestures. Gray and Sedgrave claimed and afterwards so testified that Lewis said the Protestant ministers were ministers of the devil and that Protestant books were made an instrument of the devil and commanded them henceforth not to keep or read such books. This they took to be a wrongful interference with their right of Christian worship. Thereupon the Protestant servants proceeded to take action that would bring about the punishment of Lewis. This proceeding took the form of a petition to the Governor and Council for the redress of their grievances which it was intended to be signed by all the Protestant colonists.

To show how seriously these Protestants regarded this situation, how eager they were to have their right to worship protected, and for the benefit of those who may claim that the question of religion rested rather lightly with the non-Catholic colonists, it is well to reproduce the words of the petition:

> Beloved in our Lord. This is to give you notice of the abuses and scandalous reproaches which God and his ministers do daily suffer by William Lewis of St. Inigoes, who saith that our ministers are the ministers of the devil, and that our books are made by the instruments of the devil, and further saith that those servants which are under his charge shall not keep nor read which doth appertain to our religion within the house of the said William Lewis, to the great discomfort of those poor bondmen which are under his subjection, especially where no godly minister is to teach and instruct ignorant people in the grounds of religion. And as for people which cometh unto the said Lewis or otherwise to pass the creek the said Lewis taketh occasion to call them unto his chamber, and there laboreth with all vehemency, craft and subtlety to delude ignorant persons. Therefore we beseech you, Brethren in our Lord and Saviour Jesus Christ, that you who have power, that you will do in what lieth in you to have these absurd abuses and herediculous crimes to be reclaimed, and that God and his ministers may not be so heinously trodden down by such ignominious speeches; and no doubt but that he or they which strive to uphold God's ministers and word, he shall be recompenced with eternal joy and felicity to reign in that eternal kingdom with Christ Jesus, under whose banner we fight forever more, all which words aforesaid which hath been spoken against William Lewis the parties hereunder will be deposed when time and opportunity shall be thought meet.[4]

[4] Russell, op. cit., 530.

Before this petition was presented Lewis informed Captain Cornwaleys of the Governor's council that the servants had drawn a petition to Governor Harvey of Virginia that the intent of the writing was to combine the Protestants together and to send the petition under all their hands to the Governor and Council of Virginia in order that "they would send hither for William Lewis and proceed against him as a traitor." Whether the servants intended at first to present their grievances to the Governor of Virginia is not certain. The charge of Lewis that they did so intend was subsequently dismissed on "insufficient proof." Captain Cornwaleys asked Sedgrave to deliver to him the petition and it was duly presented to Governor Calvert.

On Tuesday the third of July the sheriff was commanded by warrant from Governor Calvert to bring William Lewis, Robert Sedgrave, Christopher Carroll and Ellis Beach into court, where were present the Governor, Captain Cornwaleys and Secretary Lewger, all Catholics. What the record of the Archives now discloses gives a most interesting side-light on the proceedings. The record says:

> The Governor demanded of Robert Sedgrave whether that was his writing and he confessed. Asked who moved or advised him to that course he said that himself and Francis Gray being such offended with the speeches of William Lewis, Francis Gray did with him to draw a writing to some of the Freemen and he would procure them to join in a petition to the Governor and counsell which Robert Sedgrave did accordingly the next day but Francis Gray wished him to keep it till he had spoken with Mr. Copley which was on Saturday the last June and on Sunday morning meeting with Francis Gray at the Fort he asked him whether he had spoken with Mr. Copley who said he had and that Mr. Copley had given him good satisfaction in it and blamed much William Lewis for his contumelious speeches and ill-governed zeal and said it was fit he should be punished.[5]

The "Mr. Copley," here referred to was none other than Father Thomas Copley of the Jesuit mission who was known

[5] *Archives*, IV, 36, 37.

in the society as Father Philip Fisher, the use of two names being sometimes resorted to by the English Jesuits in order to escape persecution and arrest. He had come over to Maryland the previous year. Under the conditions of plantation Father Copley received title to two thousand acres of land at St. Inigoes in the name of "Thomas Copley, Esq.," for having "transported Mr. John Knowles and thirteen others" in 1637. This land was held for the use of the mission, it being the only provision that could be made under existing conditions for the support of the missionaries. All the land used by the missionaries was thus in the name of Thomas Copley.

William Lewis was Father Copley's overseer at St. Inigoes, and it was on the Jesuit mission property that this incident occurred. The servants were really servants of Father Copley. It was because of this that Gray wished to consult "Mr. Copley" before preferring charges against his overseer. Here is the remarkable situation of a Jesuit landowner upholding his Protestant servants in seeking the punishment of a Catholic overseer for too vigorously taking exception to the readings of a Protestant sermon wherein both the Pope and the Jesuits were accused of being "Anti-Christian." Full to running over was the measure of religious liberty accorded by this Jesuit priest to his Protestant servants, in agreeing that Lewis who had interrupted the reading of a controversial sermon "was fit to be punished" for his over-zeal. It would really seem as if Father Copley in this practical application of an ideal had stood up so straight that he had bent over backwards.

On the trial of the case, Lewis admitted coming into the room where the Protestant servants were reading out of a book, "and the matter being much reproachful to his religion, namely that the Pope was anti-Christ and the Jesuit anti-Christian ministers, etc., he told them that it was a falsehood and came from the devil, as willful lies did, and that he that writ it was an instrument of the devil, and further he said not." Sedgrave and Gray testified that Lewis said that their ministers were ministers of the devil. Sedgrave testified at first that Lewis had forbidden them to use or have any Protestant books within his house but afterwards weakened on rebuttal when Lewis denied forbidding the servants reading any books except the book they were reading, and finally admitted that it might have been only the one book they were forbidden to read and not all Protestant books. Three other Protestant witnesses were called, there evidently having been at least five who were being preached to at the time, but they could only recall that Lewis had forbidden the reading of that particular book of sermons.

After hearing the witnesses the Governor instructed the secretary to deliver the censure of the court. The secretary found Lewis guilty of making "an offensive and indiscreet speech in calling the author of the book an instrument of the devil" but acquitted him of the accusation of using the offensive term toward all Protestant ministers. He likewise found him guilty of forbidding his servants to read "a book otherwise allowed and lawful to be read by the State of England," but acquitted him of the charge of forbidding them to have any Protestant books in the house.

The record of the judgment of the court reads:

> Because of his offensive speeches and other unreasonable disputations in point of religion tending to the disturbance of the public peace and quiet of the colony, committed by him against a public proclamation set forth to prohibit all such disputes, therefore he fined him five hundred weight of tobacco to the Lord of the Province and to remain in the sheriff's custody until he found sufficient sureties for his good behavior, in those kinds, in time to come. The Captain likewise found him to have offended against the public peace and against the proclamation made for the suppressing of all such disputes tending to cherishing a faction in religion; and therefore, fined him likewise five hundred to the Lord of the Province. But for his good behavior thought fit to leave it to his own discretion. The Governor concurred wholly in his sentence with Mr. Secretary; and so the court broke up; and William Lewis was committed to the Sheriff.[6]

[6] Russell, op. cit., 533; *Archives,* IV, 35-39.

The "public proclamation set forth to prohibit all such disputes," probably referred to Lord Baltimore's letter of instructions which may have been embodied in a proclamation of the Governor. It does not appear that this Catholic tribunal ever meted out any punishment to the Protestants for reading aloud a sermon that was calculated to offer "an unseasonable disputation in point of religion tending to the disturbance of the public peace and quiet of the colony," although a sermon branding the Pope as "Anti-Christ" might at least have been deemed disputatious if not provocative to the extent of being a breach of the peace.

The effect of the decision evidently was to allow the Protestant laity the fullest liberty to regale themselves with the reading of all sermons regardless of how controversial they might be or what manner of things might be said of the Catholic religion. With Father Copley the judges agreed in allowing the fullest measure of religious liberty, a liberty of worship and a liberty of speech. Thereafter if any Catholic overheard anything that was offensive to his religion he was to hold his peace.

It was not often that the religious peace of the colony was disturbed in the early years. Evidently the Protestants were allowed the quiet enjoyment of their religion and there is no evidence that they ever interfered with Catholic worship. It was not until four years later that another case is recorded where Protestants had reason to seek redress which was promptly given. In 1642 one Thomas Gerard, a prominent Catholic landowner, was accused of taking away the key to the building which the Protestants used for a chapel, and also with carrying off the books which were used for Protestant worship, probably the hymn and prayer books, possibly the Bible itself. Just what prompted Mr. Gerard to do this does not appear but apparently it was due to some claim of ownership to the land or building, but the very obvious result was that the Protestants were deprived of their right to worship. Again they were quick to seek redress. This time they made their petition to the Colonial Assembly which was then in session and to which all the freemen of the Province had been summoned to attend in person or by proxy. The following is the entry in the case taken from the archives:

> 23rd of March. The Petition of the Protestants was read complaining against Mr. Thomas Gerard for taking away the key of the chapel and carrying away the books out of the chapel and such proceedings desired against him for it as to justice apertaineth. Mr. Gerard being charged to make answer, the house upon hearing of the prosecutors and his defense found Mr. Gerard guilty of a misdemeanor and that he should bring the books and key taken away to the place where he had them and relinquished all title to them or to the house and should pay a fine of five hundred pounds of tobacco towards the maintenance of the first minister as should arrive.[7]

Here again is found a measure of religious liberty accorded the Protestants full to overflowing, for not only was the offender ordered to return the keys and the books to the chapel and to pay a fine, but the fine was to be used to pay the salary of the first Protestant clergyman who should arrive. It is difficult to conceive of more convincing proof of the establishment of religious liberty in early Maryland and of the determination of the Catholic authorities of the colony to afford sanctuary to Protestants and to grant them the fullest protection in the exercise of their religion than is afforded by these two cases. In one case there is an adjudication by a properly constituted legal tribunal and in the other a special act of a democratic assembly of freemen having full force and effect in the law of the colony. This was more than a mere toleration. It was real religious liberty established and recognized, practically, rationally and legally. Up to this time we are concerned only with Catholics and Protestants. There were none in the colony except those who called themselves Christians. When at a later day the Jew came to Maryland, he too was accorded the fullest measure of freedom.

[7] *Archives,* I, 119.

CHAPTER V

THE EXERCISE OF SELF-GOVERNMENT

IT WAS not long before there was manifest in all of the American colonies a spirit of independence and a jealousy of charter rights. In Maryland from the beginning there was independence of both King and parliament and a real exercise of self-government. The charter gave assurance of independence of British government, and when Lord Baltimore conceded to the freemen the right to initiate legislation they lost no time in assuming that this granted them the right to exercise self-government, and they acted accordingly.

When Lord Baltimore decided not to accompany the first settlers to Maryland and to remain in England he suffered the disadvantage of a lack of direct contact with the colonists. This resulted in a greater freedom for the latter of which they were quick to take advantage.

John Esten Cook in his *Virginia, a History of the People,* says that "never was social fabric established on a larger or more liberal basis than that of Maryland." [1] Upon this social fabric sensible law-makers were to erect the frame-work of an American form of self-government.

The first legislative assembly met at St. Mary's, February 1635. This, like some of the sessions which followed, was based on the idea of a pure democracy, all the freemen being summoned to attend either in person or by proxy. This assembly passed a body of laws for the government of the province. The records of the first assembly are lost. It is only known that one law provided that murder and felonies should be punished as in England. These laws were sent to Lord Baltimore for his approval, but whatever they were, he did

[1] Page 181.

not approve them and whatever his reasons were for not approving them is not known.

No effective legislation was enacted until the session of 1639. Therefore it appears that for five years the colonists of Maryland got along without laws of their own. The matter of legislation did not seem to concern them greatly. Neither then nor later did they have any such obsession for law-making as had the Puritans of Massachusetts. It was during these five years that the colony grew and prospered, becoming a group of happy and contented people, more interested in building homes and tilling the soil than in making laws and fixing penalties.

The people dwelt together like a patriarchal family, having little need for a written code of laws to regulate their conduct and affairs. Unwritten laws and customs were quite sufficient, and recourse could be had to the common law of England if occasion arose. By making practical application of their religion they lived peaceably and well.

As time went on, the need of some kind of colonial legislation became apparent, so in January 1638, Governor Calvert issued a summons for an assembly of the freemen to be held at St. Mary's. The councilors and several of the leading men of the colony were summoned by special writ "to assemble the freemen and persuade such as you shall think proper to repair personally to said assembly and to give full power and liberty to all the rest either to be present if they so please or otherwise to elect and nominate such and so many persons as they or the major part of them so assembled shall agree upon to be the deputies or burgesses for the said freemen in their name and stead to advise and consult of such things as shall be brought into deliberation in the said assembly." [2]

This was to be a popular assembly in which every freeman was to have a voice and vote. The number of deputies or burgesses was optional with the freemen, and these, so far

2 *Archives,* I, 1.

as they were representative, were merely proxies and so voted. Every freeman had a right to a seat if he chose to claim it. Having given a proxy he could revoke it at any time and attend in person.

The session continued from January 25th to March 24th and was well attended. The first business was the adoption of some simple rules of procedure. The house was to meet every day (Sundays and holydays excluded) at eight o'clock in the morning and at two o'clock in the afternoon. There are records of fines for being tardy. It was voted that any one not appearing at the appointed hour be "amerced twenty pounds of tobacco for such default." Fines after being imposed were remitted in several cases for good excuse, such as "want of passage over the St. Mary's river."

Every freeman not only had the privilege of attending, but it was made his duty to attend either in person or by proxy. On the first day it was "proclaimed that all freemen omitted in the writs of summons that would claim a voice in this general assembly should come and make their claim. Whereupon claim was made by John Robinson, carpenter, and he was admitted." On this first day of assembly thirty freemen were present in person and twenty-eight sent their proxies. Three were excused from attendance and seven were absent. The three who were excused from attendance were the three Jesuit missionaries, Fathers Thomas Copley, Andrew White and John Altham. They appeared by Robert Clerke, who "excused their absence by reason of sickness."

In order that there should be orderly debate it was ruled that "no man shall stand up to speak until the party that spake last before him shall have sate down, nor shall anyone speak but once to a bill at one reading nor refute the speech of another with any incivil or contentious terms nor shall name him except by some circumlocution." On the second day, ten freemen were fined for non-attendance, and again Robert Clerke appeared for the Jesuit fathers and this time "made excuse for them that they desired to be excused from giving voice in the assembly." They were excused. Thereafter no Jesuit attended the colonial assemblies. There was to be no theocracy in Maryland. In their aloofness from law-making the Jesuit missionaries set the Puritan clergy of New England an example which might well have been followed. Their desire to be excused from giving voice in the assembly may have been responsible for the fact that until this day under the law of Maryland no member of the clergy has ever had a seat in a legislative body.

This first session of the colonial assembly of which there is any record was featured by a deadlock between Lord Baltimore and the freemen. This had a most important bearing on the political development of the colony. Apparently the Lord Proprietor was given the right under the charter to initiate legislation and to submit such laws for the consideration of the freemen as he thought wise and expedient; at least he claimed this right. The freemen, imbued with the spirit of independence, took issue with him.

This assembly was composed largely of Catholics. Cobb says that it was made up entirely of Catholics, but he is clearly in error. There is no doubt, however, but that the Catholics controlled this session of the assembly as they did most of the early assemblies. Notwithstanding that the majority were Catholics and loyal to Lord Baltimore, they did not propose to be puppets for the Lord Proprietor. They insisted on the right to initiate legislation.

The first code prepared by Lord Baltimore and intended for passage by the assembly was brought over by John Lewger who had been appointed secretary of the colony. Lewger had arrived at St. Mary's in the autumn of 1637. By virtue of his office as secretary he was a member of the council. He was a graduate of Trinity College, Oxford, had been an Anglican clergyman but before his appointment had been converted to Catholicism. He brought his family with him and remained in Maryland taking an active part in colonial affairs until the death of Governor Calvert, when he returned to England.

His wife died in Maryland and on his return to England he became a Catholic priest. He died in 1665 while ministering to the victims of the London plague.

When the laws sent over by Lord Baltimore from England were voted upon, they were rejected by a vote of 37 to 14. Lewger voted with Governor Calvert and other members of the council to adopt them, but the freemen being in the majority voted against them. There were twelve acts of this draft, and each was separately debated and voted upon. Here was a dilemma. Some said, so the record reads, that they might do well to agree on some laws until they heard from England again, but Governor Calvert said there was no such power in the assembly. Captain Cornwaleys thereupon "propounded the laws of England" and the governor acknowledged that his commission gave him power in civil cases to proceed by the laws of England and in crimnal cases likewise, "not extending to life or member." A committee of five was appointed to draft a code of laws to be submitted to Lord Baltimore. Cornwaleys was chairman of this committee. Thereupon the house "brake up" and did not meet again for ten days. The committee did not complete its work in ten days and the Governor suggested a further adjournment but Cornwaleys said the freemen could not spend their time better "than in business for the country's good." Finally fourteen bills for the government of the province were reported by the committee, and after three successive readings were passed and submitted to Lord Baltimore, but they never became law.

Governor Calvert wrote to his brother that the laws he had sent over by Lewger contained so many provisions that were "unsuitable to the peoples' good" that the assembly was desirous to suspend them all, and that others had been passed by the same assembly and now "sent unto you to provide both for your honor and profit as much as those you sent us did." [3]

When Lord Baltimore became convinced that the freemen

[3] Browne, op. cit., 77.

of the colony were determined that he should not exercise the right he claimed under the charter, he gracefully yielded the right to initiate all legislation, leaving that right to the freemen. This was done in a memorable letter written to his brother, August 21, 1638. In this letter he authorized his brother as governor of the province to give assent in his name to all laws "as you may think fit and necessary which shall be consented unto and approved of by the freemen of that province or the major part of them or their deputies." [4] This was no ordinary concession that Lord Baltimore made. It was not only wise statesmanship, but it was the recognition of a right that lies at the very foundation of American democracy.

The stage was now set for the freemen of Maryland to erect their own structure of government. How well these early law makers, with slight experience in the field of legislation, did their work is shown in a remarkable but simple little code of laws which was drafted and adopted at the first session of the assembly following the concession by the Lord Proprietor of the right to initiate legislation. It was their first real venture in self-government.

Governor Calvert in February of 1639 issued a summons to the freemen of the various hundreds, St. Mary's, St. George's, Mattapanient, St. Michael's and the Isle of Kent, to elect burgesses for an assembly to be held at St. Mary's on the 25th of February. The summons concluded with the warning: "Hereof fail not at your peril."

This marks a transition to a representative democracy. The freemen however were not restricted in the number of delegates or burgesses. The summons to the freemen of the Isle of Kent directed them to choose "two or more discreet and honest men" to be their deputies or burgesses. The other hundreds were told to make such election as they should "think fit." The returns were apparently signed by all freemen voting. None of the hundreds elected more than two.

Lord Baltimore's letter conceding the right of the freemen to

[4] *Archives*, I, 31.

initiate legislation was read on the first day of the assembly. Thereupon an act was passed for "the establishing of the House of Assembly." This act provided that the delegates elected by the freemen should be called "burgesses." To all intents and purposes they should be the same as the burgesses "of any borough in England" representing the inhabitants of such borough in the English parliament.

So intent were these law-makers upon giving every freeman an opportunity to participate in the affairs of the government of the colony, that they went so far as to permit such other freemen who did not consent to any election to have a seat in the assembly. Only one instance is recorded in the archives of this extraordinary concession being taken advantage of. "Cuthbert Fenwick claimed a voice as not assenting to the election of St. Mary's burgesses and was admitted, Robert Clerke, similiter." [5]

The usual simple rules of procedure were read and adopted. These included a rule that all bills should be read three times before a final passage and be engrossed after the second reading. When a bill was finally passed it was stipulated that "the President shall be demanded his assent in the name of the Lord Proprietary and if his assent be to that bill, the bill shall be undersigned by the secretary in these words: 'the Lord Proprietary willeth that this be a law.' "

No time was to be lost in securing the assent of the Lord Proprietary through the governor or president. The latter was not to be asked to signify such assent, his assent, *"shall be demanded."* [6]

The assembly was made up as follows: Governor Calvert, and those summoned by him by special writ, Captain Cornwaleys, Fulk Brent, Giles Brent, Secretary Lewger and Thomas Green; Burgesses, Thomas Gerard and Francis Gray from St. Mary's; David Wickliff and Randall Revell from St. George's; James Cauther and John Price from St.

[5] *Archives,* I, 32.
[6] *Archives,* I, 33.

Michael's; Christopher Thomas and Nicholas Brown from the Isle of Kent and Henry Bishop from Mattapanient. In addition to these were seated Messrs. Fenwick and Clerke, making a total of seventeen, including the governor and secretary. The governor had the right to summon as many as he might choose by special summons, but he did not attempt to control a majority of the assembly in this way. The delegates chosen by the freemen formed the majority.

In the records of this assembly in the Archives are forty-one pages of laws which passed two readings and were engrossed to be read a third time.[7] These laws were not read a third time and so were not finally enacted. On page 81, is this memorandum of Secretary Lewger: "Memorandum that these laws were engrossed to be read the third time but were never read nor passed the house." Notwithstanding this, several historians have referred to these bills and commented upon them as if they had been finally adopted by the assembly. Doyle in his *English Colonies in America,* refers to this proposed legislation as if it could be taken as a fair sample of the work of the assembly and mentions the "needless elaboration and cumbrousness of much of this legislation" as showing "a tendency to reproduce the feudal character of the Mother Country." [8] It was because these proposed laws were needlessly elaborate and cumbersome that they were not finally adopted. The Maryland legislators desired a simpler code.

At various sessions from February 25th until March 8th, these bills were debated. It is significant that at this time when the assembly refused to pass this draft of laws, an adjournment was taken for one week. On March 15th there was read for the first time a bill to continue the commission for the government and for confirming the sentence of Claiborne. Thereupon adjournment was taken until the following Monday (March 18th).

[7] *Archives,* I, 40-81.
[8] Page 298.

It would be interesting to know what discussion was going on during this time. Unfortunately there is no record of the debates. It is fairly easy, however, to read between the lines. During these ten days some one was at work on a simpler code. That some one was undoubtedly Captain Thomas Cornwaleys, who was the outstanding legislative leader, a man of keen sense and discernment and who, while always loyal to the interests of the Lord Proprietary, was watchful of the interests of the freemen of the colony. He had been the chairman of the committee appointed to draft the laws at the previous assembly. The laws which were engrossed but not passed were apparently drafted by Secretary Lewger, and were based largely on the code which he brought over from England in 1637. Therefore it fell to the lot of Captain Cornwaleys to draft a simpler code which would better meet the practical needs of the new colony.

When the Assembly reconvened there was read for the first time a bill "for the government of the province." This bill had a second reading at the afternoon session. When this bill was read for the third time "all assembled assented thereto except Henry Bishop, James Cauther, Francis Gray and John Price." "Then the Lieutenant General give his assent thereunto in the name of the Lord Proprietary, and then he dissolved the assembly." [9]

The "act for the government of the province" passed the last day of the session was a masterpiece of codification. It takes up only two pages of the archives compared to forty pages covered by the larger and discarded code. The elimination of unnecessary legal verbiage was exceedingly well done. What was left was vital and essential. It was the irreducible minimum of legislation that met the needs of the colonists perfectly.

A more comprehensive set of laws has seldom been expressed in so few words. There was no useless phraseology.

[9] *Archives,* I, 39; 82-84.

To the advocates of fewer and simpler laws, this little code should make a strong appeal.

The preamble dedicates the laws to "the honor of God and the welfare of the Province." The first clause is a recognition of religious liberty. It reads: "Holy Churches within this Province shall have all her rights and privileges." It has apparently escaped the attention of the historians who have commented on the early laws of Maryland that in this clause use is made of the plural subject noun. In the longer proposed draft which failed of passage, the singular "Holy Church" is used, as is the case in the "Act for Church liberties" passed in 1640. While it is possible that this may have been a mistake of the scrivener, it is more reasonable to assume that it was intentional. The use of the words "Holy Churches" appears in the original manuscript of the laws of 1639 which is preserved in the library of the Maryland Historical Society at Baltimore.[10]

The use of the phrase "Holy Church" in the early laws of Maryland has given rise to much discussion. Some writers contend that it refers to the Roman Catholic Church, the same phrase being used in Magna Charta. It had not been applied to the Church of England since the Reformation. Others contend that it could only refer to the Church of England as this was an English colony, and the only Holy Church recognized by England was the established church; while there are some who claim that it referred to no church in particular but to all Christian churches in general.[11]

If historians have not been able to agree on what was meant by "Holy Church," it is fair to assume that the legislators in redrafting the law had the same difficulty. In order to make their intention clear, that all churches should have their rights and liberties, to change "Holy Church" to "Holy

10 Laws C. & W. H., 1638–1678—small folio bound in vellum—page 63 (the manuscript is apparently in the handwriting of John Lewger).

11 Russell, op. cit., 141.

Churches" was the obvious thing to do. The change was made so hastily that evidently the scrivener neglected to change the singular pronoun "her" to the plural "their," but grammatical mistakes were not infrequent in those early days of law-making.

Another change was made from the phraseology of the longer code which is equally significant. In the draft proposed by Lord Baltimore and Lewger the clause reads: "Holy Church within this province shall have all her rights, liberties and immunities, safe, whole and inviolable in all things." The revisers included church "rights and liberties" but omitted "immunities."

The second clause provides that all "inhabitants of this Province shall take an oath of allegiance to His Majesty." Out went the oath of supremacy and with it the established church. There was to be full allegiance to the King as temporal sovereign, but no acknowledgment of his supremacy as head of the church is admitted. The rights and prerogatives of the Lord Proprietary under the charter are recognized. This is followed by a recognition of the rights of the people. "The inhabitants of this province shall have all their rights and liberties according to the Great Charter of England." Here is a simple bill of rights. None other was needed to protect the privileges of English freemen. This is the only reference to Magna Charta in any of the early laws of the English colonies. The influence of English Catholic tradition is seen in the enactment of this clause.

A judiciary department was created by a simple enactment. The Lieutenant General of the Province and the Commander of the Isle of Kent "shall cause right and justice to be done in all causes civil according to the laws or laudable usages of this province or otherwise according to the laws or laudable usages of England in the same or like causes as he or they shall be able to judge and shall try the said causes and shall or may use, command and appoint all power and means necessary or conducing thereunto and the said

Lieutenant General and Commander shall take an oath to administer equal justice to all persons without favor or malice of anyone."

The Lieutenant General or any of the Council and the Commander of the Isle of Kent are given power and jurisdiction to hear criminal cases "and secure all offenders with any punishment as they shall think the offense to deserve except that in crimes extending to taking away of life or member, the offender shall be first indicted and afterwards tried by twelve freemen at the least."

The secretary of the province is given authority to prove wills and grant letters of administration on the estates of deceased persons.

A war department is created with ample powers in a short paragraph. "The Captain of the Military Band, at the direction of the Lieutenant General shall use and appoint and command all power and means necessary or conducing in his discretion to the safety or defense of the province and the commander of Kent shall do the like within that island."

A bankruptcy law of seven lines provides that where the "goods of or in the hands of any person sued for debt are not sufficient to pay all his debts" they are to be sold at "an outcry" and distributed among his creditors. Taxes and public charges are to be preferred and "debts for wine and hot waters be not satisfied till all other debts are paid." Corn was the staff of life of the colonists, but tobacco was more profitable. For many years tobacco was the medium of exchange and served as colonial currency. There was danger that it would be cultivated at the expense of the corn crop, so a sensible regulation was made that every person planting tobacco should "plant and tend" two acres of corn.

It was provided that the General Assembly should consist of "gentlemen summoned by special writ" and the burgesses chosen by the freemen.

The last clause of the code created a needful public utility. "Any bargain," it reads, "the Lieutenant-General (the Governor) and Council shall make with any individual for the setting up of a water mill for the use of the colony shall be levied upon the inhabitants," but not to exceed 10,000 wt. of tobacco in a year for two years only.

"The freemen have assented. The Lord Proprietarie willeth that this be a law. Verum Recordum" is the final entry of the secretary, John Lewger.[12]

Thus began the exercise of self-government.

[12] *Archives*, 82, 84.

CHAPTER VI

THE LEAVEN OF DEMOCRACY

WHILE it may be said that the first Lord Baltimore was a monarchist and did not intend to establish a democratic form of government in Maryland, yet it is clear that he did intend to establish a most liberal form of colonial government, and that the rights secured to the people in his charter were greater than in any other charter which had then been granted.[1] The provisions for a popular assembly and for the safeguarding of the rights of the colonists as English freemen, together with the requirement that laws could only be enacted by and with the assent of the freemen made possible the expression of the democratic spirit found in the early assemblies and fostered the growth of democratic institutions of government.[2]

There was nothing in the system of land tenure to retard the growth of democracy or to give feudalism a foothold in the colony. Many of the first settlers were granted large tracts of land but these were fee simple estates of inheritance. Each tract of one thousand acres or more was erected into a manor with the right to hold court-barons, with privileges belonging to manors in England. The English manor was not a feudal institution but an evolution of the German Mark where every freeman had his place in the assembly called the Mark Moot, from which descended the English township and the New England town meeting.[3] The manors that were erected in Maryland became nothing more than

1 Winsor, *Narrative and Critical Hist. of America,* III, 522.

2 "But this 'miniature kingdom of a semi-feudal type' was affected by the leaven of democracy from the beginning." Henry William Elson, *History of the United States,* 78.

3 Johnson, op. cit., 42-47.

political subdivisions. The Lord of the manor was on an equal footing with his tenant when it came to participating in the making of laws for the government of the colony.

Every inducement was made to encourage ownership of property, and liberal terms were given to small landowners. To every settler was given one hundred acres of land; if married, his wife received a hundred acres, and for each child he received an additional hundred acres. By the law of 1640 each indentured servant upon completing his term of apprenticeship was given a farm of fifty acres, together with supplies of food, clothing, and farming utensils. Each woman servant received a year's provision of corn and the same amount of land and clothing as the men. Furthermore, the indentured servants on the completion of service were given the freeman's vote. As early as 1637 several of those who were brought over in the *Ark* and the *Dove* as servants took their seats in the assembly as planters.

This class of immigrants came over on every ship from England. They were mostly farmers and artisans. Some were men of quality and education. George Alsop, who himself had come to Maryland as an indentured servant, wrote a few years later to his father in England that the servants in the province "live more like freemen than most mechanical apprentices in London, wanting for nothing that is convenient or necessary and according to their several capacities are extraordinarily well used and respected."[4] They gained their freedom within three to five years, being able in that time to earn enough by work to pay back what their masters had paid for their passage. The giving of the vote to the former indentured servants without restriction was eventually to place Catholics in the minority, for the large majority of the servants were Protestants. Lord Baltimore had never schemed to place or keep the control of the colonial government in the hands of those of his own faith. He could easily

[4] Hall, op. cit., 378.

have accomplished this if he had restricted the franchise to large landowners.

While it may have been possible under the charter to have established a landed aristocracy with a privileged class, conditions were such as to prevent it. In an address delivered before the Maryland Historical Society in 1850, Judge George William Brown, an eminent member of the Baltimore bar, in discussing the "Origin and Growth of Civil Liberty in Maryland," said:

The intention of the charter to establish in Maryland a mixed form of government of which a hereditary nobility was to be a prominent feature, was overruled by circumstances. Such a class can be sustained only in a country where the ownership in the soil is mainly vested in them, and where the masses are reduced to the condition of tenants, dependent on the landholders for support. But in Maryland there were vast uncultivated tracts of land, lying in their primitive state, which the proprietary was more anxious to sell than the people were to purchase. Every man who chose, became a landholder, a proprietor in his own right. He had no occasion to look up to any other man for patronage, and still less for support or protection. Labor was the passport to independence and wealth. There was no place, then, for an aristocracy, for there was nothing to support it.[4]

Later in the same address Judge Brown said:

The people opposed a steady resistance to the exercise of everything approaching arbitrary power. They were uniformly quick in perceiving, and prompt and tenacious in resisting the slightest infringements of what they considered their rights—which they claimed to be not only those which were conferred by the charter and laws of the province, but all those, in addition, which were enjoyed by English subjects at home. No right or privilege once acquired by them was ever relinquished, but on the contrary, became a means of increasing their power in all future controversies. The consequence was, that although Maryland continued to have a hereditary executive, it became, in essential

[4] *A Discourse delivered by George William Brown before the Maryland Historical Society, Baltimore, April 12, 1850, being the Fifth Annual addres to that Association,* Baltimore, printed by John D. Toy, 1850. To be found in New York Public Library, in "Maryland Historical Society Discourses."

matters, republican, and instead of being subjected to an arbitrary government, enjoyed one of mild and equal laws. The people were protected in their persons and property, and the latter was so distributed, that few were found who were either very rich or very poor—a condition of things most favorable to the growth and maintenance of civil liberty.

To prevent what had happened in England where there had been no session of parliament for ten years a provision was made in the code of laws sent over by Lord Baltimore in 1639 for the approval of the freemen, that an assembly should be called at least once every three years.[5] There was no provision of this kind in the short code but it so turned out that it was not necessary. Assemblies were called oftener than once in three years. In 1642 no less than three assemblies were convened. In the case of two of these, all the freemen were summoned to attend.

A year and seven months elapsed after the session of 1639, before another session of the assembly was called. This was in August in 1640. It was found necessary to enact a few simple laws to meet needs which had become apparent since the previous session. Provision was made for the contingency of the death or absence of the governor, a necessary penalty was fixed in the case of one planting tobacco and failing to plant two acres of corn, indentured servants on the expiration of their terms of service were made landowners and given the equipment necessary to make their farms pay, artificers' wages were regulated and restrictions were placed on the exportation of tobacco and fencing of grounds.

An act concerning marriages passed at this session is most interesting for it apparently attempted to reconcile a rule of canon law with the principle of separation of state and church. No marriage could be solemnized until banns were published for three days in "some chapel" or other place where public notices were posted, or "else oath made and caution entered" that neither party to the marriage was an

[5] *Archives,* I, 75.

apprentice or ward, under government of parents or tutors, or that the parties were within the forbidden degrees of consanguinity.[6]

At a session held the following year, in August of 1641, only three laws were enacted, an act against fugitives, an act defining measures of corn and grain, and an act relating to the settlement of estates.

Early in March of 1642, Governor Leonard Calvert issued a proclamation summoning all persons "inhabitant within the province" to attend an assembly to be held at St. Mary's on the last day of the month. The code of 1639 expired by its own terms March 19th of this year and it was necessary to enact new laws. Also the warring tribes of Susquehannocks were threatening to attack. These Indians had been supplied with firearms by traders and were learning to use them. Governor Calvert was trying to arrange a joint expedition against the Indians, but like his other attempts to cooperate with the Virginians, it came to naught. It was then deemed advisable for Maryland to make an expedition of its own. These two matters were considered of enough importance to summon all the freemen to convene. The records show that seventy-seven freemen attended either in person or by proxy.

Thomas Cornwaleys was again the legislative leader and his leadership was reflected in the independent and democratic course taken by the assembly. It was voted that the determination of the matter of the expedition against the Indians should not be left to the discretion of the Governor and Council. It was also declared that the assembly should not be adjourned or prorogued except by and with the consent of the house.[7]

[6] *Archives,* I, 97.

[7] It was at this session that the petition of the Protestants asking for the punishment of Dr. Thomas Gerard for taking away the keys and books of the Protestant chapel was heard and determined. It does not appear that Dr. Gerard attended this session in person, although his name is included in the first summons as one of those called by special writ.

Governor Calvert called the July assembly apparently because of the failure of the previous session to take action on the expedition against the Indians, but this time instead of summoning all the freemen he called for the election of burgesses by the various hundreds. The hundreds were constituted units for representation in the assembly and were distinct and fairly well populated localities. As the freemen were all attached to one or another of the hundreds they were given the right to elect representatives to the assembly.

This assembly summoned to meet July 18, 1642, was in continuous session except Sundays until August. The legislators were warned of the opening of each session by drum beat. The first beating of the drum was at sunrise, the second and third at half hour intervals. Anyone not appearing on the third call, one hour after sunrise, was fined one hundred pounds of tobacco.

At these sessions the first long code of laws was enacted. It covered eighteen pages. A more elaborate system of civil and criminal procedure, of land titles and administration of estates, was adopted. The governor and council were given power to appoint judges, thus making the three departments of the government independent of each other. Offenses were specifically defined and tobacco was made legal tender. Captain Cornwaleys was chairman of the committee to prepare all bills "fit to be propounded."

Although the Governor had the power to summon to the assembly by special writ as many as he might choose, it does not appear that he ever took advantage of this to gain control of legislation. It was only in the assemblies to which burgesses or representatives were elected that he could have had such an advantage, for when he summoned all the freemen to attend, as he frequently did, he could not have possibly gained control by the exercise of the special writ. The only session where the relative voting strength was so close that this matter came up for discussion was at this session of July-August 1642. Eleven burgesses were elected and seated but their voting strength might have been offset by the nine who were summoned by special writ, with the Governor and Secretary each having a vote. The record of those actually in attendance, however, showed that the burgesses were in the majority, ten burgesses as against the Governor, Secretary and six summoned by special writ.[8] Robert Vaughn "desired that the house might be separated and the burgesses to be by themselves and to have a negative vote." This was not allowed as the rules already adopted provided otherwise. A change to the bicameral system was made some years later.

When an act providing what should be legal tender came to a vote, eight of the burgesses voted against it. Thomas Greene, a Catholic and afterwards governor of the province, objected to the passage of the bill on the ground that it was not passed "by the major part of the burgesses as it ought to be."[9] His objection was overruled as it was found that the rules provided that "the company present was a House and in this house everyone present had a voice," and that the major part of such voices present and such as were present by proxy, was to be judged the vote of the house. On this day of all those present in person or by proxy, the burgesses constituted a voting majority. Two of the burgesses, Thompson and Vaughn, who were on the committee to draft the proposed laws, apparently voted in favor of the passage of the bill.

This assembly, like its predecessor, neglected to take action on the proposed expedition against the Indians. This was largely because Governor Calvert curtly informed the legislators that he did not intend to advise with them whether there should be an expedition or not, for that decision belonged solely to him. All that he wanted the assembly to do was to determine what assistance, if any, it would contribute. The next morning the assembly on its own initiative ad-

[8] *Archives,* I, 131.
[9] Ibid, 141.

journed without taking further action. Here was an impasse, all brought about by the determination of the assembly under the leadership of Cornwaleys to exercise the right of self-government.

The governor thereupon determined to "go to the country" once again, so he summoned all the freemen to assemble for the purpose of considering the question of the defense of the colony. The Susquehannocks had made fresh depredations on some of the outlying settlements and more attacks were threatened.

Governor Calvert acting for the Lord Proprietary, had the unquestioned right, under Section XII of the charter, to declare and carry on war against the Indians, and to summon to the colonial standards any men in the province he might choose, but the freemen were so jealous of their prerogatives that they would not admit that this right could be exercised without their consent. Instead of trying to impose his will upon the colonists by force, the governor adopted the more democratic course of summoning all the freemen and asking them to adopt means for their own protection. For a second time within a year resort was had to a pure democracy to decide important affairs of the colony.

The assembly, called for September 1642, and continuing until September 13, 1642, consisted of one hundred thirty-eight freemen, most of whom attended by proxy. The first act of this assembly was to decide that a man was not required to own property in order to be a freeman. One Thomas Weston on the first roll call said "he was no freeman because he had no land nor certain dwelling here." It was voted that he was a freeman although he owned no property "and as such bound to his appearance by himself or proxy, whereupon he took his place in the house." [10]

Captain Cornwaleys was, as usual, the legislative leader. Both he and Giles Brent, who had the proxies of the freemen of the Isle of Kent, strongly objected to a bill which gave

[10] *Archives,* I, 170.

power to the governor to appoint certain officers, making it obligatory upon the appointees to accept. The office of public hangman was included in the appointments. Cornwaleys and Brent objected that it was against their liberties to be forced to take office and that it was against "common right and decency to compel a man against his will to be a hangman." The obnoxious feature of the bill was eliminated.

When the bill for the expedition against the Indians was proposed the freemen did not hesitate to give the Governor all the power he desired. He was given authority to make a selective draft choosing one out of every third man "able to bear arms such as he shall think fit to go upon the expedition." The act further provided that each hundred must pay the expenses of its own men. The governor's servants and apprentices were exempted from the draft, which provision was vigorously opposed by Captain Cornwaleys, but nevertheless adopted. It is evident that while there had been no real opposition to the proposed expedition itself, the freemen demanded the right to initiate action themselves. It was the natural expression of the democratic spirit among the colonists. A revised code of laws was adopted, but it was substantially the same as that passed by the previous assembly.

With the last assembly of 1642 these early Catholic legislators completed their task of rearing a structure of government for their colony. There were to be no more legislative sessions for three years. Proclamations were issued for sessions in 1643 and 1644, but due to the absence of Governor Calvert in England the assemblies were dismissed.

The name of Thomas Cornwaleys is no longer to appear among the law-makers of Maryland but his work was to endure. His sturdy courage and independence, his determination to have the freemen exercise the right of self-government, gave an impetus to the development of the democratic spirit among the colonists. So strong were the forces at work in this direction that when troublous times came to the colony due largely to the incursion of those who were strangers to the traditions and ideals of the founders and the first settlers, the leaven of democracy was not destroyed nor was the growth of democratic institutions seriously retarded.

CHAPTER VII

SOME CONTRASTS IN LAW MAKING

WHEN it is said that there was religious liberty, separation of state and church, independence of king and parliament and an exercise of self-government in early Catholic Maryland, this is not stating the entire case. There was something of greater importance than any of these things. There was equality of civil rights. When the early settlers and law-makers once acknowledged that no preference should be given in the exercise of religious worship, they were bound to acknowledge that there should be no discrimination in the exercise of the right to participate in governmental affairs. It has been said that religious liberty is the parent of civil liberty, but there can be no real civil liberty unless there is equality in the privileges and duties of citizens.

In no other colony was the voting franchise so freely given and so free from restriction. Here it was dependent neither on church membership nor ownership of property. Furthermore no one was taxed to support a church or clergy not of his own faith. With the exception of the simple Act for Church Liberties there was no reference made to the subject of religion in any of the early laws of the colony. No fines were imposed for non-attendance at church, and no one was punished for exercising any particular form of church worship. No provision was made for the subsidy of any church nor for the support of the clergy of any church. Like the Royal Charter of Maryland, the early codes were as remarkable for what they omitted as for what they contained.

The contrast between Puritan Massachusetts and early

Catholic Maryland is the contrast between a theocracy and a democracy. What has been called the Puritan Commonwealth and the Puritan Republic was in reality a theocracy, a government of the clergy, by the clergy, and for the clergy. There, the power of the government was in the control of a small minority and this ruling minority was the Puritan clergy. In Maryland, the Catholic missionaries who were the only clergy in the colony, abstained from all legislative activity and excused themselves from attendance at the assemblies.

The power of the clergy was early made manifest in the proceedings of the Massachusetts General Court. It was seldom that a measure was carried over their objection and no man sat in the assembly who was obnoxious to them.[1] At the head of the Puritan theocracy was the Reverend John Cotton who has been described as "the unmitered pope of a pope-hating commonwealth." [2] It was this same John Cotton who said he did not concede that God ever ordained democracy "as a fit government either for church or commonwealth; as for monarchy and autocracy, they are both of them clearly approved and dictated by scripture." [3]

The power of the clergy in Massachusetts was supreme over the legislature, the courts and the people. The clergy made the laws. The magistrates were little more than sheriffs to execute the laws. The people were made to conform to the rule of the clergy by all manner of penal statutes which invaded the privacy of their homes, regulated their dress, and attempted to control their thoughts. The magistrate decided cases "according to rule of scripture," but if no rule of scripture could be found to fit a particular case, then he had recourse to the advice of the clergy. Frequently men were banished for no other reason than that "they were not fit to live with us." It was the clergy who decided the question of

[1] Howe, *The Puritan Republic,* 208.

[2] Moses Coit Tyler, in the *History of American Literature.*

[3] Cotton's letter to Lord Say and Seal in appendix to Vol. I, Hutchinson's *History of Massachusetts.*

fitness. The clergy was sustained by the magistrates, and the magistrates in turn supported the clergy.

The law-makers were the clergy, and their guide was not the English common law, but the Mosaic code interpreted to conform to their own ideas. The Puritan clergy had a fondness for legislation that became an obsession. They believed the law to be a panacea for all ills. Laws were passed demanding church attendance, enforcing respect for churches and ministers, prohibiting the building of any but the orthodox meeting houses, and prohibiting the preaching and practice of any kind of religion except what was strictly orthodox. No man was given the voting franchise unless he was a member of the orthodox church in good and regular standing.

On Sunday nothing was lawful except to go to church. Absence from church service was punishable by a fine and in order to prevent back-sliding the constables were enjoined to "duly make search throughout the limites of their towns" for absentees during the time when services were being held, and if any were found, to hale them within the church portals. Attendance at church service was not enough. A man must not fall asleep during the sermon and the sermons were long, never less than an hour, sometimes two hours. In 1643, a man was fined for falling asleep in church and striking the man who woke him up. Later the same culprit was severely whipped for falling asleep again. After that he evidently kept awake during the sermon, for there is no record of any further conviction.

A man could not kiss his wife in public on Sunday. A sea captain who had returned from a voyage of three years, on a Sunday morning did not wait until he entered his house before kissing his wife, but indiscreetly kissed her on the door step in full sight of passersby. He sat in the stocks for two hours for his "lewd and unseemly behavior on the Sabbath Day." [4]

[4] Earl, *The Sabbath in Puritan New England,* 247.

Against other sects, the Puritans directed their legislative shafts, Baptists, Quakers and Catholics receiving particular attention. Baptist ministers were fined, imprisoned and flogged for attempting to hold services. Laws were passed for the banishment of all Quakers, Catholic priests and Jesuits, and for the hanging of those who might return after banishment. Four Quakers, including a woman, returned from banishment and were hung on Boston Common. The law against Catholic priests was never invoked, for the missionaries in America had the good sense not to intrude where they were not wanted and where apparently their services were not needed. They never entertained any hope of converting the Puritans. Ministering to those of their own faith and attempting to convert the Indians were their chief concern.

The only record of a member of the Catholic clergy invading the sacred precincts of the Bay Colony during the early days of the theocracy was in the case of Father Gabriel Druilletes, a Jesuit missionary, who was sent to Boston with credentials from the Governor-General of Canada to negotiate with the Massachusetts authorities a proposed alliance against the warring tribes of the Iroquois. Armed with credentials from his government, he was exempt from the law providing for banishment of a priest. He was received kindly and graciously, invited to dine with Governor Dudley at Roxbury and with Governor Bradford of the Plymouth colony. When he dined with Bradford it was on a Friday and the governor "considerately gave him a dinner of fish." [5] He was also the guest of the Reverend John Eliot, Puritan missionary to the Indians, who invited him to spend the winter. Father Druilletes' mission apparently failed but the incident showed that the Puritan could tolerate a Catholic priest even if he were a Jesuit, when the law allowed him to do so.

[5] Parkman, *The Jesuits in North America,* 425. The leaders of the Plymouth colony were far more tolerant than those of Massachusetts Bay.

A study of the early Maryland codes will show that they were more constructive and remedial than penal. There were far more laws for the encouragement of husbandry, the security of property rights and the protection of the liberties of the people than there were for the restriction of liberties and the punishment of offenders. While the laws of Massachusetts fairly bristled with definitions of criminal offenses, only a few of the early laws of Maryland related to crimes and penalties. Of the eighteen pages of the code of 1642 only two relate to crime. The list of capital offenses was practically the same as recognized in England, and both the civil and criminal codes were but restatements of English law, reduced and modified to meet the simple needs of the young colony.

While Massachusetts was building jails in every county to harbor those who violated her many penal laws, there were no jails in Maryland. In 1642, eight years after the landing of the *Ark* and the *Dove,* when Captain Ingle was arrested for piracy and treason he escaped from the sheriff at St. Mary's. The sheriff excused his apparent neglect of duty by reporting that there was no public jail "but his owne hands." He was expected to entertain prisoners in his home.[6]

The Puritans were a long time finding out that men could not be re-created by legislation. The theocracy lasted for over a half century and it is amazing how this rule by a minority could have survived as long as it did. A large number of the people of the colony were deprived of the vote, not being members of the established church in good and regular standing. This number kept increasing until in the last days of the theocracy fully five-sixths of the people were disfranchised.

Coming down to Virginia, there will be found the same laws of compulsory church attendance as in Massachusetts, except that the Church of England was substituted for the church of the Puritans. Wilstach says:

[6] Andrews, *Founding of Maryland,* 115.

Church attendance on the Maryland side of the river was enforced by the Catholics in their own way. It was a matter of moral discipline. To miss Mass was a sin. The offender punished himself. On the Virginia side failure to attend church was made a wilful misdemeanor and the State punished the offender.[7]

Anyone who absented himself from church in early Virginia forfeited a pound of tobacco, and if his absence continued for a month, he forfeited fifty pounds of the same commodity.[8] All churches and ministers must conform to the Church of England and all churches were built at the public expense. Penalties were imposed on parents for not sending their children to church, and upon children for refusing to learn the catechism.

The first legislative assembly in America was introduced in Virginia, but it cannot be said that because of this the germs of real American democracy first took root in the soil of this colony. From the very beginning the Church of England was established in Virginia. The oath of supremacy was required of all inhabitants and the freeman's vote was given only to conformists.[9]

The preliminary meeting of the assembly was held in the English church at Jamestown in 1619. The assemblymen first sat in the choir of the church. The Governor was in the seat he was accustomed to occupy when attending church service. The sergeant was at the choir rail ready for any emergency. The meeting was opened with prayer by the minister of the Church of England. The members of the assembly withdrew into the body of the church, each taking the oath of supremacy before being admitted to his seat.[10]

The idea of a legislative assembly in Virginia was probably original with Sir Edwin Sandys. George Calvert was a member of the Second Virginia Company and a member of the provisional council for the management of the affairs of the

7 *Potomac Landings,* 247.
8 Hening, *Statutes at Large,* I, 126.
9 Cobb, op. cit., 75.
10 Charles M. Andrews, op. cit., 185-186.

colony after the revocation of the charter. Although in the discharge of his duties as Secretary of State in the Court of James it may appear that he was opposed to some of the policies of Sandys, yet he was in entire agreement with the latter on the question of religious liberty. As Dr. Andrews says: "What Sandys may have seen as a vision Calvert prepared to carry into practical effect." [11]

Calvert in the preparation of his charters adopted the Virginia plan of a popular assembly but his plan went further in that it granted equal rights of citizenship and allowed for separation of state and church.

The first assembly, the records of which have been preserved, was that of 1623. This assembly provided for religious conformity and uniformity. All persons must yield "readie obedience" to the canons of the Church of England "under pain of censure." [12]

In 1642 "Popish recusants" were disabled from holding office and Catholic priests arriving in the colony were to be expelled within five days.[13] At different times both Puritans and Quakers were ordered to be banished with severe penalties in the event of return. Baptists were also discriminated against. Any one who disparaged a minister of the Church of England without bringing sufficient proof "to justify his reports" incurred a fine of five hundred pounds of tobacco and must publicly ask the minister for forgiveness.

In both Massachusetts and Virginia discriminatory laws and compulsory attendance upon an established church afforded barren soil for the growth of the principle of equality before the law. Without some recognition of this principle we may look in vain for the real foundation of the American form of government.

In some of the other colonies there were later established more liberal forms of government than are to be found in

[11] *History of Maryland,* 6.
[12] Cobb, op. cit., 80.
[13] Hening, op. cit., I, 268; Anderson, *History of the Colonial Church,* II, 143.

early Massachusetts and Virginia, but in all respects not as liberal as the early government of Maryland. Thomas Hooker and his band of followers who came to the meadowlands of Hartford and Wethersfield, Connecticut, to get away from the Puritan theocracy, adopted in the exercise of self-government a set of principles and laws which formed the first written constitution in America. The one great drawback in Connecticut, however, was the fact that although church membership was not made a prerequisite for voting, the Congregational Church was the established church of the colony. The church was a public charge and all inhabitants, regardless of creed, were taxed to pay for its support; its buildings were erected at public expense and its ministers were called by the town meeting.[14]

It was near the time when the control of the government of Maryland was taken from the third Lord Baltimore that William Penn received the charter for his princely domain. His charter followed some of the features of the Maryland charter, but Penn failed to obtain two concessions which were granted to the first Lord Baltimore—the guarantee of the rights of English freemen to the colonists and freedom from taxation imposed by parliament.[15] Despite these handicaps he did all within his power to follow where Calvert had led the way, and made a substantial contribution to the cause of liberal government.

In the same year that Penn came to America, James, the Duke of York, appointed Colonel Thomas Dongan, an Irish Catholic, governor of the colony of New York. Dongan established a democratic form of government and religious freedom. John Austin Stevens in his contribution to Winsor's *Narrative and Critical History of America,* declares that "no more democratic form of government existed in America or was possible under kingly authority"; than that established

[14] Cobb, op. cit., 246.
[15] Elson, *History of the United States,* 154.

in New York by Governor Dongan.[16] The first act of the assembly in 1683 was that which bore the title of "The Charter of Liberties and Privileges granted by His Royal Highness to the Inhabitants of New York and its dependencies." The supreme legislative authority under the King and the Duke, was vested in a governor, council and the "people met in general assembly." The franchise was free to every freeholder, there was no church establishment and there was freedom of conscience and religion. It is a noteworthy fact that in the only two colonies which had Catholic governors, both civil and religious liberty were established which continued as long as these colonies were under Catholic rule. It is equally significant that both these Catholic governors (Leonard Calvert and Colonel Dongan) had Jesuits for their spiritual advisers. One of Dongan's advisers during the short time he was governor of New York was Father Thomas Harvey who afterwards came to Maryland.[17]

Professor Andrews cites as an early measure of religious liberty an act passed by the General Court of the Province of Maine in 1649, "oddly enough," he says, "but six months after the passage of the more famous and misunderstood act concerning religion by the Maryland assembly." This act declared that:

> All good people of this province who are of a church way and be orthodox in judgment and not scandalous in life shall have liberty to gather themselves into a church estate, providing they do it in a Christian way, with due observance of the rules of Christ revealed in his word and every church hath full liberty of election and ordination of all her officers from time to time, provided they be able, pious and orthodox.[18]

Assuming that the real purpose of this act was to grant religious liberty it can be seen that any of its several provisos,

[16] *The English in New York,* Winsor, III, p. 404.

[17] Hughes, op. cit., II, 145-151. See also Chapter II of Walsh, *Our American Jesuits,* under sub-title, "Governor Dongan and Religious Toleration."

[18] *The Colonial Period in American History,* I, 427.

especially the proviso as to orthodoxy, might easily stand in the way of allowing full liberty to all sects and all creeds. Then too, this act is to be interpreted in the light of the royal charter granted by Charles I to Sir Ferdinando Gorges for the Province of Maine. In the charter there was an express provision that "the religion now professed in the Church of England and ecclesiastical government now used in the same, shall be forever professed and with as much convenient speed as may be, settled and established in and throughout said province and premises and every of them." [19]

Gorges was granted proprietary rights much the same as was Baltimore, together with the "liberties and immunities as the Bishop of Durham within the bishopric or County Palatine of Durham in our Kingdom of England now hath." The charter to Gorges was not granted until 1639, some sixteen years after Baltimore received the Charter of Avalon. Evidently some of the King's advisers cautioned against any vagueness and uncertainty such as had crept into the Avalon and Maryland charters, and to take no chance with the Maine charter so far as the establishment of the Church of England was concerned, so church establishment was made mandatory. There may be toleration under church establishment but not real religious liberty.

Maryland, Pennsylvania, Maine and New York were all proprietary colonies, as were also the Carolinas and New Jersey. Professor John M. Mecklin in his recent work, *The Story of American Dissent,* says:

> The proprietary colonies were inclined to be tolerant. Founded primarily for the purpose of trade, they welcomed any group of immigrant irrespective of religious affiliations who were economic assets. Often the tolerant ways of life built up in proprietary colonies persisted after the colonies were transferred to the crown and offered the stubborn and effective resistance to all efforts to enforce a religious establishment. This was especially true of the Carolinas, New Jersey and New York where Anglican establishment was never more than a mere shell. The

[19] Baxter, *Sir Ferdinando Gorges and His Province of Maine,* II, 129.

same was also true of Maryland where, however, it was not so much the exigences of trade as the effect of liberal ideas inculcated under Lord Baltimore that later proved a hindrance to the effective functioning of the Anglican establishment.[20]

The claim to priority in the field of civil and religious liberty must after all be yielded to Maryland, for here in the early days of the colony can be found the first full recognition of the basic American principle of equality before the law.

20 Page 42.

CHAPTER VIII

AS TO ROGER WILLIAMS AND RHODE ISLAND

IT IS a preconceived idea of many that religious liberty in America first took root in the soil of Rhode Island under the watchful care of Roger Williams. Consequently, the founder of Rhode Island has been generally proclaimed as "the Apostle of Religious Liberty." Whether he really deserves this title is quite another matter.

Williams arrived in America in 1631, some three years before the sailing of the *Ark* and the *Dove*. The date of his arrival, however, is without any historical significance, for when he came he was as narrow and intolerant in his views as were any of the Puritans of his day. As a matter of fact, a strong and bitter religious prejudice dominated his whole life.

During his residence in Massachusetts there is no evidence that Williams attempted to make a direct issue of the question of religious liberty. It was not until some time after his banishment to Rhode Island that he gave expression to his own peculiar ideas of "soul liberty." [1] Professor Charles M. Andrews in his *Colonial Period of American History* has recently said:

> There is nothing to show that at this early date Williams had formulated or expressed any clear cut notions such as are customarily ascribed to him by later expositors of his place in religious thought regarding what is loosely termed "toleration" or that the question of soul liberty had any conspicuous place in the controversies that arose in Massachusetts before 1643. The time had not come either in England or in America for that burning question to take its place as a matter of first con-

[1] Charles Deane, "New England" in Winsor, *Narrative and Critical History of America*, III, 336.

cern or as something uppermost in men's minds. The banishment of Roger Williams has been invested by later writers with an importance that was not felt contemporaneously.[2]

Williams was a most pronounced dissenter from the Church of England. On his arrival in America he refused to join the Boston church because its members had not publicly repented for their former communion with the Church of England. He would have nothing to do with any church that had held communion with or gave any recognition to the established church or even allowed its members while visiting in England to attend Anglican worship. To hold any communion with "her of England" he held to be a heinous sin. He called upon the churches of the colony to disclaim the Church of England as "no church at all," and when they did not do so he called upon his own church in Salem to renounce all communion with its neighbor churches as they were "full of the pollution of anti-Christ." He professed and practised a rigid separation and admitted to membership in his church no one who had not first renounced fellowship with the Church of England. He was intolerant of the views of others and intolerant of any church that did not hold strictly to his own opinions; and as his opinions were by no means easy of comprehension it became increasingly difficult to determine what churches, if any, did conform to his views.

One of the strange vagaries of his mind was reflected in his attitude on the question of baptism. He was persuaded to believe that his infant baptism was worthless, so he was rebaptized. Then he discovered that the baptism of the man who baptized him was worthless so he decided that there was no man living who had authority to baptize and that there was no true church anywhere and that he must wait for God to send a new apostle.[3]

He preached sermons against the use of all ceremonies and symbols claiming that they came from Popery and would

[2] Loc. cit., I, 471.
[3] Schneider, *The Puritan Mind,* 56.

lead to a false religion. One particular sermon in which he declared that while the Puritans had a Christ without a cross, yet they followed the cross in the colors, resulted in Endicott making his famous display of bigotry when he cut with his sword the cross of St. George from the royal standard.

He went so far as to urge his people not to pray with unregenerates (those who had not made open profession of their own regeneration), even though they might be members of their own families. To his congregation at Salem he preached the duty of women to wear veils in church, and when his wife did not obey the order and came to church veilless, he refused to join her in family devotions. Not only did he withdraw from the society of his wife because she would not yield to his whims, he at one time refused to have anything to do with his children as he counted them "unregenerate." [4]

Williams was a born fighter and wherever he went there was a large chip on his shoulder. Dr. Twichell says that he was "the genius of social incompatibility. Everywhere he lingered there forthwith sprang up strife and in an acute form. The community in which he sojourned he invariably set by the ears and embroiled with its neighbors." [5] He took a stand on public questions that was calculated to cause trouble with the home government. He denounced the King as a blasphemer and a liar. He preached against the royal charter as a sinful instrument, and insisted that it be publicly forfeited. The colonists he said should not accept title through royal grant and all lands should be purchased from the Indians. This did not deter him, however, from owning a house and lot in Salem and from later accepting a Royal Grant in Rhode Island.

When Williams entered the realm of governmental affairs he paved the way for his banishment. "He is often spoken of as the victim of religious bigotry," said Dr. Twichell. "He

[4] Grahame, *History of the United States,* American edition, I, 167.
[5] *Life of John Winthrop,* 132.

was nothing of the sort. In his general onslaught on the errors prevailing around him—and to his view little else did prevail—he fell foul of the charter." [6] It was his attitude on the charter and a controversy with the leaders of the theocracy on trivial matters of church polity more than it was any question of religious faith that sent Roger Williams into the Narragansett wilderness.

There was no orderly form of government established in Rhode Island until 1647. In making his first settlement at Providence in 1636 Williams did not intend to found a colony or a state.[7] All that he sought was a refuge in the wilderness outside the bounds of the Puritan theocracy. Consistent with his claim that no legal title could be acquired by royal patent and acting on the advice of his friend John Winthrop "to flee into the Narragansett country free from English patents," he acquired lands from the Indians and with his followers entered into a "town fellowship." The lands were purchased in his own name and he soon became the largest landowner in New England. He was a feudal overlord and his associates became his tenants. His latest biographer says that for the first few years from a legal and commercial standpoint "Providence was a board of management for the corporate land monopoly of Roger Williams." [8] By the end of 1637, he was the most powerful man in New England. The land monopoly and proprietorship gave him autocratic power.[9] He himself admitted that his associates were in fact, bound in fee to manage his property to suit his wishes. A few years later this land monopoly was converted into a landholding company, and the town became a close corporation holding title to the land. The right to voice and vote in the town affairs was limited to those only who acquired title to property.

[6] Op. cit., 134.

[7] Ernst, *Roger Williams, New England Firebrand,* 157; Arnold, op. cit., I, 97.

[8] Ernst, op. cit., 172.

[9] Ibid, 177.

There were other settlements in Rhode Island which were welded later into the colony of "Rhode Island and Providence Plantations." One of these was at Aquedneck which had a form of government strongly resembling a Puritan theocracy. When the first freemen were admitted a pair of stocks and a whipping post were installed and three days later a prison was ordered to be built. In the settlement of Warwick made by the half mad fanatic, William Gorton, there was no form of government. Under Gorton it became a veritable hornet's nest. Gorton, who had been whipped and banished from Aquedneck, denied the right of the people to set up for themselves a form of government.

The settlements were finally incorporated under a charter from the parliamentary commissioners. The charter was granted in 1644 but incorporation was delayed until 1647, when a code of laws was adopted. This was the first legally constituted government in Rhode Island. On the question of religious liberty the charter was silent, but its broad terms gave Williams free play to carry out his peculiar ideas of "soul liberty." His principle of liberty of conscience, however, was often interpreted as freedom from all civil restraint. The colony contained a heterogeneous group of disturbers and fanatics who mistook liberty for license, and there were times when conditions bordered upon anarchy and when "anarchy was openly and freely avowed." [10] William Harris, who was one of the leaders of an armed opposition to civil authority, denied the right of the state to "punish transgressions against the private and public weal," and used the writings of Williams as the basis of his claim. Robert Williams, brother of Roger, was one of the organizers of this opposition.

In the days of Roger Williams, Rhode Island was a refuge "for all sorts of religious misfits," and as Cotton Mather expressed it, "everything in the world but Roman Catholics and real Christians." [11] As late as 1680, Peleg Sanford, gover-

[10] Ernst, op. cit., 344.

[11] Schneider, op. cit., 56-57. Mather, *Magnalia,* VII, Chap. III, sec. 12.

nor of the province, reported to the Board of Trade in England that "as for Papists we know of none amongst us."[12] There may have been reason for this. Catholics usually kept away from colonies where they believed they would not be welcome.

Historians of the state have had a hard time trying to explain away a law that was apparently passed in 1664. This law appears in the first printed revision of the laws in 1719, and purports to be an act originally adopted in March 1663. In the revision the law reads:

> All men professing Christianity and of competent estates and of civil conversation who acknowledge and are obedient to the civil magistrate though of different judgments in religious affairs (*Roman Catholics only excepted*) shall be admitted freemen and shall have liberty to chuse and be chosen officers in the colony, both military and civil.

In the original manuscript records of the proceedings of the assembly for March 1663-4, now in the office of the Secretary of State, this law is not to be found. It first appears in the Revision of 1719,[13] and then, with slight changes in phraseology, in no less than four subsequent revisions, those of 1730, 1744, 1752 and 1762. Although the revision of 1719 was previously authorized it was not subsequently ratified. The revision of 1730 was ratified and confirmed by the assembly, so this law excluding Catholics from the franchise became the law of the colony and remained so for over fifty years.

This law was not repealed until 1783. The repealing act refers to a law made and passed March 1, 1663. The cause for the repeal was the presence of the French forces in Rhode Island after France had come to the aid of the American cause in the Revolution. It was found advisable, in order "to efface any semblance of opprobrium," to have the law immediately repealed. The French allies were the first Catholics

12 Arnold, *History of Rhode Island,* I, 490.
13 Rhode Island Records, II, 36.

to receive a real welcome in the land of Roger Williams.

An apologist for Rhode Island says it really makes no difference even if this act was originally adopted in 1664, as no harm was done, there being no Catholics in the colony at the time.[14] Another says that the franchise to vote had nothing to do with religious liberty. He asks:

> Was it not natural for the founders of Rhode Island to keep the government in the hands of its friends, while working out their experiment, rather than to put it into the hands of the enemies of religious liberty? How many shiploads of Roman Catholics would it have taken to swamp the little colony in the days of its weakness? [15]

One of the reasons given for the belief that the clause excluding Roman Catholics from the franchise was not put into the law as early as 1664, is that any discrimination of this kind would be "totally at variance with the antecedents of Roger Williams." As will later appear this particular discrimination was quite consistent with Williams' bitter hatred of the Church of Rome.

Roger Williams was hopelessly addicted to controversy. John Fiske says that there was scarcely any subject upon which he did not wrangle. Little sympathy would he have had for the advice given by the young Lord Baltimore "to be silent on all occasions of discourse concerning matters of religion."

The Quakers were given sanctuary in Rhode Island, but it was not a peaceful sanctuary. Although he would allow no one else to molest the Quakers in the exercise of their religion, he molested them by a challenge to an acrimonious debate and disturbed the peace which they sought and had reason to believe they would have in this haven of refuge. He did not try to force his own opinions upon them by laws, but he did attempt to do so by words. He tried to make them see the errors of their way of thinking by a barrage of con-

[14] Cobb, op. cit., 438.
[15] Deane, op. cit., 380.

troversy that lasted four days and four nights. His challenge to George Fox, the Quaker leader, rings like a challenge to a prize fight. Accompanying the challenge were fourteen propositions which he boasted he would maintain in public "against all comers."

Williams' controversy with the Quakers throws more light on his true nature than does any other incident in his life. The debates began in the Quaker meeting house at Newport and lasted three days and three nights and then were adjourned to Providence, where they terminated after another day, with the usual result, producing no effect, as one biographer says, other "than to exasperate the friends of both parties and set them still more violently against each other." [16]

The debates were scenes of tumult and disorder and attracted large crowds of spectators who cheered and jeered in turn. There was no moderator or umpire, and he who could talk the loudest and the longest could convince himself that his views had prevailed. In this way Williams satisfied himself that he had won the debate. To celebrate his victory, he wrote out all that he said in the debate, and probably more too, which he had printed in pamphlet form and labeled *George Fox Digged out of his Burrows.* It was unfortunate for him and his reputation as "The Apostle of Religious Liberty" that he chose to triumphantly broadcast to posterity his vile and violent utterances in this debate rather than to suffer them to be buried in the eclipse of a verbal controversy of which there would otherwise have been no record. A reprint of *George Fox Digged out of his Burrows* contains some three hundred pages and may be found in volume five of the *Publications of the Narragansett Club,* first series. Anyone having any preconceived notions as to the liberality, tolerance and forbearance of Roger Williams will only have to read a few pages of this volume to suffer a rude shock.

[16] Gammell, *Roger Williams,* Vol. IV, Sparks, American Biographies, 189.

Williams' biographers have mostly ignored this written evidence of their idol's bigotry. Gammell, one of the earlier biographers, however, does say that the pamphlet "was distinguished by a bitterness and severity of language unequaled in any of his other writings," [17] and a recent biographer, Emily Easton, offers some apology for her idol's fall from grace when she says:

> The rehearsal, however, of the long and tedious argument is as tiresome and profitless as the original debate must have been. In his conduct of it, he is constantly guilty of the same faults with which he accuses his adversaries. The violent railing language is the contradiction of the gentle spirit of tolerance that has formerly characterized him, "the Apostle of Religious Liberty." *George Fox Digged out of his Burrows* and a *New England Fire Brand Quenched* are not adapted to general reading in modern times nor do they add to the greatness of Roger Williams.[18]

Williams placed Quakers and Catholics in the same category and consigned them both to the lake that burns with fire and brimstone. "The Papists and Quakers" he declared "are both spitting and belching out fire from one fire of Hell." The foundation of both "is laid deep upon the sand of rotten nature." Their fastings, penances, alms, prayers and sufferings are but "the dung of men and beasts," and other filthy things which are quite unprintable, although they are embalmed in the archives of the Narragansett Club.[19]

The peaceful Quakers he looked upon as potential murderers, for "if their spirit should ever get a sword" he would not place them above drinking the blood of all their enemies "as the Papists are justly charged with drinking the blood of the saints." The Pope and the Quakers he linked together as "horrible revilers, slanderers and cursers of the righteous."

Williams was seventy-three years of age when he debated with the Quakers, and lest it be claimed that he may have been in his dotage and that his language does not reflect

[17] Ibid, 190.
[18] *Roger Williams, Prophet and Pioneer,* 358.
[19] *Publications of Narragansett Club,* 1st series, V., 205-6, 262-4, 432-501.

the sweet, loving and charitable sentiments of his earlier years, attention must be called to a letter which he wrote some twelve years previous (1660) to the kindly John Winthrop of Connecticut. Dipping his pen in the same venom and filth he used later, he expressed to his friend the fond hope that the Catholic Church "will shortly appear so extremely loathsome in her drunkenness and bestiality that her bewitched paramours will tear her flesh and burn her with fire unquenchable." [20]

The words in this letter were written in cool deliberation and were not spoken in the heat and haste of debate. Some excuse might be offered for his resort to invectives of this nature in the excitement of a heated oral controversy, but what possible excuse can be offered when in the quiet and seclusion of his study he wrote the letter to Winthrop? Then again, it must be remembered that after the excitement of the debate with the Quakers had subsided he deliberately and laboriously wrote out for publication every vile epithet of which he could conceive to hurl at Catholic and Quaker alike.

It may be said for him that he was but "a child of the age in which he lived," and simply made use of weapons in the form of language that were used by others who played the rôle of religious reformers in his day. But when this is said in excuse for him then the mantle of a prophet or an apostle of religious liberty falls from him.

No rôle of a prophet or an apostle is claimed for George or Cecil Calvert. They were practical men, but the very practical application they made of the ideal of religious liberty marked them as men who lived in advance of their own times. In contrast to Roger Williams they left religious controversy to others, and no words indicating the slightest

[20] Ibid, VI, 307-311. This letter to Winthrop was written only four years prior to the enactment of the famous law of 1664. If Williams believed that the Catholic Church should be burned in the fires of Hell he might have welcomed a law that would keep its members from having the right to vote in Rhode Island.

dislike of or prejudice against others because of religious belief ever left the lips or pen of either.

"The Charter of Lively Experiment" was procured from Charles II not by Roger Williams but by John Clarke, a Baptist minister who had suffered from persecution in the Bay colony. Williams and Clarke went on a mission to England during the Protectorate and made an attempt to obtain a liberal charter from the Cromwell government. For some unexplained reason the mission failed. The petition was neither granted nor rejected. Williams returned to Providence in 1654, leaving Clarke to carry on the negotiations. As soon as the monarchy was restored, Clarke on behalf of Providence Plantations petitioned that "they be permitted to hold forth a lively experiment that a flourishing civil state may stand, yea and best be maintained and that among English spirits with full liberty in religious concernments."

The assembly voted to send six men including Williams to aid Clarke, but Clarke satisfied the assembly that he could secure the charter unaided and no one was sent. Ernst says that Clarke performed his work "with distinction." In 1663, a charter was granted by the King who "never said a foolish thing and never did a wise one" (save in this instance) which was the most liberal charter ever granted to an American colony. The charter permitted the "lively experiment" sought for.

This may have been a lively experiment for New England, but it would not have been a lively or any other kind of an experiment for Maryland where full religious liberty had already been observed and practised under a duly constituted government for nearly thirty years. After all, religious liberty is not established by charter or law or any other fiat of government. It is born of the spirit. The real spirit of religious liberty first came to America with the *Ark* and the *Dove*.[21]

[21] The greater part of this chapter previously appeared in an article by the author in *Thought,* December, 1931.

CHAPTER IX

A RUDE AWAKENING

With the single exception of the activities of Claiborne, the first ten years in the life of the young colony were years of peace and steady growth. Never had a colonial settlement been started under such happy auspices. A fertile soil, a mild climate, rivers and bays affording not only attractive but easy and economical means of transportation; Protestants and Catholics both enjoying the blessings of religious liberty; devout and self-sacrificing mission priests who kept out of politics and state-craft and confined themselves to the saving of souls and to good works both among Indians and white men; a beneficent and liberal minded lord proprietary conceding to the freemen every right which they claimed, and doing everything possible to promote the welfare of his colony and colonists; sensible law-makers, passing as few laws as possible, and only those designed for the betterment of all concerned; the freeman's vote freely given; courts administering equal justice; all united to transform the region about St. Mary's into a land of quiet contentment. "It was an idyllic moment," wrote Helen Ainslee Smith, "on which it is pleasant to dwell before the appearance of the all devouring monster of self-righteous Puritanism." [1]

The ascendancy of the Puritan party in England was soon to bring a repercussion in the quiet colony of Maryland. In the summer of 1642, King Charles set up the royal standard at Nottingham and rallied to it all his loyal subjects. The struggle between King and Parliament was completely to upset the affairs of Lord Baltimore's colony and rudely

[1] *The Thirteen Colonies,* 114.

awaken the good people of St. Mary's from their pleasant dream.

It was a trying time for Cecil Calvert. Although his natural sympathy and interest were on the side of the King, he had a colony to save and that he saved it was due to the great good fortune attending his efforts to keep from being drawn into the whirlpool of events rapidly bringing a crisis in the mother country. He owed it not only to himself but more to his colonists to use all the tact and diplomacy that he possessed to avoid sharing the fate of the King who had given him his charter.

In this troublous time Leonard Calvert was summoned by his brother to come to England to confer as to the policy to be followed to save the colony. He sailed for England in April of 1643, leaving his kinsman, Giles Brent, to act as governor *pro tempore*. In the following year Captain Richard Ingle, a swashbuckling parliamentarian, came to Maryland and put in to St. Mary's to discharge the cargo of his ship. Ingle arrived with a chip on his shoulder and unfortunately the acting governor knocked it off. Ingle made it known that he was "a captain for the Parliament against the king" and that the King "was no king at all." Furthermore, if he "had Prince Rupert on board his ship he would flog him at the capstan." He had a bad habit of brandishing his cutlass and making threats about cutting off heads. When his language and conduct came to the attention of Brent, he was arrested and turned over to the sheriff. Captain Cornwaleys had the good sense to see that the quicker Ingle was got rid of, the better. He saw how serious it would be to make an open issue at this time between King and parliament. With another councillor, Neale, after Ingle's apparent release, he accompanied the prisoner to his ship where he told him "all is peace," and withdrew the guard which the acting governor had placed on the ship.

Ingle lost no time in sailing his ship out of the harbor. Brent, who had been determined to punish Ingle as a traitor, now brought charges against Cornwaleys, Neale, the sheriff, and the guard who had been placed on Ingle's ship, claiming that they aided the prisoner's escape. All were exonerated except Cornwaleys who was made the scapegoat for the others and was ordered to pay a fine of one thousand pounds of tobacco, the maximum penalty, although he had acted in good faith and had supposed that Ingle's release had been approved by Brent. This affair placed Cornwaleys in a false light and there was so much ill-feeling against him that he decided to return to England in Ingle's ship and there seek vindication.

In the winter of 1644-5, Ingle returned with an armed ship, *The Reformation,* and a motley crew. This time he was determined to have things his own way. Claiborne bobbed up serenely on the old battle-ground of Kent Island, always looking for trouble when trouble was around. He saw his opportunity to get possession of the island he coveted, but the islanders who had before favored his cause were not disposed to aid him now. They had lived quietly and peaceably under the Baltimore government and were quite content to remain as they were. They turned deaf ears this time to Claiborne when he told them they were living under a tyrannical popish government. They had listened to this appeal before, but since then they had become part of the government and found that the Catholic yoke was easy. Claiborne, finding the islanders would not listen to him, sailed back to Virginia, but not for good.

In the meantime, Ingle and his crew had seized and captured St. Mary's. Governor Calvert, who had returned from England, was in Virginia at the time and Captain Cornwaleys was away, so the colonists lacked a leader. Back to Kent Island came Claiborne with a force of armed men. He took possession of Commander Brent's house, and mustering the islanders in an open field, proposed that they march on St. Mary's. They asked to see his authority, and when they saw he had none, refused to obey him. Claiborne and his men remained in possession of the island while Ingle's forces were pillaging St. Mary's. It is not known whether there was an alliance between the two, although there seemed to be concert of action. Ingle had a commission from Parliament, but Claiborne claimed to be acting under royal authority.

It would have been an incongruous combination from a political point of view, but they had one thing in common, that was their desire to take over Lord Baltimore's colony. It is probable that Ingle merely tolerated Claiborne's apparent cooperation, and that the latter took advantage of the seizure of St. Mary's to take possession of the island. Claiborne, as usual, did no fighting. Ingle's men did all the fighting that had to be done and Claiborne reaped his reward without risking life or limb. Virginia gave no help to either party. The Virginians had no sympathy with the Roundheads and did not like Claiborne's apparent alliance with Ingle. After this escapade, Claiborne's name was dropped from the roll of Virginia councillors.

For two years the province remained in the possession of the marauders who made no attempt to set up any kind of a government. Ingle and his men pillaged and plundered, stripped mills of their machinery and laid waste plantations. They impressed corn, tobacco, cattle and household goods, loaded ships with their plunder and sent it to England where they sold what they had stolen and pocketed the cash.[2] They destroyed the great seal of the colony and burned many of the records. Ingle, forgetful of what Cornwaleys had done and suffered for him when he was placed under arrest on his first arrival at St. Mary's, confiscated Cornwaleys' plantation, killed his cattle and carried off all of his household goods. Cornwaleys was still in England. Had he been in Maryland, Ingle would never have gained a foothold in the province. Cornwaleys now realized that he had been duped and imposed on by this self-styled parliamentary captain. He

[2] Fiske, *Virginia and Her Neighbors,* I, 307.

had Ingle arrested and imprisoned in England when he returned with his booty from Maryland. He complained that his whole estate had been ruined to the damage of "at least twenty-five hundred pounds," and that Ingle had confiscated goods to the value of two hundred pounds which he had entrusted him to take to Maryland on his return trip.

Ingle filed a counter petition in the House of Lords in which he alleged that on his arrival in Maryland he deemed himself bound in fidelity to Parliament to risk all to come to the aid of the distressed Protestants against "a tyrannical governor and the Papists." The petition contains the following reference to Captain Cornwaleys: "But since his, Ingle's, return into England the said Papists and Malignants conspiring together have brought fictitious actions against him at the Common Law in the name of Thomas Cornwaleys and others for pretended trespasses." He concludes by affirming that it would be "of dangerous example to permit Papists and Malignants to bring action of trespass or otherwise against the well affected for fighting and standing for the parliament." How this litigation was finally determined is not recorded, but on September 8, 1647, Richard Ingle transferred to Thomas Cornwaleys "for divers goods and valuable causes" certain debts, bills and choses in action belonging to him and made him his attorney to collect the same.[3]

Ingle posed as the champion of the Protestant cause, and his reference to the "Papists" shows that religion had entered into his activities in Maryland and that it was not wholly a political matter. According to statements made in the assembly of 1649, those who remained loyal to Lord Baltimore during this invasion were spoiled of their whole estate and sent away as banished persons out of the province; those few that remained were "plundered and deprived in a manner of all livelihood and sustenance only breathing under that

[3] "Thomas Cornwaleys, Commissioner and Councillor of Maryland" by George Boniface Stratemeier, *Catholic University Studies in American Church History,* II, 117.

intolerable yoke which they were forced to bear under these rebels." [4]

The people were tendered the oath of submission which all Catholics refused to take. In consequence of this they were severely treated, some being banished, and others voluntarily leaving the colony, taking refuge in Virginia. At this time Virginia, being still loyal to the King, willingly received the Catholic refugees from Maryland. In after years this period of trouble, when Ingle and his followers had control of the province, became known as "the plundering time."

It was the little band of Jesuit missionaries who were the greatest sufferers during the "plundering time." They bore the brunt of the attack of the marauders. There can be no doubt that Ingle and his crew designed to completely wipe out the Jesuit mission, believing that in doing this they would gain the approval of the parliamentary party. In their attack upon the mission they were prompted wholly by religious bigotry and their hatred of the Jesuit order, for the mission priests could yield little in the way of valuable plunder. The effect of what they accomplished has been little emphasized by historians. It was the greatest loss suffered by the colony during this period, for it not only retarded the great and good work the mission was doing in the field of religion and humanity, but it cut short the missionary career of Father White "the apostle of Maryland," and here was a loss that cannot be overestimated.

There was nothing that could be laid to the charge of the Jesuits. They could not even have been accused of proselyting. In one of the early letters of the missionaries it is said that "since there are Protestants as well as Catholics in the colony, we have labored for both, and God has blessed our labors." [5] In all the record of cases where the fathers tell of conversions of non-Catholics there is no evidence of any pressure being brought to bear upon the convert that would

[4] I, *Archives*, 238.
[5] *Narrative of a voyage to Maryland,* Fund Publication No. 7, p. 55.

vary from the practical principles of religious liberty outlined in the Utopia. It was by "amicable and modest ways but without bitterness," by the force of argument and reason, rather than the force of threats and persecution, that these conversions were brought about. Several cases are related where the conversion was the result of ministration in time of sickness and near-death and where the father, with the aid of a physician having saved the body, then turned his efforts to saving the soul.

The mission which had a small beginning never at any time in its early history consisted of more than five. The necrology tells a story of privation and sacrifice. With Father White on the *Ark* and the *Dove* came Father John Altham and Brother Thomas Gervase. Brother Gervase was to be the first to give his life in the mission field. In 1635, came Father Francis Rogers and Brother John Wood, but they remained only a year and returned to England the following year. In 1637 came Father Thomas Copley (Philip Fisher) and Father John Knowles to take the places of the two who had returned. Father Copley was to suffer the same fate as Father White—to be sent back to England a prisoner. Father Knowles was stricken with yellow fever the same time as Brother Gervase, and died after being in the mission but two months.

In 1639 came Father John Brooke (Ferdinand Poulton) and Brother Walter Morely. Father Brooke was shot and killed while crossing the St. Mary's River on mission work. His death was reported to have been "by accident." The details of the accident were never made known. In the same year Brother Morely became another victim to the fever. In 1641 there came Father Roger Rigbie who had been so eager for service in the Maryland mission that he had written to his superior:

> My request is only to entreat the happiness to be made partaker of that happy mission of Maryland. 'Tis true, I conceive, the mission not only happy and glorious, but withal hard and

humble in regard to the raw state things as yet are in, yet the love of Jesus neither fears labor nor low employment.

Two years later, 1643, came Fathers Bernard Hartwell and John Cooper. Father Cooper, barely past thirty, possessed of a frail body but an indomitable spirit, was fearful lest his poor health would prevent his being sent to America. He begged his superior "out of that affection you bare my soul's good, that you will value my health and life no more than I myself do value them, who shall be most happy to send a thousand lives (if I had them) in so good a cause." This letter was written in 1640 before Father Rigbie had left for Maryland and in the hope that he would be sent at the same time. Again he made an appeal, and in 1642 wrote to his superior that there had been some improvement in his health and asked to be sent where he "could employ the strength and health God hath lately given me in helping the poor and traveling a foot in that work." This time his request was granted and a short time afterwards, in company with Father Hartwell, a young man of about the same age and of no inconsiderable attainments, he joined the Maryland mission whither Father Rigbie had been sent two years earlier.

Father White, on account of his work in the more distant mission posts among the Indians, was succeeded as superior in 1639 by Father Brooke. Father White became superior again for a short time after Father Brooke's death, but on account of his age and infirmities, was succeeded in turn by Father Copley.

At the time of the Ingle invasion there were five priests in the Maryland mission. Besides Fathers White and Copley, there were Fathers Roger Rigbie, Bernard Hartwell and John Cooper. Father Hartwell was superior of the mission, having been appointed in 1643. All were driven from the mission field and the mission property was laid waste and destroyed. Ingle's men made their headquarters in an improvised fort not far from St. Inigoes, the residence of the Jesuit fathers, and from this vantage point they made frequent forays and after securing their loot, retired to the protection of their fort. Fathers Rigbie, Hartwell and Cooper were forced to flee to Virginia. It is a suspicious coincidence that all three priests died in Virginia some time during the year 1646 under what circumstances is not known.[6]

Fathers White and Copley were sent back to England to answer to the charge of treason—the treason of being Jesuit priests. Both were subjected to the wholly unnecessary disgrace and cruelty of being put in chains when there was not the slightest chance of their attempting to escape. They were not alone in their misery for two of the leading Catholics of the colony, John Lewger and Giles Brent, were also sent back to England, Lewger being sent on the same ship, but they were not put in chains, as they were not Jesuits.

The Catholic colonists were left without any spiritual guides, and the mission was practically abandoned for years. During their confinement preliminary to trial Fathers White and Copley suffered great hardships. They were both indicted upon the charge of high treason under the statute of Elizabeth [7] for having been ordained Catholic priests abroad and then returning to the country. The penalty was death by hanging and quartering. The defense of the fathers was that they had not returned to England willingly, but had been brought back as prisoners against their will, and therefore, there was no violation of the statute. This was a legal defense and the judges were obliged to direct an acquittal.

Instead of being released after their acquittal, they were detained in custody and condemned to perpetual banishment. Father Copley finally made his way back to America, but Virginia and not Maryland was his destination. Accom-

[6] Hughes, op. cit., I, 563.
[7] 27 Elizabeth, C. 11, 1584–5.

panying him was another Jesuit priest, Father Lawrence Sankey. The two Jesuits, on arriving in Virginia, to use Copley's own phrase in his letter "lay hid." In February of 1648 Father Copley, leaving Father Sankey in Virginia, entered Maryland. There he found the Catholics like sheep without a shepherd, gathered together "when he dropped in among them like an apparition." "Like an angel of God," he wrote, "did they receive me. Scattered to the four winds of heaven" as he left them four years ago, he now found them in happier condition than "the foes who had plundered them." But the Indians who had been as badly treated by the plunderers were calling for him. "I scarcely know what to do," he wrote, "since I cannot satisfy all." A road had been recently opened from Virginia to Maryland so both colonies could be comprised in one mission at the cost of only a two days' journey from one to the other. In this way the Maryland Catholics were ministered to by the Jesuits until priests could be sent direct to the colony. Father Copley died in Maryland in 1652.

Father White, after being banished from England, went to Belgium. While there he sought every opportunity of returning to his beloved Maryland, earnestly begging the favor of his superiors to allow him to spend his last days in the work of the mission he had founded. The good father was now nearly eighty years of age, and his constitution was broken down as the result of his privations in the American mission field and the sufferings he had undergone during his imprisonment. His superiors would not consent to his return to America, so he returned to England for service in his native land, knowing that his days there would be numbered and would probably end in his punishment and death.

On his return to England he was evidently arrested again, for during three years he lay in prison with the sentence of death hanging over him. He must have been subsequently liberated for he spent his last days in the house of a Catholic nobleman. The accounts of his last years are vague and uncertain. It has, however, been recorded that he foresaw and named the day and hour of his death, the Feast of St. John the Evangelist, December 27, 1656. On that day, though not more ill than usual, he insisted upon receiving the last Sacraments of the Church, and about sunset breathed his last in London, in the 78th year of his age.

It was not until three years ago that a memorial was raised in this country to commemorate the lives and services of Father White and his co-workers, Father Altham and Brother Gervase who came over with him on the *Ark* and the *Dove*. This is known as the Father White Memorial and stands on the bank of St. Mary's River, opposite and overlooking the site of old St. Mary's City. It is on a plot of two acres, a part of the manor of Abel Snow, one of the early Catholic settlers. The land was the gift of Mr. and Mrs. Warren Dunbar of St. Mary's. The monument consists of a stone altar, semicircular in shape, with brick wings extending on either side. Inserted in each of these, and arranged in the form of a cross, are bricks from the old Catholic chapel of St. Mary's. The inscription in gold letters on the face of the altar reads: "Andrew White, John Altham, Thomas Gervase and their companions of the Society of Jesus, pioneer missioners in the colony of Maryland. A tribute from the Pilgrims of St. Mary's."

The memorial was designed by Christopher L. LaFarge, of LaFarge and Son, of New York, whose uncle, Father John LaFarge, was largely instrumental in having the memorial erected. It is the gift of the Washington Chapter of the Pilgrims of St. Mary's.

CHAPTER X

THE JESUIT–BALTIMORE CONTROVERSY

THERE has been no chapter of Maryland history that has been more misinterpreted than the controversy which arose between the Jesuit missionaries and the second Lord Baltimore relating to land holdings. The Jesuits have invariably been placed in a false light and the yielding of their claims has usually been interpreted as establishing separation of state and church. As a matter of fact the final result of the controversy meant nothing of the kind. There had been separation of state and church from the very beginning. The agreement finally entered into and which closed the controversy, merely removed one great source of danger to Lord Baltimore and prevented the Society of Jesus from establishing permanent institutions of religion and education on the basis of a principle which has been recognized in this country since its early days.

The controversy originated in the acceptance of gifts of lands to the Jesuits from the Indians. The natives were grateful for all that the missionaries had done for them and for their many acts of mercy and kindness. To show their gratitude they turned over to the Jesuits several large tracts of land. The Jesuits did not anticipate that there would be any objection to their holding these lands, and built several mission stations upon them. Although Lord Baltimore claimed these same lands by royal grant under the charter, there had been some recognition of the rights of the Indians. There was a purchase from the natives of the land at St. Mary's when the first settlement was made.

This raised the question which was always a troublesome one in the colonies, whether title to land should be acquired from the Indians, or by grant from the holders of the royal charter. Lord Baltimore was legally justified in his claim that no one should acquire title except through him, while on the other hand, there was some justice in the claim of the Jesuits that they should be allowed to hold the lands which the Indians had turned over to them to better enable them to carry on their missionary work.

No provision was made for the support of the Jesuit fathers, and they were obliged to look to the lands which were given them under the original conditions of plantation for their only means of support. Under these conditions each settler was allotted an acreage proportionate to the number of men he brought with him. The Jesuits who came in under these terms were entitled to not less than 28,500 acreas. Of this, however, they claimed only 8,000 acres. The title was taken in the name of Father Copley in consideration of his bringing fifty persons into the province. These lands he held for the use of the Society of Jesus.

Father Copley, in a letter to Lord Baltimore, called attention to the fact that the Jesuits would never be able to pay the rent of twenty shillings for every thousand acres and besides furnish fifteen freemen in case of war or hostilities with the Indians. The burden of his claim was that lands held solely for religious and educational purposes should not be subject to the burden of assessment and taxation.

The statutes against mortmain in force in England at the time, which abolished the right of religious persons or societies to hold property in perpetuity, came into the controversy. The first Lord Baltimore, who drafted the Royal Charter, clearly intended that the English strictures against disposition of lands to charitable and religious uses should not apply to Maryland. The mortmain laws were wholly English, being dictated by local policy, and did not extend to Scotland, Ireland or the colonies.

Under Section XVIII Lord Baltimore and his heirs were given the right to convey property to any persons willing to purchase the same "to have and to hold" to such persons and their heirs and assigns in fee simple or fee tail and for term of life, lives or years. Later followed the abrogating clause in these words:

> The Statute Quia Emptores Terrarum heretofore published in our Kingdom of England or any other statute, act, ordinance, usage, law or custom or any other thing, cause or matter to the contrary thereof, heretofore had, done, published, ordained or provided to the contrary thereof notwithstanding.

In discussions of this kind it is well to go back to original sources. The Statute Quia Emptores Terrarum was passed during the reign of Edward I, son of Henry III. Section III and reads as follows:

> No feoffment shall be made to assure land in mortmain. And it is to be understood that by the said sales or purchases of lands or tenements or any parcels of them, such lands or tenements shall in no wise come into mortmain either in part or in whole, neither by policy nor craft contrary to the form of the statute made thereupon of late, and it is, to wit, that this statute extendeth but only to lands holden in fee simple and that it extendeth to the time coming and it shall begin to take effect at the feast of Saint Andrew the Apostle next coming.[1]

The language of this statute as above quoted should remove any doubt as to the intention of the first Lord Baltimore in drafting Section XVIII of the Charter.

Cecil Calvert's directions as to the ownership of land were contained in the conditions of plantation issued in 1641. There were two conditions that do not appear in the record, but have been preserved in the archives of the Jesuit Society at Stonyhurst. Whether they were published in the province or not, is not known. These conditions provided that no corporation, fraternity or political body, ecclesiastical or lay, should have the power of acquiring or enjoying any lands in Maryland, either immediately or held in trust for them, with-

[1] Volume I, *Great Britain Statutes at Large from Magna Charta to the End of the Reign of King Henry VI,* Runnington edition, p. 122.

out special license in each case; and that no person should give or alienate any lands or tenements to any such society or to trustees for its use, "for any of the uses prohibited in the statute of mortmain, without special license from the proprietary." The second Lord Proprietary either overlooked or deliberately disregarded the provision in the charter expressly exempting conveyances of land from the statute of mortmain.

In this dispute Leonard Calvert had sided with the Jesuits, for which he was taken severely to task by his brother. In a letter written to him in November of 1642, Baltimore called attention to certain grants of lands to the missionaries approved by the governor. These were lands at St. Inigoes and St. Mary's, and also a tract of a hundred acres near the Indian mission at Piscataway.

Captain Cornwaleys also supported the Jesuits in the controversy and championed their cause even more vigorously than did Governor Calvert. He wrote a letter to Lord Baltimore calling attention to the fact the new laws violated the liberties of the church and stated, "Your Lordship knows that my security of conscience was the first condition I expected from this government." [2]

The missionaries were well within their rights when they attempted to justify their land holdings. They were not attempting to place themselves above the law; for under the Maryland charter there was nothing that prohibited the holding of estates in perpetuity, and they recognized no principle of justice in the English strictures against mortmain. It must have been plain to them, as apparently it was not to Cecil Calvert, that the first Lord Baltimore did not intend to have the statute against mortmain enforced in his colony.

In his letters to his brother, Baltimore expressed himself

[2] Browne, *Calverts,* 108. This statement by Cornwaleys is strongly indicative of the fact that the recognition of "security of conscience" was made known to the first settlers before the sailing of the *Ark* and the *Dove*.

very forcibly in the matter of the claims of the Jesuit missionaries. At times he used harsh language and made accusations which were wholly unwarranted. He wrote as a man out of patience, and as a man would write who had cares and worries which others did not understand. At one time he was so exasperated that he went so far as to petition the Sacred Congregation of the Propagation of the Faith to grant a prefect and secular priests to take charge of the Maryland mission. Two secular priests did come from England in 1642, one of them arriving on the same ship that first brought Ingle to Maryland. These priests were Fathers Gilmett and Territt.

Baltimore had expected that the secular priests would not uphold the claims of the missionaries, but it so turned out later that they both took sides with the missionaries.[3] He finally changed his mind about sending secular priests to take the places of the Jesuits. There has been a false impression that the Jesuits objected to the sending of secular priests to Maryland. The only objection they raised was confined to other priests being substituted for them and taking over their work. Their attitude is explained in the following from a letter which one of the fathers wrote to the English provincial:

> The Fathers do not refuse to make way for other labourers, but they humbly submit for consideration, whether it is expedient to remove those who first entered into that vineyard at their own expense, who for seven years have endured want and suffering, who have lost four of their confrères, labouring faithfully unto death, who have defended sound doctrines and the liberty of church with odium and temporal loss to themselves; who are learned in the language of the Savages, of which the priests to be substituted by the Baron Baltimore are entirely ignorant, and from which it must needs be that contentions and scandals should arise and the spark of faith be extinguished which begins to be kindled in the breast of the infidels.

Historians have said that there was much mystery surrounding this controversy but the mystery, if any there be,

[3] Hughes, op. cit., I, 538.

is cleared by a single passage in Baltimore's letter to his brother, which revealed the reason for his attitude. He wrote:

And for aught you know some accident might have happened here that it was no injustice in me to refuse them grants of land at all and that by reason of some act of this state it might have endangered my life and fortune to have permitted them to have had any grants at all; which I do not, I assure you, mention without good ground.[4]

The "act of this state" which he refers to was an act passed in 1585 during the reign of Elizabeth, and reenacted in 1604 during the reign of James. This act was allowed to remain on the statute books of England for years, and was never finally repealed until the reign of Queen Victoria. It provided that all Jesuits must leave the realm of England within forty days after the end of the session of Parliament and any remaining or any returning after the expiration of forty days must suffer death. In the fourth clause of this act is the following:

And every person which after the end of the same forty days as before limited and appointed shall wittingly and willingly receive, relieve, comfort, and maintain any such Jesuit, seminary priests or other priests, deacon or religious or ecclesiastical person as is aforesaid being at liberty or out of hold, knowing him to be a Jesuit, seminary priest or other such priest, deacon or religious or ecclesiastical person, as is aforesaid, shall also for such offence be adjudged a felon without benefit of clergy and suffer death, loss and forfeit as in the case of one attainted of felony.[5]

This law hung over the head of Cecil Calvert like the sword of Damocles. One need only to look at the constantly shifting panorama of English history to realize the very real danger that faced him. The civil war between King and Parliament had begun. Only the month previous King Charles had left London, never to return except as a prisoner. If the parliamentary party gained control of the government

[4] Browne, *Calverts*, 122-3.
[5] Pickering, *English Statutes at Large*, VI, 349-50.

Lord Baltimore had every reason to believe that this law would be enforced. When it had been enforced before, both in the reign of Elizabeth and during the early part of the reign of James, full two hundred Catholics had suffered death, one hundred and twenty-four being executed for exercising the priestly functions and the others for becoming reconciled to the Catholic faith or for aiding or assisting priests.[6]

Father White had been one of the Jesuit priests banished from England under the terms of this very act. Was it any wonder, then, that Lord Baltimore feared for his life if it became known to his enemies that he was giving aid, comfort and maintenance to a Jesuit priest who had been exiled from England, and to others of his order? The year previous, Lord Baltimore's staunchest friend at court, and his father's old friend, Wentworth, the Earl of Strafford, had gone to the block, having been brought to trial on a bill of attainder in order to placate the Puritan party. Within the year the great rebellion had broken out in Ireland and the Parliamentary party was eager to punish the Irish because they were Roman Catholics.

How Baltimore sensed his danger and feared the result of his letters falling into the hands of his enemies is shown by his never referring to the Jesuits by any name by which it would be known he was having any dealings with them. He always refers to them as "those of the hill" and Father White he refers to as "Mr. White." In March of 1643, there is a record of Lord Baltimore being cited before the House of Lords and placed under bonds not to leave the kingdom. The reason for this does not appear, but it emphasizes the danger that confronted him during this period. He was several times accused of maintaining a seminary for Jesuits in Maryland, and if this were so it might have cost him his life.

[6] Butler, *Historical Memoirs of the English Catholics*, I, 174.

Little realization of his danger came to the Jesuit fathers who were so eager and zealous in their work in the fields and forests of Maryland that they gave little heed to happenings in England. Communication of news in those days came over at rare intervals and sometimes there might intervene several months between the happening of an event in England and the receipt of information in the colonies.

The failure of the Jesuits to properly interpret the news that was received, and to sense the dangers that confronted Lord Baltimore, only exasperated him the more and to some extent accounts for the hostile tone of some of his letters. Adding to his troubles and exasperations was the fact that some of the ladies in his own household were taking the part of the Jesuits, for he writes to his brother of a "bitter falling out between my sister Peaseley and me" because of her sympathy for the missionaries.

There was at least one man in the Society of Jesus who sensed the danger in the situation and that was Father Henry Moore, provincial of the order in England. He was in England at the time and fully realized that the missionaries would have to sacrifice their land holdings. He prepared and had executed a release in full of all lands acquired and all right to acquire lands from the Indians and all domains held in the province either by Indian grant or by grant to any person for the use of the society. The Jesuit fathers gave up their lands and no lands were ever possessed by them or given to them except the plot for their burial. "Give us souls," wrote the Vicar General, "and he can have the rest."

In the terms of settlement it is set forth that the continued holdings of lands by the Jesuits would tend "to the destruction of his Lordship and his heirs and their royal jurisdiction over and in the province so dearly purchased by His Lordship as aforesaid and consequently be offensive to the crown of England," and recites that Lord Baltimore "is already at very great charge and hath and doth daily undergo very great hazards and trouble both in his person and in his estates principally for the Propagation of the Christian faith in those parts and the welfare of the people having no temporal gain or profit to himself from thence as yet."

The loss of its lands was now added to the already great handicap which the mission had to bear. Of the ten missionaries who came to the Maryland colony in the first decade of its history, eight died on the mission field within the space of six years from the time of their arrival, and two were sent back in chains to England. All had come to America in high hopes and eager for the harvest of souls, to have their careers cut short by the hardship of their lot or the persecution of their enemies. The harvest was plenteous, but the laborers were few. This was not by reason of any unwillingness to answer the call, but because all those who were willing to go could not be sent, due to conditions in England and the lack of the support that the mission sorely needed.

How eager many of the young English Jesuits were to be sent to the American fields is shown in the many requests that were made for assignments. Father Hughes records that no less than eighteen young priests and two lay brothers applied for the Maryland mission, whose requests could not be granted.

The hardships of the mission, deprived as it was of even enough support to provide at times for the bare necessities of life, is shown in the letters written by Father Brooke at the time he was superior of the mission. In 1640 he wrote: "On account of the dearness of the supplies, we are sorely pinched, our expenses being increased and the resources failing us whereon we should live." And in 1641 he wrote: "For my own part I should prefer to work here among the Indians for their conversion and destitute of all human aid and reduced to hunger, to die lying on the bare ground under the open sky, than even once to think of abandoning this holy work of God, through any fear of privation." [7] This letter

[7] Hughes, op. cit., I, 476.

was written only a short time before Father Brooke met his death while crossing the St. Mary's River.

Much light has been thrown on the Jesuit-Baltimore controversy by an article on this subject by Rev. John LaFarge, S.J., associate editor of *America,* in the March 1930 number of *Thought.* Father LaFarge makes it clear that the Jesuit Missionaries in asking the privilege of holding lands for charitable and educational purposes were laying the foundations for what in later years became "the actual source of the highest type of progress in modern times." The wisdom and need of such foundations, he points out, have been unquestioned in this country "from the time of John Harvard down." And, had it not been for the restrictions imposed by Lord Baltimore, "the history of Catholic education might have had an extra year to its credit in the American colonies."

It was the intention of Father White to establish a Jesuit college at St. Mary's, but the lack of material support from which the mission suffered, followed by his forced return to England, prevented the attainment of his ambition. The early mission priests had little time to give to the work of education, but within ten years from the time of Father White's banishment there is found evidence of educational work being carried on by the mission. In his history *The Jesuits and Education* Father William McGucken, S.J., of St. Louis University says that it is worthy of note that despite difficulties "Maryland Jesuits never entirely abandoned the project of establishing a school in the colony and actually made several attempts to provide the sons of the Catholic gentry with Jesuit schoolmasters."

A school was being conducted under Jesuit auspices as early as 1650. In 1653 Edward Cotton, a wealthy Catholic planter, left in his will the bulk of his estate for the endowment of a Catholic school in Newton. Father McGucken says that this was the first bequest in Maryland and "certainly the first in the colonies in behalf of Catholic education." [8]

[8] Op. cit., 48.

To the little Maryland mission belongs the distinction of founding the first Jesuit mission within the limits of the United States, a mission which has been continued with hardly a break until the present time and constitutes the present Maryland-New York Province.

CHAPTER XI

GOVERNOR LEONARD CALVERT

VIRGINIA changed front in the "Plundering Time" and became friendly with her Maryland neighbors. The Virginians had no sympathy with the parliamentary party and disapproved of the depredations of Ingle's band. Governor Leonard Calvert, who had found a safe refuge in Virginia, was able to gather an armed force and in the early spring of 1646 returned to Maryland and took St. Mary's by surprise. He was soon in complete possession of the province. Protestants joined with Catholics in welcoming the governor back to his domain. Edward Hill, who had come from Virginia to Maryland, was either commissioned or elected governor during Governor Calvert's absence, and attempted to maintain some kind of a government which was apparently not opposed by Ingle or his following. When Calvert entered St. Mary's he deposed Hill and made prisoners of the assembly. An amicable arrangement was then made whereby Hill received some compensation for his services and retired to Virginia. No action was taken against his followers, and in fact Governor Calvert continued the assembly without issuing a summons for a new election.

At a session of this assembly held at St. Inigoes in January of 1647, the governor issued a pardon for all who had taken part in the rebellion with the exception of Ingle and his chief lieutenant Durford. This assembly was the first to sit as a bicameral body with an upper and lower house. The record in the archives shows testimony given that the Governor, after coming from Virginia, declared that if he found the inhabitants of St. Mary's had accepted his pardon for their former rebellion and were in obedience to the government, the soldiers were to expect no pillage and he would receive the inhabitants in peace. This was given in a deposition signed by six freemen. There is a further entry that the Governor declared to the burgesses, whom he had sent for, that they were called as freemen to consider and advise in assembly "touching all matters as freely and boldly without any awe or fear and with the same liberty as at any assembly that they might have done heretofore and that they were now free of all restraints of their persons." The only law passed was "An Act touching Judicature." [1]

The last act of Governor Calvert was to issue a commission for the command of Kent Island to Robert Vaughn, under date of May 31, 1647. The return of the governor to St. Mary's was wholly unexpected to Claiborne. There was no one now to do his fighting for him, so letting valor give way to discretion, he decamped, but to return once more when trouble came again.

Leonard Calvert was a comparatively young man when he died at St. Mary's, June 6, 1647. The exact date of his birth is not known. His elder brother, the second Lord Baltimore, was born in 1606. If it is to be assumed that he was not more than a year younger than Cecil, he was only twenty-six when he led the voyage to Maryland on the *Ark* and the *Dove,* and only forty years of age when he died. His term as governor was a little less than fourteen years. These were trying years for the colony and its young governor. In the face of many difficulties he showed a firm determination to carry out the high purposes and ideals of his father. Notwithstanding that it was mainly his duty to execute the orders of his brother, depending upon him in the more weighty matters that concerned the government of the colony, there were times when by reason of the slow means of communication, heavy responsibility rested upon him, and he had to use his own discretion and judgment in many perplexing situations. It must be admitted that because of his closer contact with

[1] *Archives,* I, 210.

LEONARD CALVERT, FIRST GOVERNOR OF THE PROVINCE OF MARYLAND

the Jesuit missionaries and his better understanding of the work they were doing, his judgment of them was wiser and his treatment of them more just than that shown by his brother.

The irrepressible Claiborne gave him many vexing problems to solve and to solve quickly. A letter written by Governor Calvert to his brother in 1638, reveals how he used every fair means to placate Claiborne and his followers, offering them every inducement to become friendly subjects, and even after they had made armed resistance, granting a general pardon and inviting the inhabitants of Kent Island to make free choice of delegates for the General Assembly at St. Mary's.[2]

He was wholly unselfish and did nothing for his own profit. When he died, his personal estate amounted to but one hundred and ten pounds sterling. Outside of the real estate which he held through deed from his brother, this small personal estate was all that he had been able to save for himself after thirteen years of faithful service to the colony. He was a good servant of his people.

By his will, Governor Calvert appointed Thomas Greene his successor in office, and his kinswoman, Mistress Margaret Brent, he made executrix of his estate. In view of subsequent occurrences, Browne in his *History of Maryland* says if he had reversed his testamentary dispositions and made Greene his executor and Mistress Brent governor, it would have been on the whole a better arrangement.

Of Mistress Margaret Brent there is much that can be said to her credit. She was a woman of such good sense and marked ability that she stands out clearly as one of the leading figures in Maryland's early history. She came to the colony in 1638 with her sister, Mary, bringing over nine colonists. They brought more settlers later and managed their affairs so well that they contributed materially to the growth of the colony.

2 Hall, *Narratives of Early Maryland,* 150.

The Brent sisters were relatives of the Calvert family. Their brother, Giles Brent, was made acting governor of the colony while Leonard Calvert was absent in England during the rebellion. Margaret's activities in the management of her own and her sister's affairs, as representatives of her brother, and as executrix of Leonard Calvert, are shown in the colonial records no less than one hundred and twenty-four times from 1642 to 1650.[3]

Nuncupative or oral wills made in anticipation of death were legal in Maryland. Leonard Calvert on his death-bed in the presence of witnesses designated Margaret Brent to be his "sole executrix" with the terse instruction to "take all and pay all." In the probate records admitting the will the name of the executrix appears as "Margaret Brent Gent."

> Indeed who but a gentleman could administer the affairs of a deceased governor? There was no person in Maryland more powerful than Margaret Brent who with her sister, was the owner of the Sister's Freehold, who was Lady of Fort Kent Manor and who by the will of Leonard Calvert had become the Lady of St. Gabriel's and Trinity Manors. Only a superwoman could have performed the tasks that were Margaret Brent's from that day forward.[4]

In securing the services of the soldiers from Virginia who wrested the control of the colony from Ingle, Governor Calvert had pledged his own and his brother's estates for their pay. He died before he could redeem his pledge. When the soldiers did not receive their pay they were on the point of mutiny. Captain Hill, who had been ousted as acting governor, had established headquarters across the Potomac River awaiting an opportunity to lead his forces into Maryland again. A mutiny at this time would have endangered the safety and peace of the colony and brought on again the dark days of the "Plundering Time." Greene, the new governor, seemed to be powerless to act in this emergency and

[3] Andrews, *History of Maryland,* 88.

[4] Endora Ramsay Richardson, on "Margaret Brent, Gent" in *Thought,* March, 1933.

the quick wit of Margaret Brent, executrix of Governor Calvert, saved the situation. She sensed the danger and made a distribution of such of the governor's property as was available and then sold enough of Lord Baltimore's cattle to complete the arrears. She had only authority to handle the affairs of the late governor, so she appeared before the council and claimed that as Governor Calvert had acted as his brother's representative and attorney that she, as his executrix, should be declared Lord Baltimore's attorney until someone else should be appointed by the proprietary.

Governor Greene, Leonard Calvert's death-bed appointee, was unwilling to take upon himself the responsibility of naming a woman to such a position and she appealed to her brother, Giles Brent, a member of the council. Brent replied that his sister should be looked upon as "His Lordship's attorney" for recovering rights, paying debts out of the estate and of taking care of the preservation of the estate "but not further." Thereupon the governor decreed that the "executrix of Leonard Calvert aforesaid shall be received as his Lordship's attorney to the intents stated by Mr. Giles Brent." [5]

It seems that Lord Baltimore, not being in possession of all the facts and apparently not cognizant of his brother's pledge, took exception to the distraining of his cattle. The assembly of Maryland came to the support of Mistress Brent. In a forcibly worded resolution the assembly informed Lord Baltimore that the affairs of the colony were better in Margaret Brent's hands than "in any man's else in the whole province" after the death of Governor Calvert. The soldiers would never have treated anyone else with the same courtesy and respect, and although they were ready for mutiny, she pacified them and had she not been "your Lordship's attorney by an order of court" the result would have been ruinous for the colony.[6]

[5] *Archives,* IV, 313-314.
[6] *Archives,* I, 238.

In the proceedings of the Assembly of February 29, 1648, is found an entry which indicates that Margaret used her own funds to settle some of the soldiers' claims. William Whitle, Stannop Roberts, and William Hungerford petitioned for themselves and several soldiers against the estate of Margaret Brent for their wages. "And the Mistress Margaret Brent promised to send down to Virginia with all speed ready tobacco to be procured by her to buy provisions of diet of them most importuned and desired by them." [7]

It was not until August of 1650 that Lord Baltimore sent his confirmation of the sale of his "neat cattle and personal estate."

Margaret Brent legally adopted the daughter of the chieftain of one of the friendly Indian tribes who had been converted by Father White. The child had been given the Christian name of Mary Brent Kittamaqund. The converted chieftain, contrary to the custom of his people, named his daughter as heiress to all his lands, whereupon Giles Brent, old enough to be her father, married her. If he had had any idea that his bride would have a rich inheritance he was doomed to disappointment, for Lord Baltimore refused to recognize her right to hold title to her father's lands. Some years later Margaret, looking after the interests of the children of Leonard Calvert, was successful, after having recourse to the courts, in restoring to William Calvert, one of the sons, the house at St. Mary's which had been the home of the former governor.

Mistress Brent has been described as "America's first woman suffragist." It does not appear that she had any advanced ideas about the rights of women to vote, but she did ask to be allowed to vote in the assembly of freemen, acting as attorney for Lord Baltimore, and as executrix for Governor Calvert, and so she was the first woman in America to demand a vote. The following is the assembly record of this historic incident:

[7] Andrews, op. cit., 89.

Came Mrs. Margaret Brent and requested to have vote in the house for herself and voice also; for that at the last court 3rd January, it was ordered that the said Mrs. Brent was to be looked and received as his Lordship's attorney. The governor denied that the said Mrs. Brent should have any vote in the house. And the said Mrs. Brent protested against all proceedings in this present assembly unless she may be present and have a vote aforesaid.[8]

She was never given the right to vote and it does not appear that she did more than make a formal protest against being denied that privilege.

The mortal remains of Maryland's first governor lie in an unknown grave and here again is a Calvert suffering the fate of Moses for "no man knoweth his sepulchre unto this day." A monument has been erected at St. Mary's to his memory, and on the south front is the following inscription:

By his wisdom, justice and fidelity he fostered the infancy of the colony, guided it through great perils and dying left it in peace. The descendants and successors of the men he governed here record their grateful recognition of his virtues.

Governor Calvert's thirteen years of rule mark the period when the growth of democratic institutions was nurtured and fostered and when Maryland became the most typically American of all the colonies on the Atlantic seaboard. While there were occasions when his policies and recommendations were opposed by the freemen yet he was seldom insistent in using his prerogatives and invariably respected the expression of the democratic spirit shown in the action of the various assemblies he called. His frequent resort to the calling of the entire electorate of the colony to enact legislation was his greatest contribution to the work of government that was accomplished in the early and formative years. He did his part and did it well.[9]

8 *Archives* I, 215—the prefix "Mrs." is used although she was not a married woman.

9 Helen Ainslie Smith in her *Thirteen Colonies* (II, 116), says of Leonard Calvert: "His thirteen years in America had been occupied, not for his own profit, but in establishing the most enlightened and rapidly successful colony of his time, already ranking with the best on the coast."

CHAPTER XII

AN ACT CONCERNING RELIGION

IN THE year 1649 there was passed by the Maryland Assembly the so-called Religious Toleration Act. The correct title was "An Act Concerning Religion." Altogether too much importance and emphasis have been given to this law. It was more narrow and restricted and far less liberal than the policy of the Lords Baltimore which had been adopted and followed by the Governor and freemen of the colony since the voyage of the *Ark* and the *Dove*.

Maryland's claim to priority in the field of religious liberty most certainly cannot be based on this law. Religious liberty was not established in Maryland by the force of any law, much less by this one. Unless the spirit of good-will had governed and ruled the founders and early settlers of Maryland no law would have been of any avail. Laws can easily be disregarded and as easily repealed. Even this act concerning religion was repealed by a rump assembly of Puritans soon after it was enacted, reenacted again when the rule of Lord Baltimore was restored, only to be subsequently repealed after the Protestant Revolution of 1688.

The act began with ordaining death and confiscation of estate for blasphemy and denial of the doctrine of the Holy Trinity. This bears a strong resemblance to the opening provisions of a law passed by the long parliament in 1648 entitled "An act for the Punishment of Blasphemies and Heresies." [1] It was the Presbyterian party then in control of parliament that sponsored this measure. Green says it was

[1] *Acts and Ordinances of the Interregnum,* Firth & Rait, I, 1133.

"the fiercest blow at religious freedom which it had ever received." [2]

The English act provided that any man who asserted that "the Father is not God, or that the Son is not God, that the Holy Ghost is not God, or that the three are not Eternal God" should suffer the pain of death. In the Maryland act is found the provision that any person who shall deny "our Saviour to be the son of God, or shall deny the Holy Trinity, the Father, Son and Holy Ghost, or the Godhead of any of the said Three Persons of the Trinity or the Unity of the Godhead" should be punished with death and his estate forfeited. The similarity ceases with the first paragraph. While the Parliamentary act went on to provide penalties for denying the tenets of Calvinistic theology, including predestination, and for declaring, among a long list of other errors, that there was a purgatory and that images were lawful, the Maryland act provided that any one who uttered "reproachful words or speeches concerning the Blessed Virgin, the mother of our Saviour, or the Holy Apostles or Evangelists" should be fined, publicly whipped or imprisoned. This was followed by a prohibition against using in an offensive and reproachful manner the terms: "Heretic, Schismatic, Idolator, Puritan, Independent, Presbyterian, Popish priest, Jesuit, Papist, Lutheran, Calvinist, Anabaptist, Brownist, Antinomian, Barrowist, Roundhead and Separatist." This list included about every known sect and denomination existing at the time, the intent apparently being to avoid all religious controversy that the use of these terms would start in motion.

The fourth section of the Maryland act was plainly a concession to the Puritan element in the colony for it provided for a Puritan Sabbath, and imposed fines and penalties upon all who profaned or violated in any way the "Sabbath or Lord's Day called Sunday."

After making these concessions the act further provided:

[2] Op. cit., III, 246.

Whereas, the enforcing of the conscience in matters of religion hath frequently fallen out to be of dangerous consequences in those commonwealths where it hath been practised, and for the more quiet and peaceable government of this Province and the better to preserve mutual love and amity amongst the Inhabitants thereof: Be it therefore also by the Lord Proprietary, with the advice and consent of the Assembly, ordered and enacted (except as in this present act is before declared and set forth) that no person or persons whatever within this Province professing to believe in Jesus Christ shall from henceforth be anyways troubled, molested, or discountenanced for, or in respect to, his or her religion nor in the free exercise thereof within this province, or the islands thereunto belonging, nor in any way compelled to believe or exercise any other religion against his or her consent, so that they may be not unfaithful to the lord proprietary or molest or conspire against the civil government.[3]

It can readily be seen that this law was not an advance from what had been the practice and policy of the colony since the landing of the Pilgrims at St. Mary's. In some respects it was a step backward. Lord Baltimore would never have barred a Unitarian or a Jew from his colony, yet under the law there was no room for either. Nevertheless, as narrow as it was when judged in the light of the present day, it was exceedingly broad for the time in which it was enacted and far broader than the so-called toleration act of William and Mary forty years later.

There is no record of either the death penalty having been invoked for blasphemy or a fine ever having been imposed for violation of any of the provisions of the act. Under the mild forbearance of the Proprietary the first section of the act with its dire penalties became a dead letter.

It is not certain whether the act as finally adopted was in the form sent over by Lord Baltimore or whether it was changed and amended by the assembly itself. When he sent over the entire code of laws to be passed by the assembly of 1649 he specified that the laws should be passed "without alteration." The assembly in keeping with the democratic spirit of previous assemblies refused to comply with this re-

[3] *Archives,* I, 244.

quest and in a letter of protest bluntly told Lord Baltimore to "send over no more such bodies of laws." [4] The proposed code was rejected *in toto* and the assembly passed some nine acts including the Act concerning religion. That this act was not passed in the form sent over by Lord Baltimore but was changed and probably amplified by the assembly is indicated by the notation in the record that although it was passed April 21, 1649, and at once approved by Governor Stone in accordance with the power previously given him, it was not finally confirmed by Lord Baltimore until over a year later, August 26, 1650, "by an instrument under his hand and seal." [5]

The act was clearly a compromise and was intended by Lord Baltimore to continue and secure freedom of worship in the best manner and by the best methods possible. An attempt to placate both the Parliamentary and Puritan parties can be seen in the first four sections of the act. Recognizing that the majority of the freemen were Protestants, Lord Baltimore was now concerned with protecting his coreligionists as best he could in the exercise of a right which had never been denied to non-Catholics. He had already appointed William Stone, a Protestant, governor of the colony, and he gave the Protestants a majority in the council.

Baltimore was not only concerned by the trend of affairs in his colony, he also had to guide his course by events in England. No one at that time knew what the future of England was to be and he was sorely pressed to save the colony and preserve the principles that governed its foundation.[6] It is not surprising, therefore, that there is found in a measure prepared during this critical period, such a strange mixture of narrow and liberal provisions. It was not altogether such a law as he would have sponsored in ordinary times and

[4] Ibid, 238-243.

[5] Ibid, 244.

[6] After King Charles was beheaded in 1649 all of the property of Lord Baltimore was ordered seized. It does not appear that the order was ever carried out, but this shows the danger of the times. Pollen, "Baltimore House near Tisbury, Wiltshire" in *Catholic Historical Review,* III, 72.

under normal conditions nor would such a law in its entirety have been adopted by previous assemblies under the leadership of Thomas Cornwaleys.

Except as a compromise measure prepared in a period of stress and strain in an attempt to reconcile conflicting opinions and ideas and to salvage all that was possible of the old spirit of religious liberty in early Maryland, the act concerning religion is without historical significance or interest.[7]

[7] Matthew Page Andrews, in commenting on the Act of 1649, says that "it was but a delimiting expression forced upon the ideals or wishes of the Proprietary and the actual practices of the early settlers" and it was "the response to the threat of a powerful outside force inimical to the principles of toleration, and this force was, for awhile, held off by means of this enactment." *History of Maryland*, 93.

CHAPTER XIII

PURITAN INGRATITUDE

THE year the Act Concerning Religion was enacted saw the entry of Puritan intolerance into Maryland. In 1619 a small group of Puritans immigrated to Virginia. Other groups followed, and in 1642 their numbers had so increased that they sent to Massachusetts for additional ministers. They had a hard time of it after Governor Berkeley arrived, for he wanted no "preaching parsons" and believed that to tolerate Puritans was to resist the King. The ministers were forced to return to Massachusetts and were very glad to get back there. Berkeley soon found that while he had broken up formal church services, the Puritans resorted to private houses for worship. He then procured the passage of an act requiring "the governor and council to take care that all non-conformists be compelled to depart the colony with all conveniences." Soon after he invited the Puritans of Massachusetts to come to Maryland, Lord Baltimore sent a like invitation to the Puritans of Virginia, promising absolute freedom of worship. They did not accept the invitation at first, but when Berkeley began his persecution they thought better of it. In 1649 an advance body of three hundred Puritans came to Maryland. Those who remained behind feared that Catholics would be no better neighbors than the royalists. When in October the Virginia assembly declared that the beheading of the King was an act of treason which nobody could speak in defense of, under penalty of death, they decided to avail themselves of the Catholic sanctuary and before the end of the year the total Puritan population in Maryland increased to over a thousand.

With this large influx of Protestants there came a change

in Maryland, and it was not a change for the better. Lord Baltimore made every effort to satisfy the Puritan refugees and make them happy and contented in their new homes, but herein he was undertaking the impossible. Puritans could not be happy and contented unless they exercised the exclusive privilege of enjoying these felicities, barring all others from the state of contentment who did not agree with their theological views. This was their idea of religious liberty. Lord Baltimore not only gave them the right to worship as they pleased, he also gave them the right to vote, and in doing this, he made those of his own faith a minority party. Little could he have realized what the consequences were to be.

The year of the migration of the Puritans from Virginia to Maryland saw the execution of King Charles and the overthrow of the monarchy. The Puritans in Maryland now believed their time had come, and unmindful of any debt of gratitude to their benefactor, who had saved them from persecution, they began plotting to seize the colony which had afforded them a refuge. Soon there is to be pictured the basest act of ingratitude and intolerance in the annals of American history.

In England Lord Baltimore was trying to save his colony by acknowledging allegiance to the new Parliamentary government, but stories were coming to England that the Puritans were not safe under his rule and were not enjoying freedom of religion. In order to refute these claims there was drawn up in 1650 what is known as the *Protestant Declaration*. This was signed by Governor Stone, the Protestant councilors and burgesses and thirty-eight Protestant freemen who had been loyal to Lord Baltimore. The signers declared that they had enjoyed "all fitting and convenient freedom and liberty in the exercises of our religion under His Lordship's government and interest and that none of us are in any ways troubled or molested for or by reason thereof."

Then followed a series of events in rapid succession which finally resulted in the temporary overthrow of Lord Baltimore. Richard Bennett had become leader of the Puritan party in Virginia and Maryland, and now Claiborne bobbed up serenely, this time as the champion of the Puritan cause. Under the leadership of these two men, Virginia yielded to the Parliamentary government and Governor Berkeley resigned the governorship. Bennett became governor of the colony and Claiborne was restored to his old office as secretary of state. They now turned their attention to Maryland. Armed with commissions from Parliament and a frigate, they arrived at St. Mary's and demanded that Governor Stone and his council acknowledge the new Commonwealth of England. This request was at once granted. They demanded that all writs and warrants should run no longer in Lord Baltimore's name, but in the name of the "Keepers of the Liberty of England." This request was refused whereupon Governor Stone was removed from office and a provisional government established. This was in 1652. Stone, after a little delay, agreed to comply with the second request and was restored to office.

When in the next year Cromwell turned out the Rump Parliament, otherwise called the "Keepers of English Liberties," Governor Stone began issuing writs in the name of Lord Baltimore. Bennett and Claiborne returned to Maryland, again deposed Stone and placed the government in the hands of a Puritan council with William Fuller as its president. They issued writs for the election of an assembly and these writs provided that no Roman Catholic could either be elected as a burgess or vote at the election. In this way the house of assembly became unanimously Protestant.

In October of 1654 the Puritan rump assembly, for the first time in Maryland by force of law, enthroned bigotry and intolerance. An act was passed securing to all persons freedom of conscience *provided* such liberty were not extended to "popery, prelacy or licentiousness of opinion." Their idea of toleration was to tolerate no one but themselves. It is impossible to condone the action of these Puritans in their treatment of Lord Baltimore and his co-religionists who had given them homes and liberty. Cobb, in his *Rise of Religious Liberty in America,* says that the Maryland Puritan "played the part of a viper stinging the bosom that had warmed him and made the most disgraceful chapter in the history of Puritanism and religious liberty." [1]

The authority of Bennett and Claiborne expired with the Rump Parliament. Cromwell was now Lord Protector and on his own authority became assignee of the crown and successor of its rights and obligations. Baltimore's charter was therefore valid and intact and knowing that Cromwell recognized this he wrote to Stone to resume the government of the colony.

Flying the Baltimore colors of gold and black, Stone with one hundred and thirty loyal men, both Catholic and Protestant, attempted to surprise the rebels. They were overwhelmed by a force of twice their number, aided by the fire of the *Golden Lion,* an armed merchantman lying in the harbor of St. Mary's. This was the famous battle of the Severn fought on March 25, 1655. One-third of Stone's men lay dead or wounded on the field and as one of the Puritans exultingly recorded "their papist beads" were scattered broadcast. Stone himself was wounded. Although quarter was promised to all who surrendered, Stone and nine others were tried by drum-head court-martial and sentenced to be shot. Even an appeal to Cromwell as Protector was disallowed, and four were executed, all being Catholics. The Puritan soldiers refused to take the life of Governor Stone, and the intercession of the women caused the lives of the others to be spared. They were however kept in confinement and their estates were confiscated.

The Jesuit missionaries who had returned to the colony willing to face the dangers of Puritan control were able to escape to Virginia, but their lot as exiles there was well nigh unendurable. One of them wrote the following year:

[1] Page 378.

The governor and others surrendered on the assurance of their lives, but these conditions were treacherously violated and four of the prisoners were shot. The Virginians rushed into our house and demanded that the imposters, as they called them, should be given up to slaughter. By God's mercy the Fathers escaped, but their books and other property were seized. With the utmost hazard they escaped into Virginia where they still are, sorely straitened and barely able to sustain life; living in a little low hut, like a cistern or tomb.

Virginia Stone, the wife of Governor Stone, wrote a letter to Lord Baltimore telling of her troubles when her husband was imprisoned after being sentenced to be shot. The letter is in the possession of the Maryland Historical Society and a copy is printed in the *Narratives of Early Maryland*.[2] She gives the names of the four men who were shot and one of them was Captain William Lewis, the Catholic overseer of Captain Cornwaleys, who in 1638 was fined for interfering with the reading of Protestant sermons.

The Puritans felt confident of the support and approval of Cromwell in all that they had done. As he had waged ruthless war against the Roman Catholics in Ireland they reasoned they could easily count on his support for the manner in which they had turned on the Catholics of Maryland. They did not feel they were taking the slightest chance in their high-handed course. Great was their surprise and deep their chagrin when the Lord Protector of England sent back word that the persecution of Catholics must cease, that the former act of Religious Toleration must be reenacted and Lord Baltimore be restored to his rights.

The worst blow of all came when Cromwell curtly informed them "not to busy themselves about religion." He gave to them the same sensible advice that Lord Baltimore gave to the Pilgrims of St. Mary's when they set forth on their voyage to America.[3] As a result Baltimore was fully restored

[2] Page 265.

[3] There is reason to believe that Cromwell had become inclined to support the Maryland principle of religious liberty and believed that it should not be interfered with. See Andrews, *History of Maryland*, p. 7.

to his rights and Maryland came out of the dark shadows of bigotry and intolerance and once more became the land of sanctuary.

No sooner had Lord Baltimore been restored to his province, than he granted immunity to all offenders in the late rebellion, assuring them that they should have their lands or be permitted to leave the colony if they wished to do so. The Puritans had been given a whole county of the richest land which they had called "Providence." Few of them left. They knew that they would be better off in Maryland than in any other colony. They were restored to all the rights and privileges they had previously enjoyed, including the right to hold office. This was the most magnanimous act of Baltimore's life.

Captain Josias Fendall was appointed governor on the restoration, but Lord Baltimore made a mistake in this appointment. He had been favorably impressed by Fendall's active support of Governor Stone when the latter attempted to regain possession of the colonial government, and so he rewarded him with the appointment of governor, believing he could be trusted. Fendall turned out to be a traitor. He had hardly taken office when he began to plot secretly with some of the Puritan leaders with the intention of forming a commonwealth with himself as governor, holding his commission from the assembly rather than from the Lord Proprietary. The whole plot was nipped in the bud on the accession of King Charles II, who issued a proclamation commanding the magistrates, officers and subjects to recognize the rights and jurisdiction of Lord Baltimore in his province. Philip Calvert, a younger brother of Baltimore, was appointed governor in place of Fendall and as usual a general pardon was granted to all the plotters except Fendall and one John Hatch, both of whom were subsequently released.

In the negotiations between the Puritan commissioners and Lord Baltimore which settled the affairs of the province and turned it over to its rightful Proprietor, the Puritans were far more concerned regarding the agreement pertaining to property and the validity of past official acts than they were respecting any guarantee of religious liberty. It was Baltimore who insisted on liberty of worship and in his instructions to the governor he stipulated the "Act concerning religion and passed heretofore with his Lordship's assent, whereby all persons who profess to believe in Jesus Christ have liberty of conscience and free exercise of their religion, be duly observed in the said province by all the inhabitants thereof." In the proposals of agreement signed November 30, 1657, he promised "that he will never give his assent to the repeal of a law established heretofore in Maryland by his Lordship's consent, whereby all persons professing to believe in Jesus Christ have freedom of conscience." [4]

There was no need for Baltimore to have given any such assurance, for law or no law, religious liberty under his rule would continue in Maryland. The Puritans apparently had no fear that Baltimore would change his policy for they did not think it necessary to have a clause guaranteeing religious liberty inserted in the terms of the final agreement. They were willing to take him at his word.

After Fendall's attempt to supplant Lord Baltimore had failed there was a long period of peace and tranquillity in the province. When there were no influences injected from outside sources there was always freedom from trouble and disaffection. No colony was better or more wisely governed than was Maryland when Lord Baltimore was able to administer its affairs without hindrance.

[4] *Archives,* III, 324-325.

CHAPTER XIV

A LAND OF SANCTUARY

HISTORY had little to record of the daily life of the colonists in times of peace and quiet. It was only during times of strain and stress that history left its record. There have been some letters preserved which were written during the period following the restoration of the colony to Lord Baltimore, by one of the humble folk who embarked for Maryland without being able to pay passage and so came as indentured servants. The name of this letter writer was George Alsop, a young English artisan.[1] His letters written home to his friends and relatives, were printed in London in 1666, and have been reprinted by the Maryland Historical Society. Alsop served, according to the customary indenture agreement, for four years upon the plantation of Thomas Stookett in Baltimore County. He described in his letters the lot of an indentured servant in Maryland as being both easy and alluring, and in marked contrast with the struggle for life among the poorer classes in London.

In one of these letters Alsop writes:

> He that desires to see the real platform of a quiet and sober government extant, superiority with a meek and yet commanding power sitting at the helm, steering the actions of state quietly, through the multitude and diversity of opinionous waves that diversely meet, let him look on Maryland with eyes admiring and he will then judge her the Miracle of this Age. Here the Roman Catholic and the Protestant Episcopal, whom the world would persuade, have proclaimed open wars irrevocably against each other, contrarywise concur in an unanimous parallel of friendship and inseparable love unto one another; all inquisition, martyrdom and banishments are not so much as named but unexpressibly abhorred by each other. The several opinions and

[1] Hall, op. cit., 338.

sects that lodge within this government meet not together in mutinous contempts to disquiet the power that bears rule, but with a reverend quietness obeys the legal commands of authority. And truly where a kingdom, state or government keeps or puts down the weeds of destructive opinions, there must certainly be a blessed harmony of quietness. And I really believe this land or government of Maryland may boast that she enjoys as much quietness from the disturbance of rebellious opinions as most states or kingdoms do in the world, for here every man lives quietly and follows his labor and employment desiredly.

The people he declares are free from the operation of "great and eating taxes," and "harboring places for criminals" are unknown. There is no delay of justice, trials are quickly ordered and soon completed and do not hold over for several terms of court. Consequently "if the lawyer had nothing else to maintain him but his bawling he might button up his Chops and burn his Buckrom bag or else hang it upon a pin until its antiquity had eaten it with dirt and dust."

In another letter he writes:

> Neither has youth his swing or range in such profuse and unbridled liberty as in other countries for the son works as well as the servant, so that before they eat their bread they are commonly taught how to earn it.

"I dwell now," he concludes in his final narrative, "by Providence in the Province of Maryland under the quiet government of Lord Baltimore which country abounds in a most glorious prosperity and has plenty of all things." Alsop was a man apparently of little education and some of his ideas are crudely expressed, but the truth of what he writes is supported by good authority.

Browne adds to this picture a reflection of domestic life which indicates the influence of the Catholic idea of the sanctity of the marriage relation:

> The family life was the center of all interest and devotion. As children grew up they helped to extend the area of cultivation or married and settled on the land. Poor relations were

prized as valuable members of the family which prospered the more it increased. The young penniless fellow who came over in 1634 by 1660 was a prosperous country gentleman, with broad acres around him, his son's farm girdling his own and his family connected by intermarriage with his neighbors for miles around. Nowhere was the marriage bond held in higher reverence than in Tidewater Maryland; and even now, Maryland is the only state in which no marriage is legally valid without some religious ceremony.[2]

In no other colony, not even Rhode Island, were there so many different sects living together in peace and harmony. On the authority of Bancroft:

> Emigrants arrived from every clime, and the colonial legislature extended its sympathies to many nations as well as to many sects. From France came Huguenots; from Germany, from Holland, from Sweden, from Finland, I believe from Piedmont, the children of misfortune sought protection under the tolerant scepter of the Roman Catholic. Bohemia itself, the country of Jerome Huss, sent forth its sons who at once were made citizens of Maryland with equal franchises.[3]

It was not long before the oppressed Quakers came to the Land of Sanctuary. The contrast between the principles and policies of Massachusetts Bay and early Catholic Maryland is not better shown than in the treatment accorded to the Quakers. The early Quakers had strange vagaries and bore little resemblance to the peaceful Friends of a later day but even so a little kindness would have made a different people of them. Persecution made them fanatical. They seemed to thrive on persecution and courted martyrdom. The short-sighted policy of the Puritan leaders afforded them both.

The story of Wenlock Christison is one of the brightest chapters in early Maryland history. He was one of the leading spirits of the Society of Friends, but not as fanatical as some of his brethren. He was however somewhat persistent in his desire to remain in Massachusetts, for which he suf-

[2] *Maryland, The History of a Palatinate*, 167.
[3] Op. cit., II, 236.

fered floggings and imprisonment. It is recorded that he suffered "twenty-seven cruel stripes on his naked body laid on with deliberation in the cold winter season." The jailer then robbed him of his waistcoat "in that cold time of the year when he was to pass through the wilderness," took his Bible for his fees and turned him loose. He foolishly returned and just after the four executions on Boston Common. On his return he went to the town-house, walked into the court room and with uplifted hands, with the air of a prophet, said "I am come to warn you that ye shed no more innocent blood." He was seized and sent off to jail. After three months he was brought to trial. Public resentment had been aroused to such an extent that the court had lost all heart for its work. He would have been acquitted had it not been for the fury of the stern Endicott who upbraided the judges for their weakness and pounding his fists on the table, shouted, "You that will not consent, record it. I thank God I am not afraid to give judgment." Here was the Puritan theocracy personified in a man who gloried in sitting on the seat of judgment. The other judges weakly submitted and Christison was sentenced to death. The sentence was never carried out. The tide had turned; the theocracy was tottering on its throne. The General Court yielded to public clamor and the law was modified.

Christison then went to Rhode Island, but for some reason he was not altogether happy in the colony of Roger Williams, and a few years later he came to his journey's end and found a safe refuge on the eastern shore of the Chesapeake in the "Land of Sanctuary." Here, after years of wandering and persecutions, being driven from one New England town to another "with many lashings" and after being sentenced to death, he established a happy home and very appropriately named it "The End of Controversie." In his home on the Chesapeake was held the first meeting of Friends of which there is any record in the colonies. Six years later he was elected a member of the Maryland House of Burgesses, for not only were the Quakers afforded sanctuary in Maryland, they were given the right to vote and to hold public office. There were other Quakers than Christison who held office in Maryland and also were appointed on important commissions.[4]

Some of the Quakers did cause trouble because of their refusal to take oaths, to doff their hats in court and to submit to bear arms for the common defense, and for these reasons Governor Fendall in 1659 issued an order that Quakers disturbing the peace should be whipped and banished from the colony. This order was never carried out as it was never sanctioned by Lord Baltimore. There was never any active persecution of the Quakers in Maryland.

After Fendall's régime every possible concession was made to the Quakers in order that they should be happy and contented in their new home. They were granted exemption from taking the oath, from taking off their hats in court and from military duty.

In 1672 the Quaker leader, George Fox, visited Maryland and was granted freedom of worship, being allowed to conduct his meetings wherever and whenever he wished. His diary which has been published in the annals of the Maryland Historical Society, records his activities, tells of his many conversions and of the largely attended meetings which he held, many of them being attended by the magistrates and leading men of the province. "The truth," he writes, "was received with reverence and gladness." There was no colony in America at this time, not even Rhode Island, where the Quakers were given greater freedom and greater rights and privileges than in Maryland, and here indeed for the oppressed Friend there was not only a land of sanctuary, but an end to all controversy.

During the last days of the Puritan régime a Jew had come to Maryland evidently not knowing that it was no longer a land of sanctuary and that there was a law against blasphem-

[4] Andrews, op. cit., 137.

ing the Holy Trinity, for which he could be put to death. His name was Jacob Lumbrozo, and he was a doctor. It is not known why he came, or where he came from, but fortunately for him, he came not long before the Puritan party lost control of the government and sanctuary was restored under the rule of Lord Baltimore.

Several zealous Puritans put their heads together when they discovered a Jew in their midst. As a result he was arrested and charged with blasphemy. The records in the case clearly show that he was deliberately trapped into making the admissions that led to his arrest. In modern police court parlance, he was the victim of a "frame-up." No Catholic sought his arrest nor made any complaint against him. Both of the complaining witnesses were Protestants. He was invited to the house of one Richard Preston who had taken an active part in the overthrow of the Baltimore government and was speaker of the Puritan assembly which repealed the religious toleration act and enacted the law disfranchising Catholics. The doctor was asked questions as to the divinity of Christ. He innocently replied that Christ was a man. Being then asked how he explained the miracles, he said that Christ performed the miracles by practising "art magic." The next day complaint was made against him. He was placed in custody of the sheriff until "he could put into security, body for body, to make answer to what should be had to his charge concerning these blasphemous words and speeches at ye next Provincial Court." The case came before the court on February 23, 1658. In his own defense, Dr. Lumbrozo admitted that he did have some talk with the witnesses, including Preston, who had testified against him, and answered "to some particular demands they urged," but "said not anything scoffingly or in derogation of him whom Christians acknowledge as their master." The case was finally dropped. The governor of the province at the time was the Roman Catholic Philip Calvert, brother of Lord Baltimore. Lumbrozo was released under a general proclamation of amnesty issued by Governor Calvert, and was allowed the quiet exercise of his religion. A few years later he sat on a jury with no objection being made to his faith. In 1663 he was made a naturalized citizen of the province with power to exercise the full rights of a citizen and to practise his profession. Here again it is shown that the spirit is greater than the law. Notwithstanding the law against blasphemy and the denial of the Holy Trinity, Maryland became the land of sanctuary for the Jew as well as for the Christian.[5]

Shortly before the execution of Charles I, a committee of Parliament held a secret meeting at which Lord Baltimore and several other prominent Catholics were present. A last effort was made to save Charles from himself. A message was sent to the King in prison that if he would recede from his stand and acknowledge that he had been in some measure wrong, they would save his life and if possible his crown. It is said that the association of Baltimore and other moderate Royalists with members of Parliament was meant as a guaranty of sincerity, but Charles was stubborn and the attempt was fruitless.[6]

After the execution of the king, his son and heir to the throne took refuge in the island of Jersey. He had already been proclaimed by the royalists as Charles II. Lord Baltimore, although he had been loyal to his King, wisely recognized the authority of the new parliamentary government. To have done otherwise would have meant the loss of his colony and the forfeiture of his charter. From his refuge Charles II granted a commission to the poet, Sir William Davenant, to proceed to Maryland, dispossess the proprietary and take over the government himself, justifying this action on the ground that Baltimore "doth visibly adhere to the rebels of England and admit all kinds of skismatics and sec-

[5] There is evidence that a Jew came over on the voyage of the *Ark* and the *Dove* as a redemptioner and later he was made a freeman, sat in the assembly of 1641, also that there were Jews or men of Jewish lineage among the first settlers. See Andrews, *The Founding of Maryland,* 156-7.

[6] Browne, op. cit., 72.

taries and other ill-affected persons into the said plantation of Maryland." The poet-governor never reached Maryland. He was captured by a parliamentary ship and thrown in prison. His life was saved by his fellow poet, John Milton. When he came to the throne ten years later Charles forgot this incident, confirmed the Maryland patent and recognized Lord Baltimore as proprietary.

In 1661 Charles Calvert, only son of Lord Baltimore, succeeded his uncle, Philip Calvert, as governor, the latter remaining as deputy governor. The assembly was organized into two houses, the governor, secretary and members of the council forming the upper house and the burgesses the lower. The members of the upper house could be expected to serve as a check on hasty legislation while the burgesses gave expression to the popular will. This system of government continued as long as the colony remained under the proprietary government.

In 1675 Cecil Calvert the second Lord Baltimore died without ever having had the opportunity of visiting his American colony. The outstanding achievement of his career was the fact that he was the first man in history to establish a form of government where all religious sects were absolutely equal before the law. For this alone he is entitled to immortal fame.[7]

[7] Non-Catholic historians have not failed to pay tribute to the second Lord Baltimore but perhaps no more deserved tribute was paid to him than by Dr. Hawkes in his *Rise and Progress of the Episcopal Church in Maryland,* where he said:

"The course of government in Maryland under Lord Baltimore has been truly described as one 'which tolerated all Christian churches and established none.' To one conversant with the history of the times and therefore but too familiar with many a bloody enactment elsewhere made, by which persecution was elevated into piety, it is refreshing to find in the bosom of a little colony, scarce known by name to the native of the old world, the blessed influence of a holier principle proving its goodness by its effects and presenting a picture from which the legislatures of ancient empires might have caught a lesson of wisdom and learned if not to condemn the wickedness of persecution, at least to avoid its folly."

CHAPTER XV

THE END OF CATHOLIC RULE IN MARYLAND

CHARLES CALVERT, who succeeded his father as Lord Proprietary and thereby became the third Lord Baltimore, did not prove in all respects as wise a ruler as his father. He was a bit too jealous of his prerogatives but when it came to the freedom of religion, his policy showed a scrupulous regard for the traditions of the House of Baltimore. A short time after his father's death he made a report to the Lords of Trade in answer to complaints that had been made by certain Anglican clergymen. In this letter he explained the reasons for the foundation of the colony:

> At the first planting of this Province by my father, albeit he had an absolute liberty given him and his heirs to carry thither any persons out of any of the dominions that belonged to the Crown of England who should be found willing to go thither; yet when he came to make use of this liberty he found very few who were inclined to go and seat themselves in those parts but such as for some reason or other could not live with ease in other places and of these a great part were such as could not conform in all particulars to the several laws of England relating to religion. Many there were of this sort of people who declared their willingness to go and plant themselves in this province so they might have a general toleration settled there by a law by which all sorts who professed Christianity in general might be at liberty to worship God in such manner as was most agreeable with their respective judgments and consciences, without being subject to any penalties whatsoever for their so doing, provided the civil peace were preserved; and which were generally observed to happen amongst such as differ in opinions, upon occasion of reproachful nicknames and reflecting upon each other's opinions, it might by the same law be made penal to give any offence in that kind. These were the conditions proposed by such as were willing to go and be the first planters of this Province and with-

out complying with these conditions, in all probability this Province had never been planted.[1]

Cecil Calvert had ruled the province for over forty years and his son was to rule for only fifteen years. Then was to come an end to the rule of the Catholic Lords Baron in Maryland. The Protestant Revolution of 1688 brought this about. Apparently the time was not ripe for making permanent the Baltimore program of religious freedom. It had come ahead of its time. It was so little understood that its overthrow was accomplished very easily.

Rumors of "popish plots" in the old country always reverberated in the colonies. When Titus Oates became a national hero because of his wild tale of a Catholic plot to assassinate King Charles II and turn the country over to the Jesuits there was a reaction in Maryland. Oates had been an Anabaptist preacher and then an Anglican clergyman and had been unfrocked by both denominations. Conceiving the idea of informing against the Catholics he pretended to become a Catholic convert and studied for the priesthood at Vallalodid and St. Omer's and was expelled from both institutions. He bore all the ear-marks of an imposter. His story, very apparently a pure fabrication, was swallowed at first by that class of Protestants who were over-credulous when it came to stories of Catholic conspiracies and eager to believe they were true. He was finally exposed and punished, but not before thirty-five innocent people had been judicially murdered.

At about the time of the first excitement over the so-called revelations of Oates the Reverend John Yeo came to Maryland. Being of the Anglican clergy he thought that a "living" would be very helpful, for with separation of state and church in the colony there was no government support for the ministers of the Church of England. So he wrote a letter to the Archbishop of Canterbury in which he stated many things which were not true and which he must have known were not true. Because there were only three Protestant ministers

[1] *Archives,* V, 267.

who conformed to the doctrine of the Church of England in the colony, religion was despised and all notorious vices committed so that it had become "a Sodom of wickedness and a pest house of iniquity." All historians now recognize the falsity of this assertion yet at the time it carried weight.

What Yeo was seeking was the establishment of the Church of England, and with the agitation against Catholics he thought it was a good time to bring it about. Lord Baltimore at once replied that all forms of Christian faith were tolerated and every denomination supported its own clergy, that the Protestant non-conformists outnumbered the Anglicans and Catholics by three to one and that to compel them to support clergy not of their own faith would be unjust. He showed that there were an adequate number of ministers of the Church of England to take care of the needs of what few Anglicans there were and that these had been given plantations of their own and were provided for in every way, that in every county there were churches and meeting houses for the Protestants and he further pointed out the difficulty in the way of inducing different denominations to consent to the support of a church other than their own.[2] This appeal despite its apparent justice fell on deaf ears. The Bishop of London, without taking the trouble to investigate the facts, reported to the Committee on Plantations that "the deplorable state of Maryland in regard to religion" was due to ministers of the Church of England being "utterly destitute of support whereby immorality reigned supreme." [3]

In refutation of the false report of Yeo the prominent and more respectable of the Protestants issued the declaration of May 13, 1682. Professing themselves to be Christians "according to the liturgy of the Church of England and Protestants against the doctrine and practice of the Church of Rome," they declared that they possessed "the free and public exercise of their religion whatsoever it be"; that they

[2] Ibid, 133.
[3] Chalmers, op. cit., 365.

enjoyed "in as full and ample manner as any of His Majesty's subjects in any part of His Majesty's dominions, the general freedom and privilege in their lives, liberties and estates according to the grand privileges of Magna Charta." They further declared:

> His Lordship's favors are impartially distributed and places of honor, trust and profit conferred on the most qualified for that purpose and service without any regard to the religion of the participants, of which generally and for the most part, it hath so happened that the Protestants have been the greatest number.[4]

Here was a complete repudiation of the calumnies of the Reverend Yeo, and further evidence of the fact that the freemen of Maryland were ever mindful that the original source of their rights and liberties was the Great Charter of England.

When Charles II died and his Catholic brother came to the throne as James II, Lord Baltimore had reason to hope that there would be an end to the petty opposition to his rule and policies, but if hope of this kind he had he was doomed to disappointment. Of the four Stuart kings, James II was the least friendly and gave the least support to the proprietary government of Maryland. In his brief reign of three years he did not evince the slightest interest in the cause of religious liberty in the Baltimore colony.

James, running true to the traditions of the Stuart dynasty, was opposed to granting political rights and privileges to his subjects anywhere. In the case of Maryland he was jealous of the palatine powers of Lord Baltimore and was determined to curb his independence and bring the colony into line with the other colonies under his direct control and subjection. In order to accomplish his purpose he was willing to sacrifice the rights of the Catholic proprietary and the comfort and well-being of the Catholic colonists.

In the last days of Charles II there was a threat of a writ

[4] *Archives*, V, 353.

of *quo warranto* against the royal charter of Maryland due to the pressure of some of the English churchmen and their desire for church establishment. Lord Baltimore, who had been in Maryland since the death of his father, returned to England to defend his rights. He probably would have been successful before the tolerant Charles but James gave ear to the appeals of the enemies of Baltimore, for they seemed to fit in for the moment with his colonial policy. In vain did the Maryland proprietary plead that his administration and that of his father had always been in strict conformity with the royal charter and that there was no just cause for declaration of a forfeiture. James gave orders for the writ to be issued but before this was done he was thrust from power. "In the whole story of American colonization," says Cobb, "there is nothing more preposterous and absurd than the outcry of lying Protestants in Maryland to a Catholic king and his readiness to listen." [5]

During the absence of Lord Baltimore in England, his enemies in Maryland had been busy. As there were no Catholic plots being imported at the time and the Titus Oates plot being a bit stale, resort was had to a plot of home manufacture. The old familiar "No Popery" cry was raised, and to give support to it a story was circulated of a plot to kill all the Protestants with the aid of hostile Indian tribes. Indian foot-prints were seen in the snow and this could only mean that the Catholics and Indians were in a conspiracy and that there would soon be a St. Bartholomew's Eve in Maryland. Help too was to be given by the French in Canada. All that was needed to fan the fire of insurrection was a story of this kind. No substantiation was needed to serve the purpose intended.

The story was investigated by some of the Protestants who had signed the previous declaration refuting Yeo's yarns and they declared all this alarm was nothing but "a sleeveless fear and imagination fomented by the artifice of some ill-minded

[5] Op. cit., 383.

persons who are studious and ready to take all occasions of raising disturbances for their own private and malicious interest." [6] This however did not have any effect on the trouble makers who were not at all interested in the truth or falsity of the reports.

John Coode who it is said had been both a Catholic and a Protestant, once a clergyman and now an atheist, was the originator of the story of the conspiracy and became the leader of the malcontents of the colony.

In 1688, James was forced to flee from England and William and Mary were proclaimed the rightful successors to the throne. Immediately Lord Baltimore, who was in England, sent a messenger to Maryland with an order to the Provincial Court to proclaim the new sovereigns. The messenger died on the voyage so while the other colonies were announcing allegiance to the new sovereigns Maryland was silent. Another messenger was sent but before he arrived the damage had been done. Coode was quick to take advantage of the situation. He sent an address to the new Protestant sovereigns extolling his own efforts to have their majesties proclaimed, and complained that Baltimore had failed to cause such proclamation to be made. He asked royal aid for the advancement of the Protestant cause, and followed this by organizing an "Association in Arms for the Defense of the Protestant Religion and assisting the rights of King William and Queen Mary."

A declaration of the reasons for the armed force was printed and circulated. In this were statements obviously false, but as the words "Papist" and "Jesuit" were used often and effectively they received full credence and fanned the fires of religious hatred to such an extent that Coode and his followers were able to oust the Baltimore officials and seize the colonial government. An assembly was called from which Catholics were excluded. To this assembly the freeholders of Calvert County headed by Sheriff Taney refused to send

[6] Andrews, op. cit., 179.

delegates, and embodied their reasons in a statement denying the charges of Coode. For this act of independence, Taney was put in jail. The minds of the members of the assembly according to Cobb were "completely filled by their frantic hatred of Roman Catholics and they kept dinning the King's ears with their insane bellowings." Not only were Catholics imprisoned but also Protestants who refused to support Coode and denied his charges against Lord Baltimore, the Catholics and the Jesuit missionaries, well knowing they were not true.

In 1690, the attorney general was instructed to proceed against the charter in an action of *scire facias.* As this would take time, and as King William was impatient to do something for his Protestant subjects, he appealed to the Chief Justice to know if he could not at once take over the colonial government. The Chief Justice said it would be better to wait until a hearing was held to determine if there were any grounds for a forfeiture of the charter, but if the case was urgent the King might take over the government and investigate afterwards.

So on this questionable advice King William seized the colony, and in August of 1691 Sir Lionel Copley was made the first royal governor of Maryland. The Commissioners of the Privy Seal doubted the legality of the decision and refused to confirm the commission without orders from the council. No legal judgment was ever obtained as in the subsequent proceedings the facts alleged were held not to have been proven.[7]

The lords of trade had recommended that a governor be sent to Maryland who should inquire into the situation of affairs and report. In the meantime, a new commission for Copley was prepared and submitted to Lord Baltimore, who objected on the ground that it was intended to deprive him of the powers of government which had been bestowed upon him by the charter. The continuance of his territorial right

[7] Browne, op. cit., 155.

was conceded and with this, as it was useless for him, a Catholic, to contest the will of the crown, he had to be content.[8] So it was that Copley's commission as governor finally bore the signature of Lord Baltimore.

Coode, who was responsible for what happened, received no recognition nor reward. There was some historic justice in this. He dropped out of sight for a while but afterwards reappeared in holy orders. Nicholson who succeeded Copley as royal governor is recorded as beating Coode with his cane for being drunk and creating a disturbance at divine worship.[9] In 1696, charges were made against him that "he did not only cheat his parish but like-wise ran away with 15,000 pounds of tobacco belonging to it." [10] As he eluded arrest a reward was offered for his capture. But when he was finally arrested and convicted, the Royal Governor and the Council agreed that "the said Coode was very serviceable to his Most Sacred Majesty, and this province upon the said revolution," and his punishment and fine were suspended. In 1700 he was pardoned in consideration of his "former services," yet according to his own statement he was actuated in bringing about the revolution by a motive of revenge toward Lord Baltimore.[11] The authorities did not seem to realize that in recognizing the services of this miscreant and acknowledging that he was chiefly responsible for the revolution which placed them in power, they were damning themselves.

Copley was a staunch churchman and brought over several clergy to aid him in establishing the Church of England. He summoned an assembly, which after thanking the king and Queen for delivering them from the "arbitrary will and pleasure of a tyrannical Popish government" proceeded to tyrannize the non-conformists and Catholics, who were in the majority, by establishing the Anglican church and im-

[8] Osgood, *The American Colonies in the 17th Century,* III, 505.
[9] *Archives,* XXIII, 452.
[10] Ibid, 451.
[11] Ibid, XXV, 80, 103.

posing a tax on all the inhabitants for its support. At this time the communicants of the Church of England were a small minority in the colony. Under the guise of an act declared to be "for the service of Almighty God," the Church of England was established in Maryland, the justices in each county were directed to lay out the county in parishes; the freeholders in each parish were to choose the vestry; churches and chapels were ordered built and a tax of forty pounds of tobacco was laid on each taxable person for the support of the clergy.[12]

The Puritans who had supported Coode and had at all times either openly or secretly opposed the rule and policies of the Lords Baltimore, now found themselves "hoist by their own petard." Their clamor against a "Popish tyranny" which never existed now deprived them of the religious freedom they had previously enjoyed and for which they came to Maryland. They found themselves taxed to support a church to which they could not conform. But they meekly submitted and there is no record of any protest being made by them. The only protests came from the Catholics and Quakers. The Quakers sent a deputation to England and also petitioned the provincial assembly for relief from church taxation as "a burden to their consciences and estates." [13]

The framers of the act of church establishment went back to the little code of 1639 for the phraseology of their law, but had substituted the Church of England for "Holy Churches." "The Church of England within this province," reads the act of 1692, "shall have and enjoy all her rights, liberties and franchises, wholly inviolable." [14] Similar phraseology is found in all the early acts of church liberties, but the departure comes when the Church of England is substituted for "Holy Churches" and "Holy Church."

Again going back to the code of 1639 the assembly was

[12] Cobb, op. cit., 386.
[13] Ibid, 388.
[14] *Archives,* XIII, 425.

careful to insert a provision that the inhabitants of the colony should have all their rights and liberties under Magna Charta and the laws of England. Governor Nicholson informed the assembly that King William desired to have no mention made of Magna Charta in the act for church establishment and would not consent to any mention being made of civil liberties, for this would be joining ecclesiastical and temporal matters. He also informed them that it was the opinion of the attorney general and other learned lawyers in England that if the people of the colony were given the enjoyment of their rights under English laws, they would have to try all their causes in Westminster Hall.[15] The assembly replied in a petition to the governor that in the Great Charter the liberties of both church and people were recognized in one grant, although in different paragraphs, and in Lord Baltimore's charter were to be found provisions both for the liberties of the people and the propagation of the church.[16] The assembly questioned the opinion of the attorney general and ordered that "several lawyers in town" return at once a written opinion "whether the insertion of the clause touching the liberty of the subject does not thereby give right *'meum and tuum'* to remove a cause to Westminster," and whether under Magna Charta a man cannot carry his cause to the Court of Common Pleas. Five lawyers of the colony responded with a letter to the governor in which they "were of the humble opinion that the clause in question does not give it to any person to remove his cause to Westminster." Here was the legal talent of St. Mary's arrayed against the attorney general and other learned lawyers of England.

All this reveals an anomalous situation. The Maryland legislators were quite willing to bring about church establishment and to abridge the liberties of all other churches, but they did insist on the recognition of the liberties of the peo-

15 Ibid, XIX, 390, 393.
16 Ibid, 415, 416.

ple. Their insistence on the recognition of their rights under Magna Charta was undoubtedly the result of Catholic influence in the colony.

The act of church establishment was passed again by the assembly but with a clause inserted that "His Majesty's subjects shall enjoy all their rights and liberties according to the laws and statutes of the Kingdom of England," leaving out any direct mention of Magna Charta.[17] Again the royal displeasure was incurred and the act disallowed. For the first time in the history of Maryland the King of England exercised a veto power on the acts of the colonial assembly, which never could have happened if the Royal Charter had been in force. After the Protestant Revolution all acts were sent to England for the approval of the King, and Maryland became wholly subservient to the English crown and lost her independence. All of this was of the most questionable validity for the charter itself was never rightfully forfeited.

Finally in 1702, an act was passed receiving royal sanction which settled the church. Every inhabitant was required to pay a tax to support the clergy and, by the collection of fines under the act, church property was to be kept in repair. Under this law the Church of England was established and remained the established church of Maryland until the American Revolution.[18] "Thus," says Cobb, "did Maryland pass under bondage. The Puritan exchanged his liberty for a grudging and burdensome toleration, while the Romanist found himself locked out of his own home." [19]

Some measure of toleration was granted to Protestant dissenters, but this special grace was denied Catholics. Not only were they excluded from all participation in political privileges, both from voting and holding office which had never been denied to Protestants when the Catholics were in power,

[17] Ibid, 426.
[18] Ibid, XXIV, 265.
[19] Op. cit., 289.

but they were debarred from worshipping in their own churches.

Not content to abridge the rights of Catholics in the exercise of their civil rights and their right to public worship, the law-makers, emulating the example of their English progenitors, invaded the province of the home. Children of a marriage between a Catholic and a Protestant could be taken from either or both parents or from a widowed mother and placed where they might be "securely educated in the Protestant religion." [20]

It was a strange picture and one not pleasant to behold. "In the land which Catholics had opened to Protestants, the Catholic inhabitant was the sole victim of Anglican intolerance." [21]

Presently the old capital of St. Mary's was abandoned. The seat of government was removed to a new capital on the banks of the Severn soon to be named Annapolis. This was to have been expected. It was far too much to expect that the new régime would keep the capital of the colony in the center of Catholicism and named in honor of the Virgin Mary. The inhabitants of St. Mary's protested and a petition was sent to the assembly praying that the change be not made. The House of Burgesses returned an answer which has been described by John Fiske as "brutal and vulgar." [22]

Perhaps it was just as well that the change was made. The soil of St. Mary's hallowed by the planting of the first seeds of religious liberty in America should not have been the seat of the government that was to follow.

[20] *Bacon's Laws,* Ch. 39, Sec. X, 1715; Ch. 24, Sec. XII, 1729.
[21] Bancroft, op. cit., III, 32.
[22] *Virginia and her Neighbors,* II, 162. See also Scharf, op. cit., I, 545-6.

BOOK III
THE HARVEST

CHAPTER I

FROM BALTIMORE TO CARROLL

DURING the first half century of its history when there was no outside interference, Colonial Maryland presents the fairest picture that can be found in any of the thirteen original colonies. After the Revolution of 1688 this picture would seem to have become entirely obliterated, leaving no trace of the influence of the ideals that guided the founders. Therefore most historians have looked upon the recognition of the principle of religious liberty in early Maryland as merely a passing phase with no lasting result, and as having no bearing whatever upon the founding of the republic. Maryland was under the shadow of bigotry and intolerance from 1688 until the dawn of national independence, but it has been entirely overlooked that during these dark days there were watchmen on the Towers of Israel.

On the eve of the revolution that overthrew the Baltimore government, there came to Maryland the first Charles Carroll. Graduate of the University of Douai in France, a student of the Inner Temple and a member of the English bar, he received the appointment as attorney general of the province from the third Lord Baltimore. As to the real reason for his migration, his illustrious grandson, Charles Carroll of Carrollton, a century and a half later, wrote:

> My grandfather, being a Roman Catholic by religion, resolved on withdrawing from the oppression of that period by emigrating to this country. He selected Maryland chiefly because toleration was by royal charter extended to it and afterwards confirmed by

Doughoregan Manor, The Home of the Carrolls

provincial statute. Upon leaving the Mother Country he changed with a felicity of thought almost prophetic, the motto of his family arms, *In Fide et in Bello fortes,* to *Ubicumque cum Libertate* in allusion to the cause which induced him to leave the shores of his native land. The Revolution of 1688 in England was succeeded by a revolution in Maryland and my grandfather was destined to experience even in the asylum he had selected, the evils of that religious persecution from which he had so recently fled.[1]

The change in the motto of the family coat of arms from "Strong in Faith and in War," to "Liberty in all things" was not "almost" prophetic; it was truly prophetic as is borne out by the life and services of the grandson who wrote the letter.

Descended from the famous clan of the O'Carrolls, the Carroll family had a proud record in Irish history. The family estate at Litterlouna overlooked the valley of the beautiful river Shannon. "We derive our descent from princes," Carroll afterwards wrote to his son, who was born to him after coming to America, "and until the Revolution of 1688 notwithstanding the sufferings under Elizabeth and Cromwell we were in affluent circumstances and respected and we intermarried with the best families in the kingdom of Ireland."

The first Charles Carroll was twenty-eight years of age when he came to America. Hardly had he become settled in his new abode, when Coode's rebellion broke out and this robbed him of the sanctuary he had sought.

He became the stalwart champion of the Catholic colonists and if the Protestant non-conformists did but realize it, he espoused their cause as well, for his opposition to church establishment was in keeping with the policy of separation of church and state adhered to by the Lords Baltimore that gave religious freedom to Protestants as well as to Catholics. He resisted the subversion of Lord Baltimore's government and wrote to him of the "strange rebellion your ungrateful people" have involved themselves in. He wrote again:

[1] Mss. letter addressed to Rev. William B. Sprague, May 12, 1830; Rowland, *Life and Correspondence of Charles Carroll of Carrollton,* I, 8.

Neither Catholic nor honest Protestant can well call his life or his estate his own and if your Lordship, according to your wonted care and tenderness of your people, by a speedy application and true representation to his Majesty of these inhuman actions, do not presume some orders whereby to allay their fury a little, all your friends here will be reduced to a miserable condition; for daily their cattle are killed, their horses pressed and all the injury imaginable done to them and to no other. Certainly your Lordship's charter is not such a trifle as to be annulled by the bare allegation of such profligate wretches and men of such scandalous lives, as Coode, Thurling, Jowles and such fools as they have poisoned by the most absurd lies that were ever invented.[2]

The struggle of the high spirited young attorney to protect the property and civil rights of his patron and his fellow-Catholics soon brought him into trouble with the leaders of the rebellion. With other Catholics he was a prisoner for "high misdemeanors" that consisted of resistance to Coode and his followers. When Governor Copley arrived and took office, he had Carroll committed "for several reflecting speeches and discourses against the Government." April 1693, he wrote to the Governor saying he had been a fortnight in the sheriff's custody and asking for bail. He was accused of ridiculing the government by saying that for a small matter he could procure a *nolle prosequi* and that for a bottle of cider he could procure the release of a fellow prisoner. If Carroll had made these boasts as he may have done, he was able to take the measure of his accusers. He and the others who were arrested were soon released, but that it took a bottle of cider to procure their release does not appear.

Although Lord Baltimore was deprived of the government of his colony he still had some prerogatives left that had to do with his land interests. Carroll's term of office as attorney general was not of long duration but the proprietary appointed him registrar of deeds, receiver of rents and surveyor-

[2] *Archives,* VIII, 125, 187-192.

general. He also acted as Baltimore's attorney and personal representative. He acquired lands in the province, naming different tracts after lands that had belonged to the family in Ireland. "Carroll's Forest" consisting of five hundred acres in Prince George's County was surveyed for him in 1689; "Elyo Carroll" a thousand acres in Baltimore County was surveyed in 1695, and soon after "Litterlouna" in the same county a tract of four hundred acres. "New Year's Gift" was surveyed in 1700, a plantation of thirteen hundred acres at a place known as Elk Ridge. In 1702 he obtained other tracts in Baltimore County of about two thousand acres, and five years later he added to his possession "Cynmalyra" an estate of five thousand acres and the domain of "Doughoregan Manor" of ten thousand acres. He owned also "Enfield Chase" in Prince George's County and later other tracts in various parts of Maryland, amounting in all to about sixty thousand acres.[3] Thus he became the largest land owner in the colony and founded a family estate that enabled him and his son to render aid to the oppressed Catholics, and his grandson to be of great material assistance to Washington and the American cause in the War for Independence. Until Maryland became a state these lands were taxed to support an established church and a government that disfranchised Catholics and disabled them from holding office. Despite these unjust burdens Charles Carroll and his descendants gave every possible aid and support to the cause of freedom and justice.

The third Lord Baltimore, who had not abandoned hope of ultimately returning to his colony, desired Carroll to live near him. In one of his letters he writes that his attorney is to have a large acreage assigned to him "as near as possible to one of the Proprietor's manors, for the benefit of his society." He granted Carroll a tract of land and a brick house at the Port of Annapolis formerly Anne Arundel town

[3] Rowland, op. cit., I, 5, 6.

"in consideration of good and acceptable services and to enable him to continue in the performance of those services." [4]

In 1693 the first Charles Carroll married Mary Darnall, daughter of Colonel Henry Darnall of Portland Manor, a blood relative of the Calverts. Carroll received the appointment from the Lord Proprietary of Judge and Registrar of the Land Office in Maryland, succeeding Colonel Darnall who died in June 1711.

In Lord Baltimore's instructions to be observed and pursued by his agent and receiver-general in Maryland Carroll is charged to pay in tobacco, yearly, various persons for their services:

> To yourself twelve thousand pounds of tobacco for your advice and trouble about my law concerns and several allowances heretofore by me made to the several persons and officers hereinafter mentioned vis: . . . to Robert Brooke and the rest of his brethren, being in all eight persons, one thousand pounds of tobacco each. To Mr. James Haddock one thousand pounds.

Robert Brooke and his brethren were the Jesuit missionaries. James Haddock was a Franciscan Friar.[5]

Carroll had trouble with Governor Seymour who attempted to exceed his power in order to persecute the Catholics, drive out the Jesuits and confiscate their property. The governor showed his hand in a letter to the Lords of Trade when he wrote:

> I must acquaint you, that my instructions in this point are different from what other governors here have had; theirs being to admit a liberty of conscience to all who behaved themselves so as to give no occasion of scandal or offence to the government; but mine to all such but Papists whom I take to be expressly excluded from that toleration.[6]

This gentleman's idea was that even if Catholics gave no scandal or offense to the government still they were not to be tolerated.

[4] Ibid, 1-7.
[5] Boyle, *Marylanders*, 79.
[6] Hughes, op. cit., II, 460.

Carroll had enough influence to hold the obstreperous governor in leash. When Fathers Hunter and Brooke were brought before the governor and council to answer to the charge of consecrating a chapel and saying Mass, they were denied the right to have counsel, but the mere fact that Carroll had attempted to appear in their behalf and had advised them as to their legal rights, was enough to save them from fine or imprisonment.

After the Hunter and Brooke episode and the closing of the chapel at St. Mary's, Seymour set about to enact a law that would have prohibited the exercise of the Catholic religion in Maryland. This was an act to "prevent the growth of Popery within the province." It prohibited priests from baptizing any child except such as had Popish parents; from saying Mass or exercising any Catholic function, and from endeavoring to convert any Protestant. It prohibited any Catholic priest or lay person from keeping school, or taking upon himself the education of youth. This act prohibited private as well as public worship.[7] For this reason the Board of Trade for the Colonies disapproved of it. The Maryland assembly thereupon passed a suspending act to the effect that a priest or Jesuit might exercise his functions in a private family of the Roman communion for eighteen months or until the Queen's pleasure should be known.[8] This was a check to the drastic policy of Seymour and it came in response to a petition of the Catholic colonists presented by Carroll to the lower house.

Seymour complained to the Board of Trade that there were some in the assembly who "were a well wishing party to the interests of Roman Catholiques." He referred to the "mediation of a great part of the house of delegates (whose interest in lands was considerable) to procure the suspension of the law," and hinted that both Catholic laymen and Jesuits had friends in the lower house. In another letter he referred

[7] *Archives,* XXVI, 340.
[8] Ibid, 431.

to Lord Baltimore's relations and agents who were using every means to propagate the Catholic religion "being constantly supplied from Europe with Jesuits and give great scandal and offense to her Majesty's government here." The scandal and offense consisted in the attempt to enjoy freedom of worship that had previously been granted to Catholics and Protestants alike.

The Council consisting of the appointees of the governor sent word to the more liberal minded burgesses that "a toleration of such liberty taken by priests may prove a discouragement to my Lord Bishop of London from sending ministers in." The hope that the Bishop of London might send more ministers of the Church of England to Maryland may not have offered strong inducement to the members of the lower house to change their attitude, as the ministers who had already been sent had not been of a caliber or character that would have caused any devout member of the church to desire the arrival of others.

In 1706, when the time limited in the suspending act was about to expire, Carroll and other Catholic colonists petitioned the assembly to further suspend the operation of the act until her Majesty (Queen Anne) should declare her pleasure without the limitation of any time. The assembly took umbrage at this and declared the petitioners had no right to demand freedom and toleration "seeing that at the time of making the act they had not the slightest assurance of such freedom or toleration" after the expiration of the time allowed.[9]

The following year the home government had an act passed by the assembly providing that, the permission for private worship be extended without limitation of time until the pleasure of the Queen be declared and signified.[10]

The small measure of liberty afforded by the suspending act was quickly taken advantage of by the Catholics. Many

[9] Ibid, 597.
[10] Ibid, XXVII, 147.

landowners built chapels adjoining their manor houses some of which have survived to this day. Doughoregan Manor built by Charles Carroll in 1717 has its chapel adjoining the house, which is still used as a place of worship by Catholic families in the neighborhood. Colonel Henry Darnall's Manor at Poplar Hill, ten miles from Washington, preserved its chapel until 1929 when it was turned into a library.[11] In the humbler homes a room was set apart for religious worship. "It was considered an honor for a family to have the Holy Sacrifice offered within the walls of the home and everything was done to give the room the appearance of a chapel or church, the temporary altar being decorated with wild flowers which the people brought in profusion." [12]

The Archives of the Maryland-New York Province bear witness to the devotion and piety of the Catholic colonists who had to conduct their worship in their own homes. One record tells of a "Perpetual Adoration of the Blessed Sacrament" at one of the manor chapels, probably St. Thomas' Manor. There is a list of subscribers representing some forty-five families who obligate themselves to employ a half hour every month during the year "on their knees in honor of the Blessed Sacrament, by meditating or saying of vocal prayers, either relating to the Blessed Sacrament or the Sacred Heart." A list of watchers of the guard of honor follows. The men are well represented but the women are in the majority. The adoration was twelve hours long from 6 A.M. to 6 P.M. "From the scattered and lonely plantations of Maryland," writes Father Hughes, "the incense of praise, adoration and spiritual mediation rose silently from morning till night." [13]

The continuance of Irish immigration that was brought about largely by Charles Carroll, was a source of great dis-

[11] Sarah Redwood Lee, in *Records American Catholic Historical Society of Philadelphia,* "Maryland Influence in American Catholicism," Dec. 1930, pp. 16 and 17.

[12] Spalding, op. cit., 123.

[13] Hughes, op. cit., II, 518-19.

turbance to Governor Seymour. He pointed out that the root of the "evil" was the fact that the owner of the soil was "the Lord Baltimore whose agents give great encouragement to their seating here." Carroll, he indicated, had been particularly active. He suggested that more radical measures would have to be taken than mere duties poll to keep these Catholics out. "Unless something more effectual be ordered by her Majesty, this province will by far have too large a share of them who in some few years may prove dangerous." How dangerous the coming of Catholics was to Maryland is shown in the early pages of the history of the colony. A tax of twenty shillings was imposed on every Irish Catholic immigrant and in Governor Hart's time the duty was raised to forty shillings. All Protestants came in free and when convicts were imported at a later time, twenty thousand of them during a period of twenty years, they too came in free.[14]

Charles Calvert, the third Lord Baltimore, died in England in 1715 at the age of eighty-five years. The government of his colony had been taken from him but he had kept the faith. He had lived to see the spirit of religious liberty supplanted by the spirit of religious bigotry and, what was even sadder for him, he had lived to see his eldest son and heir forsake the faith of his fathers to regain the lost government. The first Lord Baltimore's change of allegiance from the Church of England to the Church of Rome had been neither for worldly nor ulterior purposes, but this was not true of Benedict Calvert, the fourth Lord Baltimore, when he changed from Catholic to Anglican.

Like Henry of Navarre, who thought a kingdom was worth a Mass, Benedict Calvert regarded a palatinate well worth communion with the established church. There can be no

[14] As to Carroll's activities in the matter of Irish immigration, Governor Seymour informed the Lords of Trade that Mr. Charles Carroll had assured her Majesty's subjects in Ireland of "good tracts of land at the head of the Bay and free toleration and exercise of their superstitious worship," Hughes, op. cit., II, 483, note VI.

doubt as to the real reason for his apostasy. He laid bare his motive in a petition to King George I. In this petition presented just prior to his father's death, Benedict set forth that he had already renounced his "Romish errors" and had received the sacrament according to the rites of the Church of England, that he had placed his children who were being educated at his father's expense in "Popish seminaries," in Protestant schools and that his father, angered by his withdrawal from the Catholic church, had withheld his allowance and compelled him to live on his marriage settlement of "only six hundred pounds a year." Out of this amount he stated that he was obliged to give two hundred pounds a year to his wife for "separate maintenance." Being divorced from his wife, a granddaughter of the favorite mistress of Charles II, he was finding a divorce with alimony an expensive luxury.

In his petition, Benedict also recited the fact that the late Queen Anne had granted him a pension of three hundred pounds a year out of the revenues of the colony, and at his request had appointed John Hart, the son of an Anglican bishop, governor of the colony directing him to pay over to the petitioner five hundred pounds per annum out of the revenues of the colony. The petitioner further called attention to the fact that Maryland was a proprietary government that would soon be in his hands at the death of his father "who is now eighty-five years of age." The son was evidently anticipating his father's early demise.

The closing appeal reveals the real motive for his change of faith. "Therefore, because he has taken the oaths of the government as well as the sacrament of the Church of England," he seeks a continuance of his pension and further asks that if the royal governor is not to be continued that the king will send him, Benedict Calvert, as governor of the colony "with a saving of the rights of the patent which is his inheritance." [15] Benedict received his reward. The pen-

[15] *Archives,* XXV, 271-2.

sion was renewed. On the death of his father, the proprietary government of Maryland was revived in his behalf. He had sold his birthright for a mess of pottage.

The father's allowance to his son, which was withdrawn, amounted to four hundred pounds a year. It needs only a little arithmetic to discover that Benedict made a good bargain with Queen Anne. In lieu of his allowance from his father he received his pension of three hundred pounds and an additional five hundred pounds from Governor Hart. His net profit for turning Protestant was then four hundred pounds yearly. It is difficult to see what legal justification there was for him to have received any share of the revenues of the colony during his father's lifetime. It was a transaction that quite measures up to the modern accomplishment known as graft. The appointment of Governor Hart was made at his request, and the request was accompanied by a demand for a subsidy. The demand could not have been successfully made of course had it not been for the change, in what the son was pleased to call, his religion. It was a mixture of politics and religion that had so often blackened the pages of English history.

Benedict Calvert did not live long to enjoy the fruits of his apostacy. He survived his father by only six weeks. His son, Charles, became the fifth Lord Baltimore April 5, 1715. As Charles was only a lad of sixteen years whose change of faith had been foresworn for him by his father, no odium can be attached to his name. He was forthwith proclaimed Lord Proprietary of Maryland. As he had conformed to the established church the government of the colony was restored to the House of Baltimore.

Thus was ended the rule of the royal governors. Governor Hart, who succeeded Seymour, was for a time continued in office by virtue of the proprietary government. Charles on coming of age took over the reins of government. He had enough respect for the traditions of his family to be mildly tolerant toward his Catholic subjects but he gave little attention to the affairs of the colony. After spending two years in Maryland he returned to England to become a gentleman of the bedchamber and to take part in the intrigues and alliances of the Crown Prince doing service "disgraceful even in a court which had to wait for another reign to introduce the fashions of good morals." [16] He lacked the strength of character to give to the colony of Maryland the benefit of the wise policy of its founders. In the meantime the torch of freedom had been given to other and safer hands.

There are many evidences of the purpose of Lord Baltimore to make the first Charles Carroll his real successor in order to safeguard the family heritage from the treachery of his apostate son. Carroll was virtually the vice-proprietary of the province. He was in England at the time of Lord Baltimore's death. Subsequent events indicate that shortly before he died, the proprietary realizing that little dependence could be placed on his son gave his attorney instructions and advice as to what course he was to follow. Carroll remained in England for some time, since he acted as attorney for Lady Baltimore in the settlement of her husband's estate.

In England at this time were other Catholic gentlemen who were not idle.[17] Two papers written in French and deposited in the records of the Board of Trade contain the representations of this group headed by Carroll. These papers indicate the policy asked to be adopted was "to defend against the Protestant aggression, a liberty granted in Maryland by what is called its Magna Charta." [18] As a result, Carroll was sent back to America with even greater powers than he had before. Before he returned, Lord Guilford as Guardian for the fifth Lord Baltimore, a minor, reappointed him as the Proprietary's agent.

When Carroll returned to Maryland it was to find Governor Hart starting on a program of Anti-Catholic legislation

16 Morris' *Lords Baltimore*, 50.
17 Hughes, op. cit., II, 486.
18 Ibid.

that would have done credit to a Cecil. A factor contributing to this and subsequent legislation was the firing of a salute from the cannon at the fort of Annapolis on the occasion of the birthday of the Jacobite pretender, by some over-zealous Catholic youths, one of them being a nephew of Carroll. This was in June of 1716. This single shot alarmed the whole colony which again reverberated with the cry of a popish plot. Governor Hart had the offenders arrested and imprisoned but Carroll obtained the release of his nephew. There was no plot except a boyish prank but the incident served as a welcome excuse for more drastic legislation.[19]

As long as Hart remained governor, he never forgot this incident and several times in his addresses to the assembly he made a great point of it and took Carroll to task, who being "a professed Papist" should have the effrontery to seek to set at large criminals who had committed "so great crimes." [20]

It was unthinkable to Hart that a Catholic should be given any powers from the Lord Proprietary that might conflict with his own powers. It hurt his pride and he threatened to resign. He made all kinds of accusations against Carroll and finally wound up by demanding that he take the oath of abjuration which was then required of all office-holders. This oath no Catholic could take, for it went so far as to require anyone who took it to declare that there was not "any transubstantiation in the elements of the bread and wine, at or after the consecration thereof by any person whatsoever." [21] This oath was required by Hart for the express purpose of keeping all Catholics out of office. Carroll replied that when the Proprietary appointed him his chief agent in the colony no mention was made of religion or oaths. The assembly supported the governor. Both Hart and Carroll took their cases to England with the result that Lord Guilford mollified

[19] Browne, op. cit., 208.
[20] *Archives,* XXXIII, 481.
[21] Russell, op. cit., 403.

Hart by stating he had no intention of lessening the authority of the governor and curtailed most of Carroll's powers.[22]

This was not enough for Hart. He did not intend to allow Catholics to have any share whatever in the government either as office-holders or voters. He procured an act to be passed in 1718 that the oath of abjuration must be taken by all voters as well as office-holders. This was openly declared to be for the purpose of preventing "professed Papists" from voting at all elections and "for the better security and safety of His Lordship's dominions and the Protestant government within this province."

Hart's addresses to the assembly were all very bitter. In his address to the assembly of 1718, he said he had looked forward to be "wholly at leisure" as the last session had passed so many good laws (discriminating against Catholics) that he had been afforded much satisfaction and tranquillity, but now his peace had been disturbed because some restless and turbulent papists had persisted in persecuting and defaming him. What these papists did to annoy and persecute him was to demand an equal share in the administration of the government. To Hart this was inconceivable in a Protestant country. He accused Carroll of being the chief fomentor of the trouble for he had the audacity to set up the claim that Catholics had the right to hold office "from an instrument granted by Lord Cecilius but that he believed, it had been burned in the State House," and to declare that the Catholics of Maryland would insist upon their rights, and that if Lord Guilford would not admit them, that they would appeal to higher powers. The governor congratulated the assembly for the "many good laws" that had been passed from which he judged that there was a determination never more to give way to a "Popish administration." As for himself he was firmly resolved to do all in his power toward establishing "the Protestant interest in this province." [23]

22 Osgood, *The American Colonies in the 18th Century,* III, 8-9.
23 *Archives,* XXXIII, 119-123; 202-206.

To the assembly of 1720 he boasted that he would soon silence the clamors of the Catholics by exposing them "to the lash of those laws that were long since provided against them." He had already told the assembly that:

> As soon as his sacred Majesty condescended to restore the new Lord Proprietary, on his professing himself a Protestant, to his hereditary government, the Papists instantly laid in their claim to be also restored to their former pretended privileges, which when offered to me for my approbation by their principal agent, Charles Carroll, was dismissed with the answer that I would oppose it to the utmost of my power. Hence our troubles had their rise.

Later in the same address he said that the Catholics could be very happy in the province if they only would "not interfere with the affairs of government which did not appertain to them." The Catholics could be happy and the governor could enjoy peace and tranquillity if only they would desist from invoking the doctrine, strange to him, of equality before the law.

As for the "pretence" that Maryland was granted to Catholics as an asylum from the rigors of the penal laws of England, this was a position that had amused the world but Hart was the one to discover that it was only an imposition.[24] The Royal Charter, he said, granted no exception to Catholics for freedom in the exercise of their religion. He then proceeded to misquote and misinterpret section IV by asserting that all churches and chapels must be dedicated and consecrated according to the ecclesiastical laws of England, whereas, as has previously been pointed out, there was nothing mandatory in the charter provision relating to the dedication of churches.

After depriving Catholics of the right to vote and to hold office, Hart next tried to confiscate the property of the Jesuits. But in this project there was the question of vested property rights to be dealt with, and Carroll, well grounded in the

[24] Ibid., 478-485.

English Common Law, stood in the way. Then, too, there were certain rights of landowners under the Royal Charter and the Conditions of Plantation, to be considered. The governor under the pretext of an act of parliament giving to a commission power "to inquire of the estates of certain traitors and popish recusants and of estates given to superstitious uses, in order to raise money out of them severally for the use of the public," appointed himself a committee of one to conduct an investigation. Since the days of Henry VIII the twin phrases of "superstitious uses" and "public use" had always done service when church or monastery property was to be confiscated for the enrichment of the confiscators.

In his investigation Hart first went to "Charles Carroll, Esq." for information and subjected him to interrogatories. In answer to the question whether he knew of any lands or sums of money that were applied to superstitious uses, Carroll replied truthfully that he knew of none. He replied further that he believed some priests were possessed of tracts of land taken by them under the common conditions of plantation or by those who had paid a valuable consideration, but he verily believed that the yearly value of them was so inconsiderable as hardly to afford a bare subsistence for those who were possessed of them.[25] The answer must have been convincing for there was no confiscation, although it is plain that this was what the governor had in mind.

The first Charles Carroll died in 1720, and during the same year Hart was replaced as governor by Charles Calvert, an uncle of the proprietary. After Hart had gone there was peace and quiet in Maryland and for a time it looked as if there might come again the halcyon days of what the historian McMahon has described as "the golden age of colonial existence." This, however, was not to be. The House of Baltimore had mixed religion with politics, and the fifth Lord Baltimore now coming to his majority was not to be

[25] Hughes, op. cit., II, 482.

guided by the traditional policy of his progenitors. One must now look to the descendants of Charles Carroll to find how the spirit of liberty and equality was to be kept alive until the beginning of American Independence.

CHAPTER II

CHARLES CARROLL OF DOUGHOREGAN

THE first Charles Carroll died in 1720, leaving a son Charles, the second of his name and line. The son was receiving his education in France at the time of his father's death. It is not certain what college he attended, but within all probability it was St. Omer's. That he received a Jesuit education is indicated in a letter written by him several years later when, referring to the Jesuits, he said: "I have, thank God, been bred among them and if you do what they have taught you and nothing contrary to it, you will be happy here and hereafter." His younger brother, Daniel, was sent abroad at the same time to receive his education. The father wrote to the boys a year before his death to "prepare vigorously" for the defense of their philosophy and asked them to style themselves in their theses: "Marylando-Hibernus." [1]

The son Charles was not of age when his father died. He had intended to enter the Inner Temple, London, for the study of law, but was obliged to change his plans. He wrote that his father had directed him to go to the Temple "but he, dying just as I had finished my philosophy, my friends thought my presence in Maryland necessary and that I might study the law here. I attempted it but to no purpose." [2] Unlike his father and son, he did not have the advantage of a legal education. He returned to Maryland soon after his father's death.

The second Charles Carroll has often been referred to as "Charles Carroll of Annapolis," but Bishop Russell rightfully contends that this designation properly belongs to Dr. Charles

[1] Rowland, op. cit., I, 10; Gurn, *Charles Carroll of Carrollton*, 19.
[2] Rowland, op. cit., I, 42.

Carroll of another branch of the family and that the son of the attorney-general should be designated as "Charles Carroll of Doughoregan," because of his long residence at the manor estate of the Carrolls.

Charles Calvert, who succeeded Hart as governor, died in 1726 and on his death Benedict Leonard Calvert, younger brother of the proprietary, succeeded him. He was one of the boys who was taken from St. Omer's and placed in a Protestant school. His father was supposed to have foresworn his change of faith, yet he was suspected of being a Catholic. A letter of warning that the new governor would bear watching was sent to Lord Townsend, a part of which read:

> The new governor is going to Maryland, an educated Roman Catholic. Jesuits go over there annually to that colony and have places there much in the nature of convents, and by reason of the little care of the choice of ministers and church discipline, the R. C. increases and spreads not only over all that province but the neighboring provinces. The new governor has made choice of and is going over to his new government with a Roman Catholic commander.[8]

Governor Benedict Calvert was forced to resign in 1731 because of ill-health. He died on a return voyage to England. His successor was Samuel Ogle. During the rule of the Calvert governors and Governor Ogle, while the fifth Lord Baltimore was living, the Maryland Catholics were not molested. There was a respite for them of twenty years although during this period they were still disfranchised, disqualified from public office and were not allowed to conduct public worship.

Upon the death of the fifth Lord Baltimore, his son Frederick became his successor. The sixth Lord Baltimore was a worthless degenerate. The only interest he took in his colony, which he never visited, was to obtain from it as much revenue as possible in order to enable him to lead a dissolute life. His indifference to the affairs of his colony gave an opportunity for a clique whose religion consisted mainly in being strongly anti-Catholic, to stir up trouble. The first outbreak

[8] Hughes, op. cit., II, 490.

came when Charles Carroll of Doughoregan attempted to force his Protestant relative and co-executor, Dr. Charles Carroll of Annapolis, to make a just accounting of certain trust funds. Dr. Carroll, to save himself from liability, attempted to invoke the penal laws of England.

James Carroll, of Tingual, Anne Arundel County, made provision in his will for the education of his nephews, James and Anthony Carroll, who were devisees and legatees under the will and were also made executors. They were both minors and had been sent to France to be educated at a Jesuit college. During their minority and absence, Charles Carroll of Doughoregan and Dr. Charles Carroll of Annapolis, relatives of the testator, were to act as executors under the will. Dr. Carroll was a Catholic when the will was made, but afterwards became Protestant and was rewarded by being elected a vestryman in the established church and a member of the assembly.

The two nephews named in the will entered the Society of Jesus. Charles Carroll, when the Jesuit legatees had attained their majority, was ready to make an accounting, but Dr. Carroll was not. The latter offered to compromise by paying a lump sum of four hundred twenty pounds to the heirs. Charles Carroll of Doughoregan refused to agree to this, stating that Dr. Carroll owed the heirs at least three times this amount, and demanded an itemized account of receipts and disbursements. Thereupon "Dr. Carroll threatened Mr. Carroll with the penal statutes."

The executors went to Daniel Dulaney, Sr., an eminent lawyer of the colony, for advice. Dulaney gave a written opinion in which he held that the executors were trustees for the legatees and ought to pay the legacies with interest from one year after the death of the testator. "If the legatees were in their minority, the legacies carry interest from the end of the year," he held, "even though no demand is made, because no lapse is to be imputed to minors." [4]

[4] Russell, op. cit., 581.

In view of this opinion there was nothing for Dr. Carroll to do but to account and pay up. This he did not intend to do. He saw in the penal laws of England against Catholics and Jesuits a loop-hole for escape from liability. He had written a letter to Dulaney, trying to influence his opinion. The letter said:

> I find Mr. Carroll bent on a matter which must, if his end's gained, ruin me. As you are going to give us your opinion, or I would choose advice, I must request that you will make this an ingredient toward giving such: 1. I am appointed executor by the will, which may be proper for you to see, during the minority of Mr. Carroll's nephews only, who are now taken into orders and are priests. 2. Whether a recusant or priest can be an executor. If not what right has Mr. Carroll to call me to account or who shall have the residue of the estate?

The doctor, in his fear of financial ruin, brazenly made the claim that no accounting could be demanded by an executor who was a Catholic or by legatees who were Jesuits. In other words that it was perfectly legal and proper to steal money from a Jesuit. Dulaney, who was a Protestant, appears in a very favorable light in this transaction. He did not allow his judgment to be swayed by any such appeal as his client made. He informed the doctor that he would "not make the ability or disability of the legatees any ingredient" in his opinion. In a letter later addressed to the speaker of the assembly, he gave a full and fair statement of the whole case and laid bare the attempt of the doctor to escape making full payment by hiding behind the penal laws. He was careful to bring out every fact favorable to the cause of the legatees. He called attention to a threat made by Dr. Carroll that his co-executor "was fishing for the Society of Jesus," and that the string might be drawn so tight that it would break. He stated that the doctor had talked much about the penal laws, but he, as attorney, advised that these laws were not meant to be enforced against "Papists who behaved as became good and peaceful subjects"; that he did not apprehend any danger from them in Maryland and that it would be "ill-policy in a country like this to force any out or deter any from coming in." [5]

The most amazing part of this whole affair was the way the assembly handled the matter when Dr. Carroll appealed to that body for protection from liability. After being fully appraised by Dulaney of the facts in the case, it lent itself to the shameful course of shielding a defaulter and denying equal justice under the law. Dr. Carroll reviewed the case from his standpoint to the apparent edification of the assembly. It is not recorded what he said, but apparently the burden of his speech was contained in the letter to Dulaney. He made one statement that aroused the ire of the attorney. Having heard that his name had been made use of in the dispute, Dulaney in his letter to the speaker of the assembly, stated that he had been told that:

> Dr. Carroll asserted in the lower house that I told him in private conversation that he would be in danger of *praemunire* [6] if he paid the money, which I hope for his own sake is not true; for if he did assert it, I declare solemnly it was without foundation and that I never told him any such thing in my life.

It was well known that the Jesuit legatees would not be able to make personal use of any of the funds or property left to them under the will, because of their vows, and that they would probably assign whatever came to them to the Jesuit mission. "Who shall have the residue of the estate?" Dr. Carroll asked the lawyer. He knew that by asking this question, even if he received no satisfactory answer from the lawyer, that his colleagues in the assembly would see to it that the estate did not go for "superstitious uses." His real design was to share in the residue of the estate that might be declared forfeited, since he was one of the relatives and heirs at law of James Carroll who died a bachelor. Dr. Carroll was the only heir at law who had purged himself of Catholicism, so he would be the one to gain by preventing Catholic heirs from inheriting the property.

[5] Ibid, 582-3.

[6] The offense of aiding a foreign power—in England, the Papacy.

Charles Carroll of Doughoregan, who was disqualified from a voice and vote in the assembly, was determined that his side of the case should be presented. He adopted the bold course of preparing an "advertisement," containing the letters of Dulaney, the letter of Dr. Carroll and a short statement signed by himself, and this he nailed to the door of the state house. No end of a commotion was created. The assembly made itself ridiculous by becoming indignant. Its rights and privileges had been violated and one of its members insulted. The advertisement was declared to contain "scandalous and malicious reflections upon the proceedings of this house and a member thereof in particular." This was done in the form of a resolution which was passed by a vote of 39 to 7. Among the seven votes in the negative was that of Daniel Dulaney, Jr., son of the attorney who advised the executors. The motion of a member that the word "false" be inserted in the resolution denouncing the advertisement was lost. The truth of the statements, supported as they were by Dulaney, Sr., was only too apparent, yet the members had recourse to the English law of criminal libel. Although the statements were truthful they were nevertheless "scandalous and malicious" being uttered against a member of the august assembly.

The sergeant-at-arms was ordered to take into custody the body of "the said Charles Carroll Esq." and to bring him before the assembly that he might make due submission. A vote to confine the offender in the public jail was resolved in the negative, but Carroll was asked to sign a prepared submission. This he signed only in part, stating that he had no intention either to reflect upon the members or to violate the privileges of the house, but he refused both to retract his statements concerning Dr. Carroll and to apologize to him. The house did not dare go further.[7] Charles Carroll, however, did not allow the matter to drop. He had a bill in

[7] The entire record of these proceedings is printed in Appendix T of Russell's *Land of Sanctuary*, 580-586, and is taken from the Archiepiscopal Archives, Baltimore.

chancery filed by one of the Jesuit legatees, Father James Carroll, who had returned to Maryland to claim his rights. The bill asked for a fair account from both executors. Dr. Carroll died before there was a final adjudication. In a letter written to his son, Charles Carroll of Doughoregan said that "there was no final decree against Dr. Carroll. He died before the cause was ripe for trial but I hope his son will be obliged to pay what his father justly owed." [8]

This was not the first time that a Protestant had attempted to secure a portion of family property left to a Catholic relative. In 1729, Thomas Brooke, brother of Father Robert Brooke, brought an action to obtain possession of his mother's estate that had been left in remainder to his brother on the ground that a Jesuit was incapable of inheriting property. He lost the case.[9]

A devise of a valuable tract of two thousand acres at Whitemarsh in Prince George County, made in the will of James Carroll to his good friend George Thorald of Portobacco, for some strange reason escaped the attention of the land-sharks. The devisee was Father Thorald, superior of the Jesuit mission. In the body of his will the testator had devised this land to Charles Carroll of Doughoregan, in a confidential trust, but "through apprehension of the said Charles's death" he made a codicil devising the land directly to Father Thorald, and in this way the mission received the full benefit of the devise.[10]

The resourceful Dr. Carroll had placed himself in a class with Benedict Calvert the fourth Lord Baltimore, who changed his religion to secure the government of the colony and all its emoluments, while the doctor conformed to the

[8] Rowland, op. cit., I, 25. Letter of July 26, 1756.

[9] Hughes, op. cit., II, 527.

[10] Rowland, op. cit., II, 387-8. There was always danger of the Jesuit mission property being confiscated. When Governor Bladen in 1746 issued a proclamation against "Jesuits and Popish priests who were seducing His Majesty's good Protestant subjects," Father Richard Molyneaux made an assignment of all the property the society possessed in Maryland to John Lancaster to whom he confidentially entrusted the property under the formality of a transfer. Hughes, op. cit., II, 529.

established church, and became a Protestant to save himself from accounting to his Jesuit wards. According to the records he accomplished his purpose; at least he did not have to account during his lifetime. If there was a recovery the burden fell on his heirs after his death. As a result of the controversy the doctor acquired a standing in the halls of Maryland legislation and he used his influence to secure the passage of much anti-Catholic legislation.

In the same year that Charles Carroll of Doughoregan nailed his advertisement to the door of the state house at Annapolis, the committee of grievances represented to the lower house the growth of Popery, the education of Catholic children in foreign institutions, the return of many such as priests and Jesuits who "here live together in societies propogating with great industry and zeal" and the existence of "mass houses." Worse than this, the Jesuits taught youths and held tracts of land in the back parts of the province, referring no doubt to Bohemia Manor school. Altogether the inconvenience "which must attend this spreading evil are too many to enumerate," so the matter was humbly submitted to the Honorable House for consideration. The house, including Dr. Carroll, at once gave consideration and passed a bill rescinding the suspending act of Queen Anne which allowed private Catholic worship. The rewards provided in the act were to be paid from the public treasury to anyone "who shall apprehend any Popish priest or Jesuit," and shall prosecute such felon unto conviction for saying mass or exercising any other office or function of a priest within the province. Here the attempt was made to put in force the anti-popery laws of William III. To the governor and upper house petitions were presented by Charles Carroll of Doughoregan in his own name as well as on behalf of other Catholic remonstrants, against this threatened persecution. The council saved what was left of religious freedom in the colony. The upper house shelved the persecution bill and declined to satisfy the wrathful demands of the delegates under the leadership of Dr. Carroll.

The next year the lower house again went into action. There was a renewal of the anti-popery campaign lasting for several years with reports of grievances and depositions against Jesuits and Catholic schoolmasters. Bills were introduced aiming at persecution and confiscation. The tocsin was sounded when it was reported that the Jesuits were possessed of large tracts of land, several public chapels and were prevailing on "dying bigots to leave their estates to the Popish church." By this time the report said, "that artful society, if not timely prevented, will increase into so much property as cannot be thought of by Protestants without great concern for the consequences."

A bill was prepared under the title of "An Act for the Security of His Majesty's Dominions, and to prevent the growth of Popery within this province." Under this measure all property of Jesuits used by them since October 1, 1751, was to be taken over and vested in seven men who became commissioners with autocratic powers. Popish priests and Jesuits were to be unearthed by means of three oaths, those of allegiance, abhorrency and abjuration. The refusal to take any one of these should be full and conclusive proof that such priest or Jesuit was a Popish recusant convict and as such would forfeit all his lands, tenements and hereditaments. This law which was as elaborate and minute as it was drastic, was adopted by the lower house, but it failed to pass the council. Again the upper body called a halt to the march toward confiscation.

The citizens of Prince George's county, where the Jesuits occupied the land devised to Father Thorald under the will of James Carroll, instructed their delegates to dispossess the Jesuits of their landed estates and to exclude the Papists from places of trust and profit as executors, trustees and devisees.

In Cecil County, where Bohemia Manor lay, the Protestants manifested an anti-popery zeal and cast covetous eyes on the domain held by the Jesuits for the maintenance of their school. The influence of Carroll and other Catholics of standing and prominence, with the better and more liberal element of the freemen, was sufficient to keep the proposed legislation from being enacted. However, this did not prevent the passage of a piece of legislation in Governor Sharpe's time which laid a double tax upon the Catholic colonists. Governor Sharpe was opposed to the passage of this measure. He was not in sympathy with the faction of the lower house which carried on its work like a well oiled political machine. He called for an investigation by the magistrates, who after completing their work, reported that they could find no fault with the Catholics. The magistrates of St. Mary's county said that if they could only apprehend the ones who were industriously spreading disturbing reports, they would take "proper measures for their being brought to justice as enemies of their country's peace, and friends of a faction that labors to foment animosities amongst us to the endangering of our common security." [11]

In a letter written at this time to Lord Baltimore, Governor Sharpe said:

> It might perhaps be unknown, if not to the authors, at least to some of the propagators of these reports, that the people who first settled in this province were for the most part Roman Catholic and that although every other sect was tolerated, a majority of the inhabitants continued Papists till the Revolution, soon after which even an act was made here for the support of a clergyman of the Church of England in every parish, which is still in force, and the Papists as well as Protestants are thereby obliged to pay annually very considerable sums of money for that purpose.

"Upon the whole, my Lord," the Governor declared, "I must say that if I was asked whether the conduct of the Protestants or Papists in the province hath been unexcep-

[11] Hughes, op. cit., II, 540.

tionable since I have had the honor to serve your Lordship, I should not hesitate to answer in favor of the latter." [12]

Governor Sharpe and the members of the council, although at first opposed to the double taxation bill, finally yielded to the machine. After holding conferences with the leaders of the lower house, the bill was passed and approved. Carroll sent a final appeal praying the Governor to disapprove the bill, saying that the Catholics had almost been reduced to the "level of our negroes, not having the privilege of voting for persons to represent us in the assembly."

The governor on receiving the petition, informed Carroll that it should have been presented to the lower house which framed the bill. Carroll made reply:

> By a parity of reason if you cannot apply by petition to the Upper House and Governor against a bill passed by the lower house unless you had first applied to the lower house against the bill, the governor and the upper house ought not to reject any bill passed by the lower house. This is a doctrine so absurd that it must strike a person even of the governor's sagacity, if it were broached to serve any other purpose than to give a color to the step resolved on to oppress the Roman Catholics.[13]

The final passage of the bill so disgusted and disheartened Carroll that he proposed to obtain from the French court a large tract of land on the Arkansas river in Louisiana and to establish a colony where there would be freedom from persecution and discrimination. As France was at war with England the project was abandoned.

Up to this time the relations between Governor Sharpe and Carroll had been very friendly, but the passage of the tax bill caused a breach between them. Carroll went abroad in 1756 to visit his son who was a student there. Sharpe wrote to a friend in England that Carroll had thought of leaving Maryland and carrying his fortune to Europe. "He is a sensible man," he wrote, "has read much and is well acquainted with the constitution and strength of these

[12] Ridgely, *Annals of Annapolis,* 99-100.
[13] Georgetown Coll. Mss.; II Hughes, 543.

American colonies. If he is inclined to give the enemy any intelligence about our American affairs, none is more capable, but indeed I do not conceive he has any such intention." [14]

There were many Protestants in Maryland who did not favor discrimination against Catholics. Most of the trouble was caused by an active minority group that was guided only by its own selfish interests. It had succeeded in building up a strong political organization that was feared by others.[15]

In 1758 the upper house attempted unsuccessfully to relieve the Catholics from the double taxation law on the ground that it could "not be defended on any principle of justice or equity." Another reason given was that "the first settlement of this province was made by Roman Catholics who had been driven from their native country by the severity of its laws," and had granted tolerance to all Christian sects, "after they had been promised and allowed an asylum here." The influence of Charles Carroll, lately returned from his trip to France and England, can be seen in this action and also in the lesson in history that followed.

The lower house asked for an explanation stating that it had never discovered anything in history which disclosed that "the Papists were promised or allowed an asylum here." The upper house sent back word: "You may not have been able to discover anything in history to satisfy our assertion that the Roman Catholics were promised an asylum here. This may be so, but it is not our fault that you have not." Then they proceeded to teach a lesson in history to the members of the popular branch of the assembly, citing authorities to establish the fact that after the Maryland Charter had been granted, "Lord Baltimore, who was then a Roman Catholic, emitted his proclamation to encourage the settle-

14 Rowland, 1-33.

15 Father Hughes cites as authority on the attempt of the lower house to enact anti-Catholic laws; Georgetown Coll. Mss., Archives of the Md.-N.Y. Province and British Museum Mss. II, Text. 550, note 16.

ment of his province, promising therein, among other things, liberty of conscience to every denomination of Christians and an equal exercise of religion." The lesson was lost. It did not make the slightest impression on the lower house, and the double taxation bill remained a law.[16]

In the year 1755 five ships landed at Annapolis bringing nearly a thousand refugees to Maryland from the "land of Evangeline." The refugees being both French and Catholic, were not wanted and were not made welcome. They were neither enemies nor prisoners of war but only neutrals and could neither be paroled, exchanged nor treated according to the articles of war. They were distributed among the several counties, but it was only in the little settlement which was the beginning of the city of Baltimore that they found a sanctuary. There some of the Acadians were housed in an unfinished dwelling which was made into a chapel—the first Catholic church in Baltimore. There being no priest in the town, the refugees were visited once a month by the priest resident at Doughoregan Manor.

A temporary altar of the rudest description was erected for these services. The congregations, never consisting of more than fifty, were made up of the exiles with whom were joined a few Irish Catholics. The Catholic colonists would gladly have rendered aid and provided homes for the exiles but this they were not permitted to do by law. "We must own with shame," says a Maryland historian, "that if not treated with positive inhumanity, they were almost everywhere viewed with suspicion and dislike and even the charity which their meek wretchedness extorted, was grudgingly bestowed." [17]

In a long letter written by Charles Carroll of Doughoregan to his son, in 1756, he tells of the plight of the exiles from Acadia:

[16] Upper House Journal, Maryland, Mss. Folio; Russell, Appendix Q, 364-368.

[17] Scharf, op. cit., I, 479.

It has been the misfortune of some of these poor people to be sent to Maryland where they have been supported entirely by private charity and the little they can get by their labor, which for want of employment, has been a very poor resource to them. Many of them would have met with very humane treatment from the Roman Catholics here, but a real or pretended jealousy inclined this government not to suffer them to live with Roman Catholics. I offered the government to take and support two families consisting of fourteen souls, but was not permitted to do so. These poor people were perhaps the most unhappy of any on the globe. They manufactured all they wore and their manufactures were good; they raised in great plenty the provisions they consumed; their habitations were warm and comfortable; they were all upon a level, being all husbandmen and consequently as void of ambition as human nature can be. They appear to be very regular and religious, and that from principle and a perfect knowledge of their duty which convinces me that they were all blessed with excellent pastors. But alas, how is their condition altered! They were at once stripped of everything but the clothes on their backs; many have died in consequence of their sufferings and the survivors see no prospect before them but want and misery.[18]

In Maryland, where under Roman Catholic rule Protestant exiles from many lands found refuge from oppression, these faithful and devout people were denied Christian charity. There was one Protestant in these days, however, whose name brightens the pages of Maryland history. This was Henry Callister, a merchant of Oxford in Talbot County. He forwarded an address to the King on behalf of the exiles, petitioned Governor Sharpe to give them relief and spent large sums of money to relieve their sufferings to the serious impairment of his own modest fortune.[19] He met with opposition in finding homes, food and clothing for them as they were papists and "few have charity for them," he said, "but myself." [20] He made an appeal to the governor to be reimbursed for his outlay, but it does not appear that the request was granted. In 1757 the freemen of his county put themselves on record in a petition to their representatives,

18 Rowland, op. cit., I, 27.
19 Browne, *Maryland,* 230.
20 *Md. Historical Magazine,* VI, 237.

praying that "you use your endeavors in the assembly to have this pest [the exiles] removed from among us." [21]

Charles Carroll of Doughoregan married Elizabeth, the daughter of Clement and Jane Sewall. Of this marriage was born Charles Carroll of Carrollton. While the son was being educated in France and England, his father wrote letters to him, many of which have been preserved and published. They portray the trend of affairs in the colony and give much of its history from the time of its foundation. They show a keen appreciation of the forces that were at work to retard the growth of civil and religious liberty. At times they reveal the discouragement of the writer in the face of what seemed to him a hopeless task. In 1753 the father wrote: "We are still threatened by our assembly, but I hope by the interposition of our friends in London, it will not be in their power to hurt us. A continual calm in this life is no more to be expected than on the ocean." The Carrolls always seemed to have had friends in England with enough influence to prevent the extreme measures favored by the anti-Catholic party in the colony from being put into effect, but who these friends were, will probably never be known.

The father was proud of his Irish ancestry and advised his son to acquaint himself not only with the family genealogy but with Irish history. His letter says:

> You may, as things are now circumstanced and considering the low estate to which all the branches of our family are reduced by the struggles the ancient Irish maintained for the support of their religion, rights and properties, and which received their finishing stroke at the revolution, think my inquiry an idle one, but I do not think so. If I am not right, the folly may be excused by its being a general one and I hope for your own and my sake, you will gratify me in making as careful an inquiry as possible and giving me what light you can on the subject. As soon as there is peace I will send you the genealogy in Irish and English, and I desire you will get our family in particular traced to its origin.[22]

21 Scharf, op. cit., I, 478.
22 Rowland, op. cit., I, 48.

There was hardly anyone at this period who perceived that the seeds of civil as well as religious liberty were planted for the first time in America on the banks of the St. Mary's. For that matter there are few in this day and generation who have this appreciation. Charles Carroll of Doughoregan had made a thorough study of the foundation of the Maryland colony, and he saw clearly that with equality of civil rights and the right of franchise freely given that there had been the full realization of the changed motto on the Carroll coat of arms, *Ubicumque cum Liberate*. In a letter written to his son, Charles Carroll of Carrollton in 1760, is contained this statement: "Maryland was granted to Cecilius, Lord Baltimore, a Roman Catholic, and all persons believing in Jesus Christ, were by the charter provisions permitted the enjoyment *not only of religious but of civil liberty*." Here was the first written recognition of the dual nature of the Maryland foundation—the establishment of both religious and civil freedom.

This letter tells that Maryland was chiefly planted by Roman Catholics, and that all sects continued in "the peaceful enjoyment of their liberties until the Revolution of 1688 when a mob, encouraged by the example set them in England, rebelled against Lord Baltimore, stripped him of his government and his officers of their places." It tells how the crown assumed the government and hindered the Catholics in the free exercise of their religion and how Benedict, Lord Baltimore, on conforming to the established church was restored to his government. The writer takes Charles the fifth Lord Baltimore to task for "being mean enough" to assent to the laws which disqualified Catholics from voting for members to represent them by requiring "all the oaths taken in England to be taken here," and depriving them of the right to hold office. No act of law compelled him to do these things "and he did it to cajole an insolent rabble who were again aiming to deprive him of his government." [23]

[23] Rowland, op. cit., I, 42.

After Frederick Calvert had succeeded to the barony, Carroll warned his son against seeking the favor of the new lord, and if he should meet him, not to fail to let him know of his resentment at the treatment the Roman Catholics were being accorded in Maryland. He wrote:

> I would not have you either decline or solicit an acquaintance with Lord Baltimore or his uncle but if you should accidentally fall in their way, you may when proper let them know that you are not unacquainted with how your grandfather came to this country, after regular study of the law in the Temple, Attorney-General; that he was honored with the post of Agent, Receiver-General, judge in land affairs, Naval officer and that he had the appointment of several naval officers and land surveyors in the province; nor that after he had served three Lords Baltimore for many years with credit and reputation, he was deprived by the late Lord of his posts to gratify a faction whose aim was to divest the family of the government. You may also let him know you are not ignorant of the laws made at that time and lately to deprive the Roman Catholics of their liberties and to distress and vex them. That the memory of the favors conferred on your grandfather will always incline you to promote the interest of the Proprietary family where you can do it in honor and justice. But remember the ill treatment your grandfather met with after so long a series of services; remember the cruel usage of the Roman Catholics by the late and the present Lord Baltimore, and let that so weigh with you as never to sacrifice your own or your country's interest, to promote the interest or power of the proprietary family. It is true they have it in their power to confer some places of credit and honor with acceptance; but as you cannot hold any of them, as the laws stand, and supposing that impediment were removed, I would not wish you to hold any of them except upon honorable terms, I cannot think it will be worth your while to pay a court there or to show any other respect than such a one as is due to them as Lords of the country where your fortunes lie.[24]

After hearing that his son had met Lord Baltimore and had some discourse with him concerning the Catholics in the colony, Carroll again reminded the son to retain the self-respect of a man of principle and honor:

> My previous letters will show you that no dependence is to be had on peace for us here since in the last instance of the act

[24] Ibid, 38.

double taxing us, my Lord thought proper to assent to it though he knew us to be innocent and the charges brought against us false and malicious. I would never have you ungrateful or act dishonorably by opposing the Proprietary family merely for opposition sake, but at the same time I think you will act foolishly, if from principle you espouse the interest of a family who have plainly showed that they have no principle at all, or at least that gratitude and justice and honor have no influence on their principles.

There was no danger that young Charles would pay court to the Baltimore family or fail to show his resentment of the manner that Catholics had been treated in Maryland, if the occasion offered. He was as high spirited as his father. In a letter written in reply to the letter above quoted the son expressed very forcibly his views on Lord Baltimore's complicity in the proceedings of "legalized spoliation" in Maryland. He charged the proprietary with "passive indolence" in allowing a mob to carry out its will and in "not openly refusing his consent to laws so iniquitous even in his own opinion." [25]

In the letter telling of the plight of the Acadian exiles, the elder Carroll intimated that he was tempted to leave Maryland. He wrote to his son: "To fly from the pursuits of envy and malice and to procure a good establishment for you, I am willing to undergo and struggle with all the difficulties and inconveniences attending on a new settlement in a new climate." Then a few years later when the double taxation bill was passed over his vigorous objections, he wrote: "From what I have said I leave you to judge whether Maryland be a tolerable residence for a Roman Catholic. Were I younger I would certainly quit it, but at my age a change of climate would certainly shorten my days." He was willing to sell some of his property so that the son might feel free to leave Maryland but he would keep the most valuable to the last "that you may choose for yourself and make your-

[25] *Maryland Historical Magazine,* X, 255-6.

self as happy as possible for it is my greatest duty to make you so." [26]

The son did choose for himself. His father's letters did not discourage him, rather did they make him the more eager to return to America to help carry on the struggle for civil and religious freedom. He had caught the vision of the Founders of Maryland.

[26] Rowland, op. cit., I, 43.

CHAPTER III

CHARLES CARROLL OF CARROLLTON

Charles Carroll of Carrollton returned to Maryland at the dawn of the American Revolution. He had spent seventeen years in France and England, receiving an education that made him the most cultured man in the colonies. Not one of the leaders of the Revolutionary cause in America had the broad and thorough educational training that he had received during his long years of study at European colleges and universities, as well as under private instructors and tutors. It was an education that peculiarly fitted him for the part he was to play in American affairs.

At the age of eleven, after a year spent at Bohemia Manor school, he had sailed for France with his cousin, John Carroll, to enter the college at St. Omer's. John Carroll was to study for the priesthood, and in 1753 while at St. Omer's he took the first vows of the Jesuit order. In the same year Charles Carroll of Doughoregan wrote to his son that "Jacky, I suppose, is gone up the hill." Here is found the use of the same code that was used in the Maryland letters of the second Lord Baltimore who always referred to the missionaries as "those on the hill." Jacky going up the hill meant that John Carroll was entering the Society of Jesus.

Charles Carroll remained at St. Omer's for six years, receiving the equivalent of two years at preparatory school and a four year college course. From St. Omer's he went to the College of the Jesuits at Rheims. After finishing at Rheims, he spent a year at Bourges where he studied civil law at the university founded by Louis XI, which was famed for its department of jurisprudence. He spent several years in Paris studying under private tutors and at the College of Louis le

Charles Carroll of Carrollton

Grand. For at least eleven years he had been under the instruction of the Jesuits. This education became a permanent influence in his life, an influence that largely shaped his whole career. The life, services and character of Charles Carroll of Carrollton speak well for the *Ratio Studiorum*.

Some of his teachers had been on the American mission and so were familiar with conditions in the colonies which would soon have to be faced by the young pupil when he had completed his education. "I cannot ask to have a better account of you than what I have from Messrs. Carvall, Wappeler and Newton," his father wrote to him in 1753. Those named were all priests, Carroll following the custom of the Lords Baltimore in always referring to them in his correspondence as "Mr." or "Messrs." Father Wappeler was a German who had been in Maryland and Pennsylvania until 1748, the year that the two Carroll boys had sailed for France so it is probable that they embarked on the same ship. One of his instructors wrote to the father that his son was:

> The finest young man that ever entered the House. I should regret the loss of one who during the whole time he was under my care never deserved on any account a single harsh word and whose sweet temper rendered him equally agreeable both to equals and superiors.[1]

While at St. Omer's his father wrote to him that he did not send him "so far away only to learn a little Latin and Greek. Where you are you can lay a foundation for other studies which may hereafter be profitable to yourself and useful to your friends." He pursued a wide and varied course of reading. He did not like poetry and the correspondence between him and his father indicated that he was eager to read works of philosophy and science. His father wrote to him in 1756 that Locke and Newton, for whose works he had made a request, could probably be purchased in Paris but if not then his cousin Father Anthony Carroll who was tutoring him could procure them for him.[2]

[1] Rowland, op. cit., I, 62.
[2] Ibid, 25.

He brought home with him a valuable testimonial of his proficiency in his collegiate courses, which is now to be seen hanging on the walls of the library at Doughoregan manor. It is a list, in Latin, of the theses delivered by him at the close of his studies in Paris and is ornamented by the Carroll crest. The Reverend F. H. Richards, S. J., one-time President of Georgetown College, writes that these essays represented "a public defense covering the whole of philosophy both mental and physical. This no doubt was a great honor, as he would not have been allowed to make a public defense had he not been thoroughly conversant with the subject of his theses." [3]

He left France for England in 1759 to take chambers at the Inner Temple for the study of law. His father wrote to him:

> You must stay at least four years in the Temple. You cannot acquire perfect knowledge of the law in less, if in so short a time, and that knowledge is essential to you as I shall leave you to dispute many things which the present injustice of the times will not permit me in prudence to contest.[4]

The elder Carroll realizing his lack of a legal education desired his son to be prepared to fight for equal justice, which at times seemed to him to have vanished from Maryland. The younger Carroll remained in London nearly six years. He was not inclined at first to make any attempt to be called to the bar. He wrote to his father:

> No degree at law can be obtained without being called to the bar and being entered of the Temple is a necessary, previous and preparatory step to that ceremony which though a ceremony is an opening to all preferments in the law; 'tis attended with no other advantages but many and great inconveniences, the chief test is the frequenting with loose and dissolute companions.[5]

He was anxious to return to Maryland, but at his father's request he continued his law studies. "This I hope will be the last year I shall pass in absence from you," he wrote in

[3] Ibid, 67.
[4] *Family Papers,* Reverend Thomas Lee Sims; Rowland, op. cit., I, 39.
[5] Ibid, I, 49.

1761 and, "Tho' I am impatient to return I readily submit in obedience to your will to remain here this one year more and my impatience shall not hinder my application to the law." But he remained three years more instead of one, as he had hoped. In addition to the law his father recommended that he take up the study of bookkeeping and also acquire a knowledge of surveying, for he said "to cast up the contents of any survey is absolutely necessary to every landed gentleman here." The son, who always acted on the recommendation of his father as to his education, reported that he had mastered the theory of Italian bookkeeping and would be able to follow that method in his own business and he had engaged the services of a professor at Woolwich to teach him surveying.

The Carroll library at Doughoregan, already extensive, was considerably augmented by books purchased by the younger Carroll from time to time and sent to Maryland. He ordered a thousand armorial book plates in England to be placed in the volumes of the home library. In 1763 he wrote that he was surprised in looking over his list of English books not to find a set of Shakespeare which "if I remember you had when I was in Maryland." He was also collecting a library of law books including a compilation of English statutes.

He had little respect for the system of legal education in England. In the same letter he added:

> Nothing could be more absurd than the usual manner of young gentlemen's studying the law. They come from the university, take chambers in the Temple, read Coke Little: (Coke on Littleton) whom they cannot understand, frequent the courts whose practice they are ignorant of; they are soon disgusted with the difficulties and dryness of the study of law, law books are thrown aside, dissipation succeeds to study, immorality to virtue, one night plunges them in ruin, misery and disease.[6]

He saw the accession to the English throne of George III. He attended frequently the sessions of Parliament and heard

[6] Ibid, 54.

many of the debates on questions of American colonial policy. He witnessed the beginning of the constitutional struggle which was to end with the establishment of American independence. He made the acquaintance of Edmund Burke and was a guest at his house. Burke was not then a member of parliament for he did not take his seat until the year that Carroll sailed for America.

There appeared in the *Maryland Gazette* published in Annapolis in its issue of Thursday, February 14th, 1765, the following item of news: "Tuesday last arrived at his Father's House in Town, Charles Carroll Jun'r Esq. (lately from London by way of Virginia) after about sixteen years absence from his Native Country at his Studies and on his Travels."

It was his intention at first to avoid politics. He was disfranchised, and until the laws were changed it did not seem that he would have the opportunity to take any active part in public affairs. "I am resolved," he wrote after his return from abroad, "never to give myself the least concern about politics but to follow the sensible advice given by candid friends to improve my own estate to the utmost and to remain content with the profits a grateful soil and laborious industry will supply." [7]

Events, however, were taking place which soon forced him into the arena of politics. It was inevitable that he should be drawn into the current of affairs that was leading rapidly to Revolution. In less than six weeks after his arrival at Annapolis, royal assent was given to the Stamp Act passed by the British parliament. News of the enactment of this law came to America in May 1765 and in no colony did it arouse more indignation than in Maryland.

The assembly met and adopted a set of resolutions in the form of a bill of rights which set forth that the first settlers had brought with them and transmitted to their descendants all their rights, privileges and immunities under Magna

[7] Gurn, op. cit., 26.

Charta and that Lord Baltimore had obtained for his colonists exemption from royal taxation. The provisions of the Royal Charter relating to taxation were quoted in full, and it was declared that the "people of this province have enjoyed the right of being governed by laws which they themselves have consented to, in the matter of taxes and internal policy," and "the representatives of the freemen alone have the sole right to lay taxes." [8] It was due to the foresight of the first Lord Baltimore that Maryland was the only colony that could claim exemption from alien taxation under the terms of its charter.

Soon after the passage of the Stamp Act, one Zachariah Hood, an Annapolis merchant who was in London, secured for himself the appointment of stamp distributor. When the ship bringing him back to Maryland tied up at the Annapolis dock he regretted that he had ever sought the appointment. Assembled at the landing was a group of his angry fellow citizens who were determined that he should not get off the boat. He remained on board ship but afterwards made a secret landing. As soon as his presence was discovered, he was the object of public condemnation and his effigy was burned at several places, including Elk Ridge adjacent to Doughoregan Manor. A mob destroyed a house which Hood had prepared for the storage of merchandise. Riley, a Maryland historian, claims that this was "the first successful forcible resistance in America to King George's authority." [9]

Charles Carroll wrote to a friend in England:

> Our stamp master Zachariah Hood is hated and despised by everyone; he has been whipped, pilloried and hanged in effigy, in this place, Baltimore town and at the landing; the people seemed determined not to buy his goods. Should the Stamp Act be enforced by tyrannical soldiery, our property, our liberty, our very existence is at an end. And you may be persuaded that nothing but an armed force can execute the worst of laws.

[8] Browne, *Maryland,* 246-9.

[9] Riley, *History of the General Assembly of Maryland,* 277; Andrews, op. cit., 279.

All the wrongs and oppressions suffered by his Irish ancestors, and all the religious and political injustice visited upon his father, his grandfather and their fellow Catholics in Maryland and England, came vividly to the mind of Charles Carroll. He was awakened rudely from his dream of a life of quiet ease on his landed estates, by the passage of the Stamp Act. This tyranny aroused him to make common cause with his fellow colonists though it might lead to armed resistance. His letters at the time indicate how quick he was to sense the whole situation. He was one of the first, if not the very first, to see the probability of successful revolution and eventual independence.

Shortly he wrote another letter to England in which he expressed himself more forcibly:

> Nothing can overcome the aversion of the people to the Stamp Act and their love of liberty but an armed force and that, too, not a contemptible one. To judge from the number of the colonists and the spirit they have already shown, and which I hope to God will not fail them on the day of trial, twenty thousand men would find it difficult to enforce the law, or more properly speaking ram it down our throats. Can England surrounded with powerful enemies, distracted with intense factions, encumbered and almost staggering under the immense load of debt—little short of one hundred and fifty million pounds—send out such a powerful army to deprive a free people, their fellow-subjects, of their rights and liberties? If ministerial influence and parliamentary corruption should not blush at such a detestable scheme; if guardians of sacred liberty, and of our happy constitution, should have the impudence to avow this open infraction of both, will England, her commerce annihilated by the oppression of America, be able to maintain those troops?

He discloses not only a knowledge of the temper of the people but also an intimacy with colonial affairs that is surprisingly accurate in view of the fact that he had only just returned from Europe where he had been for seventeen years. This knowledge had come to him through the letters of his father and those of his instructors who had been identified with the American mission. His friends, who had been in Maryland and whom he met in Paris and London, kept him informed about American affairs. Then too there were Englishmen in public life, whom he had met, such as Edmund Burke, who were not unfamiliar with what was going on in the colonies and who were opposed to the policies of the parliament.

He made a bold prediction of the future of America. While England "has already arrived at its zenith, the power of this continent is growing daily and in time will be as unbounded as our dominions are extensive." He called attention to the rapid increase of manufactures and to the advancement of art and science. He hoped the day would come

> when America will be superior to all the world. Without prejudice or partiality I do not believe the universe can show a finer country—so luxuriant in its soil; so happy in a healthy climate; so extensively watered by so many navigable rivers and producing within itself not only all the necessities but even most of the superfluities of life.[10]

Imbued with such pride of country and conscious as he was of the illegality of unjust taxation, it is not surprising that Carroll took his place among the leaders of the Revolution.

In December of the same year (1765) he wrote to his English friend Bradshaw:

> The Americans are jealous of their privileges and resolved to maintain them. Corruption has not made such inroads among them that they fail to judge liberty at its true value. They are fully cognizant of its blessings and not only talk of them, but are possessed of a genuine desire for their preservation. The surest way to defeat oppression is to make the oppressors feel it.

He recommended a boycott of British goods such as called for by the resolution adopted by the merchants and shopkeepers of New York and Philadelphia:

> I sincerely wish that this reasoning may be just and these measures produce the desired effect as I am convinced in my

10 Rowland, op. cit., I, 74-5.

opinion that the justice of our cause and our petitions unsupported by such vigorous and reasonable resolutions would operate slowly if at all to bring about our deliverance from the jaws of death, I mean political death which poverty and slavery, the companions of the Stamp Act, will infallibly bring on.

Carrying out the idea of the boycott he joined "the army of the homespun." He wrote:

A great many gentlemen have already appeared in homespun and I hope soon to make one of the number. Many imagine the Stamp Act will be suspended for a time till some expedient may be hit on to reconcile the exemption we claim from a parliamentary taxation, with the right and power asserted of late by the Parliament. If the act be suspended until such an expedient can be found, it will be suspended for all eternity.

The Stamp Act was repealed but it was accompanied by a declaratory act which expressly rejected the claims of the colonists to the right to tax themselves and proclaimed the power of parliament to make laws binding on the colonies and the people of America "in all cases whatsoever." The repeal of the Stamp Act meant nothing to the colonists, for their claim of "no taxation without representation" was denied, and parliament proceeded to pass other bills taxing them without their consent.

Carroll took exception to the endeavor of his English friend, Graves, to draw a parallel between the conditions in Ireland and America.

Your position that Ireland and America belong to the King, Lords and Commons, is quite new and I believe not warranted by any authority nor defensible upon the principles of reason or equity. Your forcible expression of belonging applied to Ireland is proper enough... England has all along treated the innocent and injured Irish as slaves and beasts of burden. But America, thank God, is at too great a distance to be treated in that manner; the Americans have too much spirit to submit to such indignities and will in a few years have a force sufficient to repel them if offered.[11]

In the same letter he indicates that he does not belong to the Rousseau school of philosophy, for he refers to Rousseau

[11] Gurn, op. cit., 32.

as that "restless, fantastical philosopher" who "cannot live long in any place."

It was while these letters were being written that he made his first acquaintance with Washington, who visited Annapolis frequently. Washington had business relations with Carroll's father concerning property in Fairfax county, Virginia, and his diary entries show that he sometimes dined at the Carroll home. Later he was chairman of a committee of the Virginia assembly which had charge of the work of improving navigation on the Potomac river. A company was formed to carry on the work and a fund of thirty thousand pounds was raised by subscription. Charles Carroll of Carrollton was among the large subscribers.[12]

It was not until 1773 that Charles Carroll made public his views on the relations between England and the colonies. The more letters he wrote, the stronger became his conviction that the only outcome was independence but these had been views privately expressed. As soon as he entered the public arena, he became the leader of the Revolutionary party in Maryland.

Since 1739, there was a standing grievance over the levy of a special tax for the payment of the salaries or fees to the officials of the colony which was as obnoxious as the tax for the support of the clergy. In that year the assembly raised an objection to it on the ground that it was an unconstitutional tax levied, like King Charles' ship money, without the assent of the people. The tax continued to be levied and collected, but it was not without continual remonstrances from the lower house. The fees had been fixed by the assembly from year to year and paid to the officers of the province either in money or tobacco in place of salaries.

The lower house, in 1770, claimed that the fees were exorbitant and in one case an officer had been guilty of taking illegal fees. A bill was passed by the house lowering and regulating the fees. This was opposed by the council, the upper

12 Rowland, op. cit., I, 99.

house. There were several members of the council who benefited by the excessive fees, among them being Daniel Dulaney Jr., a well known attorney and son of the lawyer who advised Charles Carroll of Doughoregan and Dr. Charles Carroll in their controversy. Dulaney was secretary of the province, an appointive, not an elective office. The lower house not only insisted that the fees be lowered but ordered the arrest of the officer who had illegally taken them. This created a deadlock between the two houses. Governor Eden cut short the disagreement by proroguing the assembly and fixing the fees by proclamation.

The will of the representatives of the people being disregarded by this arbitrary action of the governor, there arose considerable discontent when it became known that the clergy of the established church had taken advantage of the situation to claim an additional ten pounds of tobacco per poll. This was allowed by the Governor. The fees of the officials and the clergy were claimed to be justified by a law passed in 1702, which the Governor claimed was now in force, as the legislature had failed to take action.

At this juncture there appeared in the *Maryland Gazette* an anonymous communication which made the claim that the law of 1702 was void because the assembly which passed it, and which met on March 16th of that year, had been summoned by writs running in the name of King William III who had died on March 8th. This was immediately followed by another communication which appeared in the form of an imaginary dialogue between two citizens, one opposing the Governor and Council and the second citizen defending them. The writer, who was ingenious, prepared the article so that "second citizen" apparently demolished the arguments made by "first citizen," and presumably carried off the honors of the debate. Everyone recognized this as the work of Dulaney, chief beneficiary of the fee system.

Thereupon a communication appeared signed by "First Citizen," claiming that his side of the case had not been fairly presented in the dialogue. He answered the arguments of Dulaney in an exceedingly able and convincing manner. When it became known that the writer of this letter was Charles Carroll of Carrollton, he at once became the recognized champion of popular rights. He had dramatically taken the role of the straw man Dulaney thought he had knocked down. He took the broad position that the fees which were to be levied were nothing more than taxes, and that no taxes could be laid except by the representatives of the people, in other words that there should be no taxation without representation. Here was first raised the battle cry of the American Revolution.

Carroll showed his knowledge of English constitutional history and law throughout the controversy. In the exchange of letters in the columns of the old *Maryland Gazette,* he was more than a match for Dulaney who, although an able lawyer, did not possess the scholarship of Carroll.

Carroll had the support of public opinion, and his cognomen of "First Citizen" taken from the dialogue clung to him so that he was later actually recognized as Maryland's First Citizen. His claim that the "settling of fees and the imposition of taxes are powers belonging to the representatives of the people" was stating in effect the case of the American colonies against Great Britain. It was apparent that he was the champion of the cause of all the colonies against the encroachments of King and Parliament as well as the cause of the Maryland colonists against the usurpations of the Governor and Council.

When the Revolution broke out, Dulaney joined the Tory camp. In the meantime Carroll became a popular idol. Letters of thanks came to him from members of the assembly and from the freemen of several of the counties. The citizens of Annapolis came to him in a body to express their gratitude. In recognition of his first letter there appeared a communication in the *Gazette* signed by "Independent Whigs" thanking him for having spoken with an "honest freedom," and saying that they had "for a long time impatiently waited for a man of abilities to set forth" and tell "our darling ministers" of the evils they had brought upon the community.

William Hand Browne says that in this contest Carroll "according to the popular opinion which regarded him as the champion of freedom against prerogative, gained an overwhelming victory."[13] His letters according to McMahon were "political essays of a high order taking a wide range through the doctrines of constitutional liberty evincing much research abounding in happy illustrations and often pointed with the most caustic satire."[14]

It was gratifying to the elder Carroll to see the long and careful education that he had planned and provided for his son now attaining fruition. He was justly proud of the ability shown by his son in the controversy. He wrote that the *Gazette* office was crowded with people eager to obtain the first copies of the paper. "All the strangers in town retired to their lodging, many to private places," to read the paper free from annoyance. "The public houses were at night as quiet as private ones," and "next morning every mouth was open in praise of the 'First Citizen.'"

Later he wrote to his son:

> A gentleman told me as you appeared at the county court on Friday, that the whisper immediately ran: "There is the First Citizen," and that every eye was fixed on you with evident marks of pleasure and approbation; that many said they did not know which to admire most, your strength of reasoning or your calm and gentleman-like style, considering Antillon's scurrilous and abusive provocation, that it was a doubt and matter of debate whether your text or conclusion was most severe, but all agreed nothing could be more applicable than both.[15]

Dulaney, who lacked the broad-mindedness of his father, after realizing that Carroll was getting the better of the argument and winning public approval, followed the example

[13] *Maryland, the History of a Palatinate,* 268.
[14] *Historical View of the Government of Maryland,* 390.
[15] Gurn, op. cit., 42.

of his father's client Dr. Carroll and took refuge behind the discriminatory laws against Catholics. He attempted to discredit his opponent by calling attention to his religion:

> After all who is this man that calls himself a citizen? Who is he? He has no share in the legislature, as a member of any branch, he is incapable of being a member, he is disabled from giving a vote in the choice of representatives, by the laws and constitution of the country, on account of his (religious) principles which are distrusted by those laws. He is disabled by an express resolve from interfering in the election of members of the same account. He is not a Protestant!

When Dulaney fired this last shot he thought to finish his opponent. An appeal to bigotry had served its purpose before but it failed this time. Charles Carroll was invulnerable to an attack of the kind Dulaney had made upon him. In regard to the injustice of the disabling laws against Catholics and the votes of previous assemblies against his coreligionists Carroll said little in his reply. He refused to allow the real point of the controversy to be concealed by a discussion of religion for in so doing he "might perhaps rekindle extinguished animosities."

On behalf of the disfranchised Catholics of Maryland he simply said: "Meminimus et ignoscimus"—"We remember yet we forgive." To the question "Who is this man?" Carroll replied:

> A man of an independent fortune, one deeply interested in the prosperity of his country; a friend to liberty; a settled enemy to lawless prerogative. What my speculative notions of religion may be, this is neither the place nor time to declare; my political principles ought only to be questioned on the present occasion; surely they are constitutional and have met I hope with the approbation of my countrymen.

"I have not the least dislike of the Church of England," he wrote in another communication, "though I am not within her pale . . . knaves and bigots of all sects and denominations I hate and despise."

To Dulaney's insinuation that "Papists are distrusted by the laws and laid under disabilities," he replied:

They cannot I know, ignorant as I am, enjoy any place or profit or trust, while they continue papists; but do these disabilities extend so far as to preclude them from thinking and writing on matters merely of a political nature? Antillon [Dulaney's *nom-de-plume*] would make a most excellent inquisitor; he has some striking specimens of an arbitrary temper, the first requisite. He will not allow me freedom of thought or speech.[16]

Dulaney in an attempt at sarcasm unwittingly hit upon a truth, when he said that the first citizen had been a pupil at St. Omer's "the best seminary of the universe of the champions of civil and religious liberty." Dulaney, like many others before and after his time, had little conception of real social philosophy as taught by the ancient school-men and interpreted by the Jesuits, which the English historian Green said "forms the theory of modern democracy."

It was not only his knowledge of law but his study of philosophy, history and the humanities that gave Carroll the weapons that were used so successfully against his antagonist and made him the exponent of civil and religious freedom. There were times when he rose to great heights in the fervor of his appeal for the doctrine of popular rights. One of his most forceful utterances was:

Not a single instance can be selected from our history of a law favorable to liberty obtained from government but by the unanimous steady and spirited conduct of the people. The Great Charter, the several confirmations of it, the Petition of Right, the Bill of Rights, were all the happy effects of force and necessity.[17]

His ringing declaration that "in a land of freedom this arbitrary exertion of prerogative will not, must not be endured" brought forth the reply from Dulaney that such bold words were dangerous, and Carroll rejoined: "In a free country a contrary doctrine is insufferable and the man who declares it is an enemy to the people."

The elections of 1773 turned on the question raised in the controversy. The supporters of Carroll were victorious, carry-

16 Rowland, op. cit., I, 127.
17 Ibid, 124.

ing the assembly by a substantial majority. There was great rejoicing. The Governor's proclamation was buried beyond recall with due ceremony in a public mock funeral. After the election there appeared in the *Gazette* an address to the "First Citizen" signed by William Paca and Matthias Hammond, the newly elected delegates to the lower house from Annapolis:

> Your many and spirited opposition to the arbitrary attempt of the government to establish the fees of office by proclamation justly entitles you to the exalted character of a distinguished advocate for the rights of your country. . . The free and independent citizens of Annapolis, the metropolis of Maryland, who have lately honored us with the public character of representatives impressed with a just sense of the signal service which you have done your country, instructed us on the day of our election to return you their hearty thanks. Public gratitude, sir, for public services, is the patriot's due; and we are proud to observe the generous feelings of our fellow citizens towards an advocate for liberty. With pleasure we comply with the instructions of our constituents and in their name we publicly thank you for the spirited exertion of your abilities!

Carroll in his acknowledgement of this tribute said: "How superior is the praise of freemen to the mercenary and interested commendation of a minister, even of a monarch, when bestowed to countenance and support oppression and injustice!"

The real historical significance of the outcome of the Dulaney-Carroll controversy lies in the fact that the struggle against bigotry and intolerance and for the return of religious liberty in Maryland carried on by the Carroll family since the overthrow of the Baltimore government by the Protestant Revolution of 1688, had been won. Dulaney's ill-advised attack on the religion of his antagonist was well warded off by Carroll and so missed its mark. It was a clumsy and ill-timed camouflage. The freemen of Maryland were in no mood to have sand thrown in their eyes. Carroll could "only wield the weapons of a brave spirit and the accomplishments of a cultivated intellect." He emerged from the controversy a victor not only for civil liberty but religious liberty as well. His magnanimous rejoinder "we remember yet we forgive" was all that was needed to turn the tide of public sentiment toward tolerance and freedom.

Although Charles Carroll was disfranchised by the law of the province and disqualified from election as a representative in the assembly, because he was a Catholic, the freemen of Annapolis did not hesitate to appoint him by resolution one of a committee of six "to join with those of Baltimore town and other parts of the province to constitute one general committee—to effect such association as shall secure American liberty." A month later, June 1774, a convention consisting of the committees appointed by the various towns and counties assembled at Annapolis to elect delegates to the first Continental Congress. After the election of the delegates to the congress the convention adjourned, but from this time on it remained the depository of the sovereign power of the people of Maryland and became the real government superseding the old assembly.[18] The convention concluded its sessions on December 12, 1774, with the following appeal to the people:

> As our opposition to the settled plan of the British administration to enslave America will be strengthened by a union of all ranks of men within this province, we do most earnestly recommend that all former differences about religion or politics and all private animosities and quarrels of every kind, from henceforth cease and be forever buried in oblivion; and we entreat, we conjure every man, by his duty to his God and his country, and his posterity, cordially to unite in defence of our common rights and liberties.[19]

With the return of Charles Carroll to Maryland had come the return of the old spirit of liberty and equality.

The Provincial Convention at its December session 1774 adopted "The Association of the Freemen of Maryland."

[18] Browne, op. cit., 261.

[19] Russell, op. cit., 488; Proceedings of the Convention of the Province of Maryland held at Annapolis, 1774–76, p. 10; "Provincial Government of Maryland" Silver, J.H.U. *Studies*, 13th Series.

This took the place of the old assembly, and became the charter of the colony until supplanted by the constitution of 1776. Carroll, who was chairman of the committee on revolutionary correspondence for Annapolis county, was elected one of the deputies to represent his county in the convention or association of freemen for one year. No question was raised as to his disqualification on account of his religion. The oath of abjuration and the old discriminatory laws against Catholics were forgotten. He had been elevated to a higher honor than could have been conferred under the old laws which did not give him so much as a vote at the polls. By a silent and unofficial vote he had been made the "first citizen" of Maryland.

In 1775, the convention took the first step toward freedom in the extension of the franchise to "all freemen having an estate of forty pounds without religious distinction." [20] Now for the first time since the rule of the Catholic Lords Baltimore, both Protestant and Catholic could go to the polls together. "The benign aurora of the coming republic lighted the Catholic to the recovery of his rightful political equality in the land which a Catholic proprietary had set apart for religious freedom." [21]

In the meantime the House of Baltimore had passed from the picture of Maryland history. The misspent life of the libertine, Frederick, the last of the Lords Baltimore, had come to an end. Having left no legitimate children he attempted to make his bastard son Henry Harford his successor as Lord Proprietary, but the succession was not recognized. Before Harford could establish his claim Maryland had become one of the thirteen United States. Long since the glory and honor of the House of Baltimore had descended to the House of Carroll.

20 Cobb, op. cit., 503.
21 Bancroft, op. cit., VIII, 76.

CHAPTER IV

PREPARING FOR INDEPENDENCE

As THE *Mayflower* has overshadowed the *Ark* and the *Dove* in American history, so has the Boston Tea Party partly eclipsed the tea party held a year later in Maryland, notwithstanding that as one writer has said "Annapolis out-Bostoned Boston." The brig *Peggy Stewart* arrived at Annapolis, October 18, 1774, having on board a consignment of tea. Anthony Stewart, the owner, paid the tax on the cargo. This was in violation of the boycott against British goods. When the ship arrived a mass meeting was held which solemnly resolved that the shipment should not be landed. Stewart offered to destroy the tea and apologize for his indiscretion. This was not enough. Both the tea and the ship must be destroyed.

Stewart went to Charles Carroll of Carrollton for advice. Carroll told him to set fire to the vessel and "burn her to the water's edge." [1] With his own hands, Stewart fired the ship with its cargo of tea and in the presence of a large concourse, there was a spectacular bonfire which outshone in brilliance the Boston Tea Party. Maryland now celebrates the anniversary of the burning of the *Peggy Stewart* as one of its state holidays.

Soon after the *Peggy Stewart* affair, Charles Carroll from Washington wrote to his father that he believed that "this controversy will at last be decided by arms." As to the final outcome he was never in doubt. He wrote again to his English friend, Graves, who had boasted that six thousand troops could easily march through the colonies from one end to the other:

[1] McMahon, op. cit., 409; Ridgeley, op. cit., 162.

So they may but they will be masters of the spot only on which they camp. They will find naught but enemies before and around them. If we are beaten on the plains, we will retreat to our mountains and defy them. Our resources will increase with our difficulties. Necessity will force us to exertion until tired of combating in vain against a spirit which victory after victory cannot subdue, your armies will evacuate our soil and your country retire an immense loser from the contest. No sir, we have made up our minds to abide the issue of the approaching struggle and though much blood may be spilt, we have no doubt of our ultimate success.[2]

Benjamin Franklin once made the remark that for several years before the signing of the Declaration of Independence, he had travelled almost "from one end of the continent to the other and kept a great variety of company, eating, drinking and conversing with them freely, yet I never had heard in any conversation from any person, drunk or sober, the least expression of a wish for a separation or a hint that such a thing would be advantageous to America." John Jay, too, made the statement that until the second petition of Congress in 1775, he had never heard any American "of any class or of any description express a wish for the independence of the colonies."

If either Franklin or Jay had conversed with Charles Carroll prior to 1775 on the subject of the independence of the colonies, neither could have made such a statement. As early as 1763, while he was a student in England Carroll wrote to his father: "America is a growing country; in time it will and must be independent." [3] In the letter of 1765 written to his friend Graves he saw a vision of an independent America. In a letter written in 1766 to this same friend he said: "Altho the colonies are not aiming at independence, yet if slavery and dependency be convertible terms," and England does not make the proper distinction, then "I believe every American would disclaim that sort of dependency."

[2] Gurn., op. cit., 53.
[3] Ibid, 80.

Charles Carroll of Carrollton was the first American patriot to express himself in favor of independence, to foresee the conflict with the mother country and to have absolute faith in the ultimate freedom of the colonies.

Charles Carroll of Doughoregan, now over seventy years of age, a vigorous champion of the rights and liberties of the colonists, shared with his son the view that America must win her independence. "I hope the colonists will be unanimous and resolute, for their freedom depends upon their being so," he wrote to his son, May 27, 1774. In a letter written a month later he said: "I am confident America will be unanimous and resolute because their all is at stake and the insolence of Great Britain so great as justly to provoke every species of resentment they can show." [4]

After Lexington, Concord and Bunker Hill had given their message of war, the freemen of Maryland, recognizing the Continental Congress as being vested with power of general supervision, created a council of safety, directed the enrollment of forty companies of minute-men, established a military code and authorized the issue of a quarter of a million dollars in currency. Charles Carroll of Carrollton was appointed a member of the Council of Safety. He bent his efforts to prepare the colony to take its part in the coming struggle for independence.

He wrote a letter to Washington soon after the latter had assumed command of the American forces at Cambridge. In this letter is revealed the confidence he had in the commander-in-chief to whom he was to give the full measure of loyalty and support throughout the war. It was written to introduce John Ross Key of Frederick County, a lieutenant in a Maryland rifle company which went to Boston in this same year. Key was a friend of Carroll and had been with him in England. He was the father of Francis Scott Key of Star-Spangled Banner fame. The letter to Washington reads:

[4] Ibid, 49.

Annapolis, 26th Sept. 1775

Sir:

At the request of the bearer, Mr. Key, I have presumed to trouble you with this letter to introduce to your notice and countenance that young gentleman who I flatter myself will endeavor to deserve your good opinion and favour. Should hostilities be suspended and a negotiation take place this winter, I hope to have the pleasure of seeing you in this city on your way to Virginia. If a treaty is but once set on foot, I think it must terminate in a lasting and happy peace; an event I am persuaded you must earnestly desire as every good citizen must, in which number you rank foremost; for you who so justly deserving of that most glorious of all titles, as the man singled out by the unanimous voice of his country, for his love and attachment to it, and great abilities, and placed in a position of the most exalted and dangerous prominence. If we cannot obtain a peace on safe and just terms, my next wish is that you may extort by force from our enemies what their policy and justice should have granted, and that you may live long to enjoy the fame of the best—the noblest deed—defending and securing the liberties of your country.

I am with the greatest esteem, Sir,
Your most obedient, humble servant,
Charles Carroll of Carrollton.[5]

It was not long after the receipt of this letter that Washington issued his famous communication discountenancing the celebration of "Pope's Day" in Massachusetts. A somewhat revised version of the celebration of "Guy Fawkes' Day," in England, observing the anniversary of the discovery of the gunpowder plot, had been transplanted to New England in the form of "Pope's Day" when numerous groups had a glorious time burning the Pope in effigy. Washington had learned that this form of celebration was to be repeated while the American forces under his command were encamped around Boston. He sent the following communication to the officers and men of the army:

As the Commander-in-Chief has been apprised of a design formed for the observance of that ridiculous and childish custom of burning the effigy of the Pope, he cannot help expressing his surprise that there should be officers and soldiers in this army

[5] Rowland, op. cit., I, 138. A fac-simile of this letter is printed in the *Magazine of American History,* XXII, 353.

so void of common sense as not to see the impropriety of such a step at this juncture. At a time when we are soliciting and have already attained the friendship and alliance of the people of Canada, whom we ought to consider as brethren embarked in the same cause—the defense of the liberty of America—at this juncture and under such circumstances to be insulting to their religion is so monstrous as not to be suffered or excused, indeed instead of offering the most remote insult, it is our duty to address public thanks to those, our brethren, to whom we are indebted for every late happy success over the common enemy in Canada.

Washington at this time was misled by a false hope. He believed that the friendship and alliance of the French Canadians had been won and that they would welcome an American army and openly lend aid to the struggle for independence. There were two factors that had already prevented the consummation of this hope.

First, was the passage of the Quebec Act of 1774 by the English Parliament, which continued in Canada the French civil law and the ancient privileges of the Roman Catholic Church. This was obviously a gesture intended to dissuade the French Canadians from making common cause with the American revolutionary party and to keep the revolution from spreading into Canada. Then came a stupid outburst from the first Continental Congress, protesting against the granting of religious liberty to the French Catholics in Canada on the ground that it would endanger the liberties of England's Protestant colonists.

This took the form of an address to the English people in which the Catholic religion was grossly insulted. It said in part:

> Nor can we suppress our astonishment that a British Parliament should ever consent to establish in that country a religion that has deluged your island with blood, and dispersed impiety, bigotry, persecution, murder and rebellion through every part of the world.

Then there came an address to "the inhabitants of the

Colonies" which was milder in tone but almost as offensive. These protests did not have the approval of Washington nor Franklin, but there were some among the revolutionary leaders at whose door the responsibility must be placed. It is only necessary to mention one and that was John Jay who was afflicted with a bitter religious prejudice. It was he who penned the address to the people of Great Britain.[6]

The Congress then executed an about face. This time looking toward Canada it addressed the French Canadians with honeyed words which could not be regarded as sincere by those for whom they were intended. "We are too well acquainted with the true liberality of sentiment distinguishing your nation, to imagine that differences of religion will prejudice you against a hearty amity with us," read the appeal. It closed with a prayer that "Almighty God may incline your minds to approve our necessary and equitable measures, to add yourselves to us, and may grant to our joint exertions an end as happy as our cause is just." [7]

A more absurd and inconsistent position was never taken by an American legislative body than that taken by the first Continental Congress in its attempt to win the support of the Canadians. Every effort was made to keep the French Catholics from knowing how their religion had been insulted, but the interpreters who gave them the friendly message in the last appeal also gave an interpretation of the address to the English people. The natural resentment which followed shattered all hopes of an alliance.

In a letter to Jefferson written some years later, John Adams, evidently ashamed of any part he had in the proceedings of the first congress admitted that he was "too shallow a politician" to realize the importance of "those compositions," that the members resembled "children playing at marbles or push-pins. America is in total ignorance or under infinite deception concerning that assembly. To draw the character of

[6] Michael Williams, *The Shadow of the Pope* (1932), 34.
[7] *Journal of the Continental Congress*, I, 112.

them would require a volume and would now be considered a caricatured print."

The picture of this first continental congress blowing hot and cold at the same time is not especially edifying to the student of American history, but it indicates the state of mind of many of the colonists in the matter of religion. Most of them were so obsessed with a prejudice against the Catholic Church that they could neither see straight nor think clearly when anything arose that in any way involved consideration for the Catholic religion. The passage of the Quebec Act had completely set them off their balance.

Dr. Guilday, in his *Life and Times of John Carroll,* places three of these documents in deadly parallel. The address to the people of Great Britain was dated October 21, 1774. Five days later, October 26, the address to the Canadians was issued which knocked the props from under the previous address. On this same day is found a petition to the King which recites, among other grievances, the establishment of "the Roman Catholic religion throughout those vast regions." It is apparent that these embryo statesmen did not quite know what they were doing. However they did have a dim realization that they were committing some kind of a blunder. To extricate themselves from a diplomatic mess they gave a remarkable exhibition of mental gymnastics.

It might have been expected that the gratuitous insults heaped upon the Catholic Church and her adherents by the revolutionary party would dampen the ardor of the Catholics who were espousing the cause of the revolution. The Reverend Jonathan Boucher, a loyalist clergyman of the Anglican Church who was trying to win the support of the Catholics of the colonies through a series of propaganda sermons preached in Maryland, brought out clearly that:

> The patient firmness of character worthy of all praise and imitation, the wisdom and virtue to respect laws more than their own personal feelings enabled the Catholics to withstand such injuries and indignities as their high spirited forefathers

would have ill brooked. Everything most dear to the human heart has been torn from them, excepting their attachment to their religion and their determination to love and bless those fellow-subjects who unmindful of the duties resulting from their religion, and unmoved by so endearing an example, foolishly and wickedly continue to regard Papists as Samaritans with whom they resolve to have no dealings.

Boucher depicted the Catholics of Maryland as first wavering and undetermined to ally themselves with the revolutionary party whose members had "in general distinguished themselves by being particularly hostile to Catholics." In his crusade to win the Catholics to the loyalist side he found one man who stood in his way. That man was Charles Carroll of Carrollton, for the preacher admitted that:

The Catholic gentleman who was possessed of one of the first fortunes in the country (in short the Duke of Norfolk of Maryland) actuated as was generally thought, solely by his desire to become a public man for which he was unquestionably well qualified, openly espoused the cause of Congress. Soon after he became a member of that body. This seemed to settle the wavering disposition of the Catholics in Maryland; under so respectable a leader as Mr. Carroll they all soon became good Whigs, and concurred with their fellow-revolutionists in declaiming against the misgovernment of Great Britain.[8]

It was the patriotism of Charles Carroll and his staunch loyalty to the American cause, unwavering in the face of bitter attacks on his religion, that finally won the respect of the leaders of the Revolution and made them heartily ashamed of the absurd attack on the Catholic Church in the protest against the Quebec Act. He saved the American Revolution from being tainted with religious bigotry.

Protests against the Quebec Act were not confined to the Congress. Protestant pulpits all over the land thundered their objections to the Act and several of the State conventions, notably that of New York, voiced their opposition. The sober-minded leaders were quick to see that a mistake had been made, a mistake that might prove costly to the American cause, and they took steps to remedy it.

[8] "Preface to a sermon, preached in 1774," Russell, op. cit., 487.

Congress met February 1776, to discuss the report of its secret committee on the Canadian invasion. This committee reported that papers printed by the Tories of New York and circulated in Canada assuring the Canadians that "our design was to deprive them of their religion as well as their possessions" had done much harm and recommended that a committee be appointed and sent to Canada to "explain *viva voce* to the people there the nature of our dispute with England." [9]

The following day, February 15, 1776, it was resolved that a Committee of three, two to be members of Congress, be appointed to proceed to Canada "there to pursue such instructions as shall be given them by Congress." The members chosen were Benjamin Franklin, Samuel Chase and Charles Carroll of Carrollton. Chase, the second member of the committee, was a Marylander who had been actively associated with Carroll in the revolutionary cause, serving with him on the same provincial committees.

It was further resolved that "Mr. Carroll be requested to prevail on Mr. John Carroll" to accompany the committee to Canada. "Mr. John Carroll" was Father John Carroll of Rock Creek. Father Carroll, following the suppression of the Jesuit order, returned to Maryland. After an absence of twenty-six years he came back to his native land with a thorough understanding of the causes that had led to the Revolution and with a determination to ally himself with the American colonists. Not only his Irish antecedents but his whole training and education had led him to take his place by the side of Charles Carroll in support of the American cause. That he was imbued with the new spirit of independence was manifest when he became the first priest to refuse to submit to the English jurisdiction of Father Lewis, the former Superior of the American mission, who, after the suppression acted as Vicar General of the London District. "This was not in a spirit of insubordination," says Dr. Guil-

[9] *Journal of the Continental Congress,* IV, 148.

day, "but with political cleavage from England John Carroll believed ecclesiastical separation went also."

In the interim between his arrival in Maryland and his departure on the Canadian mission, Father Carroll had found a field of labor in caring for the spiritual needs of the faithful of Southern Maryland. He lived at his mother's house in Rock Creek where a room was set apart for the Catholic worshippers from the surrounding country. He was at Rock Creek when he received the message from Charles Carroll notifying him of the request of the Continental Congress to accompany the Canadian mission.

It is obvious that the Carrolls were asked to go on the mission because they were Catholics in thorough sympathy with the American cause. Their long residence in France and acquaintance with the French people, language and customs, it was believed would give them the entrée that was needed for the negotiations or at least insure a sympathetic hearing.

> The standing and influence of John Carroll as a Catholic clergyman of talents and activity, it was hoped would be of essential service in the accomplishment of the mission, by removing from the minds of a Catholic population, all suspicions of interference in religious subjects.[10]

It was a hopeless task from the start, made so by the stupid action of the Congress in needlessly insulting the Canadian Catholics whose friendship and cooperation were now solicited. John Carroll deliberated long before deciding to accept the invitation. It was only his desire to aid the cause of American liberty and his sense of duty that finally prompted him to accept. In the Baltimore Cathedral Archives is the unfinished draft of a memorandum written by Carroll which indicates that he saw the futility of the mission:

> The Congress has done me the distinguished and unexpected honor of desiring me to accompany the Committee to Canada

[10] Sanderson, *Biographies of the Signers of the Declaration of Independence,* VII, 250.

and of assisting them in such matters as they shall judge useful. I should betray the confidence put in me by the Honorable Congress and perhaps disappoint their expectations were I not to open my mind to them with the utmost sincerity and plainly tell them how little service they can hope to derive from my assistance. In the first place, the nature and functions of that profession in which I have engaged from a very early period in life, render me, as I humbly conceive, a very unfit person to be employed in a negotiation of so new a kind to me, of which I have neither experience nor systematical knowledge. I hope I may be allowed to add that though I have little regard to my own personal safety amidst the present distress of my country yet I cannot help feeling that when the ministers of religion leave the duties of their profession to take a busy part in political matters, they generally fall into contempt and sometimes even discredit the cause in whose service they are engaged.

Then he stated that he does not believe from the information he has received that the Canadians have "the same motives for taking up arms against England which render the resistance of the other colonies so justifiable," and he does not conceive it to be his duty to advise them to do it. He was willing, however, to do all within his power to influence the French Canadians to remain neutral in the coming struggle and to give no assistance to British arms.[11]

One important factor that made the Carrolls willing to undertake the performance of the onerous and disagreeable duty devolved upon them by congress, was the solemn promise of religious liberty which they were authorized to make to the Catholics of Canada. In the instructions issued to the commissioners was the following clause:

You are further to declare that we hold sacred the rights of conscience and may promise to the whole people, solemnly in our name, the free and undisturbed exercise of their religion; and to the clergy, the full, perfect, and peaceable possession and enjoyment of all their estates. That the government of everything relating to their religion and clergy shall be left entirely in the hands of the good people of that province and such legislature as they shall constitute; provided however that all other denominations of Christians be equally entitled to hold offices

11 Guilday, op. cit., 96-7; *Baltimore Cathedral Archives,* Special C-F.

and enjoy civil privileges and the free exercise of their religion and be totally exempt from the payment of any tithes or taxes for the support of any religion.

The importance of this pronouncement is not to be lost sight of in the study of the rise of religious liberty in America. It was not only a promise to the Catholics of Canada, but served as a pledge of the same liberty to the Catholics of the united colonies, a very large majority of whom were loyal to the American cause and supported the revolution. As the representatives of the Catholic laity and priesthood of the colonies, the two Carrolls could well regard the promise of religious liberty that they were authorized to make to the Canadians as a pledge that full religious liberty would be the policy of the newly established American government.

Washington in his instructions to General Benedict Arnold, September 14, 1775, prior to the Canadian invasion, recognized that the principle of religious liberty must govern the relations with the French Canadians. He instructed Arnold to "protect and support the free exercise of the religion of the country and the undisturbed enjoyment of the rights of conscience in religious matters, with your utmost influence and authority." [12] There was no dissimulation in these instructions for Washington always voiced his disapproval of all displays of religious prejudice. With him religious liberty was a matter of principle more than it was a question of policy.

So far as inducing the French Canadians to join the Revolution and to take up arms against Great Britain, the mission was a failure. Much good, however, resulted in the maintenance of neutrality. It was impossible for the commissioners to convince the Canadians that the congress which denounced in scathing terms the granting of freedom to the Catholic Church in Canada could be taken at its word in promising freedom of conscience in the same breath. The

[12] Force, *American Archives*, Series III, pp. 765-6.

Canadians knew that in nearly all of the English colonies Catholics were under severe disabilities, and that it was as the representatives of those colonies that the members of the congress now held their seats.

The commissioners went as far as Montreal where several conferences were held. Father Carroll met Father Pierre Floquet, a former Jesuit, and the last of the Canadian Superiors of the French mission. The meeting was very friendly but unfortunately Father Floquet on account of his friendly attitude towards the American cause was then in disgrace with Bishop Briand of Quebec. The bishop said that Floquet had a "*Bostonnais* heart." Briand evidently knew something of New England intolerance for he was violently opposed to an alliance with a cause in which the New England colonists had a part.

The commissioners were vested with powers other than conducting negotiations for an alliance with the Canadian colonists. They were to supervise all military operations in Canada, settle disputes, administer discipline, suspend officers if they deemed necessary, negotiate with the Indians and sit and vote as a council of war. They found a sorry state of affairs soon after their arrival at Montreal; lack of discipline, insufficient funds, inadequate provisions for supplies and incompetent officers. The day after their arrival they held a council of war. It was proposed to fortify the important post of Jacques Cartier between Montreal and Quebec. They directed the opening of Indian trade and asked for 20,000 pounds specie from congress to pay the debts owed and to form a fund for a bank they proposed to open for the exchange of Continental bills for hard money. They interviewed deputies from the Indian tribes of Canada and made plans to secure their neutrality. They told congress that for want of money the commanders would have to resort to violence to provide the army with its needs which would "irritate the minds of the people." They advise "if specie cannot be obtained that the Americans should evacuate Canada and fortify the passes on the lakes to prevent the enemy from invading the northern colonies." Their demands for money were not met by congress and they were only supplied with enough for their own expenses. "The purses of those in sympathy with the Americans were drained dry, and the Tories would not trust them with a farthing." [13]

The commissioners did not go to Quebec. On the 6th day of May, the British fleet arrived with one thousand troops and six cannon. The little American army encamped on the plains of Abraham was seized with a panic. After a short skirmish a retreat was ordered which soon became a rout. The commissioners heard of the disaster and reported to Congress that "we are afraid it will not be in our power to render our country any further assistance in this colony." [14]

Franklin, whose age and infirmities made his further stay no longer possible without serious risk, resolved to return to Philadelphia. Father Carroll, realizing that he could be of no further use to the commissioners and seeing that Dr. Franklin was in feeble health and with little resistance to withstand the rigors of the overland journey, decided to accompany him on the homeward trip. "It was a severe, even a cruel task to put upon a man of his age" writes Franklin's biographer in the American Statesmen Series,[15] and "indeed the carelessness of congress was near depriving the country of a life which could not have been spared." At one stage of the journey Franklin wrote: "I begin to apprehend that I have undertaken a fatigue that at my time of life may prove too much for me. So I sit down to write to a few friends by way of farewell." This same biographer did not see fit to quote from another letter which shows that Franklin believed his life had been spared by the tender care of a Catholic priest. From New York on the homeward journey he wrote to a friend: "As to myself I find I grow daily more feeble and I

[13] Rowland, op. cit., I, 156.
[14] *American Archives*, VI, 449.
[15] Morse, *Benjamin Franklin*, American Statesmen Series, 210.

think I could hardly have got so far but for Mr. Carroll's friendly assistance and tender care." [16]

The chief object of the mission, to enlist the Canadians in the American cause, having failed, there was nothing more for the commissioners to do but to attend to the wants of the troops and restore discipline in order to consolidate the positions already held or effect an orderly retreat. Chase and Charles Carroll remained in Canada for this purpose. Their letters to the President of the Congress and their messages to the generals in command show intelligent and untiring efforts to save the little American army from further disaster.

The army suffered much from lack of supplies. The reports tell of long canoe trips by night and overland journeys on foot to visit the troops and inspect the places that had been selected for further operations. Everywhere they found confusion and disorder and "the Americans without credit and without money." The commissioners had to advance money of their own to pay for the transportation of supplies, "the officer in charge not having a shilling." They report troops at Montreal being detained from want of many necessaries, "which we were obliged to procure for them." They appointed William McCarty Deputy Quartermaster General and excused themselves for exceeding their powers as "the public good requires it." "Your generals," they say, "are now obliged to be contractors and commissaries and your commissioners who have neither abilities nor inclinations are constrained to act as generals." They emphasized the lack of discipline due largely to the short enlistments and complained that many of the officers were "not sufficiently active nor do they seem actuated by those distinguished principles and generous sentiments which might be expected from men fighting in so just and glorious a cause." They reported to Congress on the question of unfitness of one of the generals for command and "humbly advise his recall." They realized the hopelessness of the task of attempting to gain any suc-

[16] Guilday, op. cit., 103.

cess for American arms on Canadian soil but were willing to make any sacrifice if Congress would order them to continue their efforts, for they reported:

> In the present situation of our affairs it will not be possible for us to carry into execution the great object of our instructions, as the possession of this country must finally be decided by the sword. We think our stay here no longer of service to the public. We are willing, however, to sacrifice our time, labour, and even our lives, for the good of our country, and we wait with impatience the further orders of congress.

The last letter of the Commissioners to Congress was written from Montreal on the 27th of May:

> We cannot find words strong enough to describe our miserable situation; you will have a faint idea of it, if you figure to yourself an army broken and disheartened, half of it under inoculation, or under other diseases; soldiers without pay, without discipline and altogether reduced to live from hand to mouth, depending on the scanty and precarious supplies of a few half starved cattle, and trifling quantities of flour which have hitherto been picked up in different parts of the country.

The reports which were sent by Carroll and Chase reveal but dimly the great services of these patriots who were given the most difficult and disagreeable task imposed on any body of civilians by the Continental Congress. On the return journey Charles Carroll lost no opportunity to gain information that would be helpful to the American cause in preparation for the defense against the invasion of the Northern colonies which was sure to come. In his journal he tells of his arduous experiences. He set off with General Schuyler at five in the morning hauling their bateaux over the carrying places, then starting the next day at three in the morning, "rowing up the serpentine and winding river," and afterwards walking for miles through the woods to meet the horses that had been sent to them for the last stage of their journey to Albany. On arriving at New York he reported to General Washington, and from there went to Philadelphia where the commissioners made a full report to Congress. On his arrival at Philadelphia he addressed a long letter to General Gates giving him detailed information with the skill of a trained military observer. His task was well performed and although not entirely successful there was much of real accomplishment in it. It was due largely to his service on the Canadian mission that he gained the confidence of General Washington and was made a member of the Board of War.

According to the testimony of two British generals, it was because of the work of the commissioners that the great mass of the French Canadians remained neutral and refused to enlist in the British forces. To induce the Canadian Catholics to remain neutral was all that Father Carroll ever hoped to accomplish as his part in the mission and it was with this idea that he undertook the task allotted him. While in Canada he worked hard to this end. A contemporary writer thus accounts for the refusal of the Canadians to fight on the British side:

> The Yankees have had their Emiceres among the French and made them thus lukewarm to Government, besides it appears that a twelve year's peace had extinguished their martial spirit and together with the sweets of British government makes them desire to live in quiet.[17]

General Burgoyne had expected to enlist several thousand Canadians for his expedition to join General Howe and sever the American colonies, but he was able only to enlist a few hundred, many of whom deserted. In the year following the visit of the commissioners to Canada, Burgoyne wrote to the war office in London giving his reasons for the failure of the Canadians to join his forces. After reciting that he could "not speak with much confidence of the military assistance I am to look for from the Canadians," and that he had only been able to enlist three independent companies of one hundred men each, various reasons were assigned for this change in the natives since the time of the French government. "It may partly be owing to a disuse of arms but I believe principally

[17] Hudleston, *Burgoyne*, 10.

to the unpopularity of their Seigneurs and to the poison which the emissaries of the rebels have thrown into their mind." [18] General Carleton writing to Burgoyne shortly after this, says the news of Canadian desertions does not surprise him:

> It has been the same here and was no more than I expected; if Government laid any stress upon assistance from the Canadians for carrying on the present war, it surely was not upon information proceeding from us. They have imbibed too much of the American spirit of licentiousness and independence administered by a numerous and turbulent faction here to be suddenly restored to a proper and desirable subordination.[19]

General Burgoyne's army of invasion was considerably weakened and far less than its expected strength was reached due to the neutrality and lukewarmness of the French Canadians. As the tide of the Revolution was turned on the battlefield of Saratoga, the work of the commissioners was of vital consequence after all.

[18] Ibid, 128.
[19] Ibid, 129.

CHAPTER V

SUPPORTING THE REVOLUTION

WHILE Charles Carroll was absent on the Canadian mission there was backsliding in the Maryland convention. The Tory faction succeeded in having a resolution adopted, that declared a "reunion with Great Britain on constitutional principles would most effectually secure the rights and liberties and increase the strength and promote the happiness of the whole empire." Further, the resolution prohibited the Maryland delegates to the Continental Congress favoring any movement for independence.

Carroll was chagrined on his return to find that during his absence the convention has thus declared against independence. With others who shared his views, he set in motion the machinery of democracy installed in the days of Thomas Cornwaleys, but which at times since had accumulated considerable rust. True to the customs and traditions of old Catholic Maryland, the patriots went directly to the people for support. The Maryland delegates were recalled from the Congress and the freemen were asked if they favored independence. On this issue there was a return to a pure democracy. Meeting in their sovereign political capacity in their several counties, the freemen by popular and decisive vote instructed their representatives in the convention to rescind all previous instructions and to allow the delegates to congress to unite with the other colonists in declaring for independence.[1]

A new convention was called to meet June 21, 1776. Charles Carroll was in his seat June 24, and four days later, on his motion, the convention resolved that the previous

[1] Browne, op. cit., 280.

instructions given the delegates to Congress, be recalled and

> the deputies of this colony or a majority of them or any three or more of them be authorized and empowered to concur with the other united colonies or a majority of them in declaring the United Colonies free and independent states, provided the sole and exclusive right of regulating the internal government and policy of this colony be reserved to the people thereof.

This was Maryland's declaration of independence. It was the work of Charles Carroll.

To ratify and confirm the course that had been determined upon, the convention prepared and adopted a formal declaration, July 3, 1776. The first clause of this declaration recites the privilege of exemption from parliamentary taxation granted to Lord Baltimore in the Royal Charter and the right under the charter to local self government:

> To be exempted from parliamentary taxation and to regulate their internal government and polity, the people of this colony have ever considered as their inherent and inalienable right; without the former they can have no property, without the latter, no security for their lives or liberties.

The declaration continues:

> Compelled by dire necessity, either to surrender our properties, liberties and lives into the hands of a British king or parliament, or to use such means as will most probably secure to us and our posterity those invaluable blessings, We, the delegates of Maryland in convention assembled, do declare that the King of Great Britain has violated his compact with this people, and they owe no allegiance to him. We have therefore thought it just and necessary to empower our deputies in congress to join with a majority of the united colonies in declaring them free and independent states, in framing such further confederation between them, in making foreign alliances and in adopting such other measures as shall be judged necessary for the preservation of their liberties; provided the sole and exclusive right of regulating the internal policy and government of this colony be reserved to the people thereof.

William Hand Browne has said that if there is one thing in Maryland's honored history to which her sons can look back "with especial—perhaps melancholy—pride, it is the action of the convention of 1776." [2]

On the fourth day of July, 1776, when the Congress of the United Colonies at Philadephia adopted the Declaration of Independence, Charles Carroll of Carrollton was elected a delegate from Maryland to the Congress. The Declaration of Independence was not signed until nearly a month later. Carroll took his seat in Congress, July 18, and on the following day the document was ordered to be engrossed on parchment. The Declaration was signed, August 2, 1776, Charles Carroll being the last signer. The fact that he signed his name as "Charles Carroll of Carrollton" has given rise to an interesting story that has turned out to be pure fiction. There was no special significance attached to his signature. He had signed his name in this manner for years. The real facts of the signing are stated by John H. B. Latrobe in his contribution to Sanderson's Biographies of the Signers of the Declaration of Independence:

> The engrossed copy of the Declaration of Independence was placed on the desk of the secretary of congress on the second of August to receive the signatures of the members and Mr. Hancock, President of Congress, during a conversation with Mr. Carroll asked him if he would sign it. Most willingly was the reply and taking up a pen he at once put his name to the instrument. "There go a few millions" said one, who stood by; and all at the time agreed that in point of fortune few risked more than Charles Carroll of Carrollton.

The day after Charles Carroll took his seat in the Continental Congress he was appointed to the Board of War. This appointment was a signal honor. It came in recognition of his services in the cause of American Independence and of his ability to manage military affairs which he had demonstrated in connection with his services on the Canadian mission. This was a real board of war. It was invested with wide powers. The committee of Congress, appointed June 12, 1776, which was called the Board of War and Ordnance, con-

[2] *Maryland, The History of a Palatinate,* 280.

sisted of five members: John Adams, Roger Sherman, Benjamin Harrison, James Wilson and Edmund Rutledge. Richard Peters was secretary. The board was increased to six members to permit the appointment of Carroll. It was entrusted with the executive duties of the military department. It was empowered to forward dispatches from Congress to the armies in the field and to the colonies, to superintend the raising, equipping and dispatching of the armed forces, and to have charge of all military provisions. It was the War Department of the new government.

John Adams in his autobiography comments on the appointment of Carroll to the board: "Thursday July 18th. Resolved that a member be added to the Board of War. The member chosed, Mr. Carroll. An excellent member whose education manners and application to business and to study did honor to his fortune, the first in America." [3] After Carroll had been appointed to the Canadian mission, Adams sent a communication to James Warren which reveals that he was well pleased with the envoys selected. He described John Carroll as "a Roman Catholic priest and a Jesuit, a gentleman of learning and ability." Of Charles Carroll he said:

> Carroll's name and character are equally unknown to you. I was introduced to him about eighteen months ago in this city and was much pleased with his conversation. He has a fortune, as I am well informed, which is computed to be worth two hundred thousand pounds sterling. He is a native of Maryland and his father is still living. He had a liberal education in France and is well acquainted with the French nation. He speaks their language as easily as ours, and what is perhaps of more consequence than the rest, he was educated in the Roman Catholic religion and still continues to worship his Maker according to the rites of that church. In the cause of American liberty, his zeal, fortitude and perseverence have been so conspicuous that he is said to be marked out for peculiar vengeance by the friends of administration; but he continues to hazard his all, his immense fortune, the largest in America, and his life. This gentleman's character if I foresee aright will make him hereafter a greater figure in America. His abilities are very good, his knowledge and

[3] *Works of John Adams,* III, 60.

learning extensive. I have seen writings of his which would convince you of this. You may perhaps hear before long more about them.

Carroll found time while a member of the Congress to return several times to Annapolis to see that Maryland adjusted herself to the new government. At a convention meeting on August 14, 1776, he took his seat as a delegate from Annapolis. The Declaration of Independence was the first matter brought up for consideration. It was promptly resolved, "That this convention will maintain the freedom and independency of the United States with their lives and fortunes." As a member of the committee to draft a bill of rights he had a hand in framing the new state constitution.

While the state convention was in session Carroll was a member of Congress and a delegate to the Maryland legislative assembly. He returned to his duties in Congress as soon as Maryland had again declared for independence and adopted a bill of rights.

The Continental Congress did not show a marked degree of efficiency in directing practical warfare. If the members had shown as much ability in devising ways and means for an adequate commissariat and a sound system of finance as they did in drafting state papers, preparing resolutions and making speeches, Washington's task would have been far easier. They were a patriotic and well intentioned body of men but too much given to speech.

Charles Carroll took little part in the debates. He concerned himself more with his duties as a member of the War Board. In his letters to General Washington and others he showed that he had a real grasp of the problems that had to be solved. His experience in Canada had brought to him a realization of the conditions that were to handicap the Commander-in-Chief through the war—short term enlistments, incompetent officers, inadequate means of communication and of supply and a weak system of finance. In a letter to Washington he wrote:

Nothing but severe punishments will in my opinion make the commissaries and quartermasters attentive to their duties. Your excellency has the power and I hope will not want the will to punish such as deserve punishment. I hope your Excellency will excuse the freedom of this letter. My zeal for our Country and my wishes for your success have impelled me to write thus freely on a subject that claims all your attention, the reformation of the army and of the abuses prevalent in the two important departments of the quartermaster and commissary-general.

He wrote a letter to Franklin, August 1777, in which he expressed his views on the question of sound finance and the danger of a depreciated currency: "My greatest apprehension arises from the depreciation of our paper money and if we emit more bills of credit they will fall to nothing." He stressed the need of a stronger confederation "that will give weight and consequence to the United States collectively and great security to each individually and a credit also to our paper money, but I despair of such a confederacy as ought and would take place if little and impartial interests could be laid aside." Congress had resorted to the easy method of inflation and the printing presses were busy flooding the country with cheap currency. Two years later he wrote to Franklin: "The depreciation of our bills of credit is such that they scarcely answer the purposes of money. The Congress has stopped the press; this in my opinion should have been done much sooner."

He gave his support and aid to Robert Morris in organizing the Bank of North America. It was through a committee of which Carroll was a member and one of the moving spirits that Morris was induced to administer the finances of the war, and organize a banking system. Many of the colonies were contributing tobacco and other commodities but these were only serviceable until through his banking system Morris found sale for them in the ports of the West Indies. Carroll, with other wealthy men, including Washington, sent ready cash to Morris who displayed the gold in the bank windows to let the people know that his system was functioning. "Despite all criticism and antagonism the Bank of North America flourished. A large part of the success came from the selection of the right man and that selection was largely due to the careful planning and committee work of Charles Carroll." [4]

Carroll had little patience with the talkative Congress. He wrote to Governor Johnson of Maryland: "The Congress do worse than ever. We murder time and chat it away in idle, impertinent talk." He hoped that "the urgency of affairs would teach even that body a little discretion." He preferred to spend most of his time with the active forces where he could learn of conditions at first hand and be of some practical aid. Several of his published letters were written from the field of operations.

In a letter written during 1777 from Swan Creek, where he was with the Maryland first line troops, he said that the life he was leading was fatiguing and that "hard lodging and irregular hours of eating begin to disagree with my puny constitution and habits of body. But perhaps I can soon be inured to and better support the fatigue of a campaign." In the winter of 1778 he was at Valley Forge with a committee of Congress on which were also Gouverneur Morris and Robert Reed. In the following spring, in a letter to Governor Johnson, he expressed the fear that England would send over during the course of the summer and fall, at least 14,000 men. "Is it not strange," he asked, "that the lust of dominion should force the British nation to greater exertions than the desire of liberty can produce among us? If our people would but exert themselves in this campaign, we might secure our liberties forever. General Washington is weak as reinforcements come in slowly. Try for God's sake and for the sake of human nature, to rouse our countrymen from their lethargy!"

Carroll showed his loyalty to Washington by assisting to thwart the Conway Cabal which had as its objective the re-

[4] Spalding, op. cit., 184.

placement of Washington as Commander-in-Chief by the incompetent and vain-glorious Gates. Such a substitution would have been fatal to the American cause. General Conway was the instigator of the conspiracy. An interesting disclosure is made in a letter written by him to Carroll, November 14, 1777. Conway complained in this letter about the "extraordinary discourses held by you, Sir," and others on account of "my applying for the rank of major general." Carroll had very pertinently asked on what ground Conway sought a major-generalship. Conway tried to convince him that the request was "not as impertinent as you, sir, and other gentlemen have styled it." The attack on Washington came at the darkest hour of his military career, after the defeats at Brandywine and Germantown, when he needed the support and loyalty of his friends. It was due to the activities of Carroll, Gouverneur Morris and Colonel John Fitzgerald, a Catholic officer on Washington's staff, that the plot was frustrated.

Leonard in his biography of Charles Carroll says that Washington and Franklin were in favor of sending him to France to open negotiations for a French alliance. "I am the one man that must be kept entirely in the background," Carroll is quoted as saying. "It must not be known to a single soul that I am personally active in this matter." Without Carroll's aid, according to Leonard, the alliance could not have been brought about:

> Men like John H. B. Latrobe and others who knew, believed that the friendship of France never could have been secured nor the alliance formed but for the effective work done by Carroll. Mr. Bushrod Washington who had talked the matter over many times with his brother, was clearly of the same opinion and in the expression of this he doubtless reflected the views of Washington himself.

In a letter written from Morristown in 1777 to Carroll by Colonel Fitzgerald there is a significent passage. After giving the news of the arrival of the French fleet at Portsmouth with twelve thousand stand of arms and of the expected arrival at a New Jersey port of a fifty-gun ship from France, laden with heavy artillery and military stores, Fitzgerald adds that "this news will be very agreeable to you," and "I therefore sincerely congratulate you thereon and hope you will pardon the liberty on my side of beginning a correspondence with you." The reason for the congratulation is obvious—the writer believed that Carroll was largely responsible for bringing the aid of France.

The exchange of letters between Carroll and Franklin was frequent and discloses the fact that Carroll was in intimate touch with the negotiations Franklin was conducting at the French court. In a letter written from Annapolis in 1779, Carroll writes:

> I flattered myself some months ago that ten or twelve ships of the line from France with ten thousand land forces, would have joined this fall Count d'Estaing's fleet off New York. Had such an expedition taken place there is the greater reason to believe the enemy's army must have surrendered prisoners of war; such an event must have put an end to it and have produced peace of which we stand in so much need. If this winter should not bring about that desirable event cannot such an expedition be taken early next summer? If such an expedition, as I propose, should be thought of seriously, it will be necessary to dispatch a frigate very early in February or sooner to notify General Washington thereof in time, that he might fully be prepared to act immediately with the fleet on its arrival before New York.[5]

When Carroll was studying at Paris he met Vergennes and later was able to use influence with him in the negotiations. Arthur Lee, one of the commissioners of Congress sent to France, in a letter written to Samuel Adams voiced his disapproval of the manner in which Franklin was conducting the negotiations and suggested that a man of "sense, of honor and of integrity and education" be sent to the Court of France to represent the United States, and "in many respects, I should think Mr. Carroll the Catholic, a fit man to send in his place." No doubt Lee was influenced by jealousy

[5] Rowland, op. cit., II, 90.

in advocating the removal of Franklin, but the letter shows that Carroll was seriously considered as an envoy to France.

Carroll evidently feared that his usefulness to the American cause would be impaired if he were to accept the French mission and believed that an alliance with a Catholic power should be brought about by a non-Catholic envoy. He chose to remain in the background but nevertheless his advice and influence were important contributions to the success of the negotiations.

The American Tories did not miss the opportunity to raise the old religious issue as the negotiations progressed. Printed reports were circulated that the French king, for the purpose of converting America to the Catholic faith, was preparing to send over a fleet laden with "tons of holy water and casks of consecrated oil, a thousand chests of relics and bales of indulgences," together with implements for an inquisition, and with this fleet would come an army of "priests, confessors, and mendicants." The report was also circulated that Franklin had been decorated with the emblem of a Catholic order by the Pope. The infamy of such an alliance declared a Tory writer "could not be matched and to think it was done just as England was again offering the balm of peace to her ungrateful children!"

There was some misgiving on the part of many of those loyal to the American cause particularly in the northern colonies, as to the wisdom of an alliance with Catholic France but it was not sufficient to offset the sentiment in its favor. America was desperately in need of a strong ally. The aid of France not only did much to bring about the surrender of Cornwallis, but it served also to break down the old time prejudice against Catholics and the Catholic Church, and was a strong factor in the ultimate recognition of the principle of religious freedom.

That Charles Carroll was seriously considered as president of congress is revealed in a letter from Gerard, the diplomatic envoy from France to the United States, written November 10, 1778, to Vergennes in Paris:

> Congress is at present embarrassed with the choice of a new president. For that office, a man active and talented is required and with a fortune that would permit him to make some appearance. Mr. Carroll of Maryland is the one spoken of. He is a Roman Catholic but it is feared he will not accept.

Carroll had no ambition for public office. He desired only to serve his country as a private citizen. He sought neither office nor honors. He resigned his seat in Congress after it was known that the French alliance had been consummated and returned to Maryland where he resumed his place in the state senate. He was reelected to Congress but did not accept. There was another reason for his resignation and his declination of reelection. He wrote to Franklin:

> The great deal of important time which was idly wasted in frivolous debate disgusted me so much that I thought I might spend more of my time much better than by remaining a silent hearer of such speeches as neither edified, entertained nor instructed me.

He was not the only member of Congress who was disgusted with the debates which were taking place in that body. Henry Laurens, president of the Congress in the same year, tells of hours being spent in a discussion of Queen Elizabeth and Mary, Queen of Scots, and the "comparative beauty of black and of blue eyes." Carroll was sensible in his decision that he could render greater service to the American cause by leaving the Continental Congress and returning to Maryland.

The main theatre of the war was now in the South, and Maryland was to be the center of much activity, both military and naval. In the spring of 1781, Lafayette was stationed not far from Doughoregan Manor where he sought and obtained much needed supplies for his men. Congress seemed to be powerless and it was only through the aid of the States that the army could be clothed and fed. It was to Maryland that Washington looked for the principal source of supplies.[6]

6 Andrews, *History of Maryland,* 363.

In the southern campaign much dependence was placed on the Maryland line. The line troops enabled Washington to win the war. Little dependence could be placed on the militia except when they were fighting on the soil of their own states. Carroll was on the committee which drafted the bill for recruiting the quota of Maryland troops for the Continental Line and when the bill was passed for raising an additional battalion of regulars he was on the committee to prepare an address urging the people to "redouble their efforts out of gratitude to our illustrious General and to the brave troops under his command." When Gates led his ill-fated expedition to avenge the defeats at Charleston and Savannah the Maryland line troops composed the main part of the force. Carroll met them near Elkton and arranged to settle their arrears of pay and to provide them with food and clothing.

When it was proposed to confiscate the property of the Tories, Carroll wrote to Benjamin Franklin, then in France, that he believed such a measure to be "contrary to the practice of civilized nations," and "may involve us in difficulties about making peace and will be productive of a certain loss and an uncertain profit to this State, for as this business will be managed it will be made a job of and an opportunity given to engrossers and speculators to realize their ill-gotten money." He had learned so much of the evils attending the confiscation of the properties of recusants in England and Ireland that he did not wish to see the evils of this practice in his own country even if it had to do with the confiscation of the property of Tories. Some of the property sought to be confiscated in Maryland belonged to the Dulaney family. Daniel Dulaney who made Charles Carroll the first citizen in Maryland, and other members of his family had become Tories.

In the summer of 1781, Admiral de Grasse arrived in the waters of the Chesapeake at the head of a fleet of twenty-five vessels, having on board a naval and military force of 21,738 officers and men. The French admiral engaged and defeated the British fleet under Admiral Graves, brother of the man to whom Charles Carroll had written letters prior to the Revolution predicting final victory for the cause of independence. The failure of the British fleet spelled defeat for the British land forces and the surrender of Cornwallis at Yorktown soon followed.

Maryland had asked Congress to establish the permanent capital of the government at Annapolis and the Congress had voted to move the seat of government there for the time being. Congress was sitting at Annapolis when the Treaty of Peace was signed at Paris in 1783. There was a celebration to commemorate the peace and final victory. It was on the Carroll estate, "Carroll's Green," that the festivities were held. General Washington came to Annapolis to submit to Congress his resignation as Commander-in-Chief. Carroll was a member of the committee for the reception. This committee was instructed to prepare an address to Washington. The address made reference to the need of a stronger central government and declared that if the powers given to Congress by the Confederation "should be found to be incompetent to the purposes of the Union, we doubt not our constituents will readily consent to enlarge them." Andrews says that this was "a foreshadowing of the call for the Constitutional Convention of the United States." [7]

After the surrender at Yorktown the French troops under Rochambeau camped at Baltimore on the ground now occupied by the Catholic Cathedral. Here with the troops forming a hollow square, a Solemn Mass of Thanksgiving was celebrated, the Mass being sung by an Irish priest, chaplain to the French commander.

The full extent of the services of Charles Carroll of Carrollton will never be known. What little information is available is found mostly in his letters. But he was always so modest, keeping himself in the background in all that he did,

[7] Ibid, 376.

seeking neither praise nor honor, that his letters do not tell all. There was no one among those not wearing the uniform of the Continental Army, who devoted more time and money to the cause of Independence, showed more unselfish devotion to Washington and the army, and served the American people in more positions of responsibility and usefulness, than he.

CHAPTER VI

JOHN CARROLL

DURING the period from the signing of the Declaration of Independence to the session of the First Congress of the United States, Father John Carroll of Rock Creek, Maryland, was the leading exponent of religious liberty in the new republic. No member of the clergy in his day was more thoroughly American in thought and spirit. As Dr. Guilday in his *Life and Times of John Carroll,* says: "No American living caught so quickly and indelibly the spirit that created the new republic." This biographer has made a most valuable contribution to American history, for he has brought to light facts relating to the organization of the Catholic Church in the United States that have not been generally known and recognized, and as a result of his scholarly research, the church has been given a place of prominence in the early history of the nation that it did not before occupy, not even in the minds of most Catholics.

When John Carroll and his cousin, Charles Carroll of Carrollton, left Maryland for France to begin their studies at the college of St. Omer, it was to be a course of preparation for them to become men of leadership and vision, each in his own chosen field. The college was made up of young men preparing for life in the world and of young men preparing for the priesthood. It was accepted as the best school for the sons of English Catholics during the penal period and it was also the house of studies for the Jesuits who were to be sent to the English and American missions. Of all the continental schools it was "the best loved by the boys of

Archbishop John Carroll

Maryland," writes Dr. Guilday and "Maryland can be looked upon to a great extent as a St. Omer's mission." [1]

After leaving St. Omer's the lives of these two Maryland boys were to drift apart for a space of years and until their return to America, when their talents and ideals were to be welded in the building of a new nation. When Charles Carroll went to the Jesuit college at Rheims for the advancement of his secular education, John Carroll entered the Jesuit novitiate at Watten. After completing his novitiate he pursued his course of philosophy at Liege, and then returned to St. Omer's to teach the classics. When St. Omer's was confiscated by the French government and transferred to the English secular clergy, after the edict of the parliament of Paris suppressing the Society of Jesus in France, Carroll accompanied a detachment of students on a long overland journey afoot, to the college at Bruges, Belgium. Here he remained, with the exception of a year's travel in Germany and Italy, until 1773, when by edict of the Pope there came the general suppression of the Jesuits.

The act of suppression came as a severe shock to Father Carroll. He wrote to his brother Daniel in Maryland that he was not and perhaps never would be recovered from the blow of "this dreadful intelligence." The greatest blessing he could receive from God would be "immediate death but if he deny me this, may his Holy and adorable designs on me be wholly fulfilled." He wondered what would become of the flourishing congregations in Maryland and Pennsylvania. He decided to return to Maryland where he would have "the comfort not only of being with you but of being further out of the reach of scandal and defamation and removed from the scene of distress of many of my dearest friends whom God knows I shall not be able to relieve. I shall therefore most certainly sail for Maryland early next Spring if I possibly can." [2]

[1] *Life and Times of John Carroll,* 18.
[2] *Ibid.,* 44.

Father Carroll's situation was desperate for he had renounced all claim to his father's estate and there was no assurance that he would receive support from the property of the supressed Society in America. He received an invitation from Lord Arundel, descendant of Lord Baltimore's friend, to make his home in Wardour Castle and to act as chaplain to the family and to the Catholics in the neighborhood, but the news he had received from America led him to decline this offer. The life of a private chaplain in England offered no inducement to him when there was an impending struggle between the American colonists and the mother country. He set sail for Maryland in the late spring of 1774. This was a momentous decision, for had he decided not to return to America and to have remained in England, the course of events immediately following the war for independence might and probably would have been far different.

At the home of his mother at Rock Creek, Father Carroll assembled a congregation of Catholics. The little congregation grew so rapidly that it was found necessary to erect a church. St. John's, a short distance from his mother's home, became the first Catholic church in Maryland under the secular clergy erected by a congregation which supported a pastor. Until this time the Jesuit fathers had carried on the service of religion at their own expense.[3]

As Charles Carroll of Carrollton visioned the political and economic future of America, Father John Carroll looked beyond the years and foresaw the growth of his church and the place it was to occupy in the life of the nation. Under the inspiration of his leadership it became a church essentially American and at the same time truly Catholic. Previous to the revolution, the Catholic Church in America had been a mission. There was no juridic or ecclesiastical control except that of the Superior who in turn was subject to the jurisdiction of the English province. With the suppression of the

[3] Ibid, 96.

Jesuit order, the churches and chapels came under the jurisdiction of the Vicar Apostolic of London.

At the outbreak of the war a serious problem confronted the American Catholics. For ten years, writes Dr. Guilday, "the work in the American vineyard went on in a listless way as it was bound to, without a shepherd and manned by a little group of priests who had been dishonored and disbanded by the Holy See." Priests and laity turned instinctively to Father Carroll for leadership. He responded with his plan of organization of 1782. The Jesuits had control of considerable real property in Maryland and Pennsylvania and the proper administration of this property was a most vexing problem. Father Carroll, in his plan, placed upon the clergy of the two states, the obligations arising from justice and charity, of using the funds entrusted their predecessors and to themselves solely for the spiritual uplift of the faithful and for the sustenance of the clergy. An arrangement of checks and balances, such as is found in the American form of government, was agreed upon among themselves. There was to be a general meeting of the clergy, each district electing a representative.[4]

Father Carroll, aware of the unjust confiscation of the Jesuit property in Europe, was not unmindful that similar action might be taken in America. In true American spirit he wrote to his friend Father Charles Plowden in London:

> Your information of the intention of the propaganda gives me concern no farther than to hear that men whose institution was for the service of religion should bend their thoughts so much more to grasping for power and the commanding of wealth. For they may be assured that they will never get possession of a sixpence of our property here; and if any of our friends could be weak enough to deliver any real estate into their hands or attempt to subject it to their authority, our civil government would be called upon to wrest it again out of their dominion. A foreign temporal jurisdiction will never be tolerated here, and even the spiritual supremacy of the Pope is the only reason why in some of the United States the full participation of all civil

[4] Guilday, op. cit., 307.

rights are not granted to the Roman Catholics. They may therefore send their agents when they please, they will certainly return empty handed.[5]

John Carroll as a good Catholic never questioned the spiritual supremacy of the Pope, but he was at all times anxious to see that the temporal jurisdiction of the papacy would not intrude itself into the plan of organization of the church in America. His attitude was always uncompromising on all points of doctrine but in temporal matters and affairs of government he believed in rendering unto "Caesar the things that are Caesar's." The policy of separation of State and Church established in early Maryland was, so far as he was concerned, quite proper to be the policy of the new government.

In a letter written the following year to Father Plowden, Carroll told the need of establishing "regulations tending to perpetuate a succession of laborers in this vineyard, to preserve their morals, to prevent idleness and to secure an equitable and frugal administrations of temporals." He saw an immense field "opened to the zeal of apostolic men," with innumerable Catholics going and ready to go "into the new regions bordering on the Mississippi, perhaps the finest in the world and impatiently clamorous for clergymen to attend them."

On June 27, 1783, an historic meeting of the Catholic clergy was held at the old Jesuit residence at Whitemarsh on the property that was left to the mission under the will of James Carroll. Here the question of a constitution for the American church was considered. Carroll's plan was fully discussed, and the first steps were taken for a church government. A committee of five was appointed to draw up a petition to the Holy See asking that Father John Lewis who had been superior of the mission be formally constituted Superior of the Church in the United States. John Carroll was one of the committee. The petition discloses that there was

5 Hughes, I, Documents, 617.

a close contact between the leaders of the Catholic clergy and the leaders of the new government. The first paragraph of the petition addressed to the Holy Father, reads:

> We John Lewis, Bernard Diderick, Ignatius Matthews, James Walton and John Carroll, missionary priests residing in the Thirteen United States of North America, assembled together from the neighboring stations to take counsel for the good of the mission, agreeing and approving by letter in our name and in the common name of our brethren, with all respect represent to your Holiness, that we, placed under the recent supreme dominion of the United States, can no longer have recourse as formerly for necessary spiritual jurisdiction to the Bishops and Vicars-Apostolic residing in different and foreign states (for this has very frequently been intimated to us in very positive terms by the rulers of the republic) nor recognize any of them as ecclesiastical superior without open offense of this supreme civil magistracy and political government.

The petition asked the Pontiff to confirm Father Lewis as ecclesiastical superior with the necessary faculties.

When the contents of this petition became known to the rest of the American clergy it was feared by some that it was not sufficiently respectful in tone, and accordingly another committee of which Carroll was a member was appointed to draft a second petition. The second request contained the modification that the American clergy be permitted to elect their own superior and declared that the United States government would not permit the presence of a bishop in the country.[6]

In these petitions as in the subsequent negotiations and letters of Father Carroll, there is evident a strong desire to be free from any dependence on any foreign jurisdiction other than such as was necessary to recognize the spiritual supremacy of the Pope. This point is stressed and explained in a letter from Father Carroll to a friend in Rome accompanying the second petition. He wrote:

> You are not ignorant that in these United States our religious system has undergone a revolution, if possible, more extraor-

[6] Guilday, op. cit., p. 171.

dinary than our political one. In all of them free toleration is allowed to Christians of every denomination, and particularly in the states of Pennsylvania, Delaware, Maryland and Virginia, a communication of all civil rights without distinction or diminution is extended to those of our religion. This is a blessing and advantage which it is our duty to preserve and improve with the utmost prudence by demeaning ourselves on all occasions as subjects zealously attached to our government and avoiding to give any jealousies on account of any dependence on foreign jurisdiction more than that which is essential to our religion, an acknowledgment of the Pope's spiritual supremacy over the whole Christian world.

He called attention to the fact that the clergy of the Church of England, who were heretofore subject to the Bishop of London, had withdrawn themselves from obedience to that dignitary as "the umbrage taken at this dependence was so great." [7]

Meanwhile in France, Benjamin Franklin was unintentionally working at cross purposes to the American Catholic clergy. He saw what he believed was an opportunity to be of service to the Catholic church in America by having it made subject to the jurisdiction of a French bishopric. The French clergy were naturally in favor of such a plan and negotiations had made considerable progress before Franklin discovered that Father Carroll and his fellow priests did not favor the project. They refused to subject themselves to any foreign ecclesiastical jurisdiction be it French or British. If a bishopric were to be created they wished a bishop of their own choice who would be a native-born American. The negotiations were broken off as soon as Franklin realized his mistake. He decided that sound policy required him to favor the appointment of an American missionary priest as Superior of the Catholic clergy in the United States.[8]

Father Lewis being of advanced years it was decided to select a younger man. John Carroll was appointed superior.

[7] Guilday, op. cit., p. 172.
[8] Shea, vol. 2, 216-19; Guilday, op. cit., 199.

The letter announcing the appointment stated it was known that the selection of Father Carroll would "please and gratify many members of the republic and especially Mr. Franklin, the eminent individual who represents the same republic at the Court of the Most Christian King." Father Lewis' name was the first on a list submitted by the American clergy for appointment; Father Carroll's was the last.

It was explained that the appointment was only temporary, and that later a Vicar-Apostolic vested with the title and character of a bishop would be named. The letter announcing the appointment was presented by Father Carroll to his brethren at the Whitemarsh chapter. Thereupon the chapter voted that a committee be empowered to send a memorial to Rome stating that as "the majority of the Protestant population are averse to a Roman Catholic prelate, the introduction of the Episcopal office would awaken their jealousy." The appointment was not to the liking of Carroll. He was apprehensive because the American Church was subject to what he called "foreign domination," then too the appointment was made by and its duration was at the will and pleasure of the Sacred Congregation.

It was repugnant to him to accept any position that was to be held at the pleasure of a foreign body. He wrote to his fellow clergy that nothing but the "present extreme necessity of some spiritual powers here" could induce him to act under a commission that might produce, if long continued, the most "dangerous jealousy." He was urged by several of the clergy to accept without hesitation. He wrote a long letter to his friend Father Thorpe at Rome fully stating conditions as they then existed in the United States and frankly giving his objecions to the form of the appointment. He expressed his gratification that his "old and cheerful friend Dr. Franklin" suggested him to the consideration of the Pope. The appointment however was not such as he wished and could not have continued long in its present form. He wrote:

You well know that in our free and jealous government it will never be suffered that an ecclesiastical superior receive his appointment from a foreign state and only hold it at the discretion of a foreign tribunal or congregation. If even the present temper or inattention of our Executive or legislative bodies were to overlook it for this and perhaps a few more instances, still we ought not to acquiesce and rest quiet in actual enjoyment, for the consequence sooner or later would raise a spirit against us and under pretense of rescuing the state from foreign influence and dependence, strip us perhaps of our common civil rights.

Father Carroll admits that he is

well aware that these suggestions will sound ungrateful at Rome and the mention of them from us will be perhaps imputed by some of the officers of the propaganda to a remaining spirit of Jesuitism, but I own to you that though I wish to treat with them upon terms of sincere unanimity and cordial concurrence in all matters tending to the service of Religion yet I do not feel myself disposed to sacrifice to the fear of giving offence, the permanent interests of religion.

He makes two objections to the future church government as it was planned at Rome. First, that the form of church government in the United States was no longer a mission. "By acquiring civil and religious rights in common with other Christians we are become a national Catholic Clergy." He hopes that in a few years a bishop will be appointed. "We are not in immediate need of one," but when the time comes he conceives that it will "be more advantageous to Religion and less liable to give offense that he be an ordinary Bishop and not a Vicar Apostolic and to be chosen and presented to His Holiness by the American Catholic Clergy."

The second objection was:

Though our free and tolerant forms of government (in Virginia, Maryland, and Pennsylvania) admit us to equal rights with other Christians yet the leading men in our respective states often express a jealousy of any foreign jurisdiction and surely will be more offended about submitting to it in matters not essential to our faith. I hope they will never object to our depending on the Pope in things purely spiritual; but I am sure there are men, at least in this state, who would blow up a flame of animosity against us, if they suspected that we were to be so much under the government of any congregation at Rome as to receive our superior from it, commissioned only during their good will and that this superior was restricted from employing any clergyman here but such as that Congregation should direct. I dread so much the consequence of its being known that this last direction was ever given, that I have not thought it proper to mention it to several of my Brethren.[9]

There were several reasons that finally prompted him to accept the appointment. One of these, urged upon him by his fellow clergy, was that if he did not accept, a foreigner might be appointed Prefect-Apostolic.

The formal Latin letter written by Father Carroll accepting the appointment embodies the same ideas as expressed in the previous letter to Father Thorpe and explained his objections even more frankly. He gave as his reason for objecting to the American Church being subject to the Sacred Congregation, his desire to "retain absolutely the spiritual jurisdiction of the Holy See and at the same time remove all objections to us as tho we had anything hostile to the national independence." How long they were to enjoy the benefit of this toleration or equal rights he does not dare to assert.

Many of our people especially in Maryland fear that we shall be absolutely excluded from holding office, for my own part I have deemed it wiser not to anticipate evils but to bear them when they come. I cherish the hope that so great a wrong will not be done us, nay more I trust that the foundation of religion will be so firmly laid in the United States, that a most flourishing part of the Church will in time be developed here to the great consolation of the Holy See.

He gives a gentle hint at the end of the letter that if "it does not seem proper to allow the priests who have labored for so many years in this vineyard of the Lord" to propose the one of their number whom they deem best fitted for the office of Bishop that "some method will be adopted by which

[9] Ibid, 210.

a bad feeling may not be excited among the people of this country, Catholic and Protestant."[10]

The importance of this letter, Dr. Guilday says, can hardly be exaggerated. It is the first document of its kind that passed between the Church in the United States and the Holy See, and it contains for the church historian of the new republic "the most valuable synthesis of the state of religion in this country which we possess for the Revolutionary period."

With his mother's home at Rock Creek as a center, Father Carroll began his visitation under his new appointment in the summer 1785. His first visit was to the historic mission of St. Inigoes where he laid the corner stone of a new church. He visited stations and congregations in Maryland and Virginia during the summer. In the autumn he visited Pennsylvania, New Jersey and New York. He kept away from New England which up to that time had not shown a spirit of hospitality to Catholics. On the return from his visitation he wrote a letter to the Nuncio at Paris about the general situation of the Church in the new republic:

> Catholics are indeed tolerated everywhere today but so far it is only in Pennsylvania, Delaware, Maryland and Virginia that they enjoy equal advantages with their fellow-citizens. The Revolution from which we have just emerged has procured us this advantage but the circumspection we are obliged to use is extreme, so that no pretext for interfering with our rights be given to those who hate us. This is especially necessary now, because the prejudice entertained for so long a time is deep-rooted. The opinion above all which many have formed that our faith exacted a subjection to His Holiness incompatible with the independence of a sovereign state, entirely false though it be, gives us continual worry. To dissipate this prejudice time will be our best aid as also will Divine Providence and the experience of our fellow citizens in our devotion to our country and to its independence.

One important fact brought out in the correspondence was the willingness of the Church authorities at Rome to between Father Carroll and the Congregation of Propaganda

10 Ibid, 214-22.

grant the requests of the American clergy and to cooperate in every way possible so that the new church government would conform to American ideals. Cardinal Antonelli, Prefect of the Congregation, wrote to Father Carroll, July 23, 1785, announcing that ampler faculties had been granted him. He assures him that the Sacred Congregation will appoint a vicar apostolic with the title and character of bishop and will confer this dignity upon Father Carroll, but if it is thought more expedient and will be more in accordance with the constitution of the Republic for the missionaries themselves at first to recommend someone to the Sacred Congregation who might be elevated to the office of Vicar Apostolic, "the Sacred Congregation will not cease to perform what you decide to be the more suitable." He also gives the assurance that in order to remove all risk of displeasure "I have seen to it that a new copy of faculties be enclosed for you," in which the usual clause for the appointment of priests and workers by the Congregation has been removed and the power granted Father Carroll as Superior of selecting workers whom he "shall judge suitable in the Lord."

Father Carroll found as a result of his first visitation that there were more Catholics in the United States than he had realized and therefore in greater need of a bishop. Unknown to him, Franklin had discussed the matter of the appointment of a bishop with the Church authorities, said he preferred to see Carroll appointed Bishop at once and that the American Congress "would be pleased to see the Catholic Church in the United States properly organized under its own Episcopal authority." The only thing that now stood in the way of the appointment of a bishop was the question of finance. The church officials at Rome would have to know more about the temporalities of the nascent church before a bishopric could be created.[11]

Dr. Guilday states that it was "a foregone conclusion that when the constitution should be written the principle of

[11] Ibid, 239.

religious liberty or to put it more accurately disestablishment, would find a place in its clauses." Father Carroll judging from his correspondence and writings evidently did not regard it as a foregone conclusion and as a matter of fact when the constitution was first written and adopted it contained no clause recognizing religious liberty nor providing against a church establishment. In reference to religious toleration Father Carroll is always careful in his letters to limit the states where there was full toleration, Maryland, Pennsylvania, Delaware and Virginia. All of the New England States, New York, New Jersey and North Carolina were decidedly anti-Catholic. Prior to the Revolution there were legal disabilities against Catholics in nearly every colony. For a large part of the inhabitants of the thirteen original states it may be said that Protestantism and patriotism were synonymous. As Father Carroll said in one of his letters previously quoted, prejudice against Catholics was so long continued and so deep seated that time only would overcome it. It was partially and temporarily lessened by the aid that Catholic France gave to the American cause and the support that was given to the Revolution by the large majority of Catholic colonists.

Theodore Roosevelt in his *Life of Gouverneur Morris* in the American Statesmen Series, says:

> The Congress by the way showed symptoms of an advance in toleration, at least so far as Protestant sects went; for it was opened and closed by ministers of the Episcopalian, Dutch Reformed, Presbyterian, Baptist and other sects, each in turn, but as will shortly be seen the feeling against Catholics was quite as narrow-minded and intense as ever. This was natural enough in colonial days when Protestantism and national patriotism were almost interchangeable terms; for the hereditary and embittered foes of the Americans, the French and Spaniards, were all Catholics and even many of the Indians were of the same faith; and undoubtedly the wonderful increase in the spirit of tolerance shown after the Revolution was due in part to the change of the Catholic French into our allies and of the Protestant English into our most active foes. It must be remembered however that

the Catholic gentry of Maryland played the same part in the Revolution that their Protestant neighbors did.[12]

Two services held in Catholic churches in Philadelphia at the close of the war attended by officers and members of Congress did much to create a better understanding between Catholics and Protestants. On the third anniversary of the Declaration of Independence July 4, 1779, a *Te Deum* service was held at St. Mary's Church where a patriotic sermon was preached by the chaplain of the French legation, in the course of which he declared that the Revolution had placed "the sons of America among the free and independent nations of the earth." Two years later another memorial service was held in the same church. Father Bandol, the French chaplain, again preached the sermon and declared that the new American government presented "to the universe the noble sight of a society which, founded in equality and justice, secures to the individuals who compose it the utmost happiness which can be derived from human institutions."

When Charles and John Carroll were sent on the Canadian mission they were given an implied promise that religious freedom would be the policy of the new government. The great services rendered throughout the Revolution by Charles Carroll and the fact that nearly all the Catholics in the country were loyal to the American cause and had contributed brave officers and men to the Continental Army could not be forgotten nor disregarded when bigotry raised its head and demanded discrimination.

Several times John Carroll found it necessary to remind the nation's statesmen that Catholics as well as Protestants had shed their blood on the battle-grounds of the Revolution, and that a revival of the policy of discrimination and of disability would be rank ingratitude for the devotion and the loyalty of Catholic patriots. He realized how quickly the fires of persecution and bigotry could be rekindled and was not easily lulled into a sense of false security because of a

[12] Page 34.

temporary period of tolerance that had come as the result of the part played by Catholics in the Revolution.

When the Constitutional Convention was held in Philadelphia in 1787, there was published in the same city a monthly magazine called the *Columbian Magazine or Monthly Miscellany,* dedicated to "history, manners, literature and characters." Beginning with the April number there appeared a series of articles written by an anonymous writer who signed himself "A-Z." The subject of the articles was announced as "Considerations on Religion in General but more particularly on the Christian Religion." The first article was as general and as inoffensive as the subject would indicate but after the convention began its sessions in May there crept into the articles an insidious attack on the Catholic religion. The real purpose of the writer was only too apparent. Father Carroll sensing the situation determined to reply. It was not until December, however, and after the convention had adjourned that the reply appeared in print. The effusions of "A-Z" were first page articles, but the reply of Father Carroll appeared only in fine print in a supplement of the December number and in expurgated form. The reply of Father Carroll was vigorous and convincing but it appeared too late to have any effect on the convention.

The Federal Convention for the adoption of the Constitution that met in Philadelphia on May 14, 1787, adjourned on September 17th. No action was taken by the convention on the question of religious liberty other than the provision that no religious test should be required of federal office holders. This was no doubt pleasing to "A-Z," as it was disappointing to Father Carroll. Matthew Carey was one of the proprietors of the *Columbian Magazine*. He was so disgusted with the tone of the letters and with the manner in which the editors had withheld publication of Father Carroll's reply that he withdrew from the enterprise and later began the publication of another magazine known as *The American Museum*.

Father Carroll wrote a letter to Carey in which he said:

> After having contributed in proportion to their numbers equally at least with every other denomination to the establishment of independence and run every risk in common with them, it is not only contradictory to the avowed principles of equality in religious rights but a flagrant act of injustice to deprive them of those advantages to the acquirement of which they so much contributed.

In the same letter he tells Carey that he had sent "a few infusions on this subject to the *Columbian Magazine* eighteen months ago," but the editor "after violating his engagement made at the outset of his work and delaying the publication for many months printed it at length with unjustifiable retrenchment." [13]

All the writings of Father Carroll stressed two cardinal principles, liberty and equality. All that he asked for his church was what he claimed should be granted to all churches —equal rights and privileges under the law. This was but an application of the policy of early Maryland that had been put into the code of 1639 and had given to "Holy Churches" all rights and privileges free and inviolate.

His broad spirit of tolerance was shown in the part that he took in the controversy with the former Jesuit, Reverend Charles Wharton, who after the suppression of the Society left the Catholic Church and became an Anglican priest. It was a controversy that was carried on in a spirit of fairness and with no trace of bitterness. Father Carroll said he hoped that to engage in the controversy would not disturb

> the harmony now subsisting amongst all Christians in this country, so blessed with civil and religious liberty, which if we have the wisdom and temper to preserve, America may come to exhibit a proof to the world that general and equal toleration, by giving a free circulation to fair argument, is the most effectual method to bring all denominations of Christians to a unity of faith.[14]

[13] *American Catholic Historical Researches,* XV, 62.
[14] Guilday, op. cit., 352-3.

John Carroll was chosen by the freedom of election granted to the American clergy as Bishop of the Church in the United States. At a meeting of the clergy held at Whitemarsh, May 18, 1789, after the celebration of Mass, the votes of those present, as well of those who were at a distance, were taken and it was disclosed that Father Carroll had been duly elected Bishop, having received twenty-four out of twenty-eight votes, four being cast for two other candidates. Baltimore was unanimously chosen as the place for the episcopal See, being "in the center of Maryland where the greater part of the faithful and of the clergy are to be found and whence the faith has been happily disseminated through the other provinces." [15]

The election was confirmed by the Holy See and the letter announcing the confirmation stated:

> Nothing more acceptable and pleasing could happen to us than all ambition being laid aside and without being influenced by party spirit, you should be nominated by almost unanimous consent as the first Bishop of the new See of Baltimore. For since our Holy Father Pius VI was fully aware of the unblemished reputation of Mr. Carroll and of the remarkable zeal with which for many years he has strenuously labored there for the salvation of souls, His Holiness has confirmed by Apostolic Decree the liberty of this first election granted to you by special favour and which you have exercised with such rectitude and wisdom.

The choice of Carroll as bishop had the approval of both Franklin and Jefferson and also met with the approbation of Washington. Franklin in 1784 had made known to the authorities at Rome his approval. A letter written by Jefferson from Monticello discloses that he was consulted concerning the appointment of Carroll as bishop and gave his approval. The letter is written to Archbishop Marechal and is dated January 17, 1820. Jefferson refers to the death of Cardinal Dugnani who was the papal nuncio at Paris while Jefferson was minister to France. He speaks of the "intimate acquaintance" he had with the Cardinal and says: "I sincerely

[15] Ibid, 352.

regret his loss, having been consulted by him while at Paris by instruction from the Pope previous to making the appointment of Bishop Carroll to the See of Baltimore and given an assurance that he was perfectly free to make such an establishment without offense to our institutions or opinions." [16]

There is the testimony of Washington's adopted son, George Washington Custis, as to the esteem in which the first President held Bishop Carroll. In a letter written to the Reverend Charles White, D.D., he said:

> You are pleased to ask me whether the late Dr. Carroll was an intimate acquaintance of Washington. He was more, sir. From his exalted worth as a minister of God, his stainless character as a man and above all his distinguished services as a patriot of the Revolution, Dr. Carroll stood high, very high in the esteem and affection of the Pater Familias.

The letter further told of the part that was played by Bishop Carroll in stimulating enlistments in the Continental Army:

> The Catholic priesthood of the olden or of the present time had a great moral as well as religious influence over their flocks; to direct their influence in favour of the cause of American Liberty formed the untiring and patriotic labours of Dr. Carroll from the commencement of the troubles between the Mother Country and the colonies. And nobly did he succeed, Catholic Maryland responded to the call of the Patriot and the Priest and many a gallant Catholic grasped his arms and fought for the civil and Religious Liberty of generations yet unborn. The famed regiment of Smallwood, composed of the flower of the Maryland youth both Catholic and Protestant, was recruited principally in the lower counties and the eastern shore. It was the Tenth Legion in the American Army, marched into Philadelphia in 1776, eleven hundred strong, was cut to pieces at the Battle of Long Island, gallantly struggling for victory against an overwhelming foe, and at the close of the memorable campaign of '76 at the Battle of Princeton, mustered sixty men commanded by the late Governor Stone, then a captain; the prison ship and the grave had all the rest.[17]

[16] *American Catholic Historical Researches,* XVII, 162.
[17] Ibid, 49.

George Washington was inaugurated the first President of the United States and John Carroll was elected the first Bishop of the Catholic Church in the United States in the same year. This coincidence Dr. Guilday points out "ends rather than begins a striking parallel between the history of the thirteen original states and the history of the Catholic Church within the reconstruction years of 1773-1789." Many of the problems of the church were analogous to those of the new nation and were solved in much the same manner. Bishop Carroll was not only the most forceful champion of the principle of religious freedom and equality in his time, but he laid the foundations of his Church organization deep in the principles that gave birth to the new republic.

CHAPTER VII

JAMES WILSON AND DANIEL CARROLL

THE services of Charles Carroll of Carrollton were lost to the Constitutional Convention held at Philadelphia in 1787, by reason of a strong inflation movement in his own state. He had been a consistent opponent of a debased currency. During the Revolution he did not favor the methods that were frequently used to raise money for the war. With independence won but with the country practically bankrupt, he recognized, as few others did, that a system of sound finance was one of the great essentials of a permanent government. Debts were piling up, interest was in arrears, national credit was gone. The continental currency was so debased that its value disappeared altogether. There was no money in the treasury, and no means of securing any except by the unpopular method of taxation. So most of the states resorted to inflation and were soon over their heads with schemes of paper money and debt repudiation.

Washington saw the peril that would come to the new government if the states adopted inflation. In a letter, written at the time, he told of the violent agitation for cheap money in Maryland and said he had heard that the leaders of the movement had threatened secession if their favorite measure which had passed the lower house was rejected in the senate. "Thus," he said, "we are advancing."

Charles Carroll was elected a delegate to the Constitutional Convention but he declined solely because he believed he could be of greater service to his country by remaining in Maryland and leading the fight against inflation in the senate. Noah Webster said that the rage for paper money in Maryland bordered on madness.[1] The house voted for the emission of five hundred thousand pounds sterling equal to the entire circulating medium of the state. This would have driven every shilling of specie from circulation. The loss to the state would have been irreparable. The senate under the leadership of Carroll stood firmly against the action of the house. As in the days when independence hung in the balance Carroll went to the people, with the result that the specter of paper money was laid low. There was no further threat of secession. The people had spoken in favor of sound money. Much had depended on this action of Maryland, for if the vote of the lower house had prevailed the movement would have gained sufficient headway to have spread through the other states.

Although Charles Carroll did not attend the Constitutional Convention his influence was felt in one important matter. This was largely by reason of his acquaintance and association with James Wilson of the Pennsylvania delegation. Wilson was the ablest member of the convention and the man on whom Washington mainly relied to establish the policies which he believed should guide the new republic. Carroll's acquaintance with Wilson began in the Continental Congress. Wilson was a member of the committee to strengthen the American cause in Canada which sent the two Carrolls on the mission with Franklin and Chase. They were both signers of the Declaration of Independence and both were members of the Board of War. Wilson was defeated for reelection to Congress in 1777. Soon after his defeat he left Philadelphia and went to Annapolis where he practised law for a year.[2] During this time he no doubt came into frequent contact with Charles Carroll.

James Wilson's work in the framing of the Federal Con-

1 Ford, *Pamphlets on the Constitution,* 33. The man who headed the inflation movement was none other than Samuel Chase who had accompanied Carroll on the Canadian Mission.

2 Appleton, *Encyclopedia of American Biography,* VI, 550; *National Cyclopedia of American Biography,* I, 23.

James Wilson

stitution has been recognized by few historians. In influence he was second only to Madison but from the standpoint of legal education and ability he was without a peer in the convention. There was no more constructive statesman in his day. He was a native of Scotland; received a scholarship at St. Andrews and from there went to the University of Glasgow during the time Adam Smith was the rector. He finished his education at the University of Edinburgh. In 1763 at the age of twenty-three he came to America. After tutoring at Philadelphia College he studied law and was admitted to the Pennsylvania bar.

Francis Newton Thorpe, one of the few writers on American Constitutional History to recognize the real worth of Wilson, says of him:

> Of all the men chosen to make the national constitution he was the only one who understood and advocated the national idea as it has been understood and advocated since the Civil War. His place in the evolution of American democracy has been slightly recognized and his just fame has been delayed. . . If a man's greatness is commensurate with the ideas of mankind, the national ideas advanced and advocated by Wilson place him among the most eminent Americans of the eighteenth century and entitle him to the veneration of his countrymen.[3]

James Bryce says that his speeches "display an amplitude and profundity of view in matters of constitutional theory which place him in the first rank of political thinkers of his age," and that "subsequent generations of Americans have failed to do him full justice." [4]

Washington declared him to be the ablest constitutional lawyer in the convention.[5] Professor Edward Elliot of Princeton says that "for depth of learning and soundness of judgment in political affairs James Wilson of Pennsylvania was unsurpassed by any member of the Constitutional Convention." [6] Wilson's colleagues referred to him as "James the

[3] *Constitutional History of the United States,* (1901) I, 342.
[4] *American Commonwealth,* I, 665.
[5] Thorpe, *Constitutional History of the American People,* (1898) I, 121.
[6] *Biographical Story of the Constitution,* 55.

Caledonian." He was tall of stature and imposing in appearance although with a touch of sternness which gained him more respect than popularity.[7]

Many writers of constitutional history have interpreted the period of the formation of the Federal Constitution as a struggle between the large and the small states. It is true that a serious contest developed in the convention concerning the adoption of the Virginia plan which was favored by the larger states and the so-called New Jersey plan which was favored by the smaller states, but this was only a temporary phase which was soon compromised by the adoption of equal state representation in the Senate. The really important question which ultimately had to be decided was whether the United States were to be a government of the people or a government of the states. On this great issue James Wilson early took his stand for the sovereignty of the people and maintained this position all through the convention. It was his advocacy of popular sovereignty that made him the commanding figure of the convention.

Involving this issue and presenting a problem that proved to be the most difficult of solution was the question of the nature of the chief magistracy together with its powers and the mode of electing the chief magistrate. The solution of this problem brought about the division of the government into its present branches, the executive, the legislative and the judicial. The state constitutions had made the executive the weakest of the three departments. In their distrust of royal authority the people had made the state executives subordinate to the assemblies. The establishment of a national executive department therefore was an undertaking of serious import.[8]

There was a strong sentiment in the convention against a single executive. Roger Sherman and John Randolph favored an executive dependent upon the legislative depart-

[7] Farrand, *Framing the Constitution,* 21.

[8] Thorpe, *Constitutional History of the United States* (1901), I, 320.

ment and not independent of it and consisting of more than one person. Wilson favored a single executive. His argument was that it would give responsibility to the office. This was the first intimation that the executive and legislative functions should be separated.[9] Sherman said that the executive was merely an instrument for carrying the laws of the legislature into effect and for this reason the legislature should be at liberty to appoint one or more executives. Randolph regarded unity in the executive as the "foetus of monarchy." Wilson replied that unity in the executive would be the best safeguard against tyranny. This and subsequent discussion of the powers of the executive resulted in the separation of the departments of the government and the fine balance of powers which was to be one of the outstanding features of the new constitution. Wilson's idea of a single executive finally prevailed, the vote of Washington determining the vote of Virginia.[10]

In the Continental Congress the president was merely a presiding officer elected by Congress from its own membership. This plan came very nearly being adopted for the new federal government. A strong faction led by Sherman favored it. Wilson came out strongly for the election of the president by the people. When the question first arose he said he was almost unwilling to declare the mode he wished to have adopted being apprehensive that it might appear chimerical. He declared that in theory he was for an election by the people.[11]

The idea of electing the chief executive by a vote of the people was so novel to the large majority of the delegates that it did not win support. Wilson renewed his declaration in favor of an election by the people. He wished not only to have both branches of the national legislature derive their powers from the people without the intervention of the state

[9] Ibid, I, 321.

[10] Madison, *Debates on the Adoption of the Federal Constitution* (Vol. 5, supplementary to Elliot's Debates, 1866), 151.

[11] Ibid, 142.

legislatures but the executive also, in order to make them independent one of another as well of the states. Colonel Mason of Virginia favored the idea but thought it impracticable. He asked that Wilson might have time to give the matter more thought and digest it in his own form. The idea of having the president chosen by the people and deriving his powers from the people was looked upon as experimental and radical, and Wilson now realized that he would have to proceed cautiously if he expected to accomplish anything.

Wilson having prepared his plan of election at the request of Mason offered it for the consideration of the convention. This was the plan which he feared might appear to his colleagues as chimerical. He proposed that the states should be divided into districts and the voters in each to choose electors who should meet and by ballot elect an executive outside their body.[12] Wilson borrowed this idea from the Constitution of Maryland. The method of choice by electors to be chosen by the people was to be found only in the Maryland constitution and was original with Charles Carroll of Carrollton.

In the Maryland convention of 1776 which adopted a bill of rights and a state constitution, Charles Carroll proposed a mode of election of the senate that was entirely novel. The senate, consisting of fifteen members, was to be chosen by a body of electors forty in number, two to be elected by the people of each county and one each from Baltimore and Annapolis. This method of election which was a distinct departure from all other forms of state government created much favorable comment. Samuel Chase declared his approval by saying it was "virgin gold." [13] *The Federalist* commented: "The Maryland constitution is daily deriving from the salutary operation of this part of it, a reputation which will probably not be rivalled by that of any state in the Union." [14]

[12] Ibid, 143.
[13] McMahon, op. cit., 480.
[14] *The Federalist* (Edited by Lodge, 1888), 398.

That the plan offered by Wilson was original with Charles Carroll is shown in a letter which the latter wrote in 1817 to Worthington C. Ford. This letter reads:

> I was one of the committee that framed the constitution of this state and the mode of chusing the Senate was suggested by me; no objection was made to it in the committee, as I remember, except by Mr. Johnson who disliked the Senate's filling up the vacancies from their own body. I replied that if the mode of chusing senators by electors were deemed eligible, the filling up vacancies by that body was inevitable, as the electors could not be convened to make choice of a senator on every vacancy and that the senate acting under the sanction of an oath and *l'esprit de corps,* would insure the election of the fittest men for that station, nor do I recollect while I was in the senate that the power intrusted to it in this instance was ever abused or perverted to party views. I do not remember at this distance of time, whether this part of the committee report was objected to in the convention, nor any report of its debates or proceedings other than what is found in Hanson's Edition of the Laws, nor what was the understanding of that body respecting the right of the Governor of nomination to the Council.[15]

It is extremely probable that Charles Carroll suggested this plan to Wilson but in any event Wilson must have been familiar with the method of choosing senators in Maryland, for he was practising law in Annapolis the year following the adoption of the state constitution. It is safe to state, therefore, that Charles Carroll of Carrollton was the father of the electoral college. If it had not been that this plan was offered as a compromise measure, the choice of president would undoubtedly have been left to Congress and the people would have had no say in the choice of their executive.

In first offering the plan of presidential electors which was a proposed substitute for the Randolph resolution for election by Congress, Wilson urged that the choice of the executive by popular electors would produce more confidence among the people in the first magistrate than an

[15] Rowland, op. cit., I, 190-191. There was apparently no precedent for Carroll's plan of election except that which he may have found in the organization of his own church—the method of the election of the Pope by the College of Cardinals, although there is not a perfect similarity.

election by the national legislature. Wilson's motion was lost by a vote of eight states to two, this time Pennsylvania and Maryland voting in the negative.[16] The convention was not yet ready for the popular election of the president. It was to be over three months and not until near the close of the convention, that the electoral plan was to be finally adopted as part of the constitution. In the meantime there were to be marches and counter-marches and much debate.

On Monday, July 9, 1787, Daniel Carroll of Rock Creek, Maryland, elder brother of Father John Carroll, took his seat in the constitutional convention, as a delegate from his own state. He had been elected after his cousin, Charles Carroll, had declined to serve.

He soon went to the aid of Wilson in support of the cause of popular sovereignty. The Scotch Presbyterian and the Irish Catholic found they had much in common. They belonged to the same school of political philosophy and their forebears had cherished the same desire for freedom and independence. They shared with each other a firm belief in the sovereignty of the people and an unshaken confidence in republican institutions of government.

Daniel Carroll was a native of Maryland. He received his preliminary education at Bohemia Manor school, and in 1742 was sent to St. Omer's where he pursued a six years' course. When he returned to America in 1784, his brother John Carroll and his cousin Charles Carroll went to France to begin their training at the same college. He had been a member of the Continental Congress, of the Maryland Council and of the Maryland Senate, of which latter body he was at one time president. As a member of the Continental Congress he took an active part in the negotiations for the French alliance.[17]

16 Madison, op. cit., 144.

17 Daniel Carroll was chairman of a committee to which was referred the communication of Luzerne, the French minister opening the negotiations. The committee reported that there was no danger in leaving the negotiations to the discretion of the French government.

While the services of Wilson have not been fully recognized until recent years, mention has hardly ever been made of Daniel Carroll. He is the forgotten man in American constitutional history. Although he may not compare with Wilson from the standpoint of legal or forensic ability, he was swayed by the same ideas and ideals. He proved himself a man of vision with a broad conception of the science of government.

When Daniel Carroll entered the convention the debate was going on concerning the election of senators and representatives. A week later what some writers have called "the great compromise" was brought about. The important feature of this was the provision for the equal representation of the states. Pennsylvania voted against the compromise. Wilson favored the election of United States senators by the people, and in this he was a century and a quarter ahead of his time. In the debate preceding the compromise he had asked: "Can we forget for whom we are forming a government? Is it for men or for imaginary beings called states?" [18] On another occasion he asked: "Must the states alone possesss sovereignty and the people be forgotten?"

The compromise ended the so-called struggle between the large and the small states, but a more important struggle between the advocates of the sovereignty of the states and those who upheld the sovereignty of the people, was still to come. Although when Wilson first proposed the electoral college it was defeated by a rather decisive vote, the struggle did not end there. Soon after Daniel Carroll took his seat he came to the support of Wilson and they determined to secure the popular election of the chief magistrate.

Gradually some of the leading members of the convention were coming around to the idea of choosing the president by electors; Madison, Hamilton and Morris finally favoring it. Wilson said he perceived "with pleasure that the idea was gaining ground of an election mediately or immediately by

[18] Madison, op. cit., 262.

the people." [19] Just previous to this, on the motion of Oliver Ellsworth, the convention had voted in favor of choosing the executive by electors appointed by the state legislatures, but this action was later reconsidered. It was then voted that the "executive be appointed by the national legislature." This was carried by a vote of seven states to four, Pennsylvania, Maryland, Connecticut and Virginia voting in the negative.[20]

After this action was taken, Wilson in sheer desperation and hoping for a compromise, moved a substitute plan. He moved that the executive be chosen "by electors to be taken by lot from the national legislature who shall proceed immediately to the choice of the executive and not separate until it be made." Carroll seconded the motion. Wilson explained that he did not offer this as the best mode. His opinion, he said, remained unshaken "that we ought to have resort to the people for the election." He favored the suggestion of King that as "nobody seemed to be satisfied" the matter be postponed. Indefinite postponement was agreed upon.[21]

The most interesting phase of the proceedings of the convention was the slow recognition of the doctrine of popular sovereignty. There seemed to be a profound distrust of democracy on the part of most of the delegates, and a reluctance to give to the people any share in the national government except the right to elect their own representatives in the lower house, and at one time there was even opposition to this. Roger Sherman of Connecticut said, "the less the people had to do with the government, the better." Wilson compared the government to a lofty pyramid and therefore in need of as broad a base as possible.[22]

Wilson and Carroll were among the few who were at all times and for all purposes in favor of the people exercising their choice of rulers. When they made their proposals as

19 Ibid, 337. Hamilton and Madison many times were in accord with Wilson on fundamental questions and were more in agreement with Scholastic principles than with the French school of political thought.

20 Ibid, 358-9.

21 Ibid, 362.

22 Thorpe, op. cit., I, 316.

late as a month prior to the final adjournment they were not supported by the votes of the majority of their colleagues. It was not until the closing days of the convention that the majority swung to the support of the doctrine that Wilson and Carroll had advocated from the beginning.

On Friday, August 24, when a proposed article came before the convention that the president should be "elected by ballot by the legislature," Daniel Carroll was on his feet with a motion that the words "by the legislature" be stricken out and in lieu thereof there be inserted the words "by the people." By this motion he flung before the convention the direct issue of a government by the people or a government by the chosen few, of a free republic or an oligarchy. Carroll's motion was promptly seconded by Wilson. The motion failed to pass by a vote of nine states to two. Delaware was the only state voting with Pennsylvania in favor of a popular election.[23]

On the same day the Carroll motion for a popular election was lost, Morris stated his objection to the majority plan for election of the president by congress and moved that the president "shall be chosen by electors to be chosen by the people of the several states." Carroll seconded him. The motion was lost by a vote of six states to five.[24] Had the Protestant delegates from Maryland voted with their Catholic colleague the motion would have passed and the question would have been settled then and there. Under the unit rule Maryland was recorded as voting in the negative. But the popular cause was slowly gaining strength. Immediately after this and on the same day, a vote was taken on "the abstract question, shall the executive be chosen by electors." The states were equally divided, Massachusetts being recorded as absent.[25]

On August 21, it was agreed to refer all parts of the Con-

23 Madison, op. cit., 472.
24 Ibid, 473.
25 Ibid, 474.

stitution and reports of committees not acted upon, to a committee of eleven to be appointed by ballot, one member from each state. Daniel Carroll was appointed on this committee and with him Morris and Madison. It was this committee that organized the executive. It was the committee on detail of which Wilson was a member that enumerated the executive powers. These were the two most important committees of the session. Much of the real work of the convention was done in committee.

The committee of eleven made a report to the convention September 4, containing the plan of presidential electors, and this was substantially the same as was finally incorporated in the Constitution. The method of election, as recommended by the committee, was deemed so radical an innovation that Randolph and Pinckney called for an explanation. It was explained that the general disapproval of an election by congress, by the state legislatures or directly by the people, and the necessity of making the executive an independent department of the government, had induced the committee to resort to the expedient of presidential electors.[26] It is thus made clear that the plan of electors original with Charles Carroll of Carrollton, as offered by Wilson and supported by Daniel Carroll, was responsible for preventing the presidency from being bestowed by any other body than the people. It must be borne in mind, however, that both Wilson and Daniel Carroll preferred a direct election by the people and favored the electoral college as the only possible compromise.

After the adoption of the Carroll plan for the election of president, there was a long debate in which it developed that there was opposition to the clause in the proposed draft reported by the committee that gave to the senate the power to elect the president in the event of a dead-lock in the electoral college. This opposition was voiced by Wilson who said that the proposal was a "dangerous tendency to aristocracy as

[26] Ibid, 508.

throwing a dangerous power into the hands of the senate." He declared that according to the plan the president "will not be the man of the people as he ought to be but the minion of the senate." The House of Representatives was then given the power to elect in the event that no candidate received a majority of the votes of the electors.[27]

Just before the question was put upon the adoption of the engrossed constitution, Washington for the first and only time in the sessions of the convention spoke in advocacy of any measure. This was in relation to a matter brought up by Daniel Carroll and two other members, Gorham and King, and had to do with the ratio of representation in the lower house. The committee had reported in favor of one representative for every 40,000 inhabitants. It was now proposed to change this so that there would be one representative for every 30,000, thereby increasing the number of representatives. When Washington arose to put the question, he said that although he recognized the impropriety of his speaking from the chair, he felt this amendment to be of such consequence that he "could not forbear expressing his wish that the alteration proposed might take place." [28] Without a single objection being made the amendment was adopted. This same proposal which previously had had no chance of being adopted, Farrand says, shows that bringing it up at this time was "inspired." [29]

At the opening of the morning session of the final day of the convention Daniel Carroll reminded the house that no address to the people had yet been prepared. He considered it of great importance that such an address should accompany the constitution. The people had been accustomed to such addresses on great occasions and would expect one of this. He moved that a committee be appointed for the special purpose of preparing an address to the people. The members,

[27] Ibid, 519.
[28] Ibid, 555.
[29] *Framing the Constitution*, 193.

however, did not want to take the time necessary for the preparation of an address. They were anxious to adjourn and return to their homes. Rutledge objected on account of the delay it would produce. Sherman concurred with Rutledge that an address to the people was unnecessary. Carroll's motion was lost by a vote of six states to four, Pennsylvania, Maryland, Virginia and Delaware supporting the motion.[30] The members were left to explain the reasons for what had been done, to their own constituents. Carroll's plea for an address to the people was consonant with his position that the people were to be the real source of power in the new government.

[30] Madison, op. cit., 546-7.

CHAPTER VIII

SAVING THE CONSTITUTION

No two members of the Constitutional Convention worked together in closer harmony for the accomplishment of a common purpose than did James Wilson and Daniel Carroll. This was because they adhered to what they regarded as a fixed principle, that all governments derive their just powers from the consent of the governed. All through the convention they labored zealously for the cause of popular government. Their work resulted in the establishment of a free republic. In this respect they saved the constitution.

The main objection to the plan to allow the people to make a choice of the chief executive was due to what was deemed to be the incapacity of the people to select proper persons for office, a difficulty incident to the limitations set on the elective franchise at that time. Most of the members of the convention saw no prospect of a large extension of the franchise nor could they see any way by which the voters would be able to judge of the qualifications of candidates in different states. These members were dominated in thought and action by the political and economic conditions of their day.[1] Wilson and Carroll, however, had the vision to foresee an intelligent electorate and to visualize future conditions whereby the average voter would come into more or less intimate touch with the affairs of the nation.

The trust which Wilson and Carroll had in the people did not come so much from their own experience as it did from their political ideals and their philosophy of human rights. Their school of political thought was of no modern mould and much less was it that of Rousseau and the "empty

1 Thorpe, op. cit., I, 446-7.

moonshine" of the French enlightenment which Edmund Burke repudiated. Wilson's training was along the line of Scotch common-sense philosophy and the political doctrine of the Whigs in the time of Burke. The traditional Whig theory of government was formulated mainly on the basis of scholastic principles.[2] Both Locke and Hooker borrowed from the schoolmen. The writer on Hooker in the *Encyclopædia Britannica* says that the Whig philosopher based his reasoning on principles which he discovered in Augustine and Thomas Aquinas.[3] Janet did not hesitate to say that "it would not be altogether inexact to state that in the Middle Ages it was in the cloisters that the doctrine of the sovereignty of the people was born." [4] Daniel Carroll, educated at St. Omer's, was well grounded in scholastic philosophy and medieval doctrines of government.

In connection with the concept of Wilson and Carroll, that the people should be given the right to select their rulers, it is interesting to find the following passage in the writings of Thomas Aquinas in the thirteenth century:

> Accordingly the best form of government is in a state or kingdom wherein one is given the power to preside over all, while under him are others having governing powers and yet a government of this kind is shared by all, both because all are eligible to govern and because the rulers are chosen by all. For this is the best policy, being partly kingdom since one is the head of all; partly aristocracy, so far as a number of persons are set in authority; partly democracy, i.e., government by the people, in so far as the rulers can be chosen from the people and the people have the right to choose their rulers.[5]

Randolph G. Adams, who has given a remarkably clear analysis of Wilson's philosophy of government, says:

> It would require a great deal more space than I have at my disposal to trace the relationship between Wilson's treatment of the natural law and that of Thomas Aquinas. It would form a

2 "Modern Practical Liberty and Common Sense," Moorhouse F. X. Millar, S.J., in *The State and the Church,* 160-2.

3 Vol. XIII, 11th edition, 673.

4 *Histoire de la philosophie politique,* II, 2, 227.

5 *Summa Theologica,* II.II^ae^ Q 105a1.

fascinating subject for research. Yet one cannot but be struck with the parallel between Aquinas' striving to obey the dualism of the authority of the pope and the authority of the emperor, with Wilson's efforts to make clear that a man could at the same time be a citizen of the United States and a citizen of the state of Pennsylvania. Both men thought in almost universal terms, and I hope I may not be claiming too much for my subject by suggesting that it is time Americans knew a little more about their own Aquinas, particularly in these days when the dualism of federal or state jurisdiction is being complicated by the problem of an international jurisdiction.[6]

The electoral procedure set up in the constitution was soon regarded as equivalent to popular election, and the president as the one national representative of the people. The president alone was elected by the whole union and no man in the United States had the concurrent voice of the people but him.[7] The president would never have been the choice of the people had it not been for the combined work and influence of Wilson and Carroll, and could they have had their way the people would have expressed their choice directly and not indirectly through electors.

There was work to be done to bring about the ratification of the Constitution for its opponents were many and some were of influence. Daniel Carroll returned to Maryland to find a spirited opposition led by Samuel Chase. Two of the Maryland delegates, Martin and Mercer, refused to sign the document and joined the ranks of the opposition. Charles and Daniel Carroll were appointed members of a commission of four, by the Maryland Senate, to report on the action of the convention. They led the forces favoring ratification. The delegates were called before the assembly to give an account of the proceedings of the convention. Martin taking liberty with his oath of secrecy occupied three hours in a fierce attack upon the entire plan of government. A convention was then called to be held August 21, 1788.

Washington and Madison gave the full support of their

6 *Selected Political Essays of James Wilson*, 7-8.

7 "The Creation of the Presidency," Thach, *Johns Hopkins University Studies*, Series XL, No. 4, 168.

influence to the Carrolls. Madison wrote to Jefferson that "a more formidable opposition is likely to be made in Maryland than was at first anticipated," but stated that most of the characters of weight, including the Carrolls, were on the side of ratification. In a letter to Washington, Madison asked him to remail an enclosed unsealed letter to the "post-office for Georgetown or to change the address to Annapolis, if you have reason to believe that Mr. Carroll should be there." [8] Throughout the campaign the Carrolls kept in close touch with both Washington and Madison.

In the great discussion of 1787-8 over the adoption or rejection of the Constitution, the method used to influence public opinion which proved most effective was the resort to the printing press. Anonymous articles appeared in the newspapers of the period and political pamphlets were widely circulated. Paul Leicester Ford appreciating the historical value of these writings and recognizing the light they would throw on constitutional history, gathered and compiled most if not all of these in two volumes. One of these volumes (*The Essays*) presents the communications that appeared in the public press and the other contains the printed pamphlets which were circulated. Ford found that there had been a neglect of these writings as historical material, and it was with great difficulty and after long research in many public and private libraries and the files of some forty newspapers that he was able to make his compilation. What had chiefly caused this neglect was the anonymous character of the papers. It was a time of literary masks, explains Ford, "and we often find like the knights of old that when the masks were removed, they had concealed our ablest statesmen." More attention, he believes, would have been given these works by succeeding generations if they had borne the names of those who wrote them. Ford was able to identify each writer with the result that his research reveals nearly all the nation's leaders engaged in the battle of the printing presses.

[8] Gurn, op. cit., 120.

The publication of these writings and the revelation of their authorship, show the intensity of the struggle and the strong opposition that was arrayed against the constitution. In the opposition ranks were Patrick Henry, Richard Henry Lee, Colonel George Mason, George Clinton, Elbridge Gerry, Albert Gallatin and James Monroe. These writings appeared in the newspapers in the writers' own states. Oliver Ellsworth wrote for *The Connecticut Courant;* Roger Sherman for the *New Haven Gazette;* Elbridge Gerry for the *Massachusetts Centinel;* Alexander Hamilton for the *New York Daily Advertiser;* George Clinton for the *New York Journal* and Charles Pinckney for the *Gazette of South Carolina.* All these articles appeared over noms-de-plume.

One of the exceptions to the general rule of anonymity was the address of James Wilson defending the Constitution delivered at Philadelphia, October 6, 1787. This was printed and circulated over his own name. Almost simultaneous with the printing of this address, Samuel Chase sent a communication to the *Maryland Journal* under the nom-de-plume of "Caution." In this he advised his fellow citizens to be cautious "when men urge you to determine in haste on so momentous a subject," for "it is not unreasonable to require their motives nor uncharitable to suspect they are improper." Daniel Carroll felt it incumbent on him to reply. In the same newspaper, October 13, there appeared a reply to "Caution" signed by "A Friend of the Constitution." Ford says that Carroll was the author of this communication, as he had written to Madison at this time stating that he had replied to Chase.

It appears that the final passage of Carroll's reply to Chase is almost identical with the closing part of Wilson's address. It is evident that Wilson and Carroll collaborated in the work of defending the constitution as they had in the work of framing it. Carroll after consulting Wilson evidently concluded that in his reply to Chase he could do no better than to use the closing words of Wilson's address which expressed his own ideas. The following taken from the Wilson address is almost the same language used in the communication in the *Maryland Journal* signed "A Friend of the Constitution":

> After all, my fellow citizens, it is neither extraordinary nor unexpected that the constitution offered to your consideration should meet with opposition. It is the nature of man to pursue his own interest, in preference to the public good; and I do not mean to make any personal reflection, when I add that it is the interest of a very numerous, powerful and respectable body, to counteract and destroy the excellent work produced by the late convention. All the officers of government, and all appointments for the administration of justice and the collection of public revenue, which are transferred from the individual to the aggregate sovereignty of the states, will necessarily turn the stream of influence and emolument into a new channel. Every person, therefore, who either enjoys or expects to enjoy a place of profit under the present establishment, will object to the proposed innovation, not in truth because it is injurious to the liberties of his country, but because it affects his schemes of wealth and consequence. I will confess, indeed, that I am not a blind admirer of this plan of government, and that there are some parts of it which, if my wish had prevailed, would certainly have been altered. But when I reflect how widely men differ in their opinions, and that every man (and the observation applies likewise to every state) has an equal pretension to assert his own, I am satisfied that anything nearer to perfection could not have been accomplished. If there are errors, it should be remembered, that the seeds of reformation are sown in the work itself, and the concurrence of two-thirds of the congress may at any time introduce alterations and amendments. Regarding it, then, in every point of view, with a candid and disinterested mind, I am bold to assert that it is THE BEST FORM OF GOVERNMENT WHICH HAS EVER BEEN OFFERED TO THE WORLD.[9]

After a vigorous contest Maryland became the seventh state to ratify the Constitution. Some of the opposition to ratification came from the failure to adopt a bill of rights. Jefferson's objection to the Constitution was "the omission of a bill of rights, providing clearly and without the aid of sophism the freedom of religion, freedom of the press, pro-

[9] Ford, *Pamphlets on the Constitution,* 161; *Essays on the Constitution,* 330.

tection against standing armies, restriction of monopolies, the eternal and unremitting force of the habeas corpus laws and trials by jury in all matters of fact triable by the laws of the land and not by the laws of nations." In the letter to Madison he "wishes with all his soul" that the first nine conventions, whichever they might be, would accept the Constitution, and thus secure the good it contained but the last four would refuse to accede till a declaration of rights was annexed. Later he expressed himself as greatly pleased with the course of Massachusetts in accepting the work of the Federal Convention and amending it afterwards.[10] In the work of amendment the Carrolls of Maryland were to play an important rôle.

10 Thorpe, op. cit., II, 212-230.

CHAPTER IX

THE FIRST AMENDMENT

WHEN Charles Pinckney of South Carolina presented to the Constitutional Convention the draft of a proposed form of federal government there was contained in Article IV a provision which read:

"The legislature of the United States shall pass no law on the subject of religion."[1]

This language was never adopted as part of the Constitution. It was not until August 20, that Pinckney moved to add to Article XX of the proposed Constitution the following:

> But no religious test shall ever be required as a qualification to any office or public trust under the authority of the United States.

There was little debate. Roger Sherman thought it was unnecessary, the "present prevailing liberality" being a sufficient security against such tests. Whatever Sherman's idea of a prevailing liberality may have been, in six states, including his own, there was Protestant church establishment. Morris and General Pinckney approved the motion. The motion was carried and then the whole article, North Carolina voting "no" and Maryland "divided."[2]

This article did not establish religious liberty. It did not even indicate that the convention was in favor of positive religious liberty or of the absolute separation of state and church.

Colonel George Mason presented to the Virginia state

1 Madison, op. cit., 131.
2 Ibid, 498.

convention of 1776 a bill of rights containing a broad religious liberty clause prepared by Patrick Henry and amended by Madison. This paved the way for a similar clause in the Federal Constitution, but when the time came no attempt was made to have the convention adopt it. Daniel Carroll had his attention and energies centered on the struggle to secure a popular election of the chief executive. Had he attempted to secure a provision for religious liberty, it is doubtful if he would have had the support of Wilson, for the latter was among those who did not believe a bill of rights was necessary, although he was in sympathy with the idea of religious toleration and freedom.

Those who favored the incorporation in the Constitution of a bill of rights that would include a recognition of the principle of freedom of conscience patiently waited for the opening of the first congress when the opportunity of introducing the amendments which they favored would be afforded. Madison and Jefferson were determined that a bill of rights should be embodied in the amendments. Washington was not averse to this plan.

Charles and Daniel Carroll were to be members of the new congress. Charles Carroll was elected to the senate and Daniel Carroll to the house. Wherever the contest was to be, whether in the senate or the house, one of the two Carrolls was sure to be in the arena of action.

The official directory showed Charles and Daniel rooming in the same house, 21 Smith Street. They took their seats soon after the session opened. Charles Carroll was appointed on the important committee on the Judiciary.

The session of the first congress opened in April but it was not until August that the matter of religious liberty was brought up for consideration. In the meantime an interesting newspaper controversy arose which had an important bearing on the action of the congress. In the issue of the *Gazette of the United States,* published at New York, May 9, 1789, there appeared a communication signed "E. C." The identity of the author is not known. The title was: "The Importance of the Protestant Religion Politically Considered." Like the article appearing in the *Columbian Magazine* in Philadelphia on the eve of the Constitutional Convention attacking the Catholic Church, it was a well-timed and well-placed piece of propaganda. The attack appeared in the opening days of the congress, immediately after Madison had made the announcement that amendments to the Constitution were to be acted upon.

The writer made an indirect attack on the Catholic religion by upholding the supremacy of Protestantism and demanding for it preemption and exclusive privileges. He began by asserting that "The religion which the citizens of America generally profess," and for the sake of which "our forefathers" left their happy homes in England to endure life in a "wilderness swarming with savage beasts and far more savage men" was the Protestant religion, "which laid the foundations of this new and great empire." Therefore, he reasoned, "this religion is entitled to our particular reverence and respect. The mass of mankind are ever captivated by external appearances and show 'and may be caught by the tinsel and trappings' of any other religion." It was worthy of consideration, he said, what might be the probable effects "of the introduction of any other religions," and how far these effects if in any way dangerous "may be counteracted consistent with the just and generous principles of toleration." It was well worth the attention of those who assent "to the importance of the Protestant religion, politically considered," to honor it with "every possible distinguishing mark of preeminence and respect, not repugnant to the true spirit of toleration, and liberally aid our religious fathers in the glorious work of supporting this Bulwark of our Constitution." The Protestant clergy he said must not "sink into contempt or neglect." The learned may decline the profession and then "Adieu to religion, morality and liberty!"

Behind the veil of a feigned spirit of tolerance, this writer in seeking the preeminence of the Protestant religion was inferentially asking either for religious establishment or national support of the Protestant clergy. There is no other way of interpreting his message. This was the interpretation given to it by John Carroll and he was therefore prompted to make reply. This time his reply was published before the question of religious liberty came up for discussion and action.

Bishop Carroll's reply was printed in the *Gazette* in its issue of June 10, 1789. It appeared over the pen name of "Pacificus," but its authorship soon became known to the leaders of congress. It was the strongest appeal for the recognition of the spirit of religious liberty that was made in his day. He began his reply:

Every friend of the rights of conscience, equal liberty and diffusive happiness must have felt pain in seeing the attempt made by one of your correspondents to revive an odious system of religious intolerance. The author may not have been fully sensible of the tendency of his publication because he speaks of preserving universal toleration. Perhaps he is one of those who think it consistent with justice to exclude certain citizens from the honors and emoluments of society merely on account of their religious opinions, provided they be not restrained by racks and forfeitures from the exercise of the religious worship which their consciences approve. If such are his views, in vain have Americans associated in one grand national union under the express condition of not being shackled by religious tests and under a firm persuasion that they were to retain, when associated, every natural right not expressly surrendered. Is it pretended that they who are objects of an intended exclusion from certain offices of honor and advantage, have forfeited by any act of treason against the United States, the common rights of nature or the stipulated rights of the political society of which they form a part? This the author has not presumed to assert. Their blood flowed as freely in proportion to their numbers to cement the fabric of independence as that of any of their fellow citizens. They concurred with perhaps greater unanimity than any other body of men in recommending a form of government from whose influence America anticipates all the blessings of justice, peace, plenty, good order and civil and religious liberty. What character shall we give to a system of policy calculated for the express purpose of divesting rights legally acquired by those citizens who are not only unoffending but those whose conduct has been highly meritorious?

In answer to the claim that America was settled in order to establish the Protestant religion, Bishop Carroll turned back to early Maryland and the settlement of some of the other colonies and asked:

> Did the Roman Catholics who first came to Maryland leave their native soil for the sake of preserving the Protestant faith? Was this the motive of the peaceful Quakers in the settlement of Pennsylvania? Did the first inhabitants of the Jerseys and New York quit Europe for fear of being compelled to renounce their Protestant tenets? Can it even be truly affirmed that this motive operated on all or a majority of those who began to settle the four eastern states? Or even if they really were influenced by a desire of preserving their religion, what will ensue from the persecution of another? Will history justify the assertion that they left their native homes for the sake of the Protestant religion, understanding it in a comprehensive sense as distinguished from every other?

The false interpretation of early American history contained in the letter of May 9, was clearly exposed in these searching questions of the Catholic bishop. He declared it was ridiculous to assert that the Protestant religion was the bulwark of the Constitution or that the establishment of the American government was the work of "this or that religion." The structure of our government arose, he said, "from the generous exertions of all her citizens to redress their wrongs, to assert their rights and to lay its foundations on the soundest principles of justice and equal liberty."

Commenting on the statement that if the Protestant clergy did not survive then it would be necessary to bid adieu to religion, morality and liberty, Carroll said:

> Thus the author attributes to his religion the credit of being the most favorable to freedom and affirms that not only morality but liberty likewise would expire if his clergy should be condemned or neglected, all of which contains a refined insinuation that liberty cannot coexist with or be cherished by any other religious institution and which, therefore, he would give us to understand it is not safe to countenance in a free government.

Then came the most forceful part of the reply:

> I am anxious to guard against the impression intended by such insinuations, not merely for the sake of any one profession but from an earnest regard to preserve inviolate forever in our new empire the great principle of religious freedom. The constitutions of some of our states continue still to entrench on the sacred rights of conscience and men who have bled and opened their purses as freely in the cause of liberty and independence as any other citizens are most unjustly excluded from the advantages which they contributed to establish. But if bigotry and narrow prejudices have hitherto prevented the cure of these evils be it the duty of every lover of peace and justice to extend them no further.

His closing words were:

> Must America yielding to these fanciful systems confine her distinguishing favors to the followers of Calvin and keep a jealous eye on all others? Ought she not rather to treat with contempt those idle and generally speaking interested speculations, refuted by reason, history and daily experience and rest the preservation of her liberties and her government on the attachment of mankind to their political happiness, to the security of their persons and their property which is independent of religious doctrines and not restrained by any?

John Carroll was at his best when he wrote this ringing appeal for equality and fair play. He wrote in the spirit of the New America, for he as much as any other man of his time had shown that he was the embodiment of that spirit. Recently elected the first bishop of his church by the free choice of his fellow clergy and the recipient of the confidence of Washington, Franklin and Jefferson, he was in a position of influence in his crusade for religious freedom. His appeal as published in the *Gazette* at the very time when the proposed amendments were being introduced in Congress did not fall on deaf ears.

According to the Reverend C. C. White in his article on "The Origin and Progress of the Church in the United States," in the American edition of Darras' *General History of the Catholic Church,*[3] a memorial was presented to Con-

[3] Vol. LX, 599.

gress signed by some of the leading Catholics representing the necessity of adopting a constitutional provision for the "protection and maintenance of civil and religious freedom, the purchase of which has cost so much blood and treasure among all classes of citizens." Father White gives as his authority a letter written by Bishop Fenwick of Boston which mentions John, Charles and Daniel Carroll, Thomas Fitzsimmons, Dominick Lynch and George Meade as the signers. The article also states that Bishop Fenwick evidently confused this memorial with the testimonial letter addressed to Washington in 1790, the reason for this being that the same men signed the letter to Washington. As a matter of fact Bishop Fenwick gives the name of one signer of the memorial which does not appear in the testimonial letter to Washington, that of George Meade, grandfather of General George Gordon Meade. Bishop Fenwick was a native of Maryland, and during his early priesthood must have come in contact with Bishop Carroll who apparently gave him information as to the memorial. Therefore a letter from him is not to be lightly set aside as evidence of the fact that such a memorial was sent notwithstanding that there may be no present record of it, which is not at all surprising.

Just before the adjournment of the House of Representatives, May 4, 1789, James Madison gave notice that he intended to bring forward the subject of amendments to the Constitution on the 25th. It was not until June that the amendments were offered. Madison on June 8, moved that the House go into committee of the whole. That amendments should be proposed at an early date was insistently demanded by at least eight of the states. The two hundred or more amendments which in one form or another represented the demands of the Anti-Federalists were taken together as an embodiment of public sentiment, which the new congress could not prudently ignore.[4] Madison had devoted himself to an exhaustive study of all the amendments proposed by

[4] Thorpe, op. cit., II, 199.

the state conventions and "of all the grievances and complaints of the newspapers." Finally, as the result of much labor and study, he introduced the expected list. He urged expedition in order that the public might be satisfied. The amendments he said "would give satisfaction to the doubting part of our citizens who had an apprehension that the public liberties were not secure." [5]

The great body of the Federalists considered the amendments untimely and unnecessary. One spoke of them as "milk and water amendments." Another compared the Constitution as it was proposed to be amended, to Joseph's coat of many colors. Washington was for peace and harmony and was known to be ready for any reasonable compromise.

The Federalists who objected to a bill of rights were theoretically right but practically wrong. A bill of rights was necessary because it was expedient. It was necessary to allay the fears of those who were jealous of the powers of the Federal government and desired to see those powers properly circumscribed. Minorities it was said must be protected while majorities can protect themselves. This reasoning was sound.[6]

In the first draft proposed by Madison was the following amendment to Article I, section 9:

> The civil rights of none shall be abridged on account of religious belief or worship nor shall any national religion be established nor shall the full and equal rights of conscience in any manner or on any pretext be infringed.

The proposed amendments were referred to a select committee of eleven which made its report on August 13. Madison's proposed religious liberty clause had suffered a change, and in the report of the committee it was made to read: "No religion shall be established by law nor shall the equal rights of conscience be infringed."

The record of the debate on August 15, 1789, when this proposed amendment came before the House sitting as a

[5] Ibid, 215.
[6] Curtis, *Constitutional History of the United States*, II, 155.

committee of the whole, appears in Benton's *Abridgement of the Debates in Congress* [7] under the caption "Freedom of Conscience." These records were evidently taken from long-hand notes made by one of the clerks. Thorpe says that "Daniel Carroll, a kinsman of a distinguished Roman Catholic family and a member of the late Federal Convention, was highly in favor of adopting the words" as part of the Constitution.[8] Madison who was leader of the House apparently allowed Carroll to open the debate for the proponents of the amendment for his speech in favor followed. Carroll explained the purpose of the measure and made the strongest plea for its adoption that is recorded.

Four representatives spoke briefly before Carroll but none of them unqualifiedly favored the amendment. Sylvester of New York had some doubts about the propriety of the mode of expression used. He apprehended that it was liable to a construction different from what had been intended by the committee. He feared it might be thought to have a tendency to abolish religion altogether. Vining of Delaware suggested the propriety of transferring the two members of the sentence. Elbridge Gerry of Massachusetts said it would read better if it was that no religious doctrine shall be established by law. Roger Sherman of Connecticut took the same attitude as he did in the Constitutional Convention. He is credited as saying that "he thought the amendment altogether unnecessary inasmuch as Congress had no authority whatever delegated to them by the Constitution to make religious establishments. He would therefore move to have it struck out." Daniel Carroll who followed Sherman was the first outspoken advocate for the amendment as proposed. The report of his remarks is thus given by Benton:

As the rights of conscience are in their nature of peculiar delicacy and will little bear the gentlest touch of governmental hand and as many sects have concurred in opinion that they are not

[7] Loc. cit., I, 137-8.
[8] Op. cit., II, 237.

well secured under the present constitution he said he was much in favor of adopting the words. He thought it would tend more towards conciliating the minds of the people to the government than almost any other amendment he had heard proposed. He would not contend with gentlemen about phraseology, his object was to secure the substance in such a manner as to satisfy the wishes of the honest part of the community.[9]

The fact that he is quoted as saying that "his object" was to secure the substance in such a way as to satisfy the honest part of the community, is a strong indication that he had proposed the language of the amendment which he was sponsoring. The expression "the equal rights of conscience," found in the proposal, bears the earmarks of John Carroll for this had always been the burden of his plea.

Madison followed Carroll in the debate. He conceived the meaning of the words of the proposed amendment to be that Congress should not establish a religion and enforce the legal observance of it by law or compel men to worship God in any manner contrary to their conscience, but whether the words were necessary or not he did not mean to say. They had been requested by some of the state conventions. Answering Sherman, he said Congress had the right to make laws to infringe the rights of conscience under the power to make all laws. The amendment was well expressed and he favored it.

Huntington of Connecticut feared the words might be so literally construed as to be extremely hurtful to the cause of religion. All might not understand the amendment as Madison had expounded it. It might be convenient to put upon it an entirely different construction. In New England the ministers of the congregations were sustained by the contributions of the members of their society and the expense of building the meeting houses was met in the same way. These matters were regulated by by-laws. If an action were brought in a Federal court on any of these cases the person who had neglected to pay his subscription might appeal to

[9] Benton, op. cit., I, 137; *Annals of Congress* 1789-1804, I, 758.

this amendment on the ground that he was not compelled to support a religious establishment. He called attention to Rhode Island where "no religion can be established by law." He said he could give a history of such a regulation—the people now enjoying the fruits of it. He hoped the amendment would be made in such a way as to secure the rights of conscience and the free exercise of the rights of religion but not to patronize those who professed no religion at all.

The voice of Rhode Island was not heard in this debate for the reason that not having ratified the constitution she had no representatives in Congress. Several enthusiastic Rhode Island historians have claimed that it was the influence of Rhode Island which brought about the adoption of the religious liberty amendment, when as a matter of fact the "state of lively experiment" had no voice nor vote in the first congress.

Madison suggested that if the word "national" was inserted before "religion," it would point the amendment directly to the object it was intended to prevent. Elbridge Gerry declared his aversion to the word which reminded him of the observations that had taken place in ratifying conventions. He then fired a shot at Madison saying that the latter's motion about the word national showed that he considered the word implied a consolidated government.

Livermore of New Hampshire said he was not satisfied with Madison's proposed amendment. He did not wish to dwell too long on the subject and thought it would be better if it was altered to read in this manner: "Congress shall make no laws touching religion or infringing the rights of conscience." Madison quickly withdrew his motion but observed that the words "no national religion shall be established" did not imply that the government was a national one. The question was then taken on Livermore's motion to amend which was passed in the affirmative, thirty-one for and twenty against. The closeness of the vote is significant. It was not a two-thirds vote which would have been required for final action but as the house was sitting as a committee of the whole a two-thirds vote was not required.[10]

The proposed amendments as favored were then turned over to a special committee of three which made its report August 24th. A further change was made in the language of the religious liberty clause and as it came from this committee it read: "Congress shall make no law establishing religion or prohibiting the free exercise thereof; nor shall the rights of conscience be infringed." The committee reported in favor of seventeen articles. Madison first proposed to incorporate the amendments in the body of the Constitution. The report was adopted by the house and went to the Senate the following day.

There is no record of the debates on the proposed amendments in the Senate. This body held its deliberations behind closed doors and the only record of any discussion on the measures that came before it, is to be found in the diary kept by Senator William Maclay of Pennsylvania. The amendments first came before the Senate for action on August 25. Maclay says that they were "treated contemptuously" by several of the senators and an attempt was made to have action on them postponed until the next session. This, however, was defeated and the amendments were put over until the following week.[11]

There must have been considerable debate and discussion during the first two weeks of September for all kinds of motions were made, many of them relating to the religious liberty clause. Numerous additional amendments were proposed, most of which were rejected. Maclay was ill when these amendments were discussed and absent from the Senate. The Senate Journal contains no record of debates or discussions, record only being made of the final action taken.[12]

All that we know is that the Senate strongly dis-

[10] Benton, op. cit., I, 138.

[11] Journal of William Maclay, 134.

[12] *Journal of the first Session of the Senate of the United States* (New York, 1789), 115-131; Thorpe, op. cit., II, 259-60.

sented from many of the articles, that it modified and amended them; that they went back to the House; that the House refused to recede; that the amendments were sent to a committee of conference and that on September 24, the House receded from its disagreement, provided the Senate would acquiesce in alterations of two articles, and that on the following day, the Senate concurred.[12] Senator Charles Carroll with Senators Ellsworth and Patterson was appointed on the Committee of Conference and this committee recommended the amendments which were finally adopted.[13]

A sufficient number of states did not ratify the first two articles of amendment, so the proposed article III containing the religious liberty clause became the first amendment to the Constitution. The clause surviving many changes was finally made to read: "Congress shall make no laws respecting an establishment of religion or prohibiting the free exercise thereof." The words "nor shall the rights of conscience be infringed," which were in the draft as reported by the committee of three and adopted by the house, were omitted in the final draft.

Whether Charles Carroll spoke on the question of religious liberty in the senate is not known. Leonard, one of his biographers, gives him the credit for the speech that was made by Daniel Carroll in the house and several other writers have made the same error. This was due probably to an error in the index of the first volume of Benton's *Abridgement* which refers to the remarks made by Daniel Carroll as recorded on page 137 as having been made by Charles Carroll. Daniel Carroll suffered the fate of not being as well known in history as his more famous cousin. No doubt Charles Carroll would have been heard on this question if he felt that it was necessary, and it may be that he did take some part in the senate debate. The Senate conference committee of which Charles Carroll was a member was several days in

[13] *Annals of Congress,* I, 169; Journal of the First Senate, 142.

session with the House committee. There can be no doubt but that he favored the inclusion of the religious liberty clause in the first amendment for the committee so reported. The Maryland senator had just as strong views on this subject as John and Daniel Carroll.

In a letter written some years later to George Washington Custis, Charles Carroll said:

> When I signed the Declaration of Independence I had in view not only our independence from England but the toleration of all sects professing the Christian religion and communicating to them all equal rights. . . . Reflecting as you must, on the disabilities I may truly say of the prescription of the Roman Catholics in Maryland, you will not be surprised that I had much at heart this grand design, founded on mutual charity, the basis of our holy religion.[14]

In 1827 in a letter to a Protestant minister he wrote:

> Your sentiments on religious liberty coincide with mine. To obtain religious as well as civil liberty I entered zealously into the Revolution and observing the Christian religion divided into many sects I founded the hope that no one would be so predominant as to become the religion of the state. That hope was thus early entertained because all of them joined in the same cause with few exceptions of individuals. God grant that this religious liberty may be preserved in these states to the end of time and that all believing in the religion of Christ may practice the leading principle of charity, the basis of every virtue.[15]

John Carroll Brent in his *Biography of John Carroll* (1843) calls attention to a historical sketch on "the establishment of the Roman Catholic religion in this country." On the authority of the Reverend Charles Constantine Pise, editor of the *Metropolitan Magazine,* this was written by Bishop Carroll and found among his papers after his death. The sketch was printed for the first time in 1830. It begins with the granting of the Maryland Charter to Lord Baltimore in order that "Catholics oppressed by the penal laws of that kingdom" might find "an asylum from the persecution which they suffered at home." After describing the early labors

14 Gurn, op. cit., 261.

15 Purcell, "Charles Carroll," *Studies* (Dublin), Dec. 1932.

of Father White and his mission band and the life of the early Catholic immigrants, he tells of the vicissitudes of the Maryland Catholics after the Revolution of 1688: "In 1776 the American independence was declared and a revolution effected not only in political affairs but also in those relating to religion," for by the declaration "every difficulty was removed, the Catholics were placed on a level with their fellow Christians and every political disqualification was done away."

In this interesting manuscript Bishop Carroll gives the following reasons for the adoption of the religious liberty clause in the first amendment to the Constitution:

> 1. The leading characters of the first assembly or congress were, through principle, opposed to everything like vexation on the score of religion; and as they were perfectly acquainted with the maxims of the Catholics, they saw the injustice of persecuting them for adhering to their doctrines.
>
> 2. The Catholics evinced a desire, not less ardent than that of the Protestants, to render the provinces independent of the mother country; and it was manifest that if they joined the common cause and exposed themselves to the common danger, they should be entitled to a participation in the common blessings which crowned their efforts.
>
> 3. France was negotiating an alliance with the United Provinces, and nothing could have retarded the progress of that alliance more effectually, than the demonstration of any ill will against the religion which France professed.
>
> 4. The aid or at least the neutrality of Canada, was judged necessary for the success of the enterprise of the provinces and by placing Catholics on a level with all other Christians, the Canadians, it was believed, could not but be favorably disposed towards the Revolution.[16]

The outline of these facts accurately states the real reasons for the change of feeling towards the American Catholics in the days of the Revolution, and at the same time discloses the chief underlying causes of the final recognition of the principle of religious freedom in the fundamental law of the land. There was no one better qualified to analyze these causes than Bishop Carroll.

[16] Brent, *John Carroll,* 68-9.

There is abundant proof of the very great veneration and respect in which Bishop Carroll was held by his non-Catholic contemporaries, and especially those who were in positions of influence. One of the many indications of this is to be found in an exchange of correspondence between General Timothy Pickering of Massachusetts and Dr. James McHenry of Maryland. Both of these men had been officers in the Continental Army and were made members of Washington's cabinet after the war, Pickering as Secretary of War and later Secretary of State and McHenry as Secretary of War. McHenry was also a member of the Constitutional Convention and a colleague of Daniel Carroll in the Maryland delegation.

Pickering wrote to Dr. McHenry:

> The day before yesterday I met Bishop Carroll with the fine, calm, composed but cheerful countenance which distinguishes that good man. He mentioned with tender affection and regret the situation of "my friend McHenry." There is a charm in the manners and especially in the face of Bishop Carroll of which I have rarely, if ever, seen the equal.

McHenry replied, referring to Bishop Carroll as a truly good man, and that he could safely say "from a long and social intercourse with him, that the benignity which you describe as appearing so strikingly in his countenance, is not greater than the real benignity of his heart." [17]

McHenry in another letter refers to his frequent consultations with Bishop Carroll on many matters of public interest. There is no doubt but that Bishop Carroll used his influence and very properly so, with the leaders of the nation in order to bring about a recognition of the principle of equality of religious rights which to him was a matter of the greatest solicitude.

In the correspondence of General McHenry there is to be found evidence that Charles Carroll of Carrollton was likewise held in the highest respect by some of his distinguished

[17] Steiner, *Life and Correspondence of James McHenry,* 604.

contemporaries. During the first term of Washington as President it was not at all certain that he would consider a renomination. In this period of uncertainty Charles Carroll was seriously considered as the most logical successor to Washington in the presidential office. McHenry was the first to suggest Carroll as a possible nominee although not consulting him in any way. This he did in a letter to Hamilton in 1792. In reply Hamilton wrote that he hoped Washington would submit to another election but if not "then I say unequivocally I will cooperate in naming the gentleman you mention as one of the two who are to fill the two great offices, which of the two will be first or second, must be an affair of some casualty as the constitution stands. My real respect and esteem for the character brought into view will insure him my best wishes in every respect." [18] McHenry's reply to this letter stated that he expected a visit from Bishop Carroll and would show him the paragraph in Hamilton's letter just quoted. McHenry had previously written to Hamilton that Charles Carroll was "one of the wisest, most prudent and best men in the United States." [19] There were few men in public life who knew Carroll as intimately as did McHenry.

Oliver Wolcott, a native of Connecticut, descended from Puritan ancestors, a graduate of Yale and of the famous Litchfield Law School, was Secretary of the Treasury both under Washington and John Adams, succeeding Hamilton in that office in 1795. He was later Governor of Connecticut. In 1800 while he was a member of Adams' cabinet he wrote to McHenry:

> Mr. Carroll's opinions are such as were to have been expected from a wise, virtuous, firm and experienced man. I have long considered the gentleman as one of the most distinguished props of society in our country. How greatly must we regret that our affairs have not been under the direction of such a character.

The influence and standing of Daniel Carroll and the respect which the people of his state and his colleagues had

[18] *Hamilton's Works*—edited by J. C. Hamilton, V, 536.
[19] Steiner, op. cit., 479.

for him, are best evidenced by the frequency of his elections as representative in both state and national bodies and the honors conferred upon him by his fellow legislators. John Hanson of Maryland was the first president of the Continental Congress under the provisions of the Articles of Confederation, and the claim has been advanced that this made him the first president of the United States.[20] As president of the Congress he was only a presiding officer with little if any executive power. He was elected by congress and not by vote of the people or the states. Even so the office was a distinctive honor. This honor he shared with his associate Daniel Carroll. In 1782 because of ill-health Hanson retired from the active duties of the office. A resolution providing for a vice-president was defeated, but later a motion was adopted providing that whenever the president for the time being should be prevented from attending the house, one of the members present should be chosen by ballot to take his place. When Hanson became incapacitated Daniel Carroll was elected by congress to act as presiding officer and was for the time being the president of the congress.

In the character sketches of the members of the Constitutional Convention, written by a contemporary, Major William Pierce, Daniel Carroll is described as "a man of large fortune and influence in his state. He possesses plain good sense and is in the full confidence of his country-men." [21]

It was the combined influence of these three men, Bishop John Carroll, Charles Carroll of Carrollton and Daniel Carroll, that contributed more to the recognition of the principle of religious liberty in the United States Constitution, than any other factor. Largely through their efforts the spirit of the Old Maryland became the spirit of the New America.

20 Smith, *John Hanson, Our First President,* 1932.

21 *Documents Illustrative of the Formation of the Union of American States*—Government Printing office, 104.

CHAPTER X

THE TENTH AMENDMENT

THE final accomplishment of Daniel Carroll as a statesman was the bringing about of an important change in the tenth amendment to the Constitution. This was done in the closing days of the first Congress. On August 13, the select committee of eleven to which had been referred the various amendments proposed by Madison made its report and recommended the following for adoption:

> The powers not delegated by the Constitution nor prohibited to it by the States, are reserved to the states respectively.

This proposed amendment came before the house sitting as a committee of the whole on August 18. A proposal to have the reservation relate to powers not "expressely" delegated or prohibited, was defeated. Thereupon Carroll moved that at the end of the clause there should be added the words "or to the people." This was agreed to.[1] Two days later the house took up the report of the committee of the whole and Gerry revived the motion to insert the word "expressly" in the amendment but this was lost by a vote of nearly two to one. Roger Sherman then moved to alter the entire clause making it read:

> The powers not delegated to the United States by the Constitution nor prohibited by it to the States, are reserved to the States respectively or to the people.

This was adopted without debate and as finally passed the amendment contained the change originally proposed by Carroll, with the words "or to the people" added.

How did it happen that Daniel Carroll was the only mem-

1 Thorpe, op. cit., II, 249; Annals of Congress, I, 761.

Danl Carroll

ber of the congress to sense the importance of this change and to propose it? The answer is that he had been trained in a school of political philosophy which held to the doctrine that as all powers are vested in the people, such powers as are not delegated by them they reserve to themselves. Both he and Wilson in their work in the constitutional convention had endeavored to apply the doctrine that all governmental powers are vested in the people but here was presented the question of the reservation of powers and as he saw it the proposed amendment was not complete when it came from the committee of eleven. For him it was not enough to have the powers not delegated reserved to the states. He was quick to recognize the failure to fully state what he believed to be a fundamental principle of government.

Carroll during his six years of study at St. Omer's had not only been taught Scholastic Philosophy but no doubt he had become acquainted with the teaching of the Jesuit philosophers which reinterpreted and widened the doctrine of the schoolmen. There was no philosopher whose writings were receiving more attention and study than Francesco Suarez. His monumental work on law and government, *De Legibus,* had been read for years by scholars and students, especially those in the Catholic colleges on the continent.[2] While Carroll could hardly have escaped the influence of Jesuit political philosophy during his course at St. Omer's, yet even if it had made little impression on him at the time he would have been brought well under its influence later through the contact and association with his brother, the bishop and former Jesuit, and his cousin, Charles Carroll of Carrollton who had had further training in philosophy and political science after leaving St. Omer's, and was a friend of Edmund Burke who accepted in full the Suarezian doctrine of the sovereignty of the people. As has already been brought out

[2] "He who has read the *De Legibus* of Suarez knows thoroughly all the ethics, natural law and political science of the Middle Ages." Paul Janet, op. cit., II, 176.

in the discussion of the first amendment there is no record of the debate in the senate when the constitutional amendments were considered by that body, so it is not known what if anything was said by Senator Carroll on the question of the tenth amendment. All that is known is that he was a member of the conference committee which favored the amendments as finally passed by both houses. There can be no doubt but that he was fully in accord with the idea of having the words "or to the people" added to the amendment. He and Daniel Carroll roomed in the same house during the session of Congress and very probably there was discussed between them every important matter that came up for consideration. They both took their duties as members of congress seriously.

When Daniel Carroll made use of the word "people" in his amendment it was not in any loose or general sense nor has it ever been interpreted by our courts as meaning the people *en masse,* without order or unity. Suarez for the first time gave a definite meaning to the word "people" as constituting a state. The phrase he used for "people" was "a multitude of men." In so far as a multitude of men was "a sort of aggregate wholly without order, or physical or moral union" he held it was not a body politic and so it had no power of jurisdiction. But when "a multitude of men are joined by individual will or common consent in one body politic by one bond of society, that they may be of mutual aid in due ordination to one political end," i.e., the common good, then such a body becomes a corporate moral person and is endowed with original and fundamental jurisdiction in the matter of government, and "it is not in the power of men to be thus united together and to hinder this power of jurisdiction." It would be repugnant to natural reason, he held, that "there be a human congregation as one body politic with no common power of jurisdiction to which the individuals of the community are bound in obedience." [3]

[3] *De Legibus,* III, 2, 4.

Here was an amplification of scholastic political philosophy. Aquinas had recognized that the organized state was something demanded by the nature of man but Suarez went further in order to show that when a people form an organized state they acquire a power of jurisdiction which they may in part retain, that is they may retain such powers as they do not delegate. He held that in so far as the community of people reserves power to itself, its decision is ultimate and binding. "For such communities," he said, "retain the supreme governmental power in themselves, not having transferred it to any prince. Wherefore by means of this power they can enact laws for themselves." [4] At another time he said: "Therefore if a people transfers power to a king and yet retain it in themselves for certain affairs and for things of greater moment, it is allowable for them to use it and to maintain their right." [5] The principle of the reservation of powers was thus for the first time stated and defended.

Edmund Burke whose speeches and writings had a profound influence on early American political thought gave expression to the Suarezian idea in his "Appeal from the New to the Old Whigs," which was the result of a discussion in parliament relative to the French Revolution. He said:

> A number of men in themselves have no collective capacity. The idea of a people is the idea of a corporation. It is wholly artificial and made like other legal fictions by common agreement. What the particular nature of that agreement was is collected from the form into which the particular society has been cast. Any other is not *their* covenant. When men, therefore, break up the original compact or agreement which gives its corporate form and capacity to a state, they are no longer a people; they have no longer a corporate existence; they have no longer a legal coactive force to bind within nor a claim to be recognized abroad. They are a number of vague, loose individuals, nothing more. With them all is to begin again. Alas! they little know

[4] Millar, "Hauriou, Suarez and Chief Justice Marshall," *Thought,* March 1933.

[5] *Defensio Fidei Catholicae,* III, 3, 3, 130.

how many a weary step is to be taken before they can form themselves into a mass which has true politic personality.[6]

The principle of original jurisdiction became peculiar to our American form of government and it was recognized in early decisions of the Supreme Court. In his opinion in the case of Chisholm vs. Georgia, Judge Wilson in defining a state expressed the idea of both Suarez and Burke:

> By a state I mean a complete body of free persons united together for their common benefit, to enjoy peaceably what is their own and to do justice to others. It is an artificial person.[7]

Some years later Chief Justice Marshall in the decision in Marbury vs. Madison said:

> That the people have an original right to establish for the future government such principles as in their opinion shall most conduce to their own happiness, is the basis on which the whole American fabric has been erected. The exercise of this original right is a very great exertion nor can it nor ought it to be frequently repeated.[8]

The language of the tenth amendment if not properly understood could have been open to two constructions. Were the powers reserved to the people reserved to them as constituting various and separate sovereignties or were they reserved to the people of the United States considered as a mass? The reason for using both terms "the states" and "or the people" was that the states as already organized might not be held to have yielded any of the powers which their people as politically incorporated may have reserved to themselves.[9] There is this further consideration, however, which is of far reaching importance. In the American form of government there is no such thing as state sovereignty unless it be based on the underlying sovereignty of the people. The people forming the various states cannot be considered for all purposes as inhabitants of wholly separate and inde-

6 *The World's Classics,* Oxford University Press, V, 96.
7 2 Dallas, 419.
8 1 Cranch, 137.
9 Curtis, op. cit., II, 160, note.

pendent sovereignties as they must and do act in common with the people of other states in matters of national concern. Here comes in the question of divided sovereignty.

There should have been and there would have been no confusion or misunderstanding on the question of divided sovereignty if the Constitution had been studied in the light of a sound philosophy. There has always been a great deal of loose thinking on the subject of the origin and nature of our system of government and it has been due to a misconception of the true principles that are the rockbed of our governmental structure. The question of divided sovereignty goes right back to the principle of original jurisdiction and the reservation of governmental powers. A people after uniting for a common purpose and by common consent to form a body politic have the right not only to modify the government they have established but the right to withdraw powers previously conferred and delegate these powers to a federal government in order to promote the common welfare of their own and other bodies politic. That is what the people of the various states did when they accepted the Constitution. They withdrew powers from their own state governments and conferred them upon the Federal government. These powers conferred were enumerated powers, and so to that extent limited. The states thereupon became subordinate but not subject to the Federal government. Curtis says the idea of regarding the people of each state competent to withdraw from their local government any such portions of their political power as they might see fit to bestow upon a national government was "undoubtedly a novelty in political science." [10] It may have been a novelty so far as actual practice was concerned but it was not a novelty in theory.

Daniel Carroll had no confused idea about divided sovereignty. Bellarmine was a guide to those who were familiar with Scholastic philosophy and on the question of divided sovereignty he had been clear. In his *De Summo Pontifice*

[10] *Constitutional History of the United States,* I, 337.

he explained how on the basis of consent, a division of sovereignty was not only possible but desirable.[11] This was before Suarez wrote the *De Legibus* but it was the doctrine of Suarez on original jurisdiction and reservation of powers that supplied further justification for Bellarmine's theory.

James Wilson had a clear idea of divided sovereignty. In the constitutional convention he explained how he could be a citizen of the State of Pennsylvania and at the same time a citizen of the United States.[12] In his subsequent addresses and in his opinion in Chisholm vs. Georgia, he elaborated on this idea and explained how the constitution came to be ratified by the people of the various states acting in their sovereign capacity.

Years after the constitutional convention when the question of state rights was being debated in the senate James Madison recorded the intent of the convention in the matter of a divided sovereignty. He wrote:

> It has hitherto been understood that the supreme power, that is the sovereignty of the people of the states was in its nature divisible and was in fact divided according to the Constitution of the United States, between the states in their united and the states in their individual capacities and so viewed by the convention in transmitting the Constitution to the Congress of the Confederation, so viewed and so called in official, in controversial and in popular language. Of late another doctrine has occurred which supposes that sovereignty is in its nature indivisible. . . If sovereignty be in its nature divisible, the true question to be decided is whether the allotment has been made by the complete authority; and this question is answered by the fact that it was an act of the *majority* of the people in each state in their highest sovereign capacity, equivalent to a *unanimous* act of the people composing the states in that capacity.[13]

Final judicial confirmation of the principle of a divided sovereignty came in the decision of the Supreme Court in the

[11] Loc. cit.

[12] In his *Selected Political Essays of James Wilson,* Adams sees a parallel between Aquinas and Wilson on this question of divided sovereignty. See *supra,* 380, 381.

[13] James Madison: *Sovereignty Selections: Private Correspondence of James Madison from* 1813 *to* 1836, published by J. E. McGuire, Washington, 1853, pp. 370, 372.

case of Texas vs. White (7 Wallace, 700) when the court said that "the Constitution in all provisions looks to an indestructible union composed of indestructible states."

Washington in recognition of Wilson's eminent services in framing the Constitution and aiding its ratification, appointed him a member of the first Supreme Court of the United States. In the letter tendering him the appointment, the President said:

> Considering the judicial system as the chief pillar upon which our national government must rest, I have thought it my duty to nominate for the high offices in that department such men as I conceived they give dignity and luster to our national character.

Wilson died in 1798 at the age of fifty-six, while on circuit in North Carolina. Daniel Carroll died two years earlier at the age of sixty-five after having been appointed by Washington on the important commission to lay out the new national capital. After the death of both Wilson and Carroll, their concept of the sovereignty of the people received judicial recognition in the famous decision of the Supreme Court in the case of McCulloch vs. Maryland.[14]

The opinion of Chief Justice Marshall in the Maryland case is said to have been the most important judicial utterance in the annals of American jurisprudence. There are portions of the opinion which reflect the political philosophy of Wilson and Carroll and it is these very sentences that established the juridical principles which were followed in subsequent decisions, embodying the American theory of government and becoming the fundamental law of the land. On these great questions the learned Chief Justice held:

> No political dreamer was ever wild enough to think of breaking down the lines which separate the American people into one common mass. Of consequence when they act, they act in their states. But the measures they adopt do not, on that account, cease to be the measures of the people themselves or become the meas-

[14] 4 Wheaton, 323. Wilson somewhat anticipated this decision in his opinion in Chisholm vs. Georgia when he said "for the purposes of the Union Georgia is not a sovereign state."

ures of the state governments. . . It has been said that the people had already surrendered all their powers to the State sovereignties, and had nothing more to give. But surely the question whether they resume and modify the powers granted to government, does not remain to be settled in this country. Much more might the legitimacy of the general government be doubted, had it been created by the states. The powers delegated to the State sovereignties were to be exercised by themselves. To the formation of a league, such as was the Confederation, the State sovereignties were certainly competent. But when "in order to form a more perfect union" it was deemed necessary to change this alliance into an effective government, possessing great and sovereign powers, and acting directly on the people, the necessity of referring it to the people and deriving its powers directly from them, was felt and acknowledged by all. The government of the union, then (whatever may be the influence of this fact on the case) is emphatically and truly a government of the people. In form and in substance it emanates from them, its powers are granted by them and for their benefit.

In this opinion Marshall combated the idea that the Constitution was an act of the state sovereignties and showed that it was an act of the people in each state acting in their highest political capacity, excluding the idea of the governmental power emanating from any other source.[15]

It is an interesting fact that Luther Martin who had been Daniel Carroll's colleague in the Maryland delegation to the Constitutional Convention and who, after refusing to sign the Constitution, opposed Carroll in the struggle for ratification, represented the State of Maryland in this famous case, as its Attorney-General. Martin sought to maintain the theory of absolute state sovereignty. His claim, which was not upheld by the Court, was that the constitution did not emanate from the people but was the act of sovereign and independent states. His fame has quite eclipsed that of Carroll even in his own state and yet he was the most bitter opponent of the constitution and of the principle that the supreme governmental power was vested in the people.[16]

15 Curtis, op. cit., II, 77.

16 Andrews in his *History of Maryland,* makes no mention of the services of Daniel Carroll either in the Constitutional Convention or the first Congress, and devotes two pages to eulogizing the career of Martin.

Marshall with prophetic vision foresaw the dire possibility of the issue between state and popular sovereignty having to reach a final decision by the arbitrament of arms. This question, he declared, "must be decided peacefully or remain a source of hostile legislation, perhaps of hostility of a still more serious nature." Nearly a century and a half after these words were written, the concept of the supreme power of the people in the government of the nation as invoked by Wilson and Carroll in the days of constitution making, and as promulgated by the decision of the Supreme Court in the case of McCulloch vs. Maryland, found confirmation in the immortal address of Lincoln on the battlefield of Gettysburg.

CONCLUSION

Soon after he had become a justice of the Supreme Court, James Wilson was called upon to deliver a course of lectures founding the first university law school in the United States. He had been appointed professor of law at the college of Philadelphia, now the University of Pennsylvania. These lectures are the most learned commentaries on the science of law and the clearest exposition of the American ideal government that can be found in any writings or addresses during the early period of our history. Simeon E. Baldwin, late Chief Justice of the Supreme Court of Connecticut and one time president of the American Bar Association, said that they made Wilson, the "real founder of what is distinctive in our American jurisprudence."

In the course of these lectures, delivered at Philadelphia in 1790, Wilson advocated an independent system of legal education for the United States. The vital difference between our system of government and that of any other nation, he said, was that here "the supreme or sovereign power resides in the citizens at large." He challenged the time-honored definition of Blackstone that law "is a rule of action prescribed by some superior which the inferior is bound to obey." Can there be no law, he asked, "without a superior? Is it essential to law that inferiority should be involved in the obligation to obey?" While admitting that in Divine Law, there is a Superior, in human laws, the idea of a superior is "unnecessary, unfounded and dangerous." It has in it the doctrine of the divine right of kings and is subversive of all just government. The principle of obligation in human laws, he declared, "should be the consent of those whose obedience the law requires. This, I conceive to be the true origin of the obligation of human laws." [1]

There is to be found in Wilson's opening lecture a recognition of the contribution of the founding of Maryland to American institutions of government, and a remarkable tribute to the life and services of Cecil Calvert. This coming from the man who perhaps more than any other of his time, with the possible exception of Washington, had a clearer conception of the fundamental principles of a free government, deserves more than passing consideration. There is added significance to what he said due to the fact that this lecture was attended by Washington and several of the members of his cabinet.

Wilson welcomed his appointment to the chair of law because it would afford him the opportunity "to develope and communicate some striking instances hitherto little known" on which the American character was founded, a character "distinguished by the love of liberty and the love of law." The first of these instances to which he was to call attention, had to do with the foundation of Maryland. "The doctrine of toleration," he said, "in matters of religion, reasonable though it certainly is, has not been long known or acknowledged." Wherever religious toleration had been received and established the world had been thought to owe much to the writings of Locke. While just honors are bestowed on the name and character of Locke, the lecturer asked "Why should an ungracious silence be observed with regard to the name of Calvert?"

> Indeed the character of this excellent man has been too little known. He was truly the father of his country. To the legislature of Maryland he often recommended a maxim, which deserves to be written in letters of gold: "By concord a small colony may grow into a great and renowned nation; but by dissensions, mighty and glorious kingdoms have declined and fallen into nothing." Similar to that of Calvert, has been the fate of many other valuable characters in America. They have been too little

[1] Adams, *Selected Political Essays of James Wilson,* 251.

known. To those around them, their modest merits have been too familiar, perhaps too uniform to attract particular and distinguished attention; by those at a distance, the mild and peaceful voice of their virtue has not been heard. But to their memories, justice should be done, as far as it can be done, by a just and grateful country.[2]

When America should come to erect a temple of fame to "her patriots and heroes," Wilson suggested that the name of Calvert should head the list of the nation's heroes of peace, followed by the names of Penn and Franklin, these to be placed on the right of the central portal reserved for Washington.

Some thirty years later another native of Scotland and a member of the bar, Dr. James Grahame of Glasgow, in a history of the American colonies which was so well received in this country that he was given an honorary degree by Harvard, wrote:

> Before toleration was defended by Locke, it was practically established by Lord Baltimore and in the attempts which both of these eminent persons made to construct a frame of a wise and liberal government in America, it must be acknowledged that the Protestant philosopher was greatly excelled by the Catholic nobleman. The constitutions of William Penn have been the theme of general panegyric but of those who have commended them, how few have been found to celebrate or even acknowledge the prior establishment of similar institutions by Lord Baltimore?

Dr. Grahame said, what must have been in the mind of Wilson, that the slight notice given to the policies of Lord Baltimore attested the capricious distribution of fame no doubt "occasioned by dislike of his religious tenets which it was feared would share the commendation bestowed on their votary." [3]

Whatever tribute has been paid to Cecil Calvert must be

[2] Ibid, 188. Wilson's comment on the fate of Calvert would apply to his own case, for his contribution to American history is as little recognized as that of Calvert.

[3] *History of the United States of America from the Plantation of the British Colonies to their Assumption of National Independence.* 2nd edition, (1848), I, 333.

paid also to George Calvert, the first Lord Baltimore, who was the progenitor of the policies carried out by the son and without whose foresight there would have been no accomplishment, and the same tribute must be paid to those who helped to weave the social fabric and build the political structure of colonial Maryland. Only a comparatively few historians and speakers on anniversary occasions have given serious attention to the liberal principles of government which animated the founders and early law-makers of Maryland and yet the influence of these principles was a potent factor in the formation of the union of states. One recent writer, Breckinridge Long, in his *Genesis of the Constitution,* has not failed to note the similarity between the first colonial government of Maryland and the American plan of government under the Constitution. With religious liberty, general suffrage, an elective branch of the legislature and an appointive upper branch, and three independent departments of government, this writer says "we have many elements in Colonial Maryland of our constitutional system." [4]

A studied analysis of the antecedents of Maryland liberties, which are to a great extent synonymous with American liberties, gives results somewhat upsetting to many preconceived and prevalent notions. Such an analysis will reveal a thread of influence that goes far back of the Protestant Reformation, back of Magna Charta, to the cloisters of the Middle Ages and to the ancient schoolmen whose system of social and political philosophy found reinterpretation by Jesuit scholars in the days of the Renaissance and later, when English monarchs invoked the doctrine of the divine right of kings. This same thread of influence is discernible in the Baltimore policies of government and may then be traced down through the dark days following the Revolution of 1688 to the very doors of the Constitutional Convention and the first Congress of the United States.

From the days of Cecil Calvert, Father Andrew White, and

[4] Page 96.

Thomas Cornwaleys, to the days of Charles Carroll of Carrollton, Bishop John Carroll and Daniel Carroll, there is an unbroken sequence of events through which may be seen the unmistakable influence of the broad and liberal policies of the Founders of Maryland on the American system of government. This is the glory of Maryland, a heritage received from three generations of Calverts and transmitted by three generations of Carrolls to a new and independent nation.

The *Ark* and the *Dove* emerge from the shadows which have hidden them for three centuries, renewing their message of peace and good-will. Slowly but surely comes recognition of the contribution to the American system made by the Catholic founders and the early law-makers of Maryland and those who followed them to incorporate their ideals in the fundamental law of the land. There can be no full and just recognition without a realization of the great historic fact that in the wake of the *Ark* and the *Dove* came a gradual but irresistible development of the basic principles of a government wherein the people are the ample source of power, where liberty under the law and equality before the law are the unchallenged right and possession of every citizen.

BIBLIOGRAPHY

Adams, Charles Francis, *The Works of John Adams.*

Adams, James Truslow, *The March of Democracy.*

Adams, Randolph G., *Selected Political Essays of James Wilson.*

Anderson, J. S. M., *History of the Church of England in the Colonies and Dependencies of Great Britain.*

Andrews, Charles M., *The Colonial Period in American History.*

Andrews, Matthew Page, *The History of Maryland; The Foundation of Maryland.*

Andrews, James P., *The Works of James Wilson.*

Arnold, Samuel G., *The History of the State of Rhode Island and Providence Plantations.*

Bancroft, George, *History of the United States,* divers editions.

Baxter, James P., *Sir Ferdinand Gorges and His Province of Maine.*

Belloc, Hilaire, *Charles the First; History of England.*

Bozman, John Leeds, *The History of Maryland.*

Brantley, W. T., "The English in Maryland," Vol. III, Winsor's *Narrative and Critical History of America.*

Brent, John C., *Biographical Sketch of Most Rev. John Carroll, First Archbishop of Baltimore.*

Brown, George William, *Origin and Growth of Civil Liberty in Maryland.*

Browne, William Hand, *Maryland, the History of a Palatinate; George and Cecilius Calvert.*

Bryce, James, *The American Commonwealth.*

Burke, Edmund, Works of, *World's Classics,* Oxford University Press.

Burke, John, *The History of Virginia.*

Butler, John, *Historical Memoirs of the English, Scottish and Irish Catholics.*

Challoner, Richard, *Memoirs of Missionary Priests and other Catholics of both sexes who suffered death or imprisonment on account of their religion.*

Chalmers, George, *Political Annals of the Present United Colonies from their settlement to the Peace of 1765; History of the Revolt of the American Colonies.*

Cobb, Sanford, *The Rise of Religious Liberty in America.*

Cook, John Esten, *Virginia, the History of a People.*

Curtis, George T., *Constitutional History of the United States.*

Davis, George L., *The Day Star of American Freedom.*

Deane, Charles, "New England," Vol. III, Winsor's *Narrative and Critical History of America.*

Dexter, Henry Martyn, *As to Roger Williams.*

Doyle, J. A., *The English in America, Virginia, Maryland and the Carolinas.*

Dunning, William A., *History of Political Theories from Luther to Montesquieu.*

Earle, Alice Morse, *The Sabbath in Puritan New England.*

Earle, Swepson, *The Chesapeake Bay Country.*

Easton, Emily, *Roger Williams, Prophet and Pioneer.*

Eggleston, Edward, *The Beginners of a Nation.*

Elliott, Edward, *Biographical Story of the Constitution.*

Elson, Henry W., *History of the United States of America.*

Ernst, James, *Roger Williams, New England Firebrand.*

Farrand, Max, *The Framing of the Constitution.*

Fiske, John, *Old Virginia and her Neighbors; The Beginners of New England.*

Ford, Henry J., *Representative Government.*

Fuller, Thomas, *History of the Worthies of England.*

Fulop-Miller, Rene, *The Power and Secret of the Jesuits.*

Gammell, William, "Roger Williams," Vol. IV, *The Library of American Biography,* edited by Jared Sparks.

Gardiner, Samuel R., *History of England from the accesion of James I to the Outbreak of the Civil War,* 1603, 1642: *Prince Charles and the Spanish Marriage.*

Goodman, Godfrey, *The Court of King James the First.*

Green, W. H., *A Short History of Rhode Island.*

Green, John Richard, *A History of the English People.*

Grahame, James, *The History of the United States of North America, from the Plantation of the British Colonies till their assumption of National Independence.*

Guilday, Peter, *The Life and Times of John Carroll, Archbishop of Baltimore; The English Catholic Refugees on the Continent.*

Gurn, Joseph, *Charles Carroll of Carrollton.*

Hall, Clayton C., *Narratives of Early Maryland.*

Hallam, Henry, *The Constitutional History of England; View of the state of Europe during the Middle Ages.*

Hawks, Francis C., "The Rise and Progress of the Episcopal Church in Maryland," Vol. II of *Contributions to the Ecclesiastical History of the United States; A Relation of Maryland.*

Howe, Daniel W., *The Puritan Republic.*

Hughes, Thomas, S.J., *The History of the Society of Jesus in North America.* (The foot-note references are to the two volumes of Text, unless otherwise indicated.)

Johnson, Bradley T., *The Foundation of Maryland,* Maryland Historical Fund Publication No. 18.

Johnston, Mary, *Pioneers of the Old South,* Chronicles of America, Yale Press.

Kent, James, *Commentaries on American Law.*

Lecky, William E. H., *History of Rationalism in Europe.*

Lee, Sarah Redwood, *The Maryland Influence in American Catholicism,* reprinted from Records of American Catholic Historical Society of Philadelphia.

Lingard, John, *The History of England from the first Invasion by the Romans to the accession of William and Mary,* 1688.

Long, Breckinridge, *The Genesis of the Constitution.*

Maclay, William, *Journal of William Maclay,* edited by E. S. Maclay.

Martin, Clarence E., *The Legal Aspect of the English Penal Laws.* Reprint from records of American Catholic Historical Association, 1929.

Maurice, Charles E., *Stephen Langton.*

McGucken, William, S.J., *The Jesuits and Education.*

McMahon, John V. L., *Historical View of the Government of Maryland.*

McSherry, James, *History of Maryland.*

Mecklin, John A., *The Story of American Dissent.*

Meyer, Arnold O., *England and the Catholic Church under Queen Elizabeth.*

Millar, Moorhouse F. X., S.J., *The State and the Church,* written in collaboration with John A. Ryan.

Morley, John, *More's Utopia.*

Morris, John, S.J., *Troubles of our Catholic Forefathers.*

Morris, John G., *The Lords Baltimore,* Maryland Historical Society, Fund Publication No. 8.

Mott, Rodney L., *Due Process of Law.*

Oldmixon, John, *The British Empire in America,* London, 1708.

Oliver, Peter, *The Puritan Commonwealth.*

Parkman, Francis, *The Jesuits in North America.*

Parrington, Vernon L., *The Colonial Mind.*

Perry, William S., *Historical Collections Relating to the American Colonial Church.*

Powers, J. P., *The Beginnings of English Catholic Emigration to the United States.* Reprint from records of American Catholic Historical Society of Philadelphia.

Proper, Ida Sedgwick, *Monhegan, the Cradle of New England.*

Purchas, Samuel, *Purchas his Pilgrimes,* 1625.

Rowland, Kate Mason, *Life of Charles Carroll of Carrollton.*

Russell, William T., *Maryland, The Land of Sanctuary.*

Scharf, J. Thomas, *History of Maryland.*

Schneider, Herbert W., *The Puritan Mind.*

Shea, John Gilmary, *The Catholic Church in Colonial Days.*

Simpson, Richard, *Edmund Campion.*

Smith, Helen A., *The Thirteen Colonies.*

Spalding, Henry A., *Colonial Catholic Maryland.*

Stevens, John A., "The English in New York," in Vol. III, Winsor's *Narrative and Critical History of America.*

Stratemeier, George B., *Thomas Cornwaleys, Commissioner and Councilor of Maryland,* Vol. II, Catholic University Studies in American Church History.

Streeter, Sebastian F., *Papers Relating to the Early History of Maryland,* Maryland Historical Society Fund Publication, No. 9.

Taswell-Langmead, Thomas Pitt, *Constitutional History of England* (2nd Ed.)

Taunton, Ethelred L., *The English Black Monks of St. Benedict; History of the Jesuits in England,* 1580-1778.

Thomas, John Walter, *Chronicles of Colonial Maryland.*

Thorpe, Francis N., *Constitutional History of the American People,* 1898, and *Constitutional History of the United States,* 1901.

Twichell, Joseph Hopkins, *John Winthrop.*

Van Dyke, Paul, *Ignatius Loyola.*

Walsh, James J., *Our American Jesuits; The Education of the Founding Fathers of the Republic.*

Wilhelm, Lewis W., *Sir George Calvert, Baron of Baltimore,* Maryland Historical Society Fund Publication, No. 20.

Williams, Michael, *The Shadow of the Pope.*

Wilson, Woodrow, *A History of the American People.*

Wilstach, Paul, *Potomac Landings.*

Statutes and Laws, Documents, Records and Historical Collections

The Archives of Maryland, published by the Maryland Historical Society by authority of the State.

Laws of Maryland at Large, compiled by Thomas Bacon, 1765.

The Calvert Papers, Maryland Historical Society Fund Publications, Nos. 28, 34 and 35.

Relatio Itineris in Marylandiam; Declaratio Coloniae, and extracts of letters from the missionaries. Maryland Historical Society Fund Publication, No. 7.

Statutes at Large of Virginia, compiled by William W. Hening, 1809.

The Laws and Liberties of Massachusetts, reprinted from the copy of the 1648 edition, Harvard University Press.

Rhode Island Records.

Publications of the Narragansett Club, First Series.

Abridgment of the Debates in Congress, 1789-1856, edited by Thomas H. Benton.

Annals of Congress, 1789-1804. Gates and Sexton.

Journal of the First Senate of the United States, 1789.

Debates on the Adoption of the Federal Constitution, 1789, reported by James Madison. Supplemental to Elliot's Debates.

Documents illustrative of the Formation of the Union of the American States including the debates of the Federal Convention of 1787 as reported by James Madison. Government Printing Office, 1927.

Pamphlets and Essays on the Federal Constitution, compiled by Paul Leicester Ford.

Select Charters and other Documents Illustrative of American History, compiled by William MacDonald.

Great Britain, Statutes at Large, Runnington edition.

Pickering, English Statutes at Large.

Acts and Ordinances of the Interregnum (Great Britain), 1642-1660.

Records of the English Province of the Society of Jesus, compiled by Henry Foley, S.J.

Documents relating to the Society of Jesus in North America, compiled by Thomas Hughes, S.J.

Files of the *Columbian Magazine and Monthly Miscellany*, 1787, in New York Public Library.

Files of the *Gazette of the United States*, 1789, in Sterling Memorial Library, Yale University.

INDEX

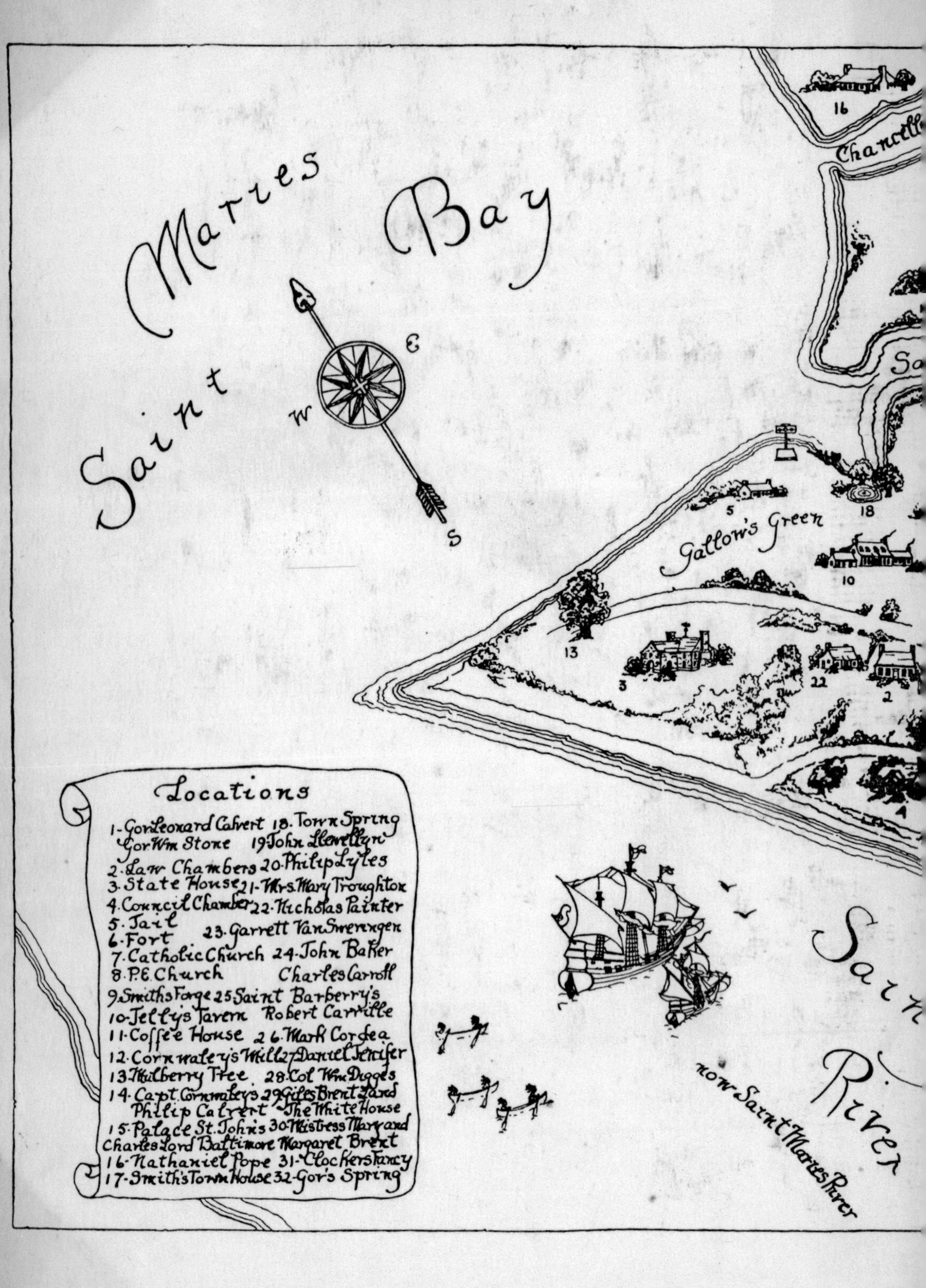
Saint Maries Bay
E
W
S
Gallow's Green
16
18
5
10
13
3
22
2
A
Saint
River
now Saint Maries River
Locations
1-Gov Leonard Calvert
Gov Wm Stone
2-Law Chambers
3-State House
4-Council Chamber
5-Jail
6-Fort
7-Catholic Church
8-P.E. Church
9-Smiths Forge
10-Jelly's Tavern
11-Coffee House
12-Cornwaley's Mill
13-Mulberry Tree
14-Capt. Cornwaley's
Philip Calvert
15-Palace St. Johns
Charles Lord Baltimore
16-Nathaniel Pope
17-Smith's Town House
18-Town Spring
19-John Llewellyn
20-Philip Lyles
21-Mrs Mary Troughton
22-Nicholas Painter
23-Garrett Van Swenngen
24-John Baker
Charles Carroll
25-Saint Barberry's
Robert Carville
26-Mark Cordea
27-Daniel Jenifer
28-Col Wm Digges
29-Giles Brent Land
The White House
30-Mistress Mary and
Margaret Brent
31-Clockers Fancy
32-Gov's Spring